D0687685

Rob Koper · Colin Tattersall (Eds.)

Learning Design

Rob Koper · Colin Tattersall (Eds.)

Learning Design

A Handbook on Modelling and Delivering Networked Education and Training

With 116 Figures

Springer

Rob Koper
Colin Tattersall

Educational Technology Expertise Centre
Open University of the Netherlands
6419 AT Heerlen

Rob.Koper@ou.nl
Colin.Tattersall@ou.nl

Library of Congress Control Number: 2004117337

ACM Computing Classification (1998): K.3.1, J.4, H.4, H.5.3

ISBN 3-540-22814-4 Springer Berlin Heidelberg New York

This work is subject to copyright. All rights are reserved, whether the whole or part of the material is concerned, specifically the rights of translation, reprinting, reuse of illustrations, recitation, broadcasting, reproduction on microfilm or in any other way, and storage in data banks. Duplication of this publication or parts thereof is permitted only under the provisions of the German Copyright Law of September 9, 1965, in its current version, and permission for use must always be obtained from Springer. Violations are liable for prosecution under the German Copyright Law.

Springer is a part of Springer Science+Business Media

springeronline.com

© Springer-Verlag Berlin Heidelberg 2005
Printed in The Netherlands

The use of general descriptive names, registered names, trademarks, etc. in this publication does not imply, even in the absence of a specific statement, that such names are exempt from the relevant protective laws and regulations and therefore free for general use.

Typesetting: By the authors
Cover design: KünkelLopka, Heidelberg
Production: LE-TEX Jelonek, Schmidt & Vöckler GbR, Leipzig
Printed on acid-free paper 45/3142/YL - 5 4 3 2 1 0

Preface

The Valkenburg Group

In March 2002, thirty-three experts in e-learning from four continents met each other for the first time in Valkenburg aan de Geul, a small village in the south of The Netherlands. Since then, the group, referred to as the Valkenburg Group, has met several times at different locations to explore how to improve the pedagogical quality of e-learning courses, in an interoperable way, with user-friendly tools. The general feeling of the experts was that most of the current e-learning offerings lack one or more of these aspects: they are of poor pedagogical quality, they lack portability, or they lack adequate tooling. Pedagogical quality is considered to be the key issue. To be successful, e-learning must offer effective and attractive courses and programmes to learners, while at the same time providing a pleasant and effective work environment for staff members who have the task of developing course materials, planning the learning processes, providing tutoring, and assessing performance.

Learning Design

The Valkenburg Group reached consensus on the idea that the Educational Modelling Language (EML) and the IMS Learning Design (LD) specification provide a good starting point towards this objective. EML was developed at the Open University of the Netherlands and was released in December 2000. EML was the input for the development of the LD specification by IMS, a consortium of global e-learning software companies and users (see imsglobal.org) and the specification was released in February 2003. Although EML and LD differ in structure, functionally they are more-or-less equivalent. With EML and LD, it is possible to develop and present advanced, interoperable e-learning courses that go beyond current implementations. The specifications were developed to describe an unlimited number of pedagogical approaches, both old and new, by abstracting from those described in the literature (eg, the collection of models described by Reigeluth in 1983 and in 1999). This abstraction level is referred to as a pedagogical meta-model (Koper 2000, 2002), and has been tested in practice in several implementations and with various courses in different settings (Koper & Manderveld 2004). For example, with EML/LD courses were described that are based on the active participation of learners in an interoperable way, such as:

- Educational role and game playing courses where multiple users perform a variety of interdependent tasks.
- Problem-based learning courses where teams of learners collaborate in problem solving and teachers have expert, assessment, coaching or monitoring roles.
- Learning community approaches based on social-constructivist principles, where the design of the learning environment stimulates collaboration and sharing of knowledge and resources.
- Performance support approaches, where learning tasks are assigned depending on assessed knowledge gaps.
- Adaptive courses where the pedagogical model, the learning processes and content are adapted to, for example, the learning needs, preferences and learning styles of learners.
- Peer coaching and assessment approaches, where learners support each other.

Koper and Van Es (in press) tested the pedagogical flexibility of LD more systematically. Their approach used an inventory of databases of pedagogical models available on the Internet (also called "lesson plans", see Van Es 2004 for an overview). Sixteen lesson plans were randomly selected from these databases, covering a variety of designs based on different pedagogical traditions (behaviorist, cognitive, social-constructivist). The lesson plans were all able to be coded in LD without any restrictions.

Learning Design provides a conceptual model for the description of teaching and learning processes. In a certain sense it works like a musical notation: it can capture the teaching and learning processes on paper. This makes the design explicit, it can be reflected upon by the designers themselves or by others, and it can be further refined and shared within a community of course developers. This feature is expected to increase the quality of courses in the long run.

IMS delivers XML Schemas (W3C 2004b) as an integral part of all its specifications. As a result, the learning designs of courses are expressed in XML to make the course machine-readable. This means that courses encoded using LD can be processed by runtime agents, making the delivery management of courses more efficient. In current e-learning systems, the teacher still has many mundane management tasks to perform to set up and maintain the environment. This can be automated to a large extent using LD.

The realisation of all these very desirable advantages of LD is, however, still a future perspective. The principles and standards are defined, but most of the tooling still has to be developed. It is exactly this aspect, namely the joint development of tools around LD, that has been the driving factor behind the Valkenburg Group. Currently the European Commission has strengthened the activity of the Valkenburg Group by funding by the UNFOLD project[1]. This book is one of the valuable resources used within this project, and some parts of the work of writing and editing this book were also sponsored by the UNFOLD project.

Development of the Ideas Behind Learning Design

It is helpful to understand the 'where, why, when and how' that went into the development of the concepts that inform LD. In 1997, the Open University of the Netherlands made a strategic decision that e-learning would be central to its future in terms of helping to innovate institutes for higher education and to renew its own educational system by implementing new competency-based models of education, integrated into an electronic learning environment. The university had to confront the fact that many different pedagogical approaches are in use in higher education and its own institution. A key issue was how these many different approaches should be expressed and supported on-line. Up to then, many interesting e-learning projects had provided innovative ways of support for particular pedagogical approaches, but were based on different systems, with different support needs, scalability, and other characteristics, each requiring its own integration effort with existing systems. The alternative of attempting to limit existing practice to the use of one or two pedagogical approaches was, if anything, even more problematic. An internally funded five-year R&D programme was therefore initiated to address this difficult dilemma.

In addition to surveying the pedagogical approaches actually in use within the university and its partners, the project team carried out extensive research into the variety of available pedagogical approaches, identifying over a hundred. The team then analysed these for common characteristics and, through a process of abstraction and experimentation, arrived at a 'pedagogical meta-language' that formed the base of EML. EML evolved in several iterations over a further two-year period of development. The development of EML went through three complete cycles of specification development, implementation in prototype software, trialling with users, evaluation of results, and redesign of the specification and prototype software. A key aim throughout these three iterations was to achieve the right balance between being sufficiently general to support the desired range of pedagogies, while at the same time being sufficiently specific to be useful and capable of supporting what was needed. EML v1.0 was released in December 2000 after three years of development and ex-

---

[1] UNFOLD (IST-2002-1_507835, January 2004 to December 2005) is funded under the European Union's Sixth Framework Programme. It is a Coordination Action within the Technology-enhanced learning and access to cultural heritage Action Line of the Information Society Technologies area.

perimentation. In 2001, the specification was accepted as the basis for the development of the new IMS Learning Design specification, and after almost two years of work and debate, the final 1.0 version of the IMS specification was made available to the public in February 2003.

The basic idea of EML and LD (we hereafter refer only to LD) is in essence simple. It represents a vocabulary which users of any pedagogical approach understand, and into which existing designs can be translated. The core of LD can be summarised as the view that, when learning, *people in specific groups and roles engage in activities using an environment with appropriate resources and services.*

Many approaches to learning expect learners to work in groups, as well as on their own. However, e-learning standards to date have only supported the model of single learners working in isolation, such as the model behind SCORM (ADL 2004b). An important capability of LD is its integration of discussions and more complex, collaborative approaches to learning into the model of content provision to the isolated individual learner. It is also desirable to integrate these two approaches so that both could be in a single unit of learning. Other requirements of EML and LD included:

- allowing learners to work in several groups so that each group could do different things at the same time to support more complex types of collaborations, as in project-based learning;
- allowing different learners to do the same things at different times, such as taking turns in different roles, or a large group accessing a limited resource (e.g. a remote telescope or other experimental equipment) in a sequence of smaller groups.

Some kinds of learning, such as those derived from programmed learning, require tight control by the system of the learning sequence, depending on the learners' response to tests; while others, such as role-plays, need to allow participants greater control over the course of events. Newer types, such as personalised learning and competency-based learning, have to respond conditionally to the characteristics of the learner, or their current state. To support such a wide variety of approaches to learning is hard, but these ideas, particularly when implemented in an open specification such as LD, make a bold attempt to lay down a foundation for the next generation of learning systems. It is also of great benefit to e-learning system developers to be able to support a wide range of pedagogical approaches using one language, rather than having to support one for each.

However, it should be borne in mind that, as with all first-generation e-learning specifications, LD can be expected to evolve and develop in response to the experiences gained from implementing and using it.

Goal of the Book

The goal of this book is to present the current state of the art in the development of e-learning courses using LD. It provides information about LD, how to implement it in practice, what tools to use, what pitfalls to avoid. It is based on the experience of members of the Valkenburg Group in building tools and using these tools in practice. The book also goes beyond the current state of the art by looking at future advancements.

It should be noted however, that LD is a fairly young specification. Large scale implementations and a full toolset for handling LD are still missing. As a consequence, we are, for example, not yet able to present rigorous summative evaluative findings, and most of the current applications aim at proving the concepts behind LD. The authors and editors are however convinced that the book will help the community of learning designers and LD tool developers to further advance the field.

Intended Audience

The handbook is designed to serve both those with an understanding of the LD specification, and those who are new to it. The target audience is e-learning *course and tool developers* interested in the innovation of e-learning. This includes people who want to improve the effectiveness and attractiveness of e-learning by applying interoperable designs in their courses, including active learning, collaborative learning, problem-based learning, gaming approaches and other multi-role learning activities. It also includes people who want to make teaching and learning using ICT more efficient, e.g. by decreasing the workload of teachers using the automated workflow possibilities of LD. And last but not least, it is intended for those who want to create truly interoperable courses, including all content, services and processes (and not only the interoperable sequenced content).

Conventions Used in the Book

Learning Design or learning design?

In the text, we use the term 'Learning Design' (with capitals) and its abbreviation, LD, when referring to the formal specification. At the time of writing, this is the IMS Learning Design Specification, version 1.0. This specification consists of three different items: an information model, a best practice and implementation guide, and an XML binding with a binding document.

We use 'learning design' (without capitals) when the human activity of designing units of learning, learning activities or learning environments is meant. This term is never abbreviated to ld. As a synonym the phrase 'instructional design' or 'instructional systems design' is used in this book, however some may argue that this has a slightly different accent in meaning. Consequently we use 'the learning design' when the result of the learning design activity is meant, i.e. a document describing the learning design in any formal or informal notation that is not LD. Furthermore, 'the Learning Design' is the part of a unit of learning that describes the XML learning design elements.

When the XML element <learning-design> is meant, we will use the notation 'learning-design' (with a hyphen).

Learning Design, Unit of Learning or unit of learning

The term 'Unit of Learning' (UOL) is used to describe an IMS Content Package that contains a learning-design element as its organisation. This use of the term is defined in the LD specification. We use the term 'unit of learning' to indicate all different kinds of formal and informal learning opportunities and events. Examples are courses, workshops, self-directed informal learning events, lessons, a curriculum, etc.

Suggested Reading Path

		Course developer	Tool developer
Part I Specification, Architectures and Tools			
1	An Introduction to Learning Design	•	•
2	The Learning Design Specification		•
3	Architectures to Support Authoring and Content Management with Learning Design		•
4	An Architecture for the Delivery of E-learning Courses		•
5	An Architecture for Learning Design Engines		•
6	A Reference Implementation of a Learning Design Engine		•
7	Learning Design Tools		•
Part II Designing E-learning Courses			
8	Basic Design Procedures for E-learning Courses	•	
9	An Instructional Engineering Method and Tool for the Design of Units of Learning	•	
10	Integrating Assessment into E-learning Courses	•	
11	Collaboration in Learning Design Using Peer-to-Peer Technologies	•	•
12	Designing Adaptive Learning Environments	•	•
13	Designing Educational Games	•	
14	Designing Learning Networks for Lifelong Learners	•	
15	How to Integrate Learning Design into Existing Practice	•	
Part III Experience			
16	Applying Learning Design to Self-Directed Learning	•	•
17	Applying Learning Design to Support Open Learning	•	
18	Using Learning Design to Support Design and Runtime Adaptation		•
19	The Edubox Learning Design Player		•
20	Delivery of Learning Design: the Explor@ System's Case		•
21	Challenges in the Wider Adoption of LD: Two Exploratory Case Studies		•
22	A Learning Design Worked Example	•	•

Acknowledgements

The editors and authors wish to thank the management and staff of the Schloss Dagstuhl International Conference and Research Center for Computer Science for providing a pleasant, stimulating and well organised environment for the writing of this book. Furthermore, we would like to express our gratitude to the members of the Valkenburg Group and the members of the Technology Development Programme of the Educational Technology Expertise Centre at the Open University of the Netherlands who acted as reviewers for the book chapters. Last but not least, we want to thank Mieke Haemers for the enormous effort she put into supporting the editors.

Contents

List of Contributors

Blat, Josep
Interactive Technology Group
Department of Technology
Universitat Pompeu Fabra
Estació de França, Passeig de Circumval.lació 8
E-08003 Barcelona
Spain

Boticario, Jesús
Dpto. INTELIGENCIA ARTIFICIAL
ETSI Informática
Universidad Nacional de Educación a Distancia (UNED)
Juan del Rosal, 16 - 3ª
E-28040 Madrid
Spain

Casado, Francisco
Interactive Technology Group
Department of Technology
Universitat Pompeu Fabra
Estació de França, Passeig de Circumval.lació 8
E-08003 Barcelona
Spain

De la Teja, Ileana
CIRTA (LICEF) Research Centre
Télé-université
4750, avenue Henri-Julien
Bureau 100
Montréal (Québec)
H2T 3E4
Canada

Douglas, Peter
Intrallect Ltd.
Braehead Business Park
Braehead Road
Linlithgow
EH49 6EP
UK

Duncan, Charles
Intrallect Ltd.
Braehead Business Park
Braehead Road
Linlithgow
EH49 6EP
UK

Farooq, Umer
Penn State University
227H Computer Building
University Park
PA 16802
USA

Garcia, Rocío
Interactive Technology Group
Department of Technology
Universitat Pompeu Fabra
Estació de França, Passeig de Circumval.lació 8
E-08003 Barcelona
Spain

Gorissen, Pierre
Fontys Hogescholen
Het Eeuwsel 1-2
Gebouw S1, kamer 1.12
5612 AS Eindhoven
The Netherlands

Griffiths, David
Interactive Technology Group
Department of Technology
Universitat Pompeu Fabra
Estació de França, Passeig de Circumval.lació 8
E-08003 Barcelona
Spain

Halm, Michael
Penn State University
227H Computer Building
University Park
PA 16802
USA

Hermans, Henry
Educational Technology Expertise Centre
Open University of the Netherlands
Valkenburgerweg 177
6419 AT Heerlen
The Netherlands

Hoadley, Christopher
Penn State University
314D Keller Building
University Park
PA 16802
USA

Hummel, Hans
Educational Technology Expertise Centre
Open University of the Netherlands
Valkenburgerweg 177
6419 AT Heerlen
The Netherlands

Janssen, José
Educational Technology Expertise Centre
Open University of the Netherlands
Valkenburgerweg 177
6419 AT Heerlen
The Netherlands

Joosten-ten Brinke, Desirée
Educational Technology Expertise Centre
Open University of the Netherlands
Valkenburgerweg 177
6419 AT Heerlen
The Netherlands

Koper, Rob
Educational Technology Expertise Centre
Open University of the Netherlands
Valkenburgerweg 177
6419 AT Heerlen
The Netherlands

Kwong, KL
GTK Press
18 Wynford Drive, Unit 109
Don Mills, Ontario
M3C 3S2
Canada

Latour, Ignace
Citogroep
Nieuwe Oeverstraat 50
6811 JB Arnhem
The Netherlands

Léonard, Michel
CIRTA (LICEF) Research Centre
Télé-université
4750, avenue Henri-Julien
Bureau 100
Montréal (Québec)
H2T 3E4
Canada

Lundgren-Cayrol, Karin
CIRTA (LICEF) Research Centre
Télé-université
4750, avenue Henri-Julien
Bureau 100
Montréal (Québec)
H2T 3E4
Canada

Manderveld, Jocelyn
Educational Technology Expertise Centre
Open University of the Netherlands
Valkenburgerweg 177
6419 AT Heerlen
The Netherlands

Marino, Olga
CIRTA (LICEF) Research Centre
Télé-université
4750, avenue Henri-Julien
Bureau 100
Montréal (Québec)
H2T 3E4
Canada

Martens, Harrie
Educational Technology Expertise Centre
Open University of the Netherlands
Valkenburgerweg 177
6419 AT Heerlen
The Netherlands

Martinez, Juanjo
Interactive Technology Group
Department of Technology
Universitat Pompeu Fabra
Estació de França, Passeig de Circumval.lació 8
E-08003 Barcelona
Spain

McAndrew, Patrick
Institute of Educational Technology
The Open University
Walton Hall
Milton Keynes
MK7 6AA
UK

Morrey, Martin
Intrallect Ltd
Braehead Business Park
Braehead Road
Linlithgow
EH49 6EP
UK

Olivier, Bill
Bolton Institute of Higher Education
Deane Road
Bolton
BL3 5AB
UK

Paquette, Gilbert
CIRTA (LICEF) Research Centre
Télé-université
4750, avenue Henri-Julien
Bureau 100
Montréal (Québec)
H2T 3E4
Canada

Richards, Griff
Simon Fraser University Surrey
10153 King George Highway
Surrey
British Columbia
V3T 2W1
Canada

Sayago, Sergio
Interactive Technology Group
Department of Technology
Universitat Pompeu Fabra
Estació de França, Passeig de Circumval.lació 8
E-08003 Barcelona
Spain

Sloep, Peter
Educational Technology Expertise Centre
Open University of the Netherlands
Valkenburgerweg 177
6419 AT Heerlen
The Netherlands

Tattersall, Colin
Educational Technology Expertise Centre
Open University of the Netherlands
Valkenburgerweg 177
6419 AT Heerlen
The Netherlands

Towle, Brendon
Thomson NETg
1751 W. Diehl Road
2nd Floor
Naperville
IL 60563-9099
USA

Van Rosmalen, Peter
Educational Technology Expertise Centre
Open University of the Netherlands
Valkenburgerweg 177
6419 AT Heerlen
The Netherlands

Vogten, Hubert
Educational Technology Expertise Centre
Open University of the Netherlands
Valkenburgerweg 177
6419 AT Heerlen
The Netherlands

Weller, Martin
Institute of Educational Technology
The Open University
Walton Hall
Milton Keynes
MK7 6AA
UK

Wilson, Scott
Research Institute for Enhancing Learning
University of Wales
Holyhead Road
Bangor
Gwynedd
LL57 2PX
UK

Part I

THE SPECIFICATION, ARCHITECTURES AND TOOLS

The first part of the book contains seven chapters. Chapter 1 sets the stage for the book by introducing the concept of learning design in a rather informal way. The second chapter will introduce you to the Learning Design (LD) specification, and will guide you in reading and understanding it. Three subsequent chapters provide architectures for the development of tools that enable authoring, content management and the delivery of e-learning courses coded with the LD specification. The final two chapters provide an overview of the set of tools needed when working with LD: Chap. 6 introduces the open source CopperCore engine that serves as a reference implementation for an LD runtime engine, and Chap. 7 provides an overview of the types of tools available.

1 An Introduction to Learning Design

Rob Koper

Educational Technology Expertise Centre,
Open University of the Netherlands, Heerlen, The Netherlands

1.1 Introduction

How can we help people to learn in an effective, efficient, attractive and accessible way? There is no simple, straightforward answer to this question; depending on the specific situation, solution X will work best for person Y. However, it is generally acknowledged that we can improve learning considerably by making the conditions for optimal learning explicit, and then use this knowledge to design new learning events.

Our knowledge of learning design draws on different disciplines. It answers questions such as the following:

- What support do people need in order to learn?
- How can we assess and communicate the results of a learning process?
- How can we make learning and support as effective, efficient, attractive and accessible as possible for everyone involved in the process?

Implicit in these questions are issues related to the nature of knowledge, the nature of learning and the nature of motivation and social exchange. There are several ways to capture learning design knowledge, one of which is the instructional design approach. Here, knowledge is encapsulated in theories consisting of a set of design principles. Another approach is to identify best practices in teaching and learning, and yet another is to capture the knowledge in pedagogical design patterns. Such patterns take up a position in between theory and best practices in that they are abstracted from best practices. What a teacher believes about good teaching and learning is influenced by one or more sources. These are: prescriptions taken from instructional design theory; concrete examples of best practices; and patterns of experience. In each case, we will call the representation of this knowledge *learning design knowledge.*

A *learning design* is defined here as the application of learning design knowledge when developing a concrete unit of learning, e.g. a course, a lesson, a curriculum, a learning event. Our assumption is that the quality of a unit of learning depends largely on the quality of the learning design, and, moreover, that every learning practice (e.g. a course) has an underlying learning design that is more generic than the practice itself. This is similar to the belief that every building has an underlying architecture which is more generic than the building itself. The design can be re-used over and over again at different times and places for more or less the same course (or building). This does not necessarily mean that the design is made explicit before it is used. That may well be the case when it comes to the architecture of buildings, but it is not common practice in education. There is (still) no real tradition in education of making formal notations of course designs that can be understood by anyone who is trained to read them. The lack of a common notation makes designing courses a very local or even individual event. It hampers broader communication about effective educational practice and impedes the evaluation of existing designs. It also makes it difficult to automate some or all of the design and delivery process. A notation would increase the effectiveness of education and training and reduce the overall cost by making it possible to automate the laborious, repetitive parts of the process.

In this chapter we introduce the concept of learning design. We examine what a learning designer must know in order to create high-quality learning designs, and we discuss the nature of this knowledge, how it can be modelled in terms of rules, and how the rules are derived. We use several examples to introduce the different modelling concepts. Our informal introduction to many of the concepts used in learning design sets the stage for the rest of this book. We do not discuss the specifications for a learning design (LD 2003) in any great detail, but we do introduce most of the basic modelling concepts by comparing learning design to a theatre piece and by providing several informal examples of learning design methods or lesson plans. We conclude the chapter by describing the requirements for a learning design notation, which will then be presented in the next chapter.

1.2 The Knowledge of the Learning Designer

In this chapter, we use the term 'learning designer' to describe those who have a learning design task to perform. They can be course developers, curriculum developers, teachers, trainers, coaches, mentors or learners who design their own learning plans. A learning designer's basic task is to design a course that meets a set of learning objectives. Say, for example, that a learning designer wishes to develop a course on 'Spanish as a Second Language'. How does the designer proceed? What steps must be taken to develop an effective course? Typically, the designer should seek solutions that give learners a good chance of attaining the learning objectives of the course. However, the best solution depends heavily on the context of the course. It is possible to develop hundreds of different Spanish courses, one more suitable in situation A, and another in situation B. Solving this problem requires the designer to make use of design knowledge, i.e. a set of rules that can be applied to the design problem. One example of such a rule is: 'When learning a new language, the best approach is to present various common situations – e.g. transacting business in a shop or a hotel – and define different tasks for students to perform in that situation.' A design rule can also take the form of a specific example: 'This particular Spanish course has been used successfully in a comparable situation.' We will answer two basic questions about learning design rules in the following sections: what are they, and how are they derived?

1.3 Learning Design Rules: What Are They?

In the literature much has been written about the nature of learning design knowledge. In this section we will elaborate on the work of Reigeluth (1999, pp 5–30) to specify what learning design rules are. Reigeluth uses learning design knowledge as a synonym for instructional design theory and defines it as knowledge that offers explicit guidance on how better to help people learn and develop. The theory is not descriptive in nature, but prescriptive: it offers guidelines as to what method or methods can be used better to attain a certain learning outcome. Reigeluth states that learning design knowledge is situational rather than universal, meaning that one method may work best in one situation whereas another method works best in a different one. This means that learning design knowledge consists of a set of prescriptive rules with the following basic structure: '*If* learning situation S, *then* use learning design method M.' Furthermore, these rules are not meant to be deterministic, but probabilistic. Applying a rule does not *guarantee* that we reach the desired outcome, but it does increase the *probability* that we will. We can expand the rule to reflect this idea: '*If* learning situation S, *then* use learning design method M, *with* probability P.' It is difficult to indicate the exact probability of design rules for various reasons, and we are usually not able to do so. One reason is that probability is also situation dependent. However, although a rule does not guarantee complete success, the probability of finding a good solution increases when it has been thoroughly tested in practice. The argument is that using learning design rules will probably result in better courses than ad hoc and random decisions about a course design.

Another factor which we have to take into account, and which is also difficult to measure, is that the rules are not value free. People prefer certain learning outcomes and methods above others. There are generally several alternative methods that can be used in a given situation, and in such circumstances in particular, the learning designer has to evaluate the various methods available and choose between them.

Given the discussion above, we can now summarise the structure of a learning design rule as follows:

If learning situation S (*and* value V)
then use learning design method M (*with* probability P)

As we mentioned above, the segments between brackets in the equation are difficult to measure. We do not intend to discuss these aspects in detail, but will concentrate on the two key factors in the equation: the learning situation and the learning design method.

1.3.1 Learning Situation

The left-hand side of the equation is the learning situation. It contains all the factors that are of importance when selecting adequate learning design methods. The situational factors can be seen as the requirements that any new learning design method has to meet, or as descriptors of the situation in which an existing learning design method has been applied. The situational factors can be divided into learning outcomes and learning conditions. Learning outcomes are related to the level of effectiveness, efficiency, attractiveness and accessibility of the learning design method:

1. Effectiveness describes how well the learning objectives have been met by the learning design method. For instance, when a Spanish course is effective, 80% of the students will pass the test; when it is non-effective, only 40% will. Success is measured by the number of students who pass the test.
2. Efficiency describes the labour intensity and cost of the method, both for the learners as they work to attain the outcomes and for the teachers as they attempt to support the learners.
3. Attractiveness describes how much the activities appeal to the learners and teaching staff.
4. Accessibility describes how easily learners and staff can access the learning facilities: are the facilities location dependent or are they accessible remotely; are there time constraints or can learners work whenever they like; can the facilities be adapted to specific situational or personal circumstances; etc.?

The learning conditions can be categorised as the characteristics of the learning objective, the learners, the setting and the media. A special vocabulary is needed in each category, for example:

1. Learning objective: knowledge, skill, attitude, competence
2. Learner characteristics: pre-knowledge, motivation, situational circumstances
3. Setting characteristics: individual and/or group work, work at school and/or work and/or home
4. Media characteristics: bandwidth, synchronous/asynchronous, linear/interactive, media types.

1.3.2 Learning Design Method

The right-hand side of the equation is the key part: the learning design method (or simply 'method'). In this section we explain what a learning design method is and then analyse the overall structure of a method and its underlying components. We will use the script of a play as a metaphor to explain the various issues involved.

The Script as a Metaphor

A learning design method describes a teaching–learning process, i.e. the process undertaken by persons interacting within a learning environment. To help us model this process, we can look at examples of similar processes and take these as a metaphor for our own. One useful metaphor for learning design is the script of a theatrical play, a film or a game. A script models all kinds of realities in which actors interact with one another within the context of a defined environment (the stage; the scene). Let us look at an example from the script of the play *Street Theater* by *Wilson* (see next page).

If we analyse the structure of the script, we can identify the following components:

1. *Metadata*: the descriptive data that is not a part of the play itself, but identifies the title, author, copyright, objectives, etc.
2. *Roles*: Murfino and Jack are the roles. The roles are played by persons who are referred to as actors. In this example the role is for single persons. There are also roles, like Crowd or Jury, which are performed by a group of actors.
3. *Acts*: this play has two acts (only a fragment of the first act is quoted). The curtains usually close between acts to allow the stage crew to set up

new scenery or to give the actors a break. Acts are sequential; one follows the other.

Doric Wilson's

STREET THEATER

Stonewall 1969

in two acts

Roles for this fragment:
- MURFINO, a thug
- JACK, heavy leather, keys left

Act One

(No curtain. No scenery. The audience, arriving, sees an empty performance space in half-light. The sound system plays a medley of up beat golden oldies from the late sixties, ending with the Lovin' Spoonful's *Summer in the City*. MURFINO, a thug, enters through the audience carrying a battered garbage can.)

MURFINO: (To the audience, an unauthorized prologue.) Hot enough for you? They say we got another week of heat wave. (As he wipes his brow.) This play is all about this bunch of lowlifes. Juicebums, hopheads, weirdos, oddballs, queers—what you call your "artistic element." The usual gutter crud you got to expect to contend with down here in Greenwich Village.

(The stage lights come up as MURFINO places the garbage can downstage left. JACK, heavy leather, keys left, enters left, carrying an overly full plastic trash bag. The ominous image used to promote S&M establishments, JACK's geniality and good humor comes as a surprise to the uninitiated.)

JACK: (Giving the bag to MURFINO.) Here you go, Murfino.

MURFINO: (Investigating the bag.) What's this?

JACK: You forgot your lunch.

MURFINO: Garbage! (Emptying a wide assortment of rubbish into the garbage can, filling it to overflowing.) We gotta be this authentic?

---

4. The set-up of the stage *environment*: the descriptions between brackets provide information about the set-up: the staging (music, no scenery), the props (garbage can, trash bag), and which actor is on the stage at what time.
5. *Role-part*: the following describes a role-part: 'MURFINO: (Investigating the bag.) What's this?' A role-part describes the activities of an actor when it is his or her turn on stage.

6. *Sequence* of activities: the sequence of activities is specified in two ways. The order of the text lines suggests the order in time. However, when different activities are performed simultaneously (e.g. a crowd shouts while two knights are jousting), this is usually explained in the text between brackets.
7. *Conditions*: these are special comments between brackets that tell the actors how to adapt to specific situations. These are not shown in the fragment presented above, but an example would be: (if the audience laughs, tell them …; otherwise say …). Such constructs are generally found more in game scripts and other interactive scripts than in linear media formats such as plays and film.

In addition to these structural aspects, we can identify other important factors in our script metaphor. One is the specificity of the script: it can be very strict and detailed or more open to improvisation during performance. Specificity, in turn, is related to another factor, which is that the script of the play is different from the performance of the play itself. The script is a model of the play. It is a high-level description that focuses on some details but abstracts from others. The same script can be staged by many different theatre companies at many different locations, with different actors and for different audiences. It can be repeated over and over again, but the actual performance (a 'run' in computer terms) can be very different and have certain unique aspects to it. As a result, a script has to be instantiated and interpreted at different moments in time to create an actual play.

Another factor is that the scripting language has a particular format (roles, acts, etc.), but it does not require that the play be of any specific type (e.g. a comedy or a drama). In fact, all sorts of realities or fantasies can be modelled in a play or film. The medium puts constraints on what can be modelled, e.g. some things are possible in film that are not possible in the theatre, but these constraints only impact the quality of the representation, not its essence.

Finally, it is important to note that scripts are generally written by a specialist who is not necessarily the director or one of the actors.

Structuring Learning Design Methods as a Script

We can use the metaphor of a script to model learning design methods. Learning design methods have different names, one of which is 'lesson plan'. A search on the Internet reveals several sites with example lesson plans (see Van Es (2004) for a list). Let us look at a lesson plan for a Spanish course (Masciarelli 2004).

Title: Beginning of the Year or Semester Review for returning students
Primary Subject: Language Arts - Spanish; Grade Level - 6-8
General Goal: Student will be able to converse with peer in target language as a way of reviewing previously learned material.

Required Materials:
- Textbook (*Ven Conmigo*)
- Lined Paper
- Name sticks (for random pairing)

Anticipatory Set (Lead-In):
Show scene from accompanying video series that models student conversation. Discuss how at the end of the course last year, all students were able to converse like this.

Step-By-Step Procedures:
1. Students should be assigned partners by random pairing of name sticks.
2. Students should begin by reviewing key phrases and verbs. They should do this in pairs using a read and quiz method.
3. To reinforce the review, students should write an outline of what they'd like to say in their conversation, either as homework or in the next class. When students have completed their outline, they should create a realistic conversation.
4. After they have completed their conversation, the students should check with the teacher before memorising the dialogue. Any mistakes should be brought to the students' attention. Once correct, memorisation and practice should begin.
5. Once memorised, the conversation should be performed before the class.

Closure (Reflect Anticipatory Set): If lessons are videotaped, students may watch their videos and compare them to the series that accompanies the book.

Assessment Based On Objectives: Students may be graded using a rubric based on objectives or be given narrative feedback. Students could also use their own videos as a self-assessment tool.

We can model this lesson plan as a kind of play. The metadata is the title, author, learning objective (general goal). The roles are implicit: teacher and students. The script is told from the teacher's point of view. As no explicit acts are mentioned we can model it as a one-act play, but the grouping of activities suggests four acts (anticipatory set, step-by-step procedures, closure and assessment). The set-up of the learning environment is not described in detail, but a classroom context is implied. The role-part can be distilled from the text, for example:

Teacher: Show scene from accompanying video series…
Teacher: Assign students in random pairs, using name sticks…
Student: Review key phrases and verbs….

Note that the role-part is described using the structure ‘Role: Activity’. The sequence is indicated by the text, as in a script. Some conditions are mentioned: ‘if lessons are videotaped, …’; ‘when students have completed their outline’. Taking the script as our metaphor, we could rewrite the lesson plan as follows (in abridged form):

LEARNING DESIGN METHOD

Metadata:

Title: Beginning of the Year or Semester Review for returning students
Primary Subject: Language Arts, Spanish;
Students: Grade Level - 6-8
Setting: classroom, students grouped in pairs
Learning Objectives: Student will be able to ….

Play:

Act I (Anticipatory Set):
Teacher: Show scene from accompanying video series… (video set)
Act II (Step-by-step procedure):
Sequence:
1. Teacher: Assign students in random pairs, using name sticks… (name sticks)
2. Student: Review key phrases and verbs….(*Ven Conmigo*)
3. etc.
Act III (Closure)
Teacher: Grade students (score system) OR
Student: Use video to carry out self-assessment (video)

Conditions:

IF conversation is complete *THEN* students check with the teacher before memorising.
IF teacher wants to grade *THEN* students do not carry out self-assessment.
Etc.

Look at how the activities in the example are structured. Every activity implies certain resources that are needed to perform it, e.g. a classroom, name sticks or a book. To put it more generally: roles perform activities within an environment (e.g. classroom, stage, home). The environment is filled with resources (e.g. books, computers) that can be used. Every activity is closely related to the environment needed to perform the activity. When analysing the sentence that describes the activity, we get an idea of the resources needed in the environment. Take the sentence ‘students may watch their videos and compare them to the series that accompanies the book’. The verbs in the sentence (watch, compare) describe the behaviour students are expected to undertake. The nouns in the sentence define the resources that are needed (their videos, the series that accompanies the book). Besides these nouns, implicit resources may also be needed to perform the activity, e.g. the video player, a classroom. In the example above, we summed up the resources between brackets.

Method Components

Methods are not fixed in terms of number of components; they can be broken down into smaller methods or constituent parts. In the example above, the different acts can all be seen as smaller methods that can be reused in other contexts. The method used in the Spanish course can also be incorporated into a larger course or curriculum. This raises several intriguing questions: can we develop new methods from existing smaller ones, and what is the smallest workable, reusable unit for developing methods? The subject of reusing smaller learning objects (figures, computer programs and textbooks) is a popular one in the literature (see e.g. Littlejohn 2003). It is important to reuse learning objects, but we must bear in mind that they are not courses; they are the resources needed to perform learning activities. Reusing a learning resource in a new course still requires us to integrate the object into the course activities and method. So the exchange of learning resources can be seen as one level of reuse in education and training. Another option is to reuse learning design methods or parts of such methods. It is too early to say how far a learning design method can be broken down and what the smallest constituent part is; it may be a 'play', an 'act' or an 'activity'. We assume that all three can be exchanged to develop new courses.

Summary

In the previous sections, we analysed the structure of learning design rules. The formula takes the following format:

If Learning Situation:
Required level of effectiveness, efficiency, attractiveness, accessibility *AND*
Characteristics of learning objectives, learners, setting, media *AND*
Values of Learning Designer
then Learning Design Method:
A Play of one or more sequential Acts with one or more parallel Role-parts,
Taking into account a set of conditions for the Play, the Act or the Role-part
with A certain probability of success

1.4 Learning Design Rules: How Are They Derived?

Now that we know how a learning design rule is structured, we can answer the next question: how can we create rules that work, i.e. rules that offer a high probability that learners will indeed attain the intended learning outcomes? There are two aspects to this question: the particulars of the situation or situations in which the rule is used and its success within that specific context. The lesson plan for the course Spanish as a Second Language tells us the learning design method, for example, but we know very little about the situation in which it was used, and have no idea whether the method was successful. We need more information if we want to assess how good the rule is. For example, it would be nice to know the effectiveness of the method (percentage of students with a sufficiently high mark), or its efficiency. (How much time did it take to refresh the students' knowledge of Spanish in this way? Wouldn't other methods have been easier?) We also need more information about the underlying values or preferences of the method's designer. Did he or she include collaborative aspects because they have been shown to be more effective, efficient or attractive than other methods, or because he or she values these types of activities more than, for instance, individual work?

There are three categories of good rules: (1) those derived from instructional design theory, (2) those derived from best practices, and (3) those derived from patterns in best practices. We will refer to first type of rule as prescriptions, the second as examples and the third as patterns. The relationships and differences between the three categories are quite complex. For example, instructional design theory can be based on a rigorously empirical approach which results in approximately the same procedures as the patterns approach. Moreover, patterns can be abstracted to such an extent that the relationship between practice and pattern is lost.

We will now discuss the three types of rules briefly. We do not prefer one over another, but believe that all three are complementary.

1.4.1 Rules Derived from Theory

The romantic idea behind any theory is that it reveals an unconditional truth. When we apply this idea to learning design theory, it means that the theory would search for a learning method that can be applied universally: in every course, in every setting and for every person. To put it differently, the *If* side of the equation would be empty; there would be only one recommended learning design method. A recent example is the approach taken by Merrill (2003). He proposes some 'first principles of instruction', stating that 'the most effective learning products or environments are those that are problem centred and involve the student in four distinct phases of learning: (1) activation of prior experience, (2) demonstration of skill, (3) application of skill, and (4) integration of these skills into real-world activities'. He doesn't make this statement conditional on any particular situation: his principles are the minimum requirements for every learning product.

Leaving aside whether these principles are indeed unconditional, we do know that they are based on a review of recent research into instructional design and that using them to develop a learning design method will probably increase the effectiveness of that method. However, let us return to our wish to design a Spanish course. Do these principles provide us with enough guidelines actually to design the course? The answer is no. The principles can be used to check whether an existing design meets the requirements, but they are not practical enough for a course developer (although they can be inspiring). Course developers want more detail, perhaps even complete examples of real practice.

Besides these *universal* principles, we also come across *conditional* instructional design principles in the literature, although they tend to be hard to find for a learning designer, and sometimes contradict one another or are hard to combine. It would be useful to have a summary of current, state-of-the-art instructional design principles, using a uniform rule format such as the one presented in this book, and similar to the attempt made by Reigeluth (1999). It would provide some dozens of models and summarise them in a conditional format (*If* situation *then* use this method). One example is the rule for designing constructivist learning (abridged; Mayer 1999, see next page).

The prescriptive rule is conditional, but it still has a high level of abstraction. It can be used to explore a wide range of design problems, but it does not provide specific guidelines for the designers of our Spanish course, for example.

Desired outcomes and conditions
Foster knowledge construction through direct instruction. Primarily intended for textbook-based learning, lectures and multimedia environments in which behavioural activity is not possible.

Values
- focus on process and product of learning
- focus on knowledge transfer and retention
- focus on how to learn as well as what to learn

Major Methods
1. Select relevant information
- highlight the most important information for the learner (using headings, italics, etc.)
- use instructional objectives and/or adjunct questions
- provide a summary
- eliminate irrelevant information; be concise
2. Organise information for the learner
- structure the text in some defined formats (cause-effect structure, generalisation structure, enumeration structure, classification structure or comparison/contrast structure)
- Outlines
- Headings
- Pointers or signal words
- Graphic representations
3. Integrate information
- advanced organisers
- illustrations with captions
- animations with narration
- detailed examples
- detailed questions

1.4.2 Rules Derived from Best Practice

Another way of deriving learning design rules is to take the learning design method used in a specific example course. In this approach, our search for a learning design method ends not with a principle but with a comprehensive example. We can use several tactics to do so. The first is to set up a database of accessible and usable courses or course components (e.g. Edusource 2004; Merlot 2004), i.e. 'out-of-the-box'. The second tactic is to set up a database of learning design methods, e.g. course scripts, frameworks or lesson plans. The 'Spanish as a Second Language' lesson plan is an example. Lesson plans are more abstract than actual courses and can be used as specific guidelines for designing a new course. However, unlike in the first example, the course has yet to be developed.

One major problem with all such collections of examples is that the situational characteristics of the courses and lesson plans must be described in enough detail to support a successful search process. They must also provide an indication of the quality, and the resulting learning design method must be available in a usable format if it is to be of any practical use. Quality can be expressed by the probability of success; other methods are peer review, expert review or the average quality ratings of users.

Unlike with rules derived from theory, when rules are derived from best practice the resulting learning design method is very well defined – an advantage that also has its disadvantages. The chance of finding a successful example that matches precisely is not very great. It would take a huge number of courses and lesson plans to have a reasonable chance of identifying a suitable solution. In other words: whereas the theoretical approach is intended to be of general purpose because it excludes conditions as much as possible, the example-based approach is so highly contingent on conditions that the chance of finding a matching example is relatively small. However, it may be worth a try. Things have changed now that the Internet allows us to share course examples and lesson plans with others on a massive scale. A search on the Internet revealed at least 93,901 lesson plans in 16 different databases (see Van Es 2004). Some of these contained a large number of lesson plans (more than 35,000), while others were too small to be of any real use (fewer than 1000, some even fewer than 100). Learning designers are advised to try first try to find existing examples on one of the websites identified by Van Es. Other approaches, e.g. that of theoretical prescriptions, are preferable only when no matching examples can be found.

1.4.3 Rules Derived from Patterns in Best Practice

The third, rather new and promising approach is to analyse patterns in collections of comparable best practices, instead of using just one comprehensive example. Patterns reflect the experience of experts in the field, are described concisely and solve recurrent problems in a learning design. Patterns can be created in two ways: inductively, by analysing common structures in a set of learning design methods, or deductively, by having meetings with experienced learning designers to identify recurrent problems and generic models for solutions. The second approach is the more popular one at the moment (e.g. Bergin et al. 2000; E-LEN 2004). The following is an example of a pedagogical pattern (abridged; Eckstein 2000):

LEARNING TO TEACH AND LEARNING TO LEARN: RUNNING A COURSE

Problem: how to start a course?
Forces: you want to get to know the participants; want to break the ice; …
Solution: the participants introduce themselves in a way which at the same time provides an introduction to the topic (different variants are provided).
Discussion: for participants who seem to be aggressive, choose variant …

Problem: how can you make students less dependent on the teacher?
Forces: it's easy for students to ask the teacher, but in a work environment the teacher will not be available
Solution: assign a problem to your students. When they have a problem ask them to search for answers with their peers first.
Discussion: a group often has different skills …

etc.

The rule expressed in the example takes the format: '*if* problem situation, *then* solution'. This is similar to our approach. The problem is a widespread one in education. The solution is expressed in informal terms. This is fine for human readers, but will be difficult to support when computers are brought in. The different pedagogical patterns that can currently be found on the Internet all define their own pattern language. To allow us to search, store, adapt and use patterns, we need to adopt a single, standard notation. For example, taking the script modelling language presented above, we could develop a pattern of a learning design rule as follows:

Situation:
- Train a skill
- Setting: individual student

Method:

Play	Act I:	Student: read/study introductory information
	Act II:	(repeat for n exercises)
		Student: do exercise (1...n)
		Student: if question, then ask other student or tutor
		Student: answer questions posed by fellow students
		Tutor: if fellow students cannot respond, then answer students' questions
		Student: take test, and get feedback about test results
	Act III:	Tutor or Agent: Provide feedback about learning outcome

A pattern such as above could be used as a learning design template for many skill-learning situations. The pattern can be derived from existing examples by abstracting the learning design methods, mainly by looking at common patterns.

Patterns can also be combined. For instance, the pattern above does not describe how to prepare the introductory information or tests. This usually means that they are available in the design and are fixed. In many situations, the tutor prefers to control this information so that he or she can develop or adapt it. A pattern for texts and tests may take the following form:

Situation:
- Develop/adapt introductory information (or tests)

Method:

Play	Act I: Tutor: develop/adapt introductory information (or tests)

The methods can be combined to form the following pattern:

Situation:
- Train a skill
- Develop/adapt introductory information
- Develop/adapt tests
- Setting: individual student

Method:

Play	Act I:	Tutor: develop/adapt introductory information
	Act II:	Tutor: develop/adapt test
	Act III:	Student: read/study introductory information
	Act IV:	(repeat for n exercises) Student: do exercise (1...n) Student: if question, then ask other student or tutor Student: answer questions posed by fellow students Tutor: if fellow students cannot respond, then answer students' questions Student: take test, and get feedback about test results
	Act V:	Tutor or Agent: provide feedback about learning outcome

---

The main point here is not how correct the example is, but how to notate the patterns and the idea of composing learning design methods based on smaller pattern components. The notation can be easily translated into a more formal notation, such as that provided by Learning Design (LD 2003), as we will see later in this book. These examples also give an initial indication of the level at which the learning designs are being reused, i.e. at the level of short plays that can be combined to form longer ones. This would suggest that we should identify practical, small-scale, independent play structures with a recurrent objective (as expressed in the situation) as the building blocks for learning design methods.

It would be useful for authors to have access not only to the patterns, but also to the specific examples derived from them, preferably notated in Learning Design so that they can be adapted and reused.

1.5 Conclusion

A learning designer uses learning design knowledge to create the learning design method for a course. Learning design knowledge consists of a series of rules taking the '*if* situation, *then* method' format. These rules are derived from theory, from examples, or from patterns. To enable learning designers to search for, share and reuse learning design methods, a standard notation must be available and used.

In this chapter several design requirements have been mentioned throughout the text. To conclude this chapter we will state the requirements for a learning design notation:

1. The notation must be comprehensive. It must describe the teaching–learning activities of a course in detail and include references to the learning objects and services needed to perform the activities. This means describing:
   - How the activities of both the learners and the staff roles are integrated.
   - How the resources (objects and services) used during learning are integrated.
   - How both single and multiple user models of learning are supported.
2. The notation must support mixed mode (blended learning) as well as pure online learning.
3. The notation must be sufficiently flexible to describe learning designs based on all kinds of theories; it must avoid biasing designs towards any specific pedagogical approach.
4. The notation must be able to describe conditions within a learning design that can be used to tailor the learning design to suit specific persons or specific circumstances.
5. The notation must make it possible to identify, isolate, de-contextualise and exchange useful parts of a learning design (e.g. a pattern) so as to stimulate their reuse in other contexts.
6. The notation must be standardised and in line with other standard notations.

7. The notation must provide a formal language for learning designs that can be processed automatically.
8. The specification must enable a learning design to be abstracted in such a way that repeated execution, in different settings and with different persons, is possible.

These requirements provided the basis for the Educational Modelling Language (EML 2000; Koper 2001; Koper and Manderveld, 2004), and the later standardised version of EML, called Learning Design (Koper and Olivier 2004; Hummel et al. 2004; LD 2003). Koper and Olivier (2004) provide a first qualitative evaluation to what extent these requirements are met by the LD specification. They conclude that the specification fits the requirements well, however further research is needed to a) evaluate how well LD meets the pedagogical expressiveness requirement, b) integrate the Question and Test Interoperability (QTI 2003) specification into LD (this has since been done through an update of the QTI specification by IMS), and c) the personalization rules aspects have to be studied in more detail. The following chapter examines the LD specification in more detail.

2 The Learning Design Specification

Bill Olivier[1], Colin Tattersall[2]

[1] Bolton Institute of Higher Education, Bolton, United Kingdom

[2] Educational Technology Expertise Centre,
Open University of the Netherlands, Heerlen, The Netherlands

2.1 Introduction

The preface and the previous chapter introduced the idea of describing a learning design in terms of "people in specific groups and roles engage in activities using an environment with appropriate resources and services". To be usable by computers, this language has to be given a concrete syntax and semantics, and this is provided by the Learning Design (LD 2003) specification.

The documents which make up the specification can be quite daunting, and this chapter aims to lower the threshold to their comprehension. It starts with some historical background, examines the intended readership for the specification, then provides a reading guide to the specification documents, before giving an overview of the ideas and concepts in LD and how they are intended to work together when used to represent a Unit of Learning (UOL). The overview is intended to make it easier to understand the specification and the dynamics of a running learning design.

2.2 The Move from EML to Learning Design

IMS Global Consortium Inc.'s (IMS) work on specifications and the Open University of the Netherlands' (OUNL) R&D Programme into Learning Technologies that resulted in the Educational Modelling Language (EML 2000), both started around the same time in 1997. IMS's early work developed a number of e-learning specifications, mainly targeting support processes for learning rather than the learning process itself. By early 2001, IMS had reached the point where it recognised the need for a specification that addressed the description of learning processes and set up the Learning Design Working Group. It had an ambitious scope which could only be met in a reasonable timescale if it was based on an existing work. EML was submitted to the Working Group in the second quarter of 2001.

EML was a very complete and mature specification, focused on the entire learning process and was thus complementary to the specifications developed by IMS. Moreover, the use of SGML as the format in which to cast EML fitted well with the IMS specification development approach, which requires its specifications to be described using XML Schema (W3C 2004b). As a result, EML was accepted by the Working Group as the basis from which to develop the LD specification in August 2001.

The EML specification included both a DocBook-based (OASIS 2002) content specification for marking up materials used in the learning process, and extensions for multimedia, assessments and learner interaction with the runtime system, known as a player (see Chap. 3 for details). The content model and extensions were dropped from LD by the Working Group, which recommended the use of XHTML (W3C 2002) allowing both web content, including typical web-enabled multimedia, and XML extensions. It was agreed that Question and Test Interoperability (QTI 2003) should be used for assessment, but defining how it should integrate with LD was left until a later version of QTI was released. Separate mechanisms were introduced to allow communication between content and LD players (described later in this chapter). A further change involved the integration of LD into the Content Packaging specification (CP 2003) Organizations element. When used for an LD package, it replaces the simple Organization/Item tree structure with a richer, more developed structure.

These modifications were proposed and the IMS LD 1.0 specification was approved in February 2003. Thus, the central concepts of EML were brought into a neutral forum in which members with various business interests and decision-making criteria collaborate to satisfy real-world learning requirements for interoperability and reuse.

2.3 Who Is the Learning Design Specification for?

In understanding the LD specification and assessing its relevance and importance, it is important to distinguish between the specification itself and its application in the wider e-learning landscape. The specification is a very detailed document intended primarily for software developers who create the tools and systems that implement LD. However, it is also intended to be understood by technically aware learning and instructional designers to enable them to determine its suitability for their purposes. Generally, the XML format of LD should not normally be visible, in the same way that document formats such as RTF are not normally seen by users but are hidden and processed by software applications such as word processors. LD authoring and runtime tools should provide users with higher-level representations for carrying out their tasks.

Although the specification itself has a narrowly defined readership, its use is intended to provide a number of benefits for various e-learning stakeholders:

1. E-learning system lock-in is avoided since courses can be exported as LD Units of Learning from one system into another. The need to move courses between systems occurs both when new systems are purchased and when a heterogeneous set of tools is used at the same time, a situation not uncommon in both single and multiple learning provider situations.
2. Procurement choices are increased through increasing system interoperability, with commercial and open-source tooling being better able to be mixed-and-matched to satisfy e-learning requirements.
3. The market for buying and selling courses is made more appealing, since publishers are no longer bound to publishing for particular delivery systems.
4. Instructional and learning designers are liberated from the use of non e-learning specific (e.g. HTML) or proprietary scripting languages to create learning processes. Using the concepts described in the specification, designers are able to talk in terms of pedagogy rather than technology, making pedagogical choices explicit and subject to review, inspection and critique.
5. New avenues for educational R&D are opened, with diverse approaches to learning and teaching being better able to be compared when they are both described and delivered in a formal language defined in an open, technical specification.

The recency of the specification means that these benefits have yet to be reaped in practice. However, the use of the specification is intended and expected to lead to increases in the efficiency, effectiveness and attractiveness of e-learning, thereby improving the lot of one other important e-learning stakeholder: the e-learner.

2.4 A Reading Guide to the Specification Documents

IMS has developed a set of document types for its specifications. There are three main documents: an *Information Model*, a *Best Practice and Implementation Guide* (BPIG) and an *XML Binding document*.

The documents of the LD specification are intended to be read by technical domain specialists, learning technologists and learning and instructional designers. For almost all readers, the BPIG is the best place to start, since it is an informative, rather than a normative document. It provides background information and guidance on how the LD specification is intended to be used to represent various kinds of learning. Members of IMS submitted a range of learning scenarios, referred to as 'use cases', representing the kind of learning they would like to see supported. As part of the validation process for the specification, these were translated into LD XML representations. Some of these XML representations are included in the document but the larger ones were published as separate XML files.

The first part of the BPIG is primarily intended for more technically oriented experts in the learning domain, although it is also of value to developers, particularly those developing authoring tools, and LD editors. In addition to the BPIG, the first chapters of the LD Information Model, up to the start of the Information Tables themselves, will also be of value to learning domain experts. Unless they are familiar with XML, those focused primarily on learning do not need to read the XML Binding Document, which is intended primarily for software developers. The actual XML Schemas are published separately. Also, as various XML software toolkits and libraries are not able to handle modular XML Schemas, the OUNL has made single schemas for each level available on the website www.learningneworks.org.

The Implementer's Guide section of the BPIG is, as its name suggests, intended primarily for implementers, particularly those responsible for developing runtime systems, although it is also useful to teachers and system administrators responsible for setting up LD runtime systems and Units of Learning for use with learners.

The Implementer's Guide inevitably provides only an overview of the main issues at a fairly high level, outlining the main tasks and significant aspects of implementing an LD runtime system. A more thorough treatment can be found in Chaps. 3, 4 and 5 of this book.

Probably of more use to runtime system developers will be an open-source reference implementation such as the CopperCore runtime engine (Vogten and Martens 2004) developed by the OUNL, and described in Chap. 6.

After reading the Implementer's Guide, and the early parts of the Information Model, developers can either go to the XML Binding document and XML Schema files, using the Information Model tables to gain more details about the intended use of the various elements, or might prefer to continue on to the Behavioural Model section in the Information Model to gain a better understanding of how the different parts of the LD specification are intended to work together.

2.5 Understanding the Learning Design Specification

2.5.1 Units of Learning

The LD specification provides a framework of elements that can be used to describe formally the design of any teaching–learning process. A UOL refers to a complete, self-contained unit of education or training, such as a course, a module, a lesson, etc. The creation of a UOL involves the creation of a learning design and also the bundling of all its associated resources, either as files contained in the unit or as web references, including assessments, learning materials and learning service configuration information. As a result, a packaging mechanism is needed to pack the learning design and its associated files into a single container. The LD specification recommends the use of the CP specification for this purpose.

2.5.2 Where Learning Design Fits into a Content Package

A Content Package consists of a file structure that must include a 'manifest' and the associated files. The manifest is described in detail in the CP specification. It includes the structure of the content, described in the Organizations section which defines a simple tree hierarchy; a list of the files themselves contained in the Resources section; and a Metadata section that describes the package.

The structure of a Content Package and the manifest is shown in Fig. 2.1. The LD specification is constructed so that it can fit into a Content Package as a discrete element, effectively replacing the simple initial tree structure held in the `Organization` element (see Fig. 2.2).

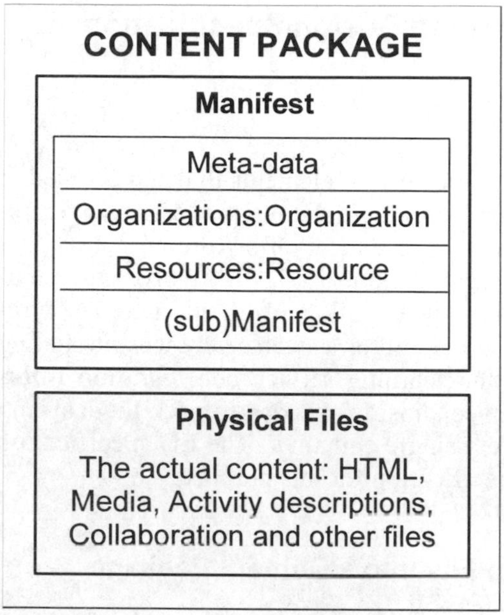

CONTENT PACKAGE
Manifest
Meta-data
Organizations:Organization
Resources:Resource
(sub)Manifest
Physical Files
The actual content: HTML, Media, Activity descriptions, Collaboration and other files

Fig. 2.1. The structure of a Content Package

Unit of Learning
Manifest
Meta-data
Organizations:Learning Design
Resources:Resource
(sub)Manifest
Physical Files
The actual content: HTML, Media, Activity descriptions, Collaboration and other files

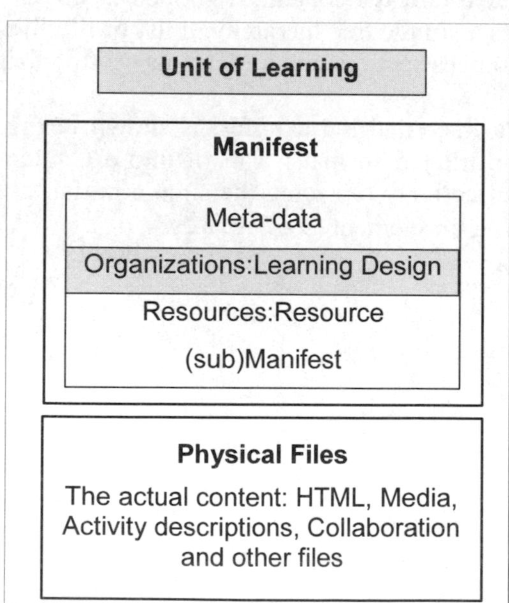

Fig. 2.2. The location of the `learning-design` element in a Content Package

2.5.3 Looking Inside the `learning-design` element

The `learning-design` element in turn has many component elements, as do they themselves. The following shows the main 'top-level' elements within the `learning-design` element.

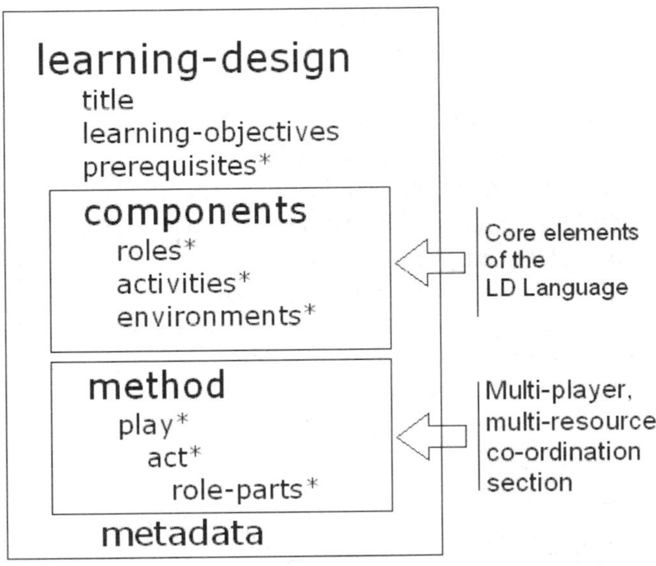

Fig. 2.3. The basic structure of the `learning-design` element

In Fig. 2.3, the `learning-design` element, as well as having a `title` (most major elements include a title but these are omitted in the figures), `learning-objectives`, `prerequisites` and `metadata` elements, also includes a `components` and a `method` element. Note that `learning-objectives` can be described using either purely textual resources or resources that are defined according to the Reusable Definitions of Competencies and Educational Objectives specification (RDCEO 2002).

The `components` and `method` elements are the two main and largest structures in LD.

The `components` includes the three components originally identified as the main elements of the language:

1. `roles`
2. `activities`

3. `environments` (which hold references to the resources and services used by activities).

The `Method` holds the workflow or 'learning flow' for the learning design, and contains three main nested elements:

- `play*`
  - `act*`
    - `role-part*`

Thus a `play` contains one or more `acts` and an `act` contains one or more `role-parts`.

While the `components` element contains the main structural elements, the `method` drives the whole process when a learning design is being run. As a result, when reading a UOL that conforms to LD, the method element provides an orientation point from which to view how the parts fit together. Since both a learning designer and a design implementer need to understand how a learning design is expected to play out with learners when it "goes live" in a player, an overview of this is given next.

2.5.4 Running a Learning Design

Once a learning design has been set up on a runtime system, the player uses the method to make the appropriate activities and environments available to the people playing the various roles. Through this, it coordinates and synchronises multiple learners as they work through a learning design. Figure 2.4 sketches the `method` and `components` of a learning design.

The `method` part is where the top-level coordination of people and activities takes place, and can be described using the metaphor of a theatrical play, following on from Chap.1. A `play`, as in a theatrical play, consists of `acts`, although there can be one-act plays.

As with theatrical plays, `acts` run in sequence, with one starting when the previous act has finished, and the play ends with the completion of the last `act`. The transition from one act to another serves as a synchronisation point for the multiple participants in a learning design, ensuring that they can all start the next act at the same time. If a given learning scenario does not require such points, then it can be designed with a single act.

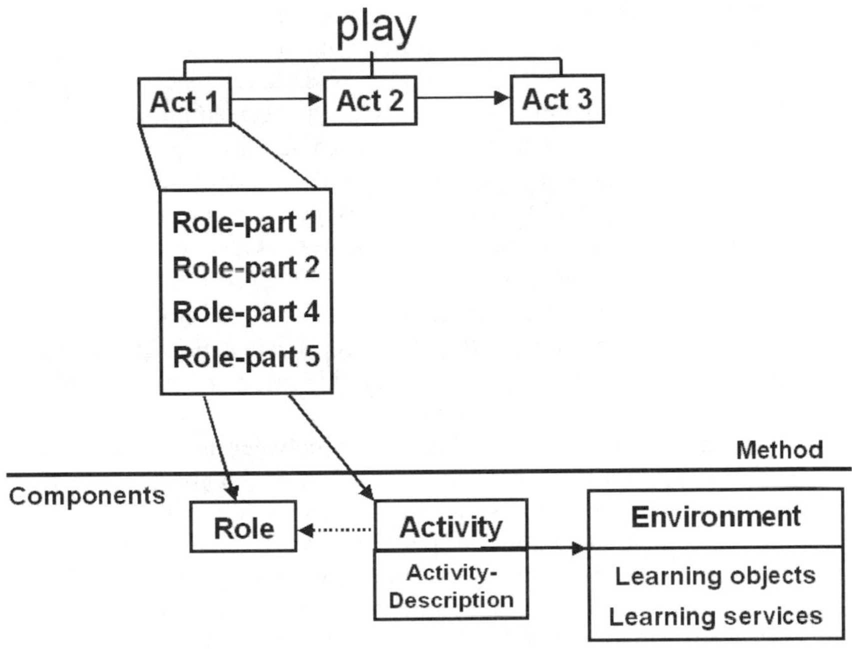

Fig. 2.4. Relating the learning flow to its constituent components

Again, as in a theatrical play, an `act` includes one or more `role-parts`, which are 'on stage' at the same time.

A `role-part` simply has two reference links; one refers to a `role` and the other to the `activity` that the role is to perform in the `act`. Effectively the `role-part` assigns an activity to a role, analogous to giving a role the script that it has to perform in the act.

An activity includes an `activity-description` and typically a reference link to an `environment`. The activity description says what the role should do with any items included in the environment.

An environment may include both learning objects (web pages or other content, Content Packages, SCORM objects (ADL 2004a), QTI-compliant tests, etc.), and/or learning services which are to be used in the activity (see Sect. 2.5.5).

The horizontal line dividing Fig. 2.4 separates the elements that are included in the `method`, which are above the line, and those included in the `components`, which are below the line. Thus `role-parts` act as the link between the method section and the components section.

This division also marks another important distinction: the method is essentially where the coordination of multiple roles takes place. The transition from one `Act` to another is essentially a synchronisation point for all the participants. In effect, it releases a new set of activities and materials to all participants in the new act's role-parts at the same time. It does not necessarily mean that those who have not finished their current activity are forced to move on, as, by default, all earlier activities and resources should continue to be made available. A designer could choose to create a `condition` whereby some or all previous material is made invisible, e.g. if the next act consists of a memory test with no referring. Equally, when an activity is assigned to a role, in practice what this means is that the activity is assigned to each person playing that role.

It is important to understand the relationship between individual participants and roles. When a UOL is *instantiated*, part of the process is assigning individuals to the role or roles they are to play. A role may have one or more participants, with the number of participants left open, or the learning designer may specify maximum and minimum numbers of participants for the role (see Chap. 4 for further information on the instantiation of UOLs). When creating a run of a UOL, the role-parts in the first act must be checked, and the activity in each role-part must be assigned to each person assigned to the corresponding role.

An activity should have learning objectives, prerequisites, a description and a reference link to an environment with learning objects and/or learning services. The player has to provide each person with access to these and track their individual use of them, so that after they log off from a session, when they next return they can be presented with the activity in the same state as they last saw it. Thus the presentation of, engagement with and progress through LD activities and their compound activity structures are done on an individual basis, although learners, teachers and other users can engage with each other and work together through shared collaborative learning services.

Although LD supports models that involve multiple learners, it can be used for models involving single learners. Used in this way, it is possible to use LD to implement programmed learning, just as easily as collaborative and multi-user scenarios.

Figure 2.5. fills out the LD structure.

Components
    Role
        learner*
        staff*
    Activities
        learning-activity*
            environment-ref*
            activity-description
        support-activity*
        activity-structure* {sequence | selection}
            environment-ref*
            activity-ref*
            activity-structure-ref*
    Environments
        environment*
            learning-object*
            learning-service*
                mail-send*
                conference*
Method
    Play*
        Act*
            Role-Part*
                role-ref
                activity-ref

Fig. 2.5. The further parts of the components and methods sections

The role-part includes: a reference to a role and a reference to an activity. In the components which precede it, roles include predefined learner and staff roles, but learning designers can define other roles of their own, derived from these basic two.

Activities include learning-activities, support-activities and activity-structures. Learning-activities and support-activities have a similar structure. As shown in Fig. 2.5. an activity can include an environment reference and an activity description. However, it also includes a title, metadata, learning-objectives and prerequisites (which, for brevity, are not shown in these diagrams).

Activity-structures contain a simple list of references to activities and/or other (sub)activity-structures. The attribute `structure-type` has two possible values: `sequence` and `selection` (the default). Using the former value indicates that the elements should be presented in sequence, separately, to each learner. The latter value indicates that the player should provide some mechanism, such as a menu or navigation tree, which allows the user to choose from the list.

Note that `sequence` and `selection` provide simple dynamics for a single user when engaging with an `activity-structure`. More sophisticated dynamics can be provided through the use of properties and conditions (if–then type rules explained below). However, as activity-structures can be nested, `sequence` and `selection` can be used to provide some degree of flexibility without the use of conditional rules. A set of activities and activity-structures may be set to run in a `sequence`, but when a particular activity-structure in the sequence is reached this could be set to `selection`, allowing the user a choice of activities at that point. One of these activities might in turn contain another sub-structure where the activities have to be worked through in a sequence, and there are many possible variations of this.

A further refinement is that the number of activities can be set for a `selection`. This means that if the `number-to-select` is set to a value of `1`, then only one of the optional activities needs to be carried out, and the user can choose which one. If the `number-to-select` equals the number of activities, this means that all activities must be carried out, but the order in which they are done is not important.

In this way, activity-structures can be used to create more elaborate sets of activities and choices to present to users on an individual basis.

2.5.5 Learning Objects and Learning Services

A learning object typically links through to a web page or other content item (making it essentially equivalent to an Item element in a Content Package).

As already described, an `environment` can contain learning objects learning-services. The selection of services reflects the most widely implemented and used services in online learning environments at the time of approval of version 1 of the LD specification: `send-mail`, `conference`, `monitor`, and `index search`. These services must either be provided by the player, or be separate services that are linked to by the player (e.g. they might be provided by standard email and Netnews servers respectively).

Underneath, what distinguishes a 'learning object' from a 'learning service' is simply that for a learning object, its location (or URL) is known at design time, whereas the location for a learning service is created when a UOL is instantiated. The reason for this is that an LD learning service includes a mapping of LD roles onto the roles in the service (e.g. for a conference this includes `participant`, `observer`, `moderator` and `ad-`

`ministrator` and usually grants participants different permissions in a conferencing system in the allocated space). At design time, not only are the actual participants unknown, but they will change every time the UOL is run. If we again take the example of using a conference system in a UOL, what a designer may well intend is a unique discussion space dedicated to the use of the actual participants in each run.

To handle this, when a UOL is being set up prior to a run with a particular group of participants, the participants have first to be mapped to the roles specified in the learning design. Typically this would be done through a management utility provided with the runtime system.

The learning design is then scanned for all learning services and, with a list of participants for each role, a dedicated instance of the service is set up using the list of participants in the relevant roles and the mapping of LD roles to the service roles contained in the UOL's service definition. Setting up the service can be done in one of two ways. If the service only has a user interface for creating instances, then setting up the service with the actual participants has to be done manually. In this case, the set-up function of the management utility should produce a human-readable list of the necessary services together with a list of people mapped to the service's roles. If, on the other hand, the service has a machine-to-machine interface, then the management utility can produce a script to automate the process of setting up the service. The ability to set up collaborative and other services automatically is of some practical importance, as without it, the load on system administrators will result in limiting the use of such services and hence conflict with the learning goals.

Once a service has been set up, the link (URL or other identifier) to this service has to be passed back to the player, along with the reference to the service in the learning design. From then on, the LD player can treat a learning service in the same way as a learning object, by simply providing, at the appropriate point, a hyperlink to it in the learner's web browser interface.

It is worth noting that where a service such as a `conference` is requested, it could be met in several ways. One of the systems available where the design is deployed could be used, or this approach could be substituted for a face-to-face meeting or a conference call with a link being made to a web page providing information about time, place, phone number and other details as appropriate.

It should also be noted that services such as computer-based conferencing systems do not have a standardised configuration interface. This means that LD management utilities are likely to produce some XML files, which will then need a further specialised transformation into the configuration calls needed for the particular service to be used. It will be of benefit if all LD management utilities produced such service configuration information in the same XML format, so a small 'adjunct' specification outlining this may well be produced. This would at least limit one side of the many-to-many translations that are otherwise necessary so that only one transformation needs to be written for any given service which all LD management utilities can use. In the longer term, a standard interface to the service may be produced for each service so that the ideal of *plug-and-play* between LD systems and services can be achieved.

2.6 Learning Design Levels A, B and C

LD has three levels:

- Level A contains the core language of LD that has been covered so far.
- Level B adds properties and conditions to Level A, allowing more sophisticated control and types of learning.
- Level C adds notifications to Levels A and B.

There were several reasons for partitioning LD into three levels:

- It gives developers the option of releasing their implementation of this large specification in stages.
- The properties and conditions of Level B can be seen as a more general capability that overlaps to some extent with the functionality of Simple Sequencing (SS 2003), which, while starting later than LD, was developed in parallel. By making the LD properties and conditions optional and allowing Simple Sequencing to be used where possible, it enables the door to reuse of Simple Sequencing in LD.
- Notifications were separated to allow those developers whose Learning Management Systems were primarily content oriented, rather than communication oriented, to choose whether not to implement this feature, or to add it at a later date.

A separate reason relates to compliance. The LD specification defines a system rather than just a collection of elements. That is to say, the elements all work together and depend on each other. Therefore, to be compliant with LD, a system is required to implement all features for a given level, whether or not they are indicated in the specification as mandatory or optional. Mandatory and optional relate only to particular instances of learning designs which, when exchanged between systems as an XML file, do not have to include optional features. Thus the conformance requirements for systems that implement LD are more stringent than for document instances.

The three levels show where this natural partitioning of LD lies, and how the main parts of LD build on each other. Thus the parts contained in Level A are seen as a whole that provides a minimum level of capability that meets the requirements of the specification. But Level A has no dependency on Level B, although Level B depends upon and extends the elements in Level A; while Levels A and B have no dependency on Level C, but Level C in turn depends upon and extends the elements in Levels A and B.

2.6.1 Level B

Level B adds Properties and Conditions. Properties enable information about learner, roles and the state of the learning design itself to be maintained. Conditions enable designers to define rules that govern the behaviour of the UOL as a whole and what gets presented to individual participants.

Properties

Properties are of two main types, 'Local' and 'Global', which can in turn be General, Person or Role Properties.

Local Properties (Table 2.1) live only for the duration of each 'run' of a UOL.

Table 2.1. Local Properties

Property Type	Description
General Property (loc-property)	attached to a UOL as a whole
Person Property (locpers-property)	attached to each individual user
Role Property (locrole-property)	attached to all members of a role

Global Properties (Table 2.2) persist across multiple runs of a UOL.

Table 2.2 Global Properties

Property Type	Description
General Property (glob-property)	attached to a UOL as a whole
Person Property (globpers-property)	attached to each individual user

Property Groups act as a container that holds a set of Properties of the same type and may also contain
(sub-)Property Groups.

Properties can be used for many different purposes, but one common use is to use Person Properties to provide more detailed information about learners to adapt a learning design to individual needs and preferences. This can be done either before a run of a UOL starts or during the run, using tests that are integrated in the LD (see Chap. 10). Another use is to maintain the state information during the run of a UOL. This can be used to determine, dynamically, when an action should be triggered (e.g. on the completion of an Act, or indeed to trigger other events).

A Property has the simple structure described in Table 2.3.

Table 2.3. The structure of a property

Structural Element	Description
A name (title)	a text string that uniquely identifies the property
A type (datatype)	a data type, such as text, integer, URL and several others
A value	a value which can be set initially by the designer or during the run
An identifier	a unique identifier that is an XML ID in the XML binding
Restrictions	a designer may constrain the permissible values
Metadata	metadata can be added to describe a property

This property structure is essentially the same as that used for handling the results of tests in QTI and as that used for handing the outcomes of activities in the Learner Information Package specification (LIP 2001). The former can be used to pass results from a separate test service or QTI runtime engine to an LD player while the latter can be used to store information generated about a learner during the run of a learning design to a separate dossier or ePortfolio repository

One main difference between these different specifications is that QTI and LIP do not limit their identifiers to XML IDs. In the LD specification, the characters that can be used to compose a Property identifier are limited to those that can be used in an XML ID (an identifier that uniquely identifies an element in an XML document). This was to facilitate automatic validation of properties and the references to them in a UOL. However, this has a potential drawback in terms of integrating with other IMS specifications, as these do not have the restrictions imposed by an XML ID, allowing any characters to be used. It is likely that these three IMS specifications will be harmonised in future (see Chap. 10 for more on integrating QTI and LD).

Properties are also associated with a further addition to the level A specification: 'Global Elements'. In essence, global elements enable properties and groups of properties to be both viewed and set by participants at runtime, and so are part of LD Level B.

In order to function through a learner's browser, global elements are provided as XML extensions to an XHTML web page. When an XHTML page includes the LD-defined `global elements`, it is given a CP type of `IMSLDcontent`. The definition of these XML extensions is provided as a small XML Schema that is separate from the main LD Level A, B and C XML schemas.

When viewing or setting a property, there is a default set to `self` which means that only the learner's own properties can be viewed or set. This can be changed to `supported-person` which allows someone given a support role to see properties of the people in a given role that they are supporting.

The particular properties or property-groups that are to be made accessible by the system are defined by the learning designer at design time.

Conditions

Conditions provide the capability for learning designers to define rules as to what should happen when certain events take place.

The simplest kind of event is provider by a timer *when the UOL's runtime clock reaches a given point in time, then carry out a specified action*.

The time can simply be checked against the current date and time, or it can be the time since the UOL or since a particular Activity started.

Rules can also be triggered when an Activity or Activity-structure, a Role-part, Act, Play or even the UOL as a whole has completed.

Another common event that can be checked for by rules is the changing of a property value. This might be when it is first given a value, when it is set to a value that is equal to, above or below a number given in the rule, or is set to a value between two other numbers. It could also be triggered if a text Property's value is set equal to a text string defined in the rule. The value of a Property can also be checked against the value of another Property, rather than against just a fixed value defined in the rule. Equally all other types of Property can be used in condition rules.

A number of types of action can be triggered from a rule. A rule can hide or show `learning-objects` and `learning-services`, `environments`, `Activities`, `Activity-structures`, or `Plays`. (there can be more than one Play running in parallel and one might be hidden unless or until a rule is triggered which reveals it). Note that it is not possible to show or hide Acts or Role-parts.

Rules can also be used to set or change Property values. This can be used to create records of what a person has done, to change what is presented to them, or to change how a live learning design functions.

In Level C, rules are extended so that they can also trigger a notification.

2.6.2 Level C

Notifications provide a greater level of interactivity and control over a live learning design, as a form of event-driven messaging system within an LD player. Notifications can be sent both to elements of the design, as well as to human participants. At Level C, a notification can be triggered by an activity completing or by a rule, but a human participant, through the global elements, can also trigger a notification to be sent, either to another human or to a design element.

Through addressing design elements, a notification can be used to make a new activity visible (or invisible) to participants in a role, or it can be used to set a property value. As rules can be triggered by property changes, setting a property value that has such a condition attached to it can trigger other actions.

Figure 2.6 shows the Level C Information Model containing all the concepts in the LD specification.

The Future of Learning Services in LD

Learning Services are a significant area that LD opens up, but that is as yet relatively undeveloped, both in the specification and in current LD practice.

Clearly many more services could be added to the LD specification, and it is desirable that they should be, from chat, instant messaging and whiteboards, through virtual classrooms and more sophisticated collaborative services, such as virtual design environments, to sophisticated simulation and multi-user game-playing systems.

The key issue that needs to be addressed is how to add services in such a way that learning designs that use them still retain a reasonable degree of portability across different LD-compliant platforms. If all the above services were included, could any system be expected to be compliant? Or should the specification stick to the lowest common denominator for services, as in LD v.1.0, only supporting them as they become commonly available in systems?

Clearly individual institutions could extend the specification to support their own services, though they would have to adapt their LD instantiation facilities in order to integrate them.

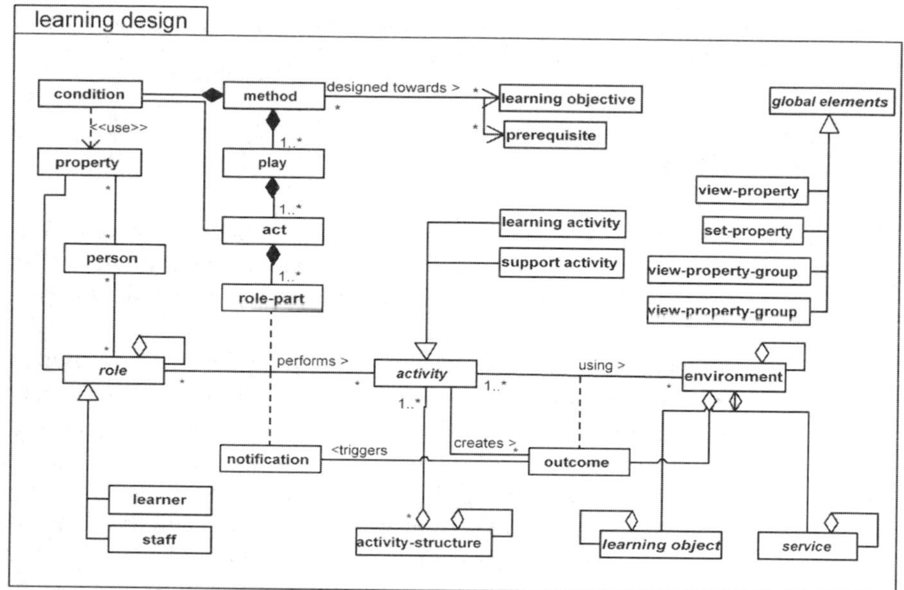

Fig. 2.6. The LD Information Model

In the meantime, this is an area that is likely to see different communities create applications profiles and optional extensions (i.e. optional for LD system implementers). The application profiles should enable both content and systems to be clearly described so that the requirements of the one and the capabilities of the other can be determined at a glance.

One hopeful avenue will be that many of these services will come to be provided by standalone services, rather than integrated into increasingly strained Learning Management Systems (LMSs) and Virtual Learning Environments (VLEs). Such loose integration would be facilitated by both configuration and service interfaces along the lines being developed by OKI (2004) and IMS. This would allow the addition of services to become independent of particular LMS/VLE providers, but presupposes the availability of at least one instance of any such service, whether open source or commercial, for each service defined, so that anyone could make use of a service specified in a learning design.

Learning services are likely to come in two varieties: those that are available as downloadable software, either open source or commercial, which are set up as part of a local environment; and those that are set up as remote web services, which again would be either freely accessible or available on a commercial basis.

To further this approach, it would be desirable to have a registry of learning services, giving their type and the service interface they used, perhaps together with an Open Service Interface Definition (OSID) type of adaptor that could be downloaded.

2.7 Conclusions

The use of general languages such as HTML or proprietary scripting languages to describe learning processes leads to unnecessary difficulty in documenting teaching strategies and reusing elements of existing teaching materials.

LD, an open technical specification, allows learning designers to model, in a generic, formal way, who does what, when and with which content and services in order to achieve learning objectives. It allows processes to be designed that include several roles, each of which can be played by several people. It enables their activities to be specified in coordinated learning flows that are analogous to groupware workflows, and it supports group and collaborative learning of many different kinds. Using the LD language, designers are able to talk in terms of pedagogy rather than technology, helping to bring learning to the forefront in e-learning.

3 Architectures to Support Authoring and Content Management with Learning Design

Scott Wilson

Research Institute for Enhancing Learning, University of Wales, Bangor

3.1 Introduction

Learning Design (LD 2003) is a complex specification, and requires a substantial supporting framework of components and services if it is to transform the experience of learning technology. In this chapter we look at some initial work to develop reference architectures for the processes of managing learning designs and their supporting materials.

Two reference models have been put forward by the Valkenburg Group: an architecture for a content management and authoring environment, including repositories and editing tools, and within that at a slightly deeper level there is a blueprint for how an LD authoring tool could be constructed. Both are presented in this chapter.

Since the development of an initial reference architecture by the Valkenburg Group there have been a number of developments in the area of architecture for e-learning, including MIT's Open Knowledge Initiative (OKI, Thorne et al. 2004), and the IMS Abstract Framework (AF 2004); there has also been a surge of interest in the use of service-oriented architectures and the role of middleware. We'll take a look at the Valkenburg Group Reference Architecture in the light of these trends.

3.2 Workflows for Learning Design

A first step towards defining a supporting architecture is to look at the kinds of task that users and tools may need to perform in working with LD.

While there may be a variety of workflows in practice, any process involving authoring and managing learning designs will most likely include several of the following tasks:

- Constrain the variety of learning designs.
- Create, edit and store learning design templates.
- Create and edit learning designs.

- Edit presentation of learning designs.
- Discover and add materials to learning designs.
- Aggregate learning designs.
- Create, edit and store materials.
- Test learning designs.
- Store learning designs in a repository.
- Search and retrieve a learning design from a repository.

This is only the set of tasks for creating and managing learning designs; there is an additional set of tasks required for delivering and using a learning design with learners, described in Chap. 4.

3.2.1 Constraining the Variety of Possible Learning Designs

LD is a very expressive specification, and enables a tremendous amount of flexibility on the part of the designer to model a wide range of educational scenarios. However, in a specific organizational context (e.g. a department within a university) it is quite likely that there will be limits that may need to be expressed to narrow this range. This could be due to policy decisions with regards to appropriate pedagogic models, or it may be simply to reduce the complexity of the authoring tools that teachers are expected to use. In any case, there is a recognizable requirement to support the handling of constraints on the possibilities of LD.

In practice, this may be a task performed by an expert user with standard XML tools to modify the base LD schema.

3.2.2 Creating, Editing, and Storing Learning Design Templates

While constraints restrict the possible learning designs, there is also a separate requirement to provide templates, acting as exemplars of particular models expressed in LD. Such templates may be very rich and well developed, requiring teachers only to modify the composition of materials within the design to suit their subject, or they may be incomplete structures designed to simplify the construction of activity sequences and conditions.

In either case, there is a requirement for the architecture to be able to support working with templates, both by editors and repositories.

3.2.3 Creating and Editing Learning Designs

It is clearly necessary for architectures to support the creation of new learning designs, whether from scratch, from an existing learning design, or based on a template. The creation and editing process may also need to be aware of the constraints imposed on learning designs. Teachers may have a variety of templates to choose from, offered by instructional designers in their organization, which they can select based on their understanding of the learning situation.

3.2.4 Editing the Presentation of Learning Designs

A possible pattern for working with learning designs is to present the design directly from XML using XSLT - the XML Stylesheet Transformation Language (W3C 1999) to convert parts of LD directly to XHTML, Shockwave, or some other presentation format.

For example, to present the current navigation options for a learner, the presentation system may ask a runtime engine to provide the activity tree for that learner as a fragment of LD XML, which is then processed by the presentation system using a stylesheet to display a navigation tree.

For authoring purposes, it may be useful to have access to these stylesheets so that the look and feel of visual authoring tools and testing tools matches that of the production environment where the design will be used.

To support these capabilities, the architecture could provide a way to create, edit and store these stylesheets. However, this is not a prescribed requirement for an LD architecture, as other presentation and rendering technologies may be used, such as directly encoding presentation methods within the runtime environment as interface objects (Java Swing components, Windows user interface elements, etc.), or by using a server-side scripting language like JSP or ASP dynamically to render the design elements.

3.2.5 Discovering and Adding Materials to Learning Designs

In addition to editing the structure of Learning Designs, it also necessary to incorporate materials within a design, such as learning objects, HTML, images, animations and so on. These materials tend to be created and managed separately from the LD, and then need to be inserted into the LD at the appropriate points.

Materials also tend to get stored in structured repositories that support search mechanisms to enable designers to discover appropriate materials.

3.2.6 Aggregating Learning Designs

Units of Learning (UOLs) can be referenced from within other learning designs, so one of the tasks that designers may undertake is to aggregate UOLs from multiple learning designs into new structures: for example, incorporating a set of designs, each of which is intended as a series of activities within a single session, into a sequence within an LD for a course or module.

3.2.7 Creating, Editing and Storing Materials

Although not strictly part of the LD workflow as such, an architecture that supports LD will typically also need to interact with the workflow for managing materials.

3.2.8 Testing Learning Designs

Designers need to be able to test their learning designs, to step through them and see how they work, and try out the various roles and pathways through the design.

Because of the flexibility of LD, there is a lot of potential for "runtime errors" emerging from the combinations of roles, activities and properties defined by the designer, so there is a need to support sophisticated debugging, validity checking and boundary testing of LDs to prevent problems occurring during use.

3.2.9 Storing Learning Designs in Repositories

Designers need to be able to store their learning designs, both in draft form for development, but also to submit finalized designs into production repositories for use by teachers.

3.2.10 Discovering and Retrieving Learning Designs from Repositories

During the creation and editing process, designers will need to be able to find and reuse previous designs (or parts of them), and locate draft learning designs for editing. Typically this is envisaged as a structured storage system that supports metadata tagging and search.

3.3 The Valkenburg Group Reference Architecture

The reference architecture developed by the Valkenburg Group embodies the workflow tasks discussed in the previous section as a set of logical architectural components (see Fig. 3.1).

Each piece of this architecture is described by a package – a logical unit of architecture, rather than as a physical software component. In actual deployment, each of these parts may be a separate software component, or be parts of the functionality of a few large applications.

This reference architecture is defined here at a very abstract level; we'll look at how this relates to some of the predominant technology platforms later in this chapter.

3.3.1 Constraint Editor

This package supports the editing of design constraints, and also provides an interface to allow the LD Editor to access constraints, so that it can check whether a design or template is valid, either by user request, or before saving. In some cases the editor may also be able to reconfigure its user interface based on the schema or application profile it is provided with.

There is no specific requirement of the reference architecture for how constraints are defined and managed; this editor could create XML Schemas derived from the basic IMS LD schemas, or the constraints could be maintained via some other means of representation, such as the Object Constraint Language (Warmer 2004). Currently there exists no standard for a constraints expression format, although if there were then this could be of potential benefit for realizing this architecture.

A possible implementation of a Constraint Editor is simply a standard XML editor capable of working with XML Schemas, such as XMLSpy (Altova 2004) or TurboXML (TIBCO 2004).

The schemas created using the Constraint Editor could then be used to configure the LD Editor, either to provide output validation, or actually to modify the behaviour of the editor itself – for example, the RELOAD editor (RELOAD 2004) generates a user interface based on an XML Schema.

3.3.2 Reference Runtime

The Reference Runtime performs the functions required to test learning designs, enabling designers to "run" a design and step through it, and debug it.

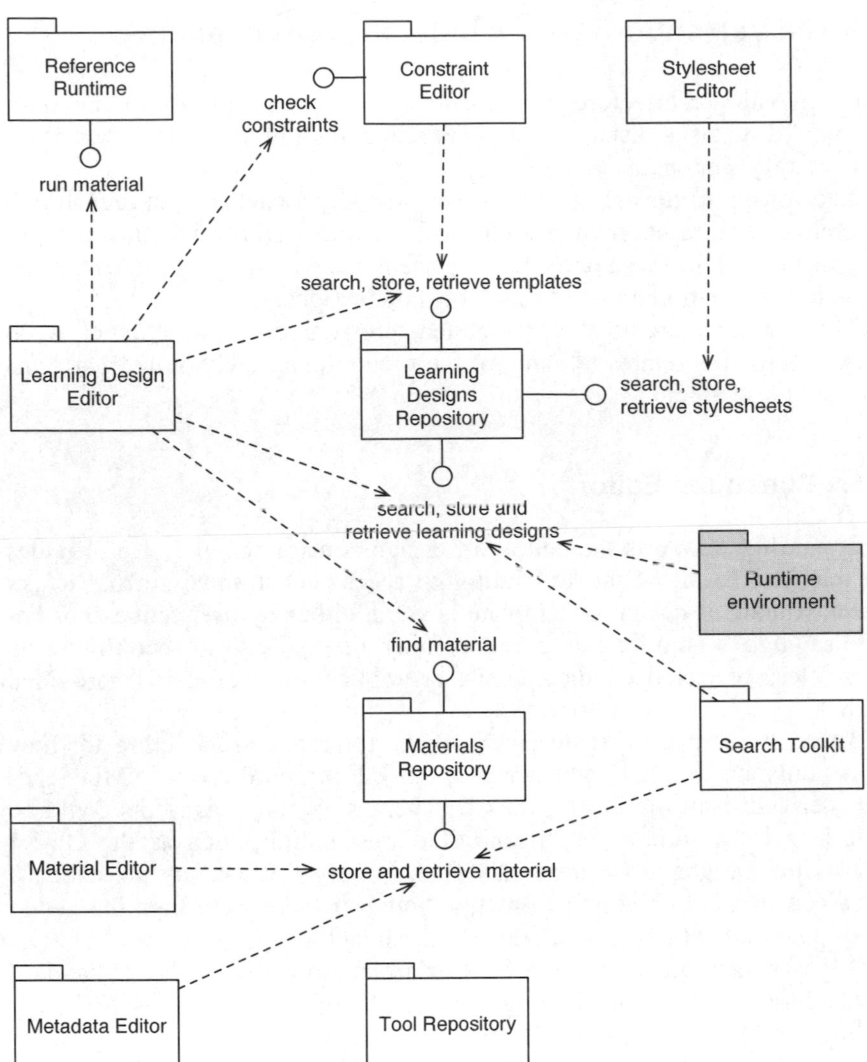

Fig. 3.1. Overview of the Valkenburg Group Reference Architecture. Note that the Runtime Environment and Search Toolkit are tinted differently; this is to indicate that these are external to the authoring and content management architecture

It is called a "Reference" runtime because it is intended to act to inform designers how their design will work in a "generic" runtime environment, even though in practice runtime environments may vary widely, especially in presentation.

The package provides an interface accessible by the LD Editor, so that the designer can take a look at how his or her design works directly from the editing workflow. This sort of interactive editing and debugging is something often found in web development software, and also in Integrated Development Environments (IDEs) such as Jbuilder (Borland 2004) or ECLIPSE (ECLIPSE 2004).

Teachers wanting to use a learning design could also use the Reference Runtime to preview it.

In either case, if stylesheets are used, it would be useful for the Reference Runtime to be able to access the set of standard stylesheets also used in the Runtime Environment so that the visual appearance of a design during testing will be closer to how it will appear in actual use.

3.3.3 Learning Design Editor

This package performs the main creation and editing duties for learning designs.

As well as providing the user interface to allow designers to create and work with learning designs, the package is additionally defined with access to the functionality of several other packages in the architecture. It can:

- Run material to test it using the Reference Runtime package.
- Search, store and retrieve templates from the Learning Designs Repository.
- Search, store, and retrieve learning designs from the Learning Designs Repository.
- Find material in the Materials Repository.
- Check that a learning design or template fits constraints defined by the Constraints Editor.
- Access stylesheets to alter the visual appearance of the learning design.

Because an LD template is essentially just a learning design with perhaps some boilerplate text or empty sections, the LD Editor also doubles up as the editing package for templates.

There is a great deal more to say about the LD Editor, and this is explored later in this chapter.

3.3.4 Learning Designs Repository

The Learning Designs Repository is a structured storage system for handling learning designs, templates and stylesheets. Although logically this is defined as a single package, in deployment this could very well take the form of a federated repository structure, distinct repositories for each type of resource, or a single multi-purpose repository (even including the functions of the Materials Repository).

The Learning Designs Repository provides interfaces to allow the discovery,[1] retrieval and storage of learning designs, templates, and stylesheets.

Because LD has a lot of reusable "parts", such as roles, activities, environments and so on, another potential role for the Learning Designs Repository is to manage these fragments so they can be accessed from the LD Editor.

In addition to the special requirements of LD, such a repository would also perform all the usual tasks associated with structured storage systems, such as version control, status management, access control, and search.

3.3.5 Materials Repository

The Materials Repository is charged with managing the workflow relating to materials (such as knowledge objects, learning objects and other media), particularly discovering[2] materials so that they may be incorporated into an LD. The Materials Repository also provides storage and retrieval functions for the Material Editor and Metadata Editor.

As with the Learning Designs Repository, the Materials Repository may in deployment actually manifest itself as a federation of repositories, and is also expected to provide generic repository-type features.

3.3.6 Stylesheet Editor

The Stylesheet Editor enables designers to create and edit stylesheets for modifying the presentation of LDs. The Stylesheet Editor uses the Learning Designs Repository for the storage and retrieval of stylesheets.

---

[1] A critical issue for the discovery of learning designs is the type of metadata used, how it is created, and how aspects of the design can be effectively described for search purposes. Although in theory the IEEE Learning Object Metadata standard could be seen as the appropriate choice of metadata format, this is not the only possible approach to support discovery; for example, in the future we may also see the use of ontologies and the semantic web as relevant to this area. Currently, there is no definitive proposal presented by the Reference Architecture for how to implement discovery of learning designs.

[2] Once again, metadata is a crucial factor here. For materials, the IEEE Learning Object Metadata standard is an obvious choice for electronic learning materials, although other options exist such as Dublin Core and its various extensions. The Reference Architecture itself is agnostic on this point, although for practical interoperability purposes the choice of metadata standard must be defined for any realization of the architecture.

In general, the rendering and presentation of LDs is handled by the Run-Time environment (e.g. the player could have a standard set of stylesheets for rendering any learning design).

In the authoring architecture, the role of stylesheets is to enable authors to view the design as it may finally appear, either with a visual editor or through the use of the Reference Runtime.

As noted previously, the use of stylesheets is only one possible means of managing presentation, and is not a required part of any architecture to support authoring learning designs.

3.3.7 Search Toolkit

The Search Toolkit represents an external discovery mechanism used to find learning designs or materials. This could manifest itself as a federated search mechanism such as XGrain (JISC 2003) or Splash (Edusource-Splash 2004), a search harvesting engine based on the Open Archives Initiative metadata harvesting specification (OAI 2004), or simply a web search engine like Google.

The Search Toolkit represents, abstractly, the means by which the LD management workflow interacts with a broader information environment, such as the JISC Information Environment (JISC 2004a), or the broader set of resources within an enterprise.

In the reference architecture, the LD Editor searches the Learning Designs Repository and Materials Repository directly through an interface offered by these packages; however, it would also be perfectly reasonable for the editor to have access to external search capabilities also.

3.3.8 Material Editor(s)

Material Editors allow materials to be created and edited, and stored in the Materials Repository. In deployment, the existing wide range of image, animation and web editing tools would most likely provide the functions of this package.

3.3.9 Metadata Editor

This package enables users to tag materials with metadata to facilitate discovery of materials for use within learning designs. This editor is envisaged as being able to access external classification schemes and taxonomies, but not necessarily able to define or modify these schemes itself.

3.3.10 Runtime Environment

For learning designs actually to be deployed and used, it is necessary to have a runtime environment access the Learning Designs Repository and retrieve designs. The architecture of the Runtime Environment (and its other packages and services) is not explored in this chapter.

3.4 The Architecture of a Flexible Learning Design Authoring Tool

The LD Editor needs to perform two sets of functions: it needs to provide a means of creating pedagogic scenarios, defining the flow of activity along with the various branching conditions, for use either as a single design or as a template. There is also a quite distinct requirement that calls for an LD Editor to be able to populate a design with specific resources and services.

These sets of requirements overlap, but tend to have some specialization in the form of the actors that perform the tasks; in the former case there is a role of an "educational specialist" who defines a pedagogic scenario, while in the latter case it is often the teacher who "fills" the scenario with what is needed for a particular session.[3] The key distinction between these actors may not necessarily be the different functions they use, but the usability requirements for the tool interface.

These overlapping requirements are expressed as coarse-grained UML use cases in Fig. 3.2.

One interpretation of these requirements is to create specialized user interfaces that manage the tasks of "Create Pedagogic Scenario" and "Fill Scenario" and their various sub-tasks, perhaps in a predefined order, such as in a "wizard".

Alternatively, the requirements could be expressed as individual fine-grained use cases, which can be performed in any order or combination, allowing more flexibility (Fig. 3.3).

These are not the only two possible roles, or sets of use cases, but are a useful reference set for defining what an LD Editor does. As more tools appear, it may be the case that different models for managing the authoring process emerge.

---

[3] Note that this is not the same as populating a design with learners for execution at runtime (see Chap. 4).

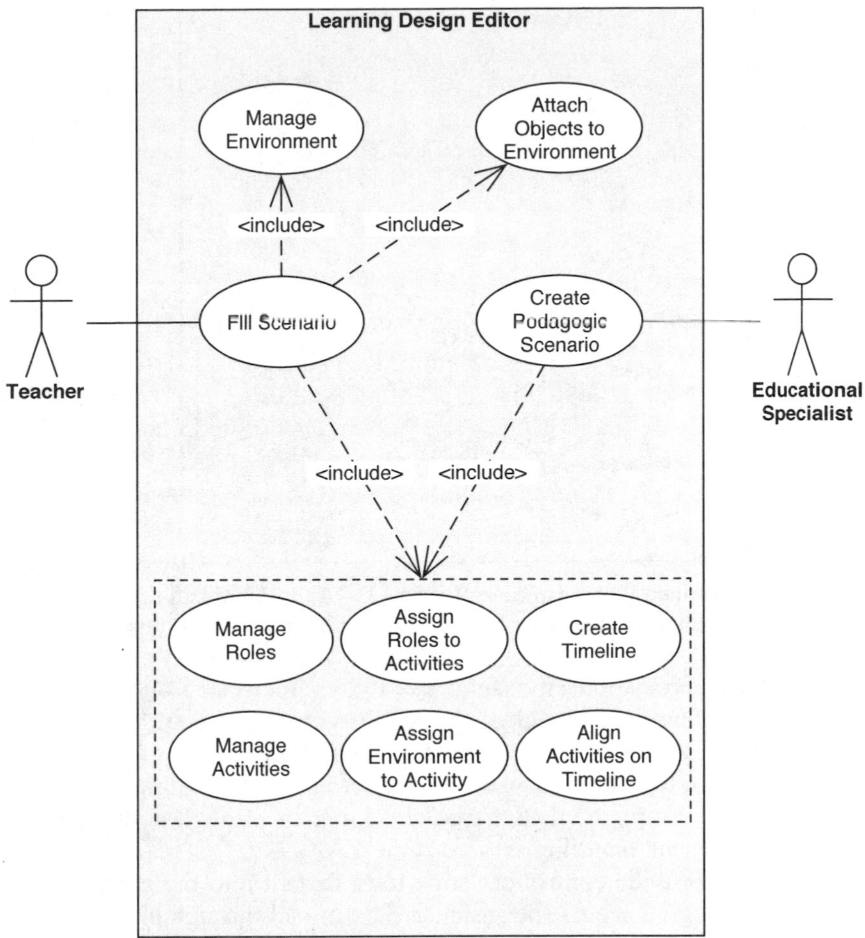

Fig. 3.2. UML use cases for an LD Editor. Note that the weak verb "Manage" in this instance means to create, read, edit and delete that type of object. So, "Manage Environment" means to create, read, edit and delete Environment elements of a learning design

3.4.1 Constructing an LD Editor

The LD Editor is a large package, and it could be a difficult task to construct it completely in one development project.

However, it may be possible to create a framework in which the various components of the editor can be "plugged in" as one approach to collaboratively developing an editor.

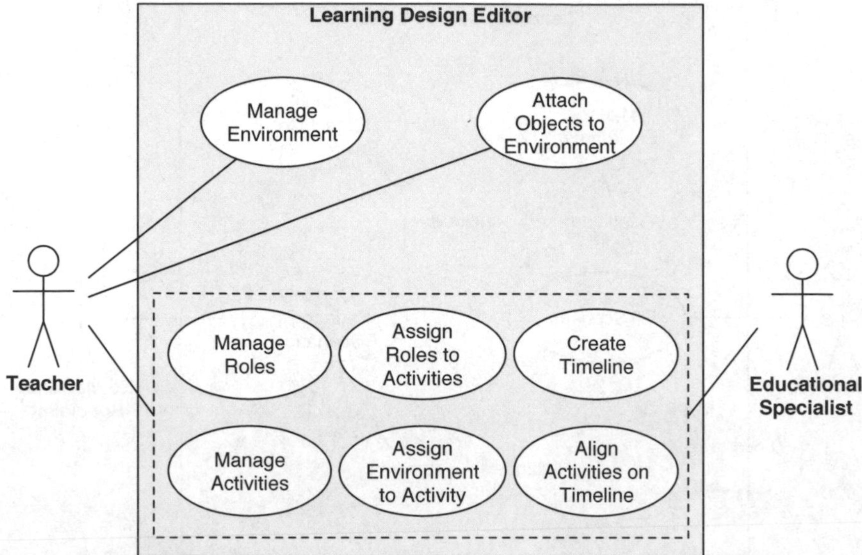

Fig. 3.3. Small-grained UML use cases for an LD Editor. Note that the weak verb "Manage" in this instance means to create, read, edit and delete that type of object

The kind of application envisaged has two frameworks: one that controls the underlying data model of the LD instance, and one that handles the management of the user interface. The data model layer is also a logical point at which to enforce constraints, either embedded within the application by incorporating XML Schema checking, or through delegation to an external constraint handling service.

Plug-in tools provide controllers and views that fit into the presentation layer framework, and access the instance data model through the Learning Design Model Framework. This architecture is shown in Fig. 3.4.

Each plug-in would provide a particular kind of authoring capability, such as managing roles, activities or environment (see Fig. 3.5). Variations on the same authoring task could also be provided for different levels of user. For expert users, the editor could also have a "Raw Learning Design" plug-in that simply allowed direct editing access to the underlying XML representation.

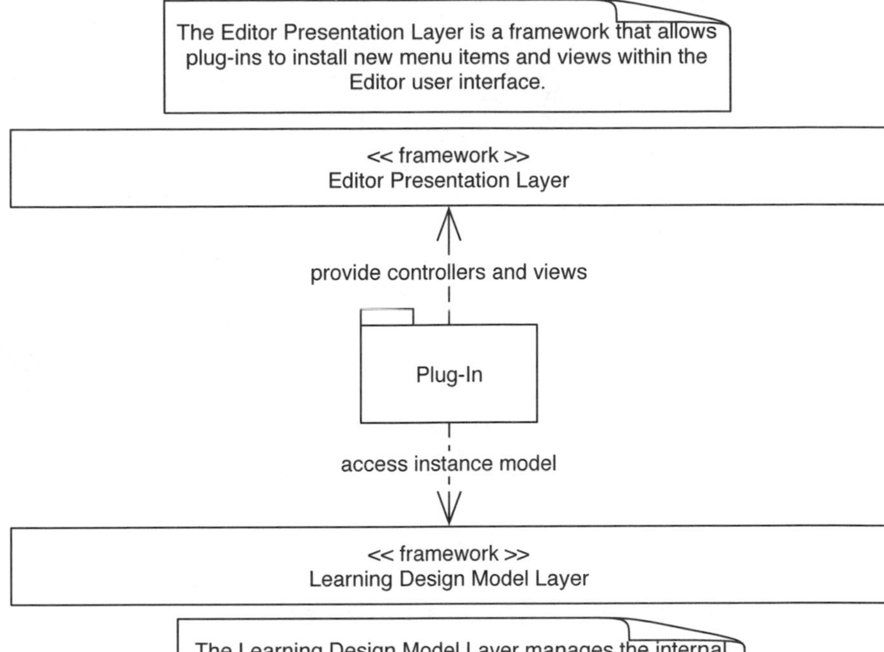

Fig. 3.4. Plug-in framework for an LD Editor

Other types of plug-in might include a package that provides import and export of SCORM (ADL 2004b) files, and a package to support access to the Learning Designs Repository and Materials Repository.

This type of application architecture has a number of real-world examples in practice. The RELOAD e-learning editor is an example, and one that draws explicitly on this framework model (this is covered in more detail in this book in Chap. 7). The ECLIPSE development environment is also constructed in a very similar fashion (ECLIPSE 2004) Its strength is that, while allowing a wide variety of functionality and user experiences for different types of users in various organizations, the validity and integrity of the learning designs they create can still be ensured.

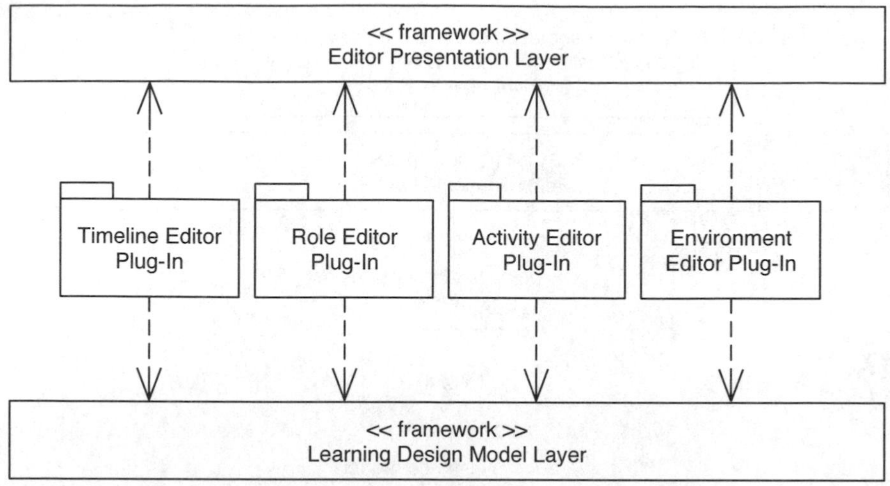

Fig. 3.5. Example of an LD Editor with a set of plug-ins

3.5 The Reference Architecture in Context

Since this framework was first created in 2002, there have been several major developments, both in e-learning and the wider field of system architecture. The most critical developments that need to be looked at are:

- The emergence of web services technology, and its adoption across all major technology platforms, with Service-Oriented Architecture an emerging approach to tackling system design.
- The ongoing efforts from MIT's OKI to create common interfaces for e-learning components.
- The publishing of the IMS Abstract Framework.
- The creation of the JISC e-Learning Framework Programme (JISC 2004b) to investigate and promote a common architectural approach in UK e-learning development

3.5.1 Web Services

Web services has finally emerged as a mainstream technology, with mature specifications from W3C, OASIS and others, and toolkits available for the major programming environments of Microsoft's net and Sun's Java platform.

The maturity and wide adoption of SOAP (W3C 2003) and the Web Services Description Language (W3C 2001) have resulted in the approach to system design known as Service-Oriented Architecture.

3.5.2 Service-Oriented Architecture

Service-Oriented Architecture (SOA) is an approach to joining up systems within enterprises. It is a relatively new approach, but is rapidly gaining popularity because of the low costs of integration coupled with flexibility and ease of configuration. SOA builds upon the experience of using web services for integration.

In SOA, the application logic contained in the various systems across the organization – such as student record systems, library management systems, learning environments, directories and so on – are exposed as services, which can then be consumed by other applications. This "service layer" is interposed between presentation and business logic within a typical three-tier architecture (Fig. 3.6).

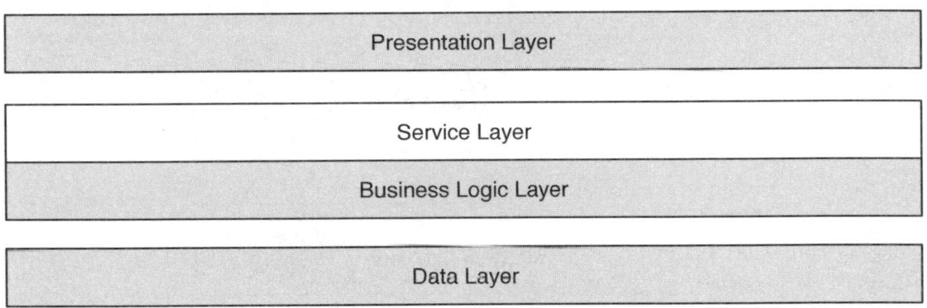

Fig. 3.6. The service layer encapsulates business logic within a three-tier architecture

This layer provides a means to encapsulate the business logic of a component (expressed in a specific programming language, such as Java) and expose it in a language- and platform-independent fashion. In this sense, SOA has a lot in common with CORBA, but has a considerably lower cost of implementation.

The service layer becomes the point in the architecture where integration agreements are made, rather than down at the data level or in the presentation layer, or even in the business layer. The problem typically with integration at the business logic layer is that it predicates a homogeneous programming environment – either Java and RMI, or Microsoft D/COM.

A service-oriented approach does not preclude also using portals or data warehouses, and is in fact agnostic about how the rest of the enterprise is configured, which is why it makes a good approach for integration in heterogeneous environments.

From an LD architecture perspective, we can look at the various functional packages defined in the Valkenburg Group Reference Architecture, and identify how those functions could be exposed as services. When looking at our earlier model from an SOA viewpoint, we find that some of our packages can be thought of as applications that are consumers of services provided by other packages, and some that are primarily providers of services to applications. This results in the service architecture in Fig. 3.7.

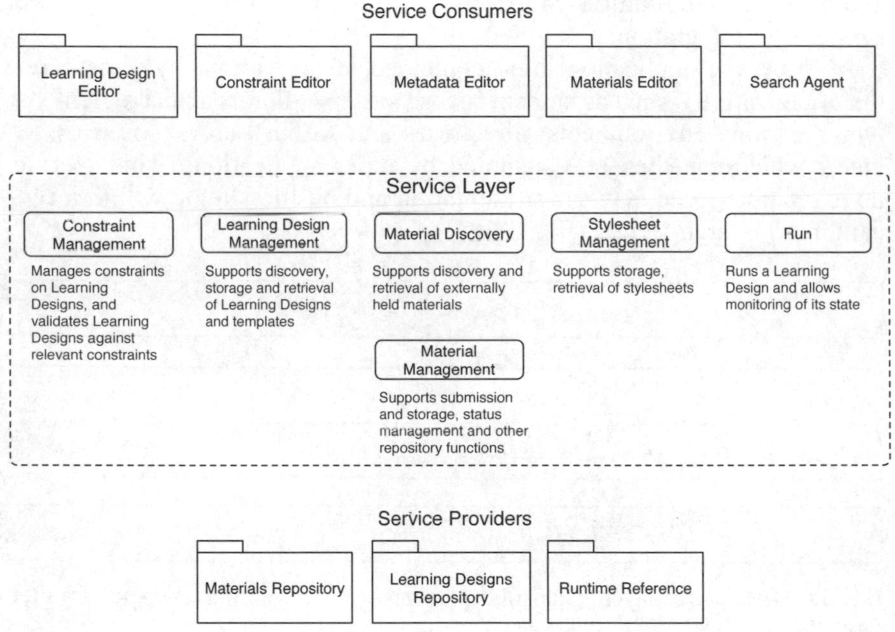

Fig. 3.7. The Valkenburg Group Reference Architecture modelled from a service-oriented viewpoint. Note that in this model, constraint management services have been split out from the Constraint Editor and into the service layer: in the original architecture, the editor provides the constraint checking service

In this view, we have interposed a set of service definitions between the "editor"-type packages, and the supporting repositories. These services would typically be defined using the Web Services Description Language (W3C 2001) and accessed using SOAP.[4]

[4] Originally, SOAP was an acronym of "Simple Object Access Protocol", but this expansion is no longer used as it is somewhat misleading with regard to what the current W3C definition of SOAP actually does.

Ideally, one would like to create standard definitions for any of these services; for example, a standard definition for a Learning Design Management Service would enable any LD Editor to readily consume services provided by any Learning Designs Repository.

Looking again at the framework for the LD Editor, we can also refactor the design to view it from a service-oriented perspective (Fig. 3.8). In this view, we are not interested in the internal behaviour of the editor as such, but the services that need to be in place in the wider environment within which the editor is being used; for example, within the set of networked services available in an educational enterprise.

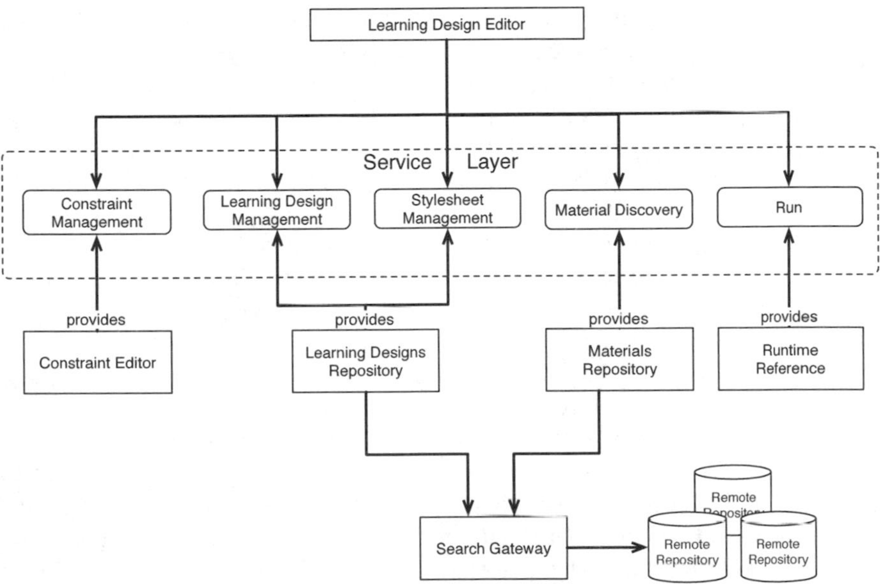

Fig. 3.8. The LD Editor modelled from a service-oriented viewpoint

In addition to the services easily identified from the original Valkenburg Group Reference Architecture (i.e. operations already defined as an interface between packages) there may be aspects of the editor packages that could be redefined as services. For example, the model layer of the LD Editor could be defined as a service rather than as an intrinsic part of the editor, as could the logic contained in some of the plug-ins. Whether or not this is to be desired remains to be seen.

Overall, the service-oriented approach and the Valkenburg Group Reference Architecture fit together quite well, and it should be perfectly possible to deploy an LD authoring workflow based on the Valkenburg Group Reference Architecture using web services.

3.5.3 The Open Knowledge Initiative

The Open Knowledge Initiative has also been developing an architecture framework. Although the OKI model does not define its architecture in terms of web services, but instead as a set of abstract Application Programming Interfaces (APIs),[5] there is a lot of commonality between the overall approach taken by OKI and service-oriented architecture. For a detailed technical discussion of how OSIDs differ from web services and other protocol-level specifications, see Kraan (2003).

The OKI model defines two large groupings of services: those referred to as "Application Services" (or sometimes "Educational Services") are focused on supporting the needs of educational applications, whether that is from a learning, administrative or information management perspective. The second grouping is called "Common Services", and is the set of services associated with access to parts of the common technical infrastructure, such as authentication and data management.

On top of these two layers of services sit the actual user applications, while beneath them sits the actual infrastructure of the organization – its databases, directories, file systems and so on. This is illustrated in Fig. 3.9.

Within the OKI framework, the Valkenburg Group Reference Architecture can best be seen as a set of (hypothetical) educational applications, and a set of educational services.

For the most part, the types of behaviour identified for the logical packages in the Valkenburg Group Reference Architecture have no direct counterparts in the OKI model. However, many of the functions of the Learning Designs Repository and the Materials Repository can be expressed using the OKI Digital Repositories OSID, which defines a set of basic repository operations, such as discovery, delivery, submission and storage, and so on. As this forms the basis of most of what would be the service layer for an LD authoring environment, then there is some integration possible using OKI specifications to support LD.

Placing the Valkenburg Group Reference Architecture in the OKI context also gives us is a picture of how the LD authoring workflow sits within the broader enterprise, particularly how it may integrate with the security infrastructure. In a sense, OKI and the activities around LD have been approaching the e-learning problem from opposite ends – while LD has been trying to tackle the pedagogic aspects of e-learning, OKI have been investigating the system management and administration components, with very little overlap.

---

[5] OKI calls its interface specifications Open Service Interface Definitions (OSIDs).

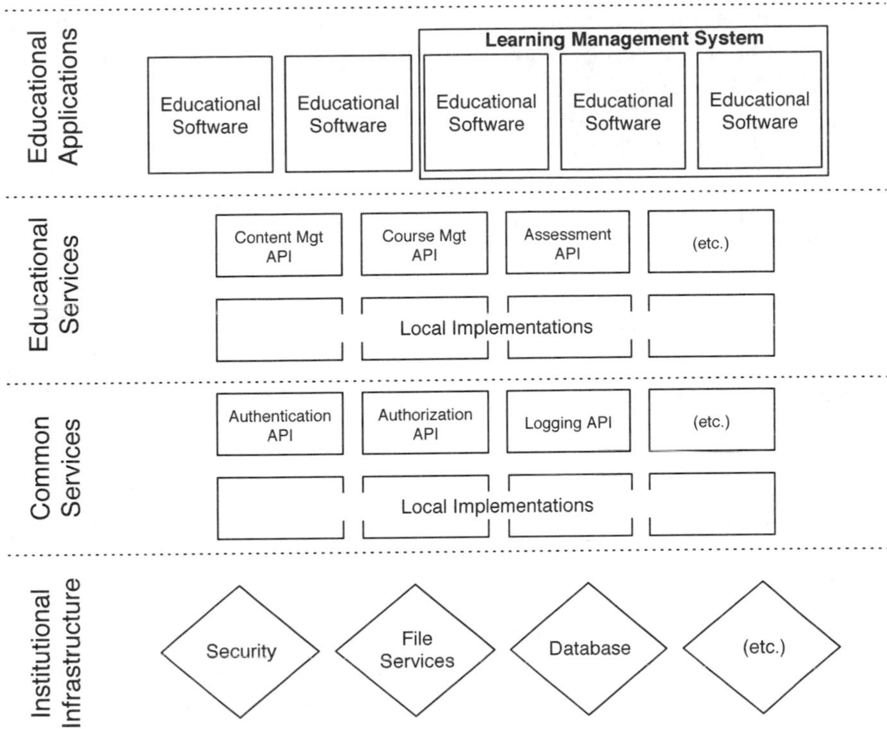

Fig. 3.9. The OKI architecture model, based on a diagram by Thorne et al. (2004)

It may be possible in the future to devise OSIDs for the services identified for the Valkenburg Group Reference Architecture beyond repository integration; at present the two approaches are not in any conflict, however, and it should be possible to create a deployment architecture that draws on both sets of work.

3.5.4 IMS Abstract Framework

The Abstract Framework is a document published by the IMS Global Consortium Inc., the body with responsibility for the LD specification. In it, IMS defines at an abstract level the components of a standards-based e-learning architecture. This framework is not intended to guide development or implementation as such, but to provide a model that can be referred to as new specifications are proposed or developed.

Structurally, the IMS Abstract Framework has a great deal in common with the OKI architecture model, with the same four layers (Fig. 3.10).

IMS provides a great deal of information about modelling and binding services and components, with an overall goal of being able to create specifications for use within SOA.

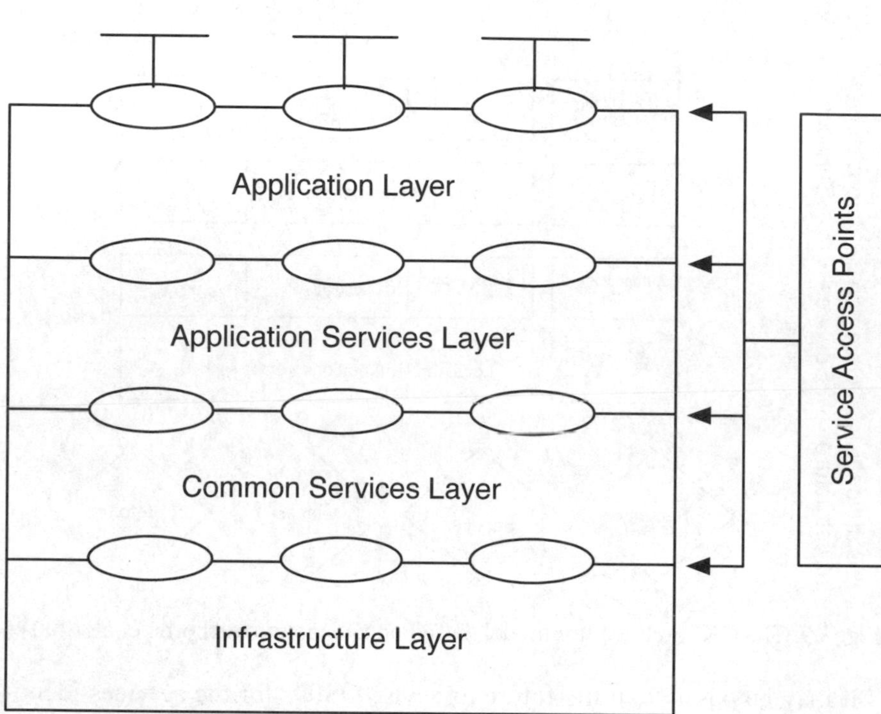

Fig. 3.10. IMS Abstract Framework, high-level overview, based on a diagram by IMS (AF 2004)

IMS works very closely with the OKI Group at MIT, and there is a conscious effort to relate the IMS Abstract Framework and the OKI architecture.[6]

At the specification level, IMS has developed a range of specifications – in addition to LD itself - that relate to some of the aspects of the Valkenburg Group Reference Architecture:

- The Digital Repositories specification (DR 2003) defines a set of operations for working with repositories.

[6] The IMS Abstract Framework draws upon a wide range of architectures in addition to the OKI framework, such as the work of the Carnegie–Mellon Learning Systems Architecture Lab, and so there is not necessarily a direct correspondence between the two models.

- The Meta-Data specification (MD 2001), now the IEEE Learning Object Metadata standard (LOM 2002) specifies how to describe learning resources to aid discovery.
- The Enterprise Services specification (ES 2004) defines a set of web services for working with information about students, courses and group membership.
- The Learner Information Package specification (LIP 2001) defines a detailed model for describing learners and profiling their achievements.
- The Content Packaging specification (CP 2003) provides a means to encapsulate, transport and store learning resources.
- The Simple Sequencing specification (SS 2003) provides a sequencing and ordering mechanism that can be used to make adaptive learning objects.
- The Question and Test Interoperability specification (QTI 2003) defines formats for exchanging and rendering electronic assessments and returning results.
- The Sharable State Persistence specification (SSP 2004) defines the mechanism for exchanging state representations between simulations and learning systems.
- The Resource List Interoperability specification (RLI 2004) defines services for exchanging reading lists.
- The Vocabulary Definition and Exchange specification (VDEX 2004) is a model for defining controlled vocabularies.
- The Reusable Definitions of Competencies and Educational Objectives specification (RDCEO 2002) can be used to define competencies for exchange between systems.

Other specifications by bodies other than IMS are also under development, and some of these specifications are being formalized as international standards by the Institute of Electrical and Electronics Engineers (IEEE) and the International Organization for Standardization (ISO). Most of these specifications relate more closely to the runtime environment than to the authoring and content management area.

The areas of the Valkenburg Group Reference Architecture not addressed by the IMS Abstract Framework, or its current set of specifications, are some of the specific operations of the Learning Designs Repository (such as working with fragments, templates and, potentially, stylesheets), the handling of constraints, and the functions of the Reference Runtime.

These service types do not conflict with any existing parts of the IMS framework, and there is some effort underway through the IMS International Conformance Programme to develop a set of recommendations for expressing constraints on IMS specifications.

3.5.5 JISC e-Learning Framework

The JISC e-Learning Framework is an initiative to focus the efforts of UK educational development activities around a common set of architectural concepts. Instead of creating service definitions itself, JISC has instead taken a pragmatic approach and is referencing existing work wherever possible, including both OKI, IMS and SCORM.

Strategically, LD plays an important role in the JISC framework as one of the main "workflow" specifications that links together at runtime a range of educational tools, such as synchronous chat, content delivery, collaboration and so on. For LD authoring and content management, the JISC framework is identifying the key services needed by drawing on the work of the Valkenburg Group as well as OKI, IMS, and the wider set of bodies creating technical standards and specifications. Unlike OKI and IMS, however, JISC is an organization that conducts development activities rather than specifications, so it can use its framework to target efforts such as technology demonstrators and common code libraries to support the implementation and deployment of the packages defined by the Valkenburg Group Reference Architecture.

3.6 Conclusion

The Reference Architecture proposed by the Valkenburg Group is a useful framework for identifying and specifying the components of an architecture for authoring and managing learning designs. It is sufficiently abstract to support a wide range of implementations (such as a single integrated authoring and content management application, a distributed network of web services and thin clients, or a collection of standalone generic applications used in a particular fashion) yet it still provides a useful framework to assist in the design of authoring and content management environments. The models proposed are also congruent with current frameworks for learning technologies, including the OKI and the IMS Abstract Framework.

It is important to note that, although this reference architecture specifies a number of packages, many of these packages can be provided by existing generic software components, rather than requiring the development of new specialist LD tools. Where specialist tools are needed – for the LD Editor, the Learning Designs Repository and the Reference Runtime – there has been a great deal of effort by Valkenburg Group members to research and develop the relevant technologies, using models like the flexible LD Editor architecture model as a point of reference. Again, this is something explored in subsequent chapters. Chapter 7 explores the topic of LD tooling in more depth.

4 An Architecture for the Delivery of E-learning Courses

Colin Tattersall, Hubert Vogten, Rob Koper

Educational Technology Expertise Centre,
Open University of the Netherlands, Heerlen, The Netherlands

4.1 Introduction

In distance learning, production processes are used to create courses for delivery to many hundreds or thousands of students over several years. One of the most powerful drivers for the use of e-learning in distance learning is an economic one, following the well-established economics of the publishing world—courses can be created once and delivered many times. Although each delivery incurs costs, these are marginal and more than covered by the fees and subscriptions paid by the material's consumers. In this way, over time, high initial production costs are first recouped and subsequently exceeded by revenues, yielding course profit. Substantial initial costs can be justified by informed market forecasting and used to invest in high-quality learning experiences which might otherwise be impossible to finance.

These opportunities have sparked a proliferation of commercial and open-source course delivery systems, also known as (web-based) course management systems, courseware delivery systems, on-line educational delivery applications and learning management systems (for an overview, see Brusilovsky and Millar 2001).

Although the 'create once, deliver many times' approach is one of the foundations of e-learning economics (Molyneux 2000; Sloep 2003), it is often overshadowed and overlooked in the wider debate on reuse in e-learning. There, the focus is squarely on reuse to support the creation of new courses and is dominated by discussions of learning object repositories, and methods and techniques to support the creation of new materials (Downes 2001; Friesen 2001).

Consideration must nevertheless be given to the concepts required for successful application of the 'create once, deliver many times' approach in the design and development of integrated e-learning systems (Koper 2003a). Without such attention, processes and systems for the delivery of courses can lead to a 'create once, deliver once' situation where each delivery is associated with its own unique variant production. The consequences of this situation are often not felt immediately, since copies of productions can be made instantly and at negligible cost. However, the seeds are sown for future course administration and management difficulties which ultimately undermine the original economic case.

This chapter provides an analysis of the requirements for reproducibility in e-learning, where reproducibility refers to repeated delivery of e-learning courses in different settings with different participants. Thereafter, the chapter describes the design for part of an integrated e-learning system which meets the requirements, followed by a description of a production level implementation of the design. We conclude with a discussion of the approach.

4.2 Requirements Analysis

The requirements presented here have been derived from production experience at the Open University of the Netherlands delivering courses to thousands of students via the Internet from 1996 onwards. We distinguish between course enrolment, when learners sign up to participate in e-learning courses, and course delivery, the process by which learners are engaged in learning processes supported by e-learning systems. The problem area addressed by this chapter is the combination of course creation and management, and course delivery policy. The latter concerns the manner in which those enrolled for a course have their education delivered, focusing on when delivery occurs and how (in terms of cohorts and sets of learners).

The distance and open learning worlds are associated with a variety of delivery policies. Learning Providers (LPs) must cater for a variety of situations, including those where:

1. a course is run once only (then discontinued), with a single set of learners.
2. a course is run for several sets of learners. The rationale behind the dividing of learners into sets is here a logistical one for the LP. The availability of staff resources to act as (remote) tutors might be constrained by institutional policy that the staff-to-learner ratio must never rise above a certain advertised maximum. Alternatively, the division might reflect simple physical constraints, such as classroom size for blended learning courses where groups of more than 40 cannot be accommodated for face-to-face sessions. In contrast, it might reflect the targeting of different geographical areas or market segments (e.g. running the

course in the winter months and marketing to those seasonal workers fully employed in the summer months, and vice versa).

3. a course is run for (possibly several sets of) learners and the learners are divided into groups. In contrast to the previous possibility, the rationale here is pedagogical, reflecting a choice to pursue, for example, a group-based learning approach in which learners are divided into competing teams, or a problem-based learning approach (Nulden 2001). Similarly the use of computer-supported collaborative learning (CSCL) technologies might be associated with working in small groups.
4. a course is run only when, but as soon as, there are enough learners enrolled on it. Here, the decision might be a pedagogical one (group learning) or might reflect economic reasoning, such as the need to have a minimum number of learners to break even.
5. a course is run for each individual learner as soon as the individual's enrolment has been finalised.

LPs may wish to adopt different delivery policies, either to gain competitive advantage through flexibility of delivery, or to reflect the stage of development of the organisation (starting with limited flexibility but increasing as the organisation's logistical processes mature).

Without an appropriate approach to delivering e-learning providing adequate separation between courses and their delivery to learners, LPs run the risk of being forced down a path of creating course variants each time a course is run. This results in a 'create once, deliver once' situation. In situations involving large numbers of learners (see Daniel (1998) for some extreme cases) this situation becomes unmaintainable.

While targeting flexibility of delivery, providers must also be aware of legal obligations on retaining information in cases of dispute with learners. Information on both the structure and content of a course, together with that concerning its time-of-delivery and cohort size must be preserved, and the obligation may exist long after learners' participation in courses has ended. Providers making modifications to courses on-the-fly without paying sufficient attention to version management run the risk of losing lawsuits filed by learners who dispute their failing of course examinations.

Notwithstanding the need for effective version management of courses, providers need to be able to make minor modifications (i.e. without legal significance) to materials being used in running courses. Such modifications include correcting spelling errors in course materials, improving the readability of materials following learner feedback, and the updating of links to time-dependent material used in courses such as company yearbooks and governmental surveys.

We identify four requirements to be met by LP processes and systems in the area of reproducibility:

1. The same course must be able to be delivered to different sets of learners without resorting to duplication of course structure and contents.
2. Deliveries must be able to be handled in an efficient way, and, where possible, partly or wholly automated. Meeting this requirement further reduces delivery costs thereby strengthening the 'create once, deliver many times' case.
3. Effective version control must be applied to courses.
4. Minor updates to running courses must be possible without disrupting on-going learning processes.

E-learning practice has not always taken these requirements into account, as noted by Porter (2001):

> In many cases the instructor is given training in a particular on-line development, delivery and management tool and then the instructor proceeds to craft a course for on-line delivery. The pedagogical structures embedded within the instructional delivery tool are tweaked to suit the needs of the class, the content or the particular instructional problem. In most cases, the courses are hand tooled and kept current through the intervention by the instructor over time.

This point is echoed by Abdallah et al. (2002) who note that in a commercial course delivery system each module, lesson, Web page has to be duplicated in each course if needed. Similarly faculties' resentment of the time required to load and reload course materials is noted as one of the factors which leads to reduction in faculty use of course management systems (Morgan 2003).

Such practice contrasts sharply with the publishing-world-inspired production systems required to realise the 'create once, deliver many times' promise.

4.3 Design

The above analysis points to the need to distinguish between a course in the abstract, and its deliveries to different sets of learners. The LD specification (LD 2003) provides an appropriate context within which to view this distinction.

LD provides a notational system to describe a Unit of Learning (UOL), an abstract term used to refer to any delimited piece of education or training, such as a course, a module, a lesson, etc.

One of the requirements the LD specification is designed to meet is that of reproducibility—the specification must describe the learning design abstracted in such a way that repeated execution in different settings with different persons is possible.

In a UOL, people act in different roles in the teaching–learning process.

Through its use of roles, LD abstracts from the details of specific learning situations and provides an appropriate concept to describe a course in the abstract: the UOL. It is UOLs that are created once, then delivered many times.

4.3.1 Moving from an Abstract Course to Specific Deliveries

The 'creation versus delivery' distinction reflects that between design time and runtime. The formal description of a learning process which results (at design time) from the use of the LD notational system is interpreted (at runtime) by an LD-aware software component, or LD Player, in the same the way HTML is interpreted by a browser. Taking into account the requirements identified in the previous section, it is clear that the design time concept (the UOL) must be augmented with an additional, runtime concept in order to satisfy the requirements.

The need to establish a specific runtime concept related to the abstract design time concept of a UOL can be informed by the world of object orientation. Although the link between e-learning systems and object orientation has been examined in other work (Douglas 2003; Permanand and Brooks 2003; Virvou and Tsiriga 2001), such work has tended to focus on the reuse of learning objects at design time; that is, in creating new UOLs. In the context of reproducibility, the focus is on the move from design time to runtime. This is the process of instantiation, whereby an object class, modelling an abstraction, is used as the basis from which to create specific object instances. Following this line, we view a UOL as describing a class of possible instances, and we use the term instantiation to describe the process of transforming an abstract UOL into deliveries for learners. The specific instances of a UOL are referred to as runs, defined as the combination of a particular UOL with an assigned community of users. Each run is assigned to exactly one UOL, but a particular UOL may have zero or more runs assigned to it.

Additionally, we exploit the notion of a publication, which is introduced to allow pre-processing of the contents of a unit of learning for a run. Publications are not strictly necessary to meet reproducibility requirements, since the processing can also be achieved on-the-fly, but have proven useful in several situations in practice. The first involves the selection of alternative resources in different languages, as is the case when a course is run for different sets of learners with different mother tongues. Here, the pedagogical approach remains identical for the two groups but the resources utilised in the learning design differ, including instructions to learners and staff, materials to be read and exercises to perform. The content package representing the UOL consists of a single learning design with multiple alternative resources. These alternatives are split out during pre-processing for linking to particular sets of learners and staff in a run (e.g. a run with French contents and a run with English contents in the Canadian context). In a similar vein, alternative resources can be selected for different media, such as a course offered both in printed form and over the web, or for different (mobile) devices, perhaps with differing display sizes and capabilities. Finally, publications can be exploited to accommodate variety in the formatting and styling of UOLs for different sets of learners, meeting both accessibility and re-branding requirements on course content. A full examination of the utility of publications is outside the scope of this chapter, but we note recent interest in the need to support re-branding of e-learning material (Canadian Department of National Defence 2003).

This resulting combination of concepts is illustrated by the UML class diagram shown in Fig. 4.1.

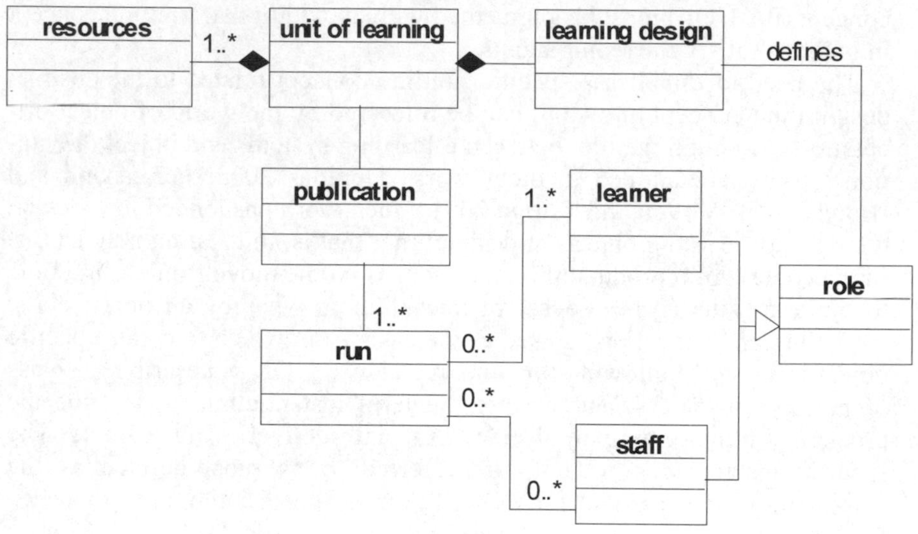

Fig. 4.1. The relationships between UOLs, publications, runs, roles, staff and learners

A run adds runtime information to a UOL by defining a start and end date and binding specific individuals into the roles modelled in the learning design part of the UOL.

The same UOL can have an unlimited number of runs. The notion of an abstract class (UOL) from which specific instances (runs) can be spawned is at the heart of the solution to reproducibility problems. Various delivery policies can be realised by creating multiple runs from a single UOL. In all cases, the 'parent' UOL is frozen and archived for future reference, with each 'child' run maintaining a link to its parent. The unique identification of a UOL using a Uniform Resource Identifier (URI) which is mandated by the LD specification is also applied to each run.

4.3.2 Constraints on Run Creation

Mechanisms are provided in the LD modelling language to help designers (at design time) indicate constraints on the creation of runs (at runtime). The mechanisms provide the basis for automation of run creation and build on the two general roles inherent in the specification: learner and staff..

Two of the constraint mechanisms are the min-persons and max-persons attributes associated with a role. The former specifies the minimum number of persons which must be bound to the role before starting a run and the latter specifies the maximum. Runs are generated using the constraints until the enrolled population of learners is exhausted. Note that if the attribute is not used, no restrictions apply to the number of individuals who can fill a role. This can be useful in situations where the number of individuals participating in a UOL is unimportant, such as is the case with fully individualised, self-taught courses.

By combining these attributes with the notion of a default run, the delivery process is opened to partial or full automation. If only one run is created for a UOL and it is designated as the default run, learners can be automatically assigned to participate in runs according to any min-persons and max-persons constraints. Therefore, we extend the definition of a run to include an attribute indicating whether or not it is the default run. Only one run for a learning design may be a default run.

To illustrate the utility of default runs, consider a cohort of 200 learners for a given UOL which has constraints indicating a minimum of 10 and maximum of 20 individuals in the role of learner. A software tool could be written to create runs automatically, so that as soon as the run is made available, 10 runs could be spawned automatically, each with 20 learners. Alternatives to full automation are also possible, whereby humans in the loop are used to couple learners to runs.

Finally, a run progresses through a lifecycle, mirrored by its changing status – namely waiting, active, stopped or archived. When a run is first created it has the status 'waiting', meaning that users have still to be assigned to the run from the pool of enrolled learners before delivery starts. Delivery starts when the run status changes to 'active'. As soon as all users have finished, the run gets the status of 'stopped', meaning that users can still access the learning design and the corresponding content contained in the UOL but no more interactions will be allowed. Finally, a decision can be made to archive the run, meaning that it is no longer available to the learners and staff, but all information is stored in an archive for future reference.

The final design is reflected in the UML domain model shown in Fig. 4.2.

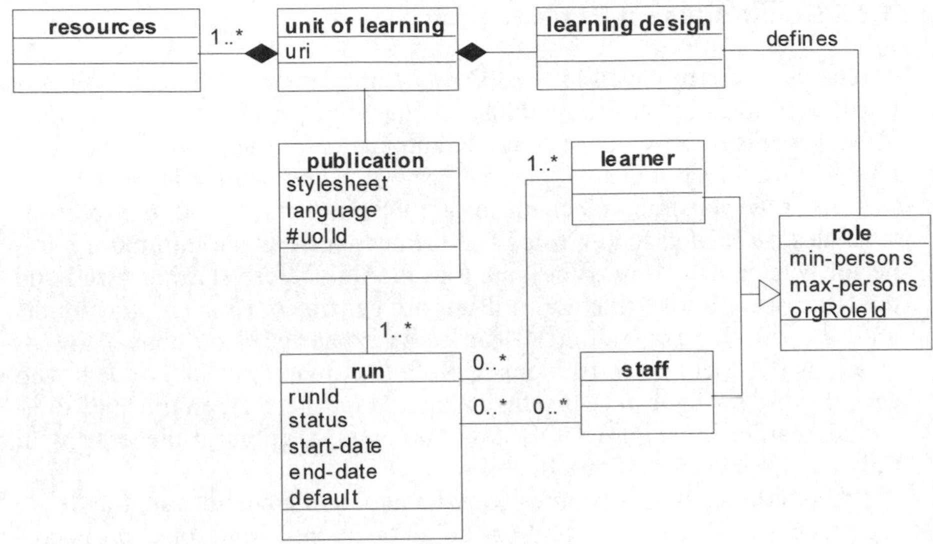

Fig. 4.2. The full UML class diagram for the design

In summary, the design of an approach to ensuring reproducibility in integrated e-learning systems involves coupling the concept of a UOL to that of a run, which links individuals in particular roles to a UOL delivered in a given time period.

4.4 Implementation

Implementation of the design occurs within the context of the production sub-system of integrated e-learning systems (Koper 2003a). Within this sub-system, a process is introduced, namely run management.

Our organisation implemented the design in its production processes a number of years ago and is successfully operating with enrolment numbers in excess of 1000 learners per course (i.e. UOL), coupled to multiple runs, following different delivery policies, varying from tens to hundreds of learners per run.

The run management process, incorporating the creation and management of publications, is supported by a run tool, the positioning of which is shown in Fig. 4.3.

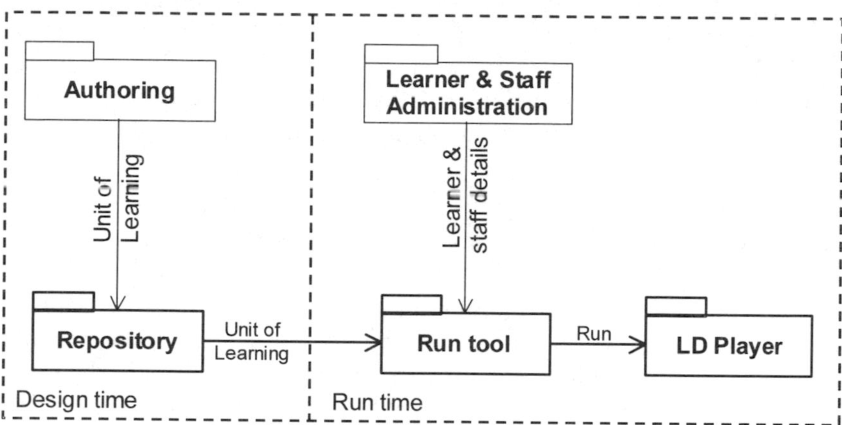

Fig. 4.3. Positioning the run tool in its immediate architectural context

Using the tool, course administrators can access a repository and upload UOLs previously created in an authoring process. The repository stores the frozen 'parent' UOLs and implements version control mechanisms. Once the abstract course description is available in the run tool, multiple instances can be spawned by linking to learner and staff details pulled in from the appropriate enrolment and administrative systems.

For users (staff or learners) using the player, support is offered in several situations. First, if the user has been assigned to exactly one run for a given UOL he or she can be directed to the run (e.g. through a hyperlink). If the user has been assigned to multiple runs of the same UOL, a choice between the available runs is offered. This mechanism can be used, for example, to give learners a choice of starting date, or staff a choice of which run to support when several are running in parallel. If the user has not been assigned to a run but is enrolled for a UOL for which a default run is available, the user is assigned to the run automatically. A fourth possibility exists in which the user is not enrolled for a UOL (and so is not assigned to a run) but requests access to a run (perhaps through sharing of hyperlinks between learners). In this case an enrolment form could be presented to the user, requesting enrolment. This aspect is not implemented in our context, where users are instead denied access and directed to the traditional enrolment process.

The run tool is used as the mechanism by which the status of a run is changed by course administrators. However, the opportunities for automation are evident, such as using timed events to move the status from waiting to active at the start of an academic year.

In rounding off this description of the design's implementation, we note that the current implementation in our organisation is based on LD's precursor, the Educational Modelling Language, or EML (Koper and Manderveld 2004). Although EML and LD differ in certain respects, the differences do not alter the requirements or design described in this chapter, and have only minor repercussions for the implementation.

4.5 Conclusion

Introducing the UOL/run distinction is a simple yet effective way of achieving flexibility of e-learning delivery while preserving efficiency and traceability of administration. The distinction mirrors that used in the book and record publishing industries where similar production and delivery economics apply.

Returning to the example delivery policies outlined in the requirements analysis, we outline how each is addressed by the design:

1. a course is run once only (then discontinued), with a single set of learners. The UOL which represents the course in the abstract is mapped to a single run which is delivered once only.
2. a course is run for several sets of learners for logistical reasons, such as staff resource limitations, physical room constraints or marketing purposes. Here, the LP creates as many runs as needed from the single parent UOL given the specific constraints, and at the times the runs are needed.
3. a course is run for (possibly several sets of) learners and the learners are divided into groups on pedagogical grounds. This example is addressed in a similar manner to the previous one, with the LP assigning learners to groups (e.g. teams) used in the learning design.
4. a course is run only when, but as soon as, there are enough enrolled learners. This is a slightly more complex situation but one which underlines the power of the approach described here. Runs can be created by LPs with appropriate constraints on min-persons and given the status of active. This means that although active, the run will not start until the constraints are met. Learners may enrol at any time and are placed into a queue until sufficient numbers are gathered, at which point an alert is issued to learners and staff that learning can begin (the queue can of course be monitored to help with staff planning). Note that runs will continue to be generated from the pool of enrolled learners each time the constraints are met. For example, if min-persons=50, then as soon as 50

learners enrol, a run will start, and as soon as the 100th learner enrols, a second run commences.
5. a course is run for each individual learner as soon as the individual's enrolment has been finalised. Here a single, constraint-free run is created to which enrolled individuals can be directed.

Archiving and version management run across these examples. The UOL which is the basis for each of the runs remains frozen in the repository, and the link between individuals and a uniquely identified run of a particular UOL is logged in learner administration systems.

Turning to the issue of making minor modifications to runs which are in progress, the link between a UOL and its runs is maintained, making it possible to apply minor modifications across all runs in one action (although institutional archiving policies may require storage of the various versions of the runs).

The approach also opens new avenues when used together with linking technologies. A UOL can contain resources, and indeed other UOLs, either directly in the content package or by reference using URIs. The use of referencing rather than direct inclusion in a content package makes it possible to deliver UOLs while referenced sub-components are still under development—a link is created in a UOL to a location in which another resource will be placed when completed. The UOL can be frozen, since it will not be modified, and runs can be spawned to reach the market before production has completely finished.

The design meets the four requirements outlined in the Requirements Analysis and has been implemented in a production level environment. We believe the distinction between an abstract description and its specific instantiations is important for the realisation of e-learning's economic promise, yet straightforward to implement, and Chaps. 5 and 6 explore the architecture in more detail.

5 An Architecture for Learning Design Engines

Hubert Vogten, Rob Koper, Harrie Martens, Colin Tattersall

Educational Technology Expertise Centre,
Open University of the Netherlands, Heerlen, The Netherlands

5.1 Introduction

Learning Design (LD 2003) is a *declarative* language, meaning that it describes what an implementation supporting LD must do. LD does not state how this should be done. Furthermore, LD is an *expressive* language, which means that it has the ability to express a learning design in a clear, natural, intuitive and concise way, closest to the original problem formulation. This expressiveness and declarative nature complicate the implementation of an engine that can interpret the specification. As a result, the main objective of this chapter will be to describe how such an engine can be implemented. We will provide guidelines which go beyond the published specification to help implementers incorporate LD into their products. The approach is generic in nature and has been tested in the CopperCore engine described in Chap. 6 of this book. We note, however, that the user interface aspects of the engine are considered to be out of scope for this chapter. These considerations are heavily influenced by the environment in which the engine is incorporated, and are not easily able to be generalized. LD specifies few requirements that have a direct impact on the user interface design.

To illustrate both the declarative and expressive nature of LD, consider the following XML code fragment.

```
<imsld:roles identifier="roles">
 <imsld:learner identifier="novice" min-persons="5"
   max-persons="10">
 <imsld:title>Novice students</imsld:title>
 </imsld:learner>
 <imsld:learner identifier="advanced" min-persons="1"
   max-persons="5" create-new="allowed">
 <imsld:title>Advanced students</imsld:title>
 </imsld:learner>
</imsld:roles>
```

Two roles, novice and advanced learner, are declared with attributes stating the minimum and maximum number of members for each defined role. For the second learner role it is possible to have *N* instances of this role during execution time due to the declaration of the `create-new` attribute. LD does not make any assumptions about how, when and who should be assigned to these roles nor does it state how and when the mentioned constraints should be checked. It merely declares valid states.

Another example Unit of Learning (UOL) fragment shows how LD can express dynamic behavior in a very declarative manner:

```
<imsld:complete-act>
 <imsld:when-condition-true>
 <imsld:role-ref ref="tutor"/>
 <imsld:expression>
  <imsld:complete-support-activity-ref ref="mark-assignment1"/>
 </imsld:expression>
 </imsld:when-condition-true>
</imsld:complete-act>
```

This example states that an act will be completed when all tutors have completed a certain support activity with id `mark-assignment1`. The LD specification makes the assumption that the completion of activities will be tracked during runtime (at least for the activity with id `mark-assignment1`) and that the activity will be completed for all users in role tutor. Again, how this is achieved is left up to those implementing the specification. LD merely specifies valid state transitions.

An engine is needed to present the learning activities to learners as expressed by a UOL. The output of the engine will be a personalized version of the UOL in XML format according to the rules defined by LD. The approach we take in this chapter is to demonstrate how an LD engine implementation can benefit from the perspective of *finite state machines,* FSMs (Sipser 1997). FSMs offer a logical, methodical approach towards sequential input processing, which is relatively easy to design and implement and which avoids error-prone conditional programming. They are a proven concept that allows for efficient and effective implementations.

5.2 Learning Design Engines as Collections of Finite State Machines

At the heart of LD are *interactions* between users in particular roles or between users and the LD system. The results of these interactions can be captured in *properties* which can be declared explicitly in LD. We further distinguish properties which are not declared but which are assumed to exist, such as a property capturing the completion status for activities for every user. We will call these properties *system-defined properties.*

The property mechanism defines an FSM for each *individual user*. An FSM consists of a set of states, a start state, an input alphabet and a transition function that maps an input symbol and current state to next state. An engine will always deal with multiple users, and so the engine is a collection of FSMs.

Each state in LD is represented by the set of values of all the properties that are either defined by the author or defined by the system. The start state of the FSM is defined by the initial value of all properties for this user. The system-defined properties are created during a socalled publication process (see also Chap. 4). A UOL is parsed and analyzed by the engine and all properties are created and stored in a database. All users have their own values for these properties representing their state at any time. Execution of the UOL consists of personalizing it for the user; in other words, adapting the UOL according to the property values of this user. A state represents the position of a user with respect to his or her progress in the UOL. The start state is defined by the initial values of the properties. These initial values are either given in LD or set as the result of executing other UOLs at earlier stages. The input alphabet is made up of all LD constructs and the transition functions are defined by LD constructs dealing with interactions. When, for example, the engine provides feedback on completion of an activity, the engine is reacting to a user action, namely completing an activity. In terms of an FSM, this can be formulated as follows: the engine responds to a change of state that is caused by the user completing an activity.

There are a number of cases defined in LD where a change of state should cause another change of state. A fairly obvious example is the `change-property-value` LD construct that can be triggered by the completion of an activity. In order to cope with these LD constructs when using an FSM, the definition of an FSM must be extended to allow each state to have an output that itself can be an input for the FSM. This type of FSM is also known as a *Moore machine*. By introducing this feedback loop, we are able to deal with chains of state changes that can occur through several LD constructs.

The following sections explain in detail how the concept of an FSM is implemented in the engine. First the concepts of runs and roles are introduced; these concepts together with the user are the primary key when accessing a single FSM from the collection of FSMs. The subsequent section shows how each state is stored by the use of properties. A number of property types can be distinguished each with its own characteristics and use. The following section deals with the transition function of the FSM. The concept of an event is introduced as the core of both alphabets. It will become clear how the engine is capable of dealing with these events. Then we will return to the start of the process, explaining the importance of the pre-processing of the UOL. Finally, bringing all the previous concepts together, personalization will be shown to have become a straightforward XML transformation.

5.3 Populating the Unit of Learning

Before a UOL can be 'executed', users (learners, staff, etc.) have to be assigned to it. LD does not refer to users directly, but uses the notion of roles for this purpose. It is the engine's responsibility to bind actual users to abstract roles.

A 'run' is introduced as a pedagogically neutral term for binding a group of users to a UOL via a publication (see Chap. 4). Each run has one or more users assigned to it, forming the community of users taking part in the UOL together at the same time. Users can enroll for a particular UOL and are assigned to one or more runs for the UOL. A run has exactly one publication assigned to it, which in turn is associated with exactly one UOL. For now, it is sufficient to understand that a publication is the result of pre-processing a UOL so it can easily be processed by the engine during execution of the UOL. For each publication one or more runs may exist, allowing parallel execution of the same UOL.

Runs provide a mechanism for binding users to the UOL, allowing at the same time multiple reuse of the same UOL, both sequentially and in parallel. Furthermore, it allows users to be grouped together in cohorts. However, individual users still must be mapped to the roles defined in the UOL. Two constructs are responsible for this requirement: 'role-participation' and 'run-participation'. Role-participation defines what roles a user may assume when participating in a run. Run-participation defines the active role for a user in a run at any moment in time.

Figure 5.1, which extends Figure 4.2, shows the relationships between the various concepts.

LD specifies that it is possible to have multiple instances for some roles. Role instances can be created dynamically during execution of the UOL as defined by LD. For a UOL to be reusable, these newly created instances of the roles cannot be associated with the publication since they are different for each run. As a result, some of the roles are associated with the run and should be considered copies (or instances) of roles defined in the UOL. The difference between roles associated with the publication and those associated with the run is reflected in the way information about them is stored.

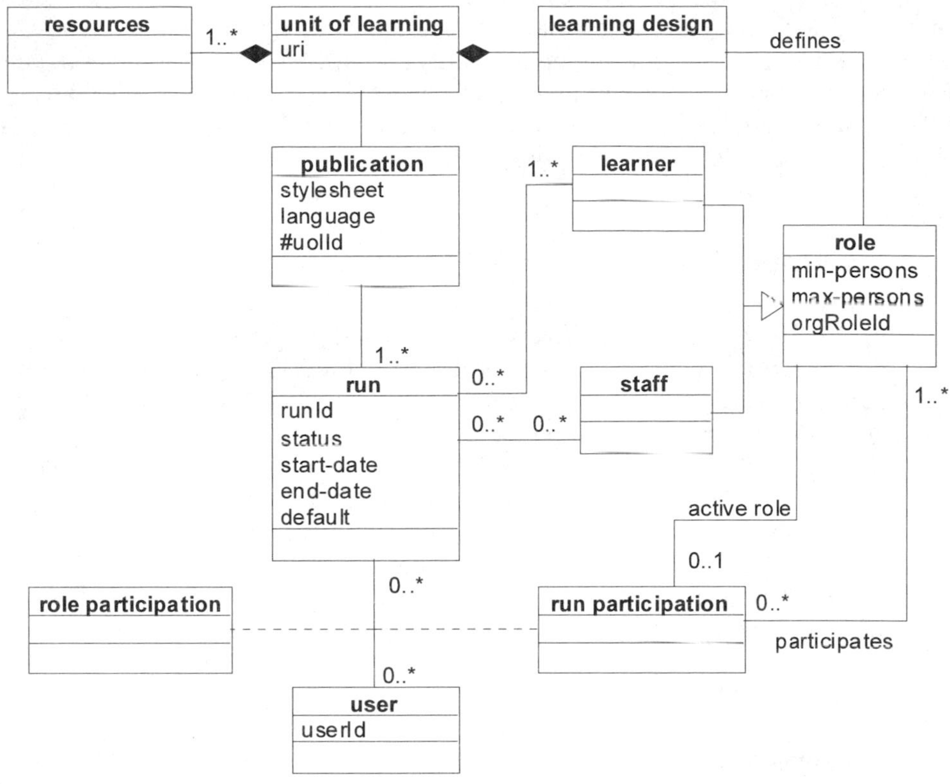

Fig. 5.1. The relationship between run and role

Information about roles associated with the publication is stored through global UOL properties, whereas information about roles associated with the run is stored through local UOL properties. The difference is explained in more detail in the following section, but for now it will suffice to say that global UOL properties have the same value for all runs of the same UOL, and that in contrast, local UOL properties can have different values for each run of the same UOL.

With the addition of role-participation and run-participation, all members of a particular role can be determined, thereby satisfying the last remaining requirement with regard to user population, i.e. assigning individual users to roles.

How, why, when and by whom users are assigned to roles is not part of the functionality of the engine, which merely provides the interfaces allowing the manipulation of the model presented in Fig. 5.1. When doing so, the engine enforces the rules implied by both the model and the UOL preventing the system getting into a state not allowed by the UOL.

We will see that the engine is a collection of FSMs and that the user, run and role are the primary key when determining which FSM is being referred to at any point in time during execution. Before going into more detail, we first describe LD's property mechanism.

5.4 Properties

Properties represent data to be stored and each property consists of a property definition with one or more property values. The property definition determines the type, the default value, the scope and owner of each property. The type restricts the possible values and provides some implicit semantics on the interpretation of the data, in a similar way to the variable types found in most computer programming languages. Initial values are used as the initial state for the FSM. The scope of a property is either local, which means that it is bound to the context of a run, or global, which means there is no direct relation with a run. The owner defines to whom or what a property belongs. The combination of scope and owner determines when and how properties are instantiated. The term 'instantiated' is derived from the world of object orientation. A property is instantiated when a new instance of a property, here a new persistent data store, is created according to its definition. The new property is assigned the initial property value of its corresponding property definition. The value 'null' is assigned when no initial property value is defined. This is only needed for user-defined properties as system-defined properties always have an initial value which is set by the engine when creating this property.

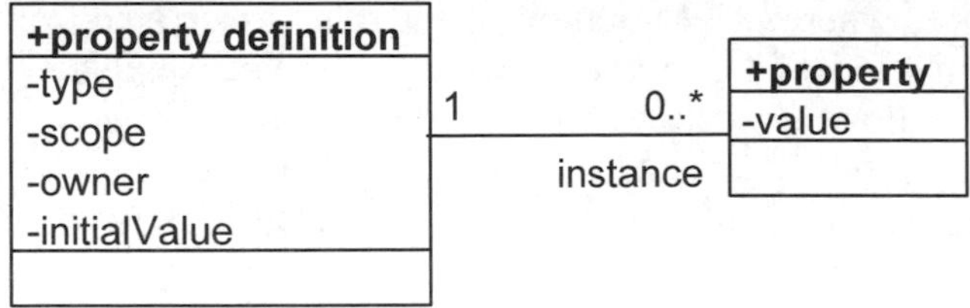

Fig. 5.2. Property definition and properties

Figure 5.2 shows a class diagram of a property definition and its instantiated properties. How and when properties should be instantiated is determined by the scope and owner. Table 5.1 shows valid combinations of scope and owner and describes the instantiation moment and the impact of this for the state.

There are several interesting points to note from this table. First of all, it becomes apparent that the state of a user comprises a number of sets of properties. Some sets are unique per individual, others for each individual in a run, and yet others are common between groups of persons in a particular role or to individuals in a run. Note that scope and owner apply to all types of properties.

Table 5.1. Property types by scope and owner

		Scope	
		Local	Global
Owner	User	A property is instantiated for every user for every run. Parallel runs can result in different states per run as the values may vary per run.	A property is instantiated once for every user. This part of a user's state is the same for every run.
	UOL	A property is instantiated for each run. The property is a part of the state of all users of a run.	A property is instantiated for each UOL and is used for persisting results from the parser. This property isn't part of anyone's state.
	Role	A property is instantiated for each role in each run. The property is part of the state for all the users in the group.	
	None		A single property is instantiated once and typically contains information about the environment. This property isn't part of anyone's state.

Figure 5.3 shows how the different sets of properties make up the state for a particular user. Note that part of the state is shared amongst users and that a user can have more than one state at any moment in time if we view the engine as a collection of FSMs. This can be explained from the fact that the state is not purely related to the user, but also to the run and the role in which the user is participating. So, when viewing the engine as a collection of FSMs, the user, run and role are the primary key when determining which FSM is being referred at any point in time. The collection of all states for a user is also known as the user's dossier. Since the FSMs in part make use of the same properties, modifications to the properties propagate to all the involved FSMs. This also explains why the initial state for one FSM could be influenced by the final state of another FSM.

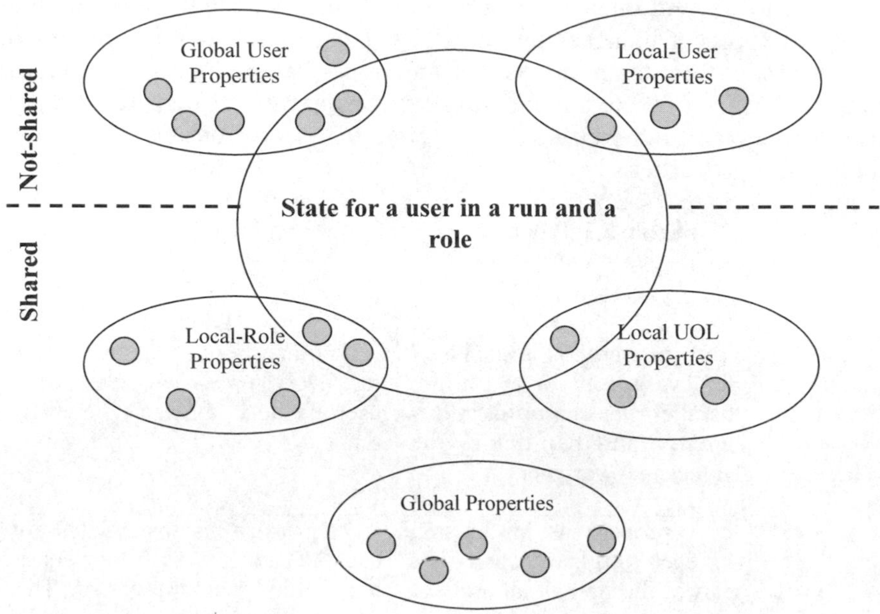

Fig. 5.3. State as combination of sets of properties

The interlocking of FSMs provides a mechanism for dealing with group behavior in the engine.

It is important to understand that the engine is responsible for determining the scope and owner for each of the system-defined properties it defines. The example at the beginning of this section mentions that the engine is responsible for adding completed properties for a number of constructs. The engine is also responsible for determining what the ownership and scope of each of the completed properties should be. For example, the engine needs to keep track of state for each user with respect to constructs like `learning-activity`, `support-activity`, `activity-structure`, `role-part`, `act`, `play`, and `unit-of-learning`. The owner and scope for all these completed properties should be user and local. This is true for all except for `unit-of-learning`. The completion of the UOL can be relevant beyond the run, e.g. in a curriculum, and its scope should therefore be global. Careful consideration of these aspects is needed for each system-defined property introduced.

The second issue arising from Table 5.1 is that a new type of property, the global UOL property, has been added in addition to the ones that are defined in LD. It is a special category of global UOL property used by the engine to facilitate persistence of the parsing results during the pre-processing. Parsing converts the UOL into a format that can be easily interpreted during the personalization stage. The results of this parsing consist of XML documents derived from the original UOL. The newly created XML documents are stored in global UOL properties. By doing so, the engine extends the use of properties as a mechanism for persisting FSM state towards a more generic store. The extension allows an efficient implementation of the engine with minimal code and optimal reuse.

5.5 Event Handling

We have seen that properties provide the means to describe the state of a user (even multiple states). In order to complete the FSM concept, we need a transition function capable of changing the state on the basis of an input alphabet. As noted earlier, the engine is a Moore machine, making it necessary to have a mechanism that can react to a change of a state in the manner required by LD for some of its constructs. These reactions will form the output alphabet.

LD provides some instructions allowing the user to manipulate properties, and thereby state, directly. Examples are the `set-property` or `user-choice` instructions. However, most constructs change property values in a more indirect fashion.

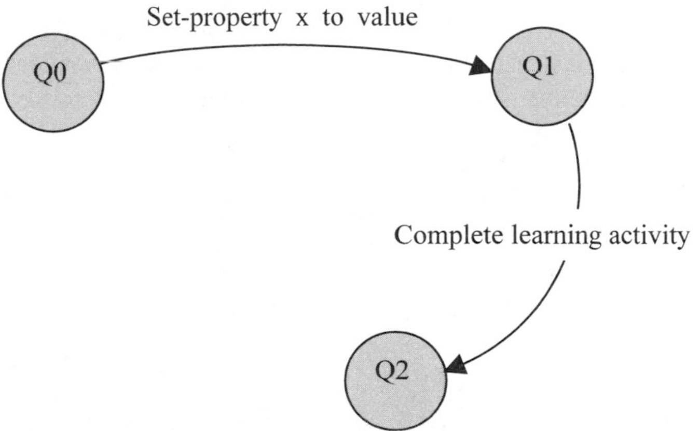

Fig. 5.4. An example state diagram

Figure 5.4 shows an example FSM responding to the input alphabet. Q0 represents the start state for the state machine for a particular user, run and role. The user interacts via the engine by manually setting a property and thereby changing state. The input is represented by the edge between Q0 and Q1. We assume that the UOL for which this state machine is drawn contains a conditional construct stating that setting property x to value y should result in the completion of learning activity Z. The result of this output is state Q2 and the output itself is represented by the edge between Q1 and Q2.

What are the alphabets and how can they be 'read' and 'written'? Everything that can change the state of an FSM is considered to be an event and the collection of events thus forms the input alphabet of the FSM. The output alphabet consists of the input alphabet extended with additional events as a result of the LD semantics. The events making up the input alphabet can be classified and are limited to only two classes: property events which trigger whenever a property value is changed, and timer events, which trigger after a defined duration of time.

The output alphabet consists of events triggered on the basis of changed property values and a number of events that will not cause any state changes. Among the latter are events triggering *notifications* and *email messages.* The remainder of this section deals with the implementation of the event processing mechanism in the engine. Figure 5.5 shows the architecture of the event handling mechanism of the engine. The property store contains all states of all users. Whenever a property value is changed the property store raises a new event, which is captured by the event dispatcher.

Although the event dispatcher reacts to all events from the input alphabet, not all of these events trigger a state transition. Those events which cause a state transition are defined by LD. This is either done by explicitly defined LD level B conditions or by the more implicit LD business rules. The pseudo LD fragment below shows an example of an explicit condition:

```
<imsld:if>
  <imsld:is>
    <imsld:property-ref ref="integer_prop_x"/>
    <imsld:property-value>1</imsld:property-value>
  </imld:is>
  <imsld:then>
    <!-- action causing new event -->
  </imsld:then>
</imsld:if>
```

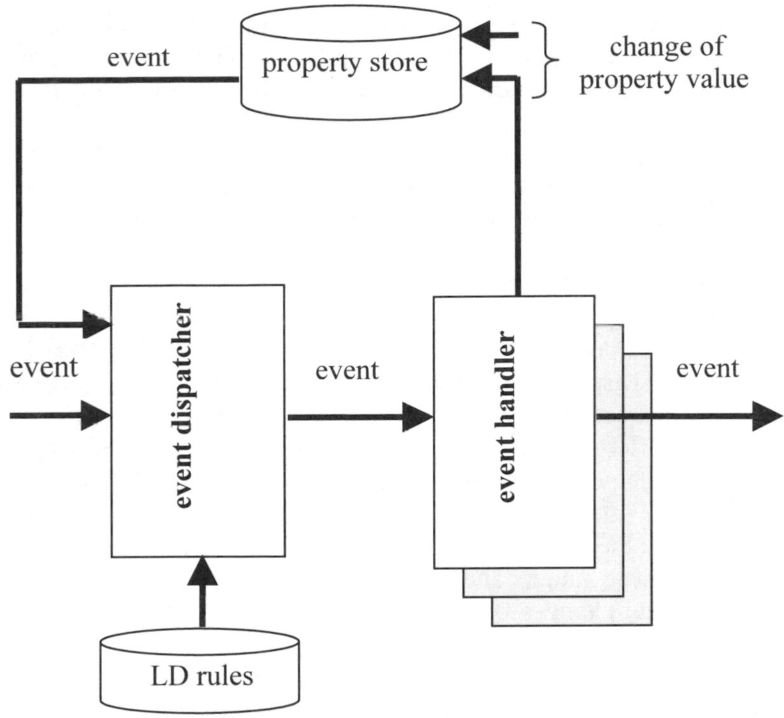

Fig. 5.5. Overview of the event handling mechanism

An example implicit condition is expressed by Fig. 5.4. In this example, a learning activity is completed when a property is set to a particular value. Each condition, being either implicit or explicit, determines if an incoming event leads to a state transition. These conditions which filter the events are known as guards.

During the pre-processing of the LD instances, all explicit and implicit conditions are expressed as guards using an extended version of the LD level B condition language. This collection of pre-parsed guards is stored as XML using a global system property. Whenever the event dispatcher receives an event this system property is read and the event is checked against all the guards. Each event for which a guard evaluates to true will cause a state transition.

The way in which the engine processes an event is defined by LD. For this purpose, a limited set of transition functions is defined in LD. These transition functions include operations regarding visibility, notifications, completions and properties. Each class of transition function is implemented by one event handler. To perform a state transition, an event handler requires additional data such as the identifier of the property that will be changed and its new value. The type of transition function and its associated additional data are defined by LD via the `then` element. The `then` element is re-used and extended and stored in a system property similar to the guards.

The event handler may trigger one or more new events thereby forming a chain of events. The event handlers do not necessarily react by changing property values. They may raise events triggering notifications or email messages. Note that an event can trigger zero, one or more event handlers and that an event handler can change zero, one or more properties. Furthermore, the change of properties can supersede the scope of a single FSM because the same properties can be shared amongst different FSMs. Therefore multiple FSMs can change state simultaneously as a result of a single event. This characteristic ensures propagation and, as a result, the synchronization of different roles and groups working together. Propagation can occur from the perspective of a single user having multiple FSMs (one for every role the user may assume) or from the perspective of groups within a run or even at the level of the whole user community known to the engine. It is important to understand that in order for this mechanism to function properly, state changes propagating over several FSMs are considered as atomic actions.

Timer events do not start with a change of a property value, but are raised by a timer. The rest of the event handling mechanism is exactly the same as for events raised through change of a property value. Clearly, there is a risk of recursion causing endless loops and it is the responsibility of the validation process in the pre-processing stage to detect such situations (this point is elaborated later in the chapter).

5.6 Publication

A publication is the result of pre-processing a UOL and the part of the engine responsible for this process is called the publication engine. We have already seen that the properties and event handling mechanisms depend on the outcome of this process.

Figure 5.6 shows a sequence diagram representing the publication process. The first step of the publication process is to check the UOL validity. Validation covers a numbers of aspects. The UOL is checked for completeness; that is, whether all locally referenced resources are also included in the UOL package. The UOL manifest is validated against the LD schema using a validating parser such as *Xerces* (2004). These types of validation are straightforward and revolve around XML technology. More interesting types of validation cover the semantics of a UOL.

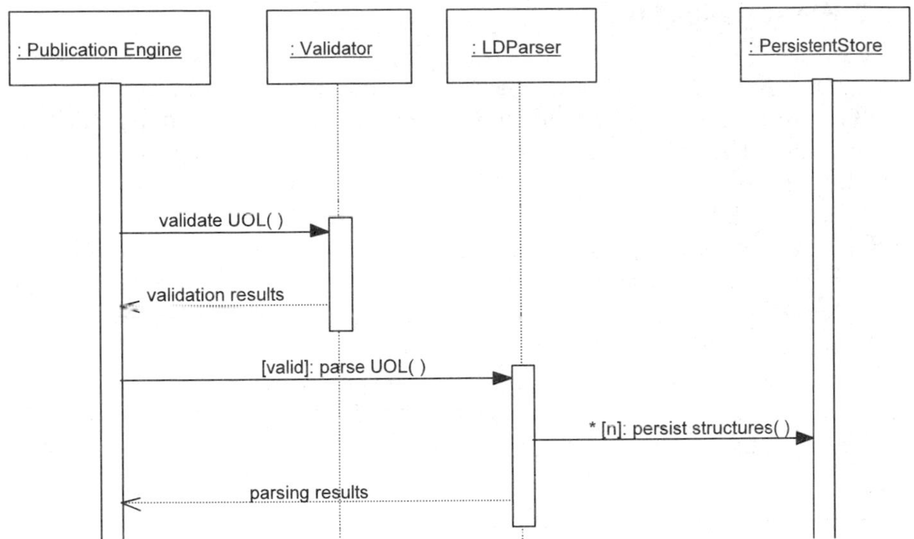

Fig. 5.6. The publication process

All references are checked to determine if no erroneous cross-references have been made.

Examples of such errors would be a `role-ref` referring to a `property`. Another type of semantic validation includes the checks for invalid attribute values: for example, if the minimum number of people specified in a role exceeds the maximum number.

Recursion can occur whenever and wherever elements can include other elements by reference, such as with the `environment` element. Checking for recursion is especially important for preventing event handlers falling into endless loops. Determining whether an UOL represents meaningful education can not be done by automated validation but will involve the expertise of the human author.

If the validation is successful, the LD parser is invoked. The LD parser converts the LD into a format that can be easily interpreted during the execution phase. This intermediate XML format is used during the personalization stage. As noted earlier, global UOL properties are used to store these small XML documents. It is important to highlight that the actual resource is not part of such an XML document but is stored separately on a web server and is referenced from the XML documents.

Another result of the parsing process is the store containing rules that should be applied for a UOL. These entries are retrieved by the event dispatcher in order to determine what actions need to be taken when an event occurs. Finally the publication process is responsible for creating all relevant property definitions for all properties.

5.7 Personalization

A UOL is executed when a user accesses a run of a UOL in a role, and results in an adapted view of the UOL according to the role and user's property values. This adaptation process is known as personalization and is one of the core requirements of LD. Personalization involves adaptation of the LD according to rules defined by LD, which describe how the engine should react to certain states. An example is feedback, which should only be provided when the corresponding activity has been completed, in other words, when a certain state has been reached (states are constructed by sets of properties).

Once the FSM is in place, personalization and execution of LD becomes relatively straightforward as most of the work has already been done by the event handling mechanism.

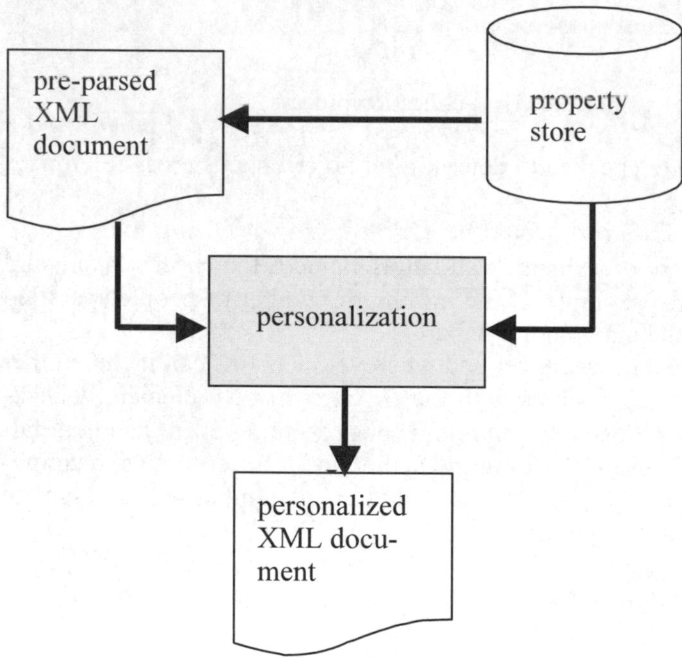

Fig. 5.7. The personalization process

The result of the personalization process, as shown in Fig. 5.7, is a personalized XML document. This is achieved by merging the XML document that was stored as result of the publication with the property values from the persistent property store. Note that the original XML document is stored as a global UOL property. How the pre-parsed XML document is merged with the property values varies slightly depending on the type of element and corresponding rules. The process can result in the replacement, addition or removal of some XML elements. Although there are a number of personalization types defined in LD, we can classify them into the following three classes:

- Personalization of the activity tree. An activity tree is the combination of all *plays* and their sub-elements. The current activity tree is selected on the basis of the run and the current role of the user and contains only the relevant subset of the activity tree. This subset is the same for all users in the same role. Personalization is the process of applying the values of the FSM for the completed and visibility properties to the current activity tree. The outcome is a personalized XML representation of the activity tree reflecting the state of the user.
- Personalization of the environment tree associated with an activity. The environment tree is adapted using visibility properties in a similar way to the activity tree, resulting is an XML representation of the environment tree.
- Personalization of the content of various LD constructs. References to properties are replaced by their actual values and parts of the content may be hidden on the basis of the value for the different class properties. Class properties are system-defined properties created during publication which reflect the visibility status (hidden or visible) for classes of content.

In conclusion, once the FSM mechanism is in place, personalization is reduced to a simple XML transformation applying the values defined in the FSM according to the rules defined by LD.

5.8 Conclusions

In this chapter we decomposed LD to a few basic constructs allowing elegant and relatively lightweight implementations. This decomposition is accomplished by exploiting the property mechanism in LD, extending it with system-defined properties. The use of these properties helps harmonize the different kinds of rules defined in LD, and reduces them to simple property operations. Furthermore the property mechanism acts as a store for the result of the publication process for the pre-parsed XML content. The event mechanism helps break down the large number of rules to a limited number of transition functions. The event handlers implementing these transition functions each have a dedicated task, dealing with different aspects of the rules laid down by LD, but all have the same basic mechanism which again helps reduce the complexity enormously. Reduction of the complexity is essential and is achieved by the fact that implementers only have to focus on the proper implementation of the event handlers themselves. Implementers of an event handler do not have to worry about the bigger picture as it is dealt with by the event handling mechanism. The same event handling mechanism ensures that reactions to certain events are adequately propagated throughout the whole system. By doing so, all group and role dynamics are automatically incorporated into the engine without additional effort as the engine is considered as a collection of FSMs. The introduction of runs and roles provides the primary key for each of the FSMs. We have shown that by selecting the right owner and scope of the properties, we can interlock the FSMs, resulting in correct, automatic propagation of state changes. Again no additional efforts have to be made because the event handling mechanism propagates state changes throughout all interlocked FSMs. Using these constructs, the implementation complexity of LD engines can be reduced significantly.

6 A Reference Implementation of a Learning Design Engine

Harrie Martens, Hubert Vogten

Educational Technology Expertise Centre,
Open University of the Netherlands, Heerlen, The Netherlands

6.1 Introduction

From the moment the Learning Design specification (LD 2003) was published there has been a need for software capable of processing LD-compliant content. LD is a powerful and complex specification, and it is not a trivial matter to implement an LD player. In response to this need, the Educational Technology Expertise Centre of the Open University of the Netherlands launched an initiative to develop a reusable kernel dealing with the intricacies of processing LD. Since this kernel should be able to be used in different settings, it is not a standalone product but needs to be integrated in a learning management system. The kernel, known as CopperCore, has been developed under the GNU General Public License and is available through SourceForge at http://www.coppercore.org.

CopperCore has the following features:

- A validation routine for the manifest file containing the LD ensuring only valid LD is processed. Validation includes both technical and semantic checks and the validation results are reported.
- An administrative backend with regard to publications, user management, runs and roles. These concepts are discussed below.
- Interpretation of LD and delivery of personalized content according to the rules defined in LD. This is achieved by keeping track of the user's progress and settings.
- Platform independence, based on a strategic choice for Java and J2EE.

This chapter provides background information for implementing an LD-compliant player based on CopperCore. First a conceptual overview is given of the two major functional Application Programming Interfaces (APIs) dealing with administrative tasks and runtime delivery. The next section gives a brief technical overview of the architecture of CopperCore and discusses the technical design decisions. This helps the reader understand the final section dealing with implementation strategies.

6.2 Conceptual Overview

In order to process LD successfully, CopperCore functionality has been divided into two major parts. The CourseManager handles administrative functionality such as users, roles, runs and publications. In contrast, the LDEngine forms the heart of CopperCore and deals with the runtime delivery of the personalized content as defined in the LD. Well-defined APIs are available for both parts to developers who wish to integrate CopperCore into their own products. The next section provides an overview of the functionalities found in the APIs.

6.2.1 CourseManager

The CourseManager deals with all administrative tasks required in order for the LDEngine to work. The CourseManager covers user management, role assignments, run management and publications. All these concepts are discussed next.

Publications

According to the LD specification a learning design needs to be packaged in a content package (CP 2003) which is a ZIP file containing all resources. This content package must contain a file named `imsmanifest.xml` containing the learning design itself. All other files in the package are additional resources. A content package containing LD is called a Unit of Learning (UOL). Before a UOL can be deployed, CopperCore creates a publication for the UOL, taking care of several aspects needed during deployment.

First, the UOL is validated to make sure no syntactic or semantic errors are present in the package. Validation includes validation against schemas, validation of the package itself with regard to the resources included, and validation of semantics of the learning design. Detected errors are stored in a list of messages which can be reported back to the user.

Second, CopperCore breaks down the learning design into more manageable parts such as activities, environments, learning objects, roles, etc. Third, CopperCore analyses the roles that are declared in the learning design. This is necessary since users need to be assigned to particular roles before they can start using the system. Finally all content contained in the UOL is copied to a web server directory for retrieval during deployment.

Publishing a UOL can be done by simply calling an API method called `publishUOL`.

User Management

LD focuses on delivering personalized education. This is achieved by describing a learning design through profiles using the role. CopperCore deals with this personalized delivery by creating a dossier for each user. In order to do so, CopperCore requires users to be defined. For this purpose a user may be added to CopperCore using the *createUser* API call. The only parameter passed is the user id. All other user information needed should be defined in LD as global personal properties and stored in a user's dossier. Once defined, users cannot be deleted.

Run Management

LD may refer to all users in a role, i.e. a grouping of users (see Chap. 4 for further discussion of this point). A grouping mechanism is required that allows the division of the user population into smaller cohorts working together in one particular learning design. A group could, for example, represent a classroom, or a number of students participating in a distance learning course. The term "run" is used in this context.

Users are never assigned directly to a publication but they are enrolled for a particular learning design by adding them to a specific run. Therefore each publication must have at least a run. If necessary, more runs can be added depending on the particular circumstances. A new run can be created in CopperCore using the `createRun` API call passing the id of the publication as one of its parameters.

The next step is assigning the users to a particular run. As stated earlier, who should be assigned to which run depends very much on the circumstances. It is important to understand that only participants of the same run can cooperate and are "visible" to each other in the same learning design. So when LD refers to all users, in effect it refers to all the participants in a specific run. Users can be added to a run by calling the method `addUserToRun`. Users may be removed from a run by calling `removeUserFromRun`.

Role Management

Roles are the main personalization mechanisms of LD and are essential for creating different paths through a learning design. Roles may be seen as a representation of users with a certain profile. It is the task of role management to populate these roles with actual users of a run. Users can be assigned to a role using the method `addUserToRole` and can be removed using `removeUserFromRole`.

Different users can be assigned to different roles, but it is also possible to assign an individual user to multiple roles. However, when the LDEngine delivers the learning design to a user it personalizes the design using the role of the user. Therefore only one role may be active at any moment for each user. This role is called the active role. A user can switch roles at any time by selecting a new active role from the list of roles he or she is assigned to. The method `setActiveRole` sets the active role for a user.

LD defines a hierarchy of roles. This has an impact on the interpretation of the roles. A sub-role is considered to inherit all the properties of its ancestor roles. For example, a sub-role of the role "learner" will inherit the properties of this "learner" role and everything available to the "learner" is also available to its sub-role. CopperCore states that a user may only be assigned to a sub-role when the user is already assigned to the parent of that sub-role. The hierarchy of roles starts with a common root and all users must be assigned to this common root before doing any further role assignments.

LD supports the runtime creation of new roles. For example, if a role is used to group users together with a maximum of ten users, a new role may be created during runtime whenever this maximum is exceeded. In LD these roles have an attribute "`create-new`" with the value "`allowed`". A new instance of a role can be created by calling the method `createRole`. Users can be assigned to these roles in the same way as with regular roles.

The UML class diagram of CopperCore is that shown in Fig. 5.1.

6.2.2 LDEngine

After the UOL is published, users are assigned to the run and to their roles and the delivery of the learning design can start. LD defines a hierarchy of activities to be performed by a role in the method section. For each activity there are a number of resources, learning objects and services, grouped in an environment. Environments are also hierarchies.

CopperCore defines a number of concepts and API calls for retrieving the information contained in these hierarchies which are discussed in detail in the following sections.

Activity Tree

An activity tree is an XML representation of the method section of LD personalized for a user. Personalization consists of two parts. First, the active role of the user requesting the activity tree is taken into account. Only those activities associated with the active role, or one of its parent roles, will be included in the activity tree. CopperCore deals with this personalization during the publication stage by splitting the method hierarchy up into a number of smaller hierarchies based on the defined roles, using the role part constructs in LD.

Second, personalization deals with the individual progress of users. This mainly involves keeping track of the completed activities for a user. CopperCore deals with all defined rules in LD, such as the completion of activity structures, acts, plays and the unit of learning. The resulting XML tree is based on the application of these rules on a personal basis. A personalized activity tree can be retrieved by calling the method *getActivityTree*. This method is called in the context of a user in a specific run and returns an XML representation of the activity tree for this user. A visual representation of the underlying schema of this XML response (an activity tree schema) is shown in Fig. 6.1.

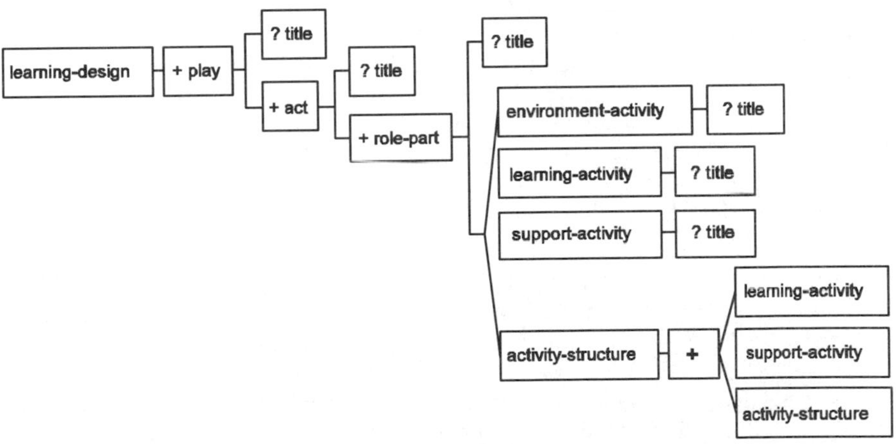

Fig. 6.1. Activity tree schema

The schema closely resembles the original LD. However, there are some differences, especially when reflecting the user's progress. The root element of the activity tree is the learning design itself. It contains one or more plays. A play contains one or more acts and an act is made up of role parts. A role part itself contains an activity which is a `learning-activity`, `support-activity`, `activity-structure` or an environment-activity. The last is not an activity as such but represents an environment with an implicit activity, such as an activity that instructs the learner to read the documents in the environment. Each of the elements may contain a title which can be used in the user interface when representing a node of the activity tree.

The activity tree contains only those nodes available to the user at the moment of retrieval, which is a major difference from the original learning design containing all potential nodes for all users. This filtering of nodes is only one result of the personalization. Another aspect of the personalization can be seen when examining the attributes of the nodes. Table 6.1 describes each of the attributes.

Table 6.1. Activity tree node attributes

Attribute	Description
completed	This attribute may have the value true, false or unlimited. The attribute indicates if a user has completed the node or, if the value is unlimited, that the node should be considered completed. The following nodes have a completed attribute: act, activity-structure, environment-activity, learning-activity, learning-design, play, support-activity.
environment	This attribute contains a space-separated list of ids belonging to environments of the activity represented by the node. The values of this attribute should be passed when retrieving the environment via the getEnvironmentTree API call. This attribute is used in the following elements: activity-structure, environment-activity, learning-activity, support-activity.
identifier	This attribute is the identifier of the object represented by the node. Note that this is not the identifier of the node itself and therefore multiple nodes may have the same identifier value if they are pointing to the same object. This identifier should be used when retrieving the content of the object represented by the node via the getContent API call. The identifier attribute is used in activity-structure, environment-activity, learning-activity, learning-design, play, role-part, support-activity.

`isvisible`	This attribute indicates if a node is visible for the user or not. For Level A it means that this value is identical to the value defined initially in the learning design because there are no constructs allowing the value to be changed. The attribute may occur in `learning-activity`, `play`, `support-activity`.
`role`	This attribute contains the role name which was the basis for generating this activity tree. The attribute occurs only in the `learning-design` node.
`structure-type`	This attribute can have the values sequence or selection indicating which type of activity structure is represented by the activity-structure node in which the attribute occurs.
`time-limit`	This attribute indicates that the completion of a node is dependent on a timed event. It occurs in an act, learning-activity, play, support-activity.
`user-choice`	This attributes indicates that a user must indicate when an activity has been completed. There should be a means in the user interface allowing for this. When a user indicates completion of the activity, `completeActivity` should be called. The attribute may occur in `learning-activity`, `support-activity`.

Environment Tree

An environment tree is a representation of the environment and the learning objects and services belonging to one or more activities. The environment tree may be retrieved by calling `getEnvironmentTree` which results in an XML document according to the schema shown in Fig. 6.2. The root element is `environments` which can contain one or more environments. An environment consists of zero or more learning object, environments and services. There are three types of services: send-mail, conference and index search. `Send-mail` contains the `send-to` element representing the recipients of the mail and the `from` element representing the sender of the mail. The content of the title element should be used to represent a node in the user interface. In LD Level A there is no personalization of the environment tree.

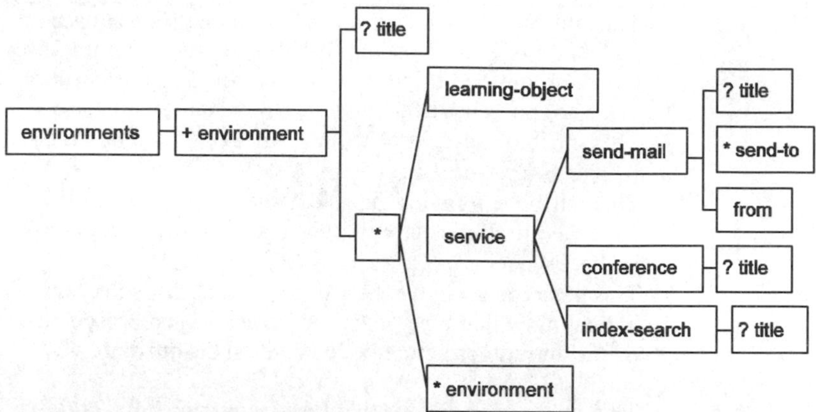

Fig. 6.2. Environment tree schema

The attributes in Table 6.2 may be defined for these elements:

Table 6.2. Environment tree node attributes

Attribute	Description
`class`	The class attribute allows the nodes to be typed by a space-separated list of types. For LD Level A this attribute should be considered merely as documentation. From Level B onwards it can be used to hide or show these nodes. The attribute may occur in `conference`, `index-search` and `send-mail`.
`conference-type`	This attribute indicates what type of conference is referenced by the conference element. Allowed values are synchronous, asynchronous and announcement. It is the responsibility of the integrating module to provide a link to a service having the appropriate features.
`identifier`	This attribute is the identifier of the object represented by the node. Note that this is not the identifier of the node itself and therefore multiple nodes may have the same identifier value if they are pointing to the same object! This identifier should be used when retrieving the content of the object represented by the node via the `getContent` API call. The identifier attribute is used in `index-search`, `learning-object` and `send-mail`.
`isvisible`	This attribute indicates whether a node is visible for the user. For level A it means that this value is identical to the value defined initially in the learning design because there are no constructs allowing the value to be changed. The attribute may occur in `conference`, `environment`, `index-search`, `learning-object`, `send-mail`.

`parameters`	This attribute contains the parameters defined in a learning design for a service. The attribute may occur in `conference, index-search, send-mail.`
`select`	This attribute defines who should receive the mail defined by the send-mail element. Allowed values are `person-in-role` and `all-persons-in-role.`
`type`	This attribute contains the type of the learning-object element as defined in LD.
`user-id`	This attribute is used in the `send-to` and `from` elements and contains the user ids of the receivers and sender of the mail. In Level B this will be extended with the email addresses of the sender and receivers of the email. This explains why the `from` element is available here already (for Level A it could be omitted as the sender's identity is known as he or she is typing the mail).

Content

All nodes in both the activity tree and the environment tree may contain content. The content can be retrieved by calling the `getContent` method while passing the identifier of the object to be retrieved as parameter. Content is returned as personalized XML resembling the original learning design content. All content may include a title and metadata if these were defined in the UOL to which the content belongs. The `getContent` call does not return the actual content of the items. Each item contains a fully qualified URL to the location of the resource representing this content. So retrieving the complete content of any element consists of a two-stage process which involves as a first step the retrieval of a personalized XML structure of the content, followed by the retrieval of the resources referenced by the items.

Figure 6.3 shows the schema for the content model of a learning activity (the Learning-activity schema). Like all content objects, a learning activity may contain a title and metadata. Furthermore it may contain learning objectives, prerequisites and an activity. All these elements have exactly the same content structure, starting with one or more item elements which may be surrounded with an optional title and metadata. An item may have zero or more sub-items. Again, an optional title and metadata may be present. An item represents a kind of paragraph structure where the title element should be used as a heading. How this hierarchy is presented in the user interface is left to the integrator of CopperCore. An item has a required Uniform Resource Identifier (URI) attribute that contains an absolute Uniform Resource Locator (URL) to the location of the associated resource. A resource may be any resource that can be rendered in a web browser.

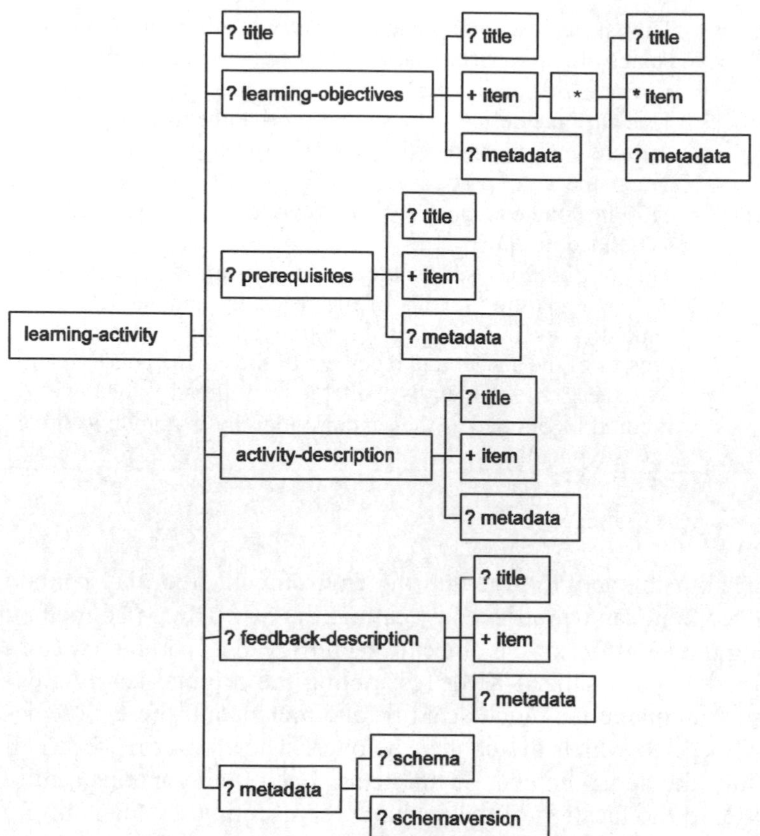

Fig. 6.3. Learning-activity schema

The learning-objectives and prerequisite elements can also occur in the content model of a learning design. The feedback-description is only shown when it is present in the original UOL and if the user has completed the learning activity. `Feedback description` may also occur in the content models of the learning design the play and the act and will be present only if the corresponding element has been completed by the user.

Figure 6.4 shows the content model for a learner role (the learner schema). Clearly, the main structure of the content model is very similar for all elements. The information element that may be presented to the user as additional information is new. The information element may also occur in the staff and act element.

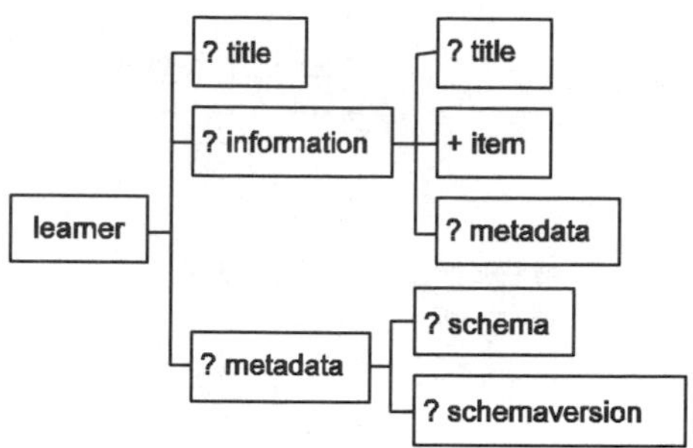

Fig. 6.4. Learner schema

The content elements can contain a number of attributes included for reference only. The most relevant are presented in Table 6.3..

Table 6.3. Learner tree node attributes

Attribute	Description
`Identifier`	The identifier of the object. It occurs in the elements `act`, `activity-structure`, `environment`, `item`, `learner`, `learning-activity`, `learning-design`, `learning-object`, `play`, `roles-to-support`, `send-mail`, `staff`, `support-activity`.
`isvisible`	This attribute holds an integer value indicating if an object was visible or not. This attribute may occur in the elements `act`, `item`, `play`, `learning-activity`, `support-activity`, `learning-object` and `send-mail`.
`url`	This attribute contains the absolute URL to an resource for which an item is a placeholder. The attribute occurs in the `item` element only.
`Class`	The class attributes assign an element to one or more categories. The visibility of these categories may be manipulated via conditions in Levels B and C of LD. The class attribute can occur in `send-mail` and `learning-object`.

Overview

Figure 6.5 gives an example of a typical calling sequence of the LDEngine API.

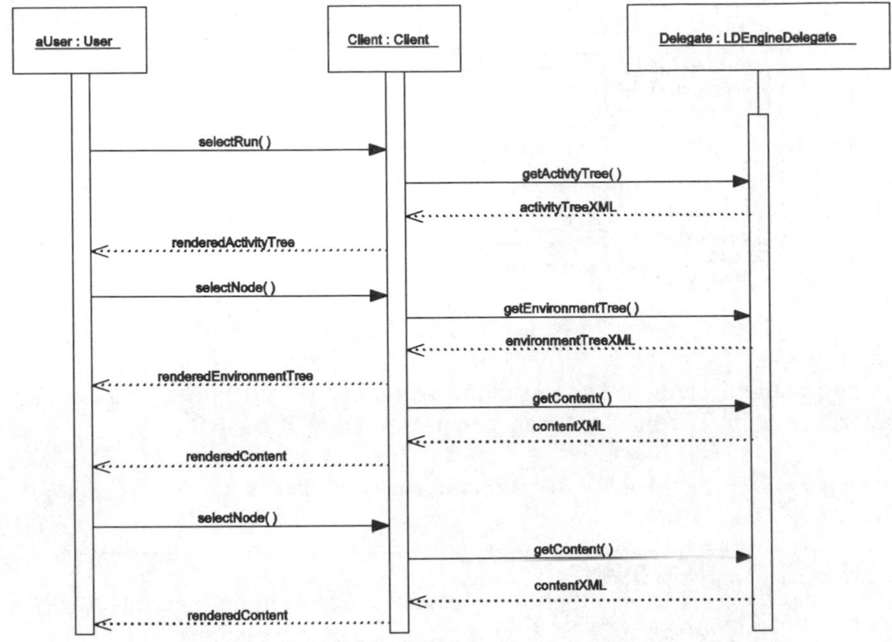

Fig. 6.5. Sequence diagram of LDEngine calls

There are three "swim lanes" representing the user, the client integrating CopperCore and the CopperCore LDEngine API. In the example, a user starts by selecting one of the runs, probably from a list of runs for which the user is enrolled. After the user selects the run, the client application retrieves the activity tree for the user and run combination. The activity tree is returned as an XML file as discussed earlier. The client transforms this XML data in such a manner so that the user may select one of its nodes. After the user has selected a node from the activity tree, the client retrieves the environment tree belonging to this node. Both the identifier of the node in the activity tree and the list of environment objects are passed as parameters. As a result, CopperCore responds with the XML representation of the requested environment trees. The client renders this tree into a format suitable for the user. Next, the client retrieves the content for the node selected from the activity tree. The content is returned as XML and the client parses this content so it may retrieve all the needed resources referenced from the item inside the content. These resources are merged or linked and also presented to the user.

The user may now select a node from the environment tree. The client acts on this request by fetching the content from the CopperCore API and rendering the content in a similar fashion to the rendering of the content of the selected activity node.

This is merely a short example of the type of interaction which takes place between the user, client and CopperCore but it gives an idea of the dependencies between the activity tree, environment tree and content.

6.3 Technical Overview

CopperCore is implemented using Sun's Java 2 Platform, Enterprise Edition (J2EE). The most pertinent reasons for this choice are:

- The kernel should be able to run on multiple platforms supporting multiple operating systems. Java is an obvious choice.
- The kernel should be accessible via web services or similar web-oriented technologies, but should allow for non-web-based access as well. Enterprise Java Beans (EJBs) provide a mechanism for this.
- The kernel should be scalable when necessary. This is another reason for choosing EJBs.

Figure 6.6 shows the technical architecture of the CopperCore kernel. All persisted data is stored in a relational database. CopperCore uses a JDBC driver to access the database. Using this extra layer between the data components and the actual database allows CopperCore to use different DBMSs by just switching the JDBC driver. The "Data Access Layer" is responsible for all interactions with the database and is made up of BMP entity beans. The "Database Access Layer" is split into two major parts.

The first part consists of properties. Although CopperCore currently only implements LD Level A, internally it depends heavily on the property mechanism. The other part of the "Database Access Layer" deals with course administration, which involves concepts such as users, runs, unit-of-learning etc.

The next layer of the architecture is the "Business Logic Layer" and contains all components representing the business logic of CopperCore. This layer is made up of a number of container components which are representations of the learning design that are directly or indirectly accessible through the API. Each container contains all the business logic it needs to adapt itself to the profile of the user accessing the LD component. For this purpose, the container makes extensive use of the property mechanism which contains its own business logic for retrieval and storage of properties. The EventDispatcher and EventHandler components deal with all event handling business logic occurring in the system. Finally the parser deals with the processing of an LD XML instance. It analyses and decomposes the LD into smaller parts suitable for further processing during runtime.

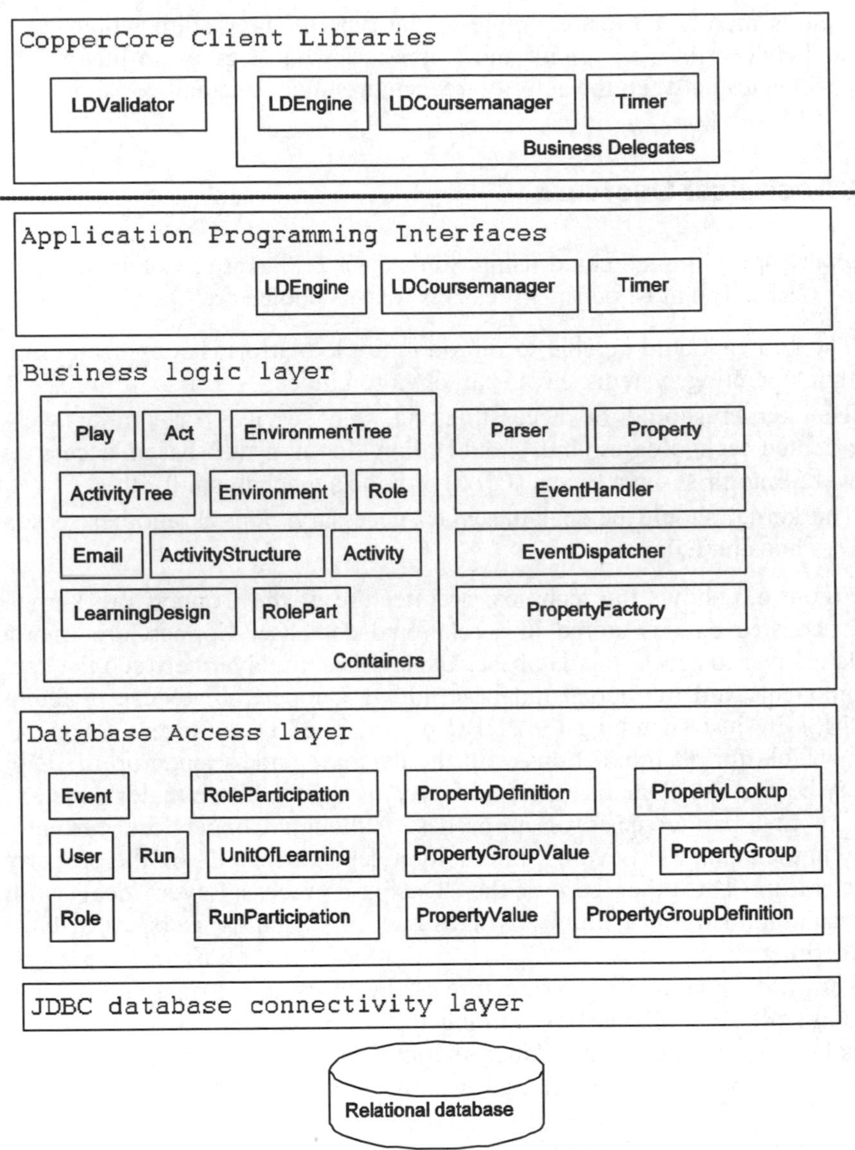

Fig. 6.6. CopperCore technical architecture

The next layer comprises three session beans. The first bean is the `LDCourseManager` bean. It deals with all administrative calls necessary to prepare delivery of an LD instance. Typical interfaces offered deal with the publication of an XML LD instance, creation of users, creation of runs and assignment of roles.

The second bean is the `LDEngine`. This is the core of the delivery mechanism. This bean handles the personalization of the LD instance for a particular user at a particular time. Calls that deal with the retrieval of personalized activity trees, environment trees and content are available.

Finally, there is a `Timer` bean which deals with all time-related events specified in the learning design. Due to implementation restrictions in J2EE the clients should generate timer events on regular intervals by calling `proces()`. CopperCore does not make any assumptions about the granularity of the intervals, by ensuring no time-related events are missed.

The final layer is the "CopperCore Client Libraries" and is not a layer in the formal sense. It is a collection of libraries that should be used by an implementation making use of CopperCore. The most important library is the validator. As the name implies, the validator validates a UOL content package. Several checks are made to see if the package is complete, if the learning design is well formed and valid against the schema, and if the learning design is semantically correct. The library should be called by all clients to make sure that everything is correct before proceeding. In addition to the validator, three business delegates are offered for the three API beans. A business delegate contains the code to make the actual connection to the enterprise bean, making life easier for implementers.

6.4 Implementation Strategies

The main design decision when building CopperCore was to give implementers maximum flexibility to use the kernel in the way they see fit. However, this also implies that CopperCore itself is not a complete LD player. To make effective use of CopperCore, the kernel has to be integrated into a larger application. This application has to implement different services, the most important being the graphical user interface (GUI), without which the kernel cannot be used by an end-user. The GUI not only gives the learners and tutors access to the LD, but should also enable administrators to manage the learning process by letting them create new publications, add new users to the system, create a run for a publication, and so on.

The other major service being offered by the application is the possibility to serve the resources which are included in the LD package to the client. CopperCore does not implement a mechanism to deliver this content directly through the kernel. It does, however, extract the resources from the package and stores them on the file system when a UOL is published. Furthermore, CopperCore changes the local references to these resources into an application-specific reference, so the application is able to serve these resources to the end-user upon request. The easiest way to implement this service is to use a web server in the application.

CopperCore has been developed using J2EE. The kernel itself is implemented as three EJBs which must be installed and run on a Java Application Server such as JBoss (JBoss 2004). This gives CopperCore the flexibility to run on different operating systems, the scalability to cope with load increases and the ability to be called from different kinds of clients (e.g. web-based clients or native Java clients). The downside of this approach is that the J2EE specification does not allow access to the underlying file system. CopperCore requires access to the file system to store the resources found in an LD package. To solve this problem CopperCore contains a CopperCore Client Library which is implemented as a set of Java classes that are used in the context of the calling application. This way access to the file system is allowed. Furthermore the library implements business delegates to hide the implementation details of accessing the remote EJBs which make up the CopperCore kernel.

Figure 6.7 shows the two main approaches to calling CopperCore. A client calls CopperCore directly via Java native calls, or an intermediate server allows clients to call CopperCore via the http protocol using a common web browser. Which approach to choose is up to the requirements of the software clients that access CopperCore. Different aspects of client software influence the decision for either a native Java client or a web browser client. When considering the ease of distributing the client application to the end-users, the web browser of course has the upper hand. No local software installation is required apart from having a recent web browser, which is the case for the majority of users. Updating the software is also easier using this web-based approach – only the web application on the server has to be updated to allow all users access to the latest version of the software. Compare this to delivering a new version of the software to individual users who may have different kinds of software configurations, different operating systems, different Java virtual machines, and so on. Furthermore, versioning becomes an issue as different users may install different versions of the client software.

Another issue is the access to the server. Since CopperCore runs on a Java application server, each client must have access to this server. In most places strict security policies exist making it easier to access the server via the most widely used port 80 for http traffic as opposed to the more obscure ports required for the native Java calls. Finally, rendering the LD content (mainly (X)HTML documents) is easier in a web browser.

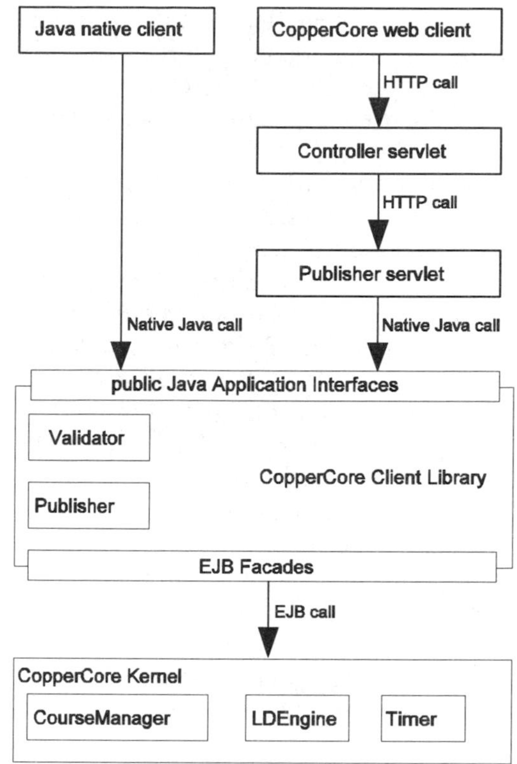

Fig. 6.7. Implementation strategies for CopperCore

A native client is usually more responsive, the GUI can be more elaborate, making handling of large amounts of data more intuitive, and avoiding port 80 can make the application more secure by not exposing some of the APIs to the Internet.

A common way of building clients for CopperCore is to create a web client to be used by end-users acting as either a student or a tutor. In other words, these users are all assigned to one or more runs and access the UOL in the context of a role. For a user who administers CopperCore a native Java client might be more appropriate. The demonstration implementation which can be downloaded from http://coppercore.org illustrates this concept. It implements a web-based player used for accessing the LD. Although the interface is rather primitive it illustrates how such a web client could be built. For administrators, a simple command line interface to CopperCore (`clicc`) is implemented as a native Java application.

Building a web client requires implementers to create a web application. A common approach to implementing a web application on the J2EE platform is using servlets to dynamically create the Internet pages that are served to the browser on the end-user's machine. These servlets call the CopperCore kernel on behalf of the client to maintain the actions performed by the user and to retrieve the personalized LD based upon the actions. To ease access to the kernel, the web application should use the CopperCore client library as is shown in Fig. 6.7.

Building a native Java client is straightforward as far as the kernel is concerned. There are a few clearly defined APIs that can be called. Using the CopperCore client library makes accessing the kernel even easier by hiding all the intricacies of connecting to the remote EJBs. There is, however, one major issue in building a management application in this way. As noted above, an EJB is not allowed to access the file system. To circumvent this problem, CopperCore accesses the file system from within the client library. This client library, however, runs in the context of the calling application. In the case of a management application like `clicc`, this implies that access to the file system is in the context of the application itself. In other words, access to the file system is relative to the location of the application instead of to the location of the server. Being aware of this problem is the major hurdle for an implementer. The problem itself can be solved in different ways: `clicc` takes the easiest approach by running the application on the server itself, another option is to store the resources on a file share on the server, and finally an intermediate server application could be created which stores the resources of a publication in the appropriate place on the server.

6.5 Summary

Since the release of LD there has been a need for a reference implementation of a player for the specification. CopperCore provides a way for implementers to jumpstart building an LD-compliant learning management system. It provides two major APIs to deal with the processing of LD. One covers administration-related tasks while the other deals with the runtime delivery of LD.

CopperCore has been implemented using J2EE and the main components are implemented as Enterprise Java Beans. The use of J2EE allows a number of different implementation strategies giving developers the choice between a pure web-based approach and a dedicated native Java client.

CopperCore is now readily available to all developers who wish to integrate LD support into their own software. It is released under the GNU General Public License and is available for free through SourceForge at http://www.coppercore.org.

7 Learning Design Tools

David Griffiths[1], Josep Blat[1], Rocío Garcia[1], Hubert Vogten[2], KL Kwong[3]

[1] Interactive Technologies Group, Universitat Pompeu Fabra, Barcelona, Spain

[2] Educational Technology Expertise Centre,
Open University of the Netherlands, Heerlen, The Netherlands

[3] GTK Press, Toronto, Ontario, Canada

7.1 Introduction

In this chapter we provide an overview of the tools required for working with the Learning Design specification (LD 2003). These include editors for creating Units of Learning (UOLs), runtime players, and repositories for storing UOLs.

We first examine the context provided by the Valkenburg Group Reference Architecture, identifying those parts which can be handled using general purpose tools, and those which require the development of tools which are specific to LD. We then move on to discuss user roles, and the tools which they require. A framework is offered which enables authoring tools to be situated in terms of their degree of specialization, and the degree to which they require the user to work directly with the specification vocabulary and syntax.

We then move on to classify and examine the tools which are specific to LD which have so far been produced, or are currently being developed. The discussion is organized as shown in Fig. 7.1, which indicates the main topics and examples.

7.2 General Purpose Tools

In Chap. 3 we saw how the Valkenburg Group Reference Architecture provides a set of subsystems which define the structures and expected behaviors required by authors and learning managers. It is not necessary to develop specialist LD tools for all these functionalities, as some can be met by general purpose tools.

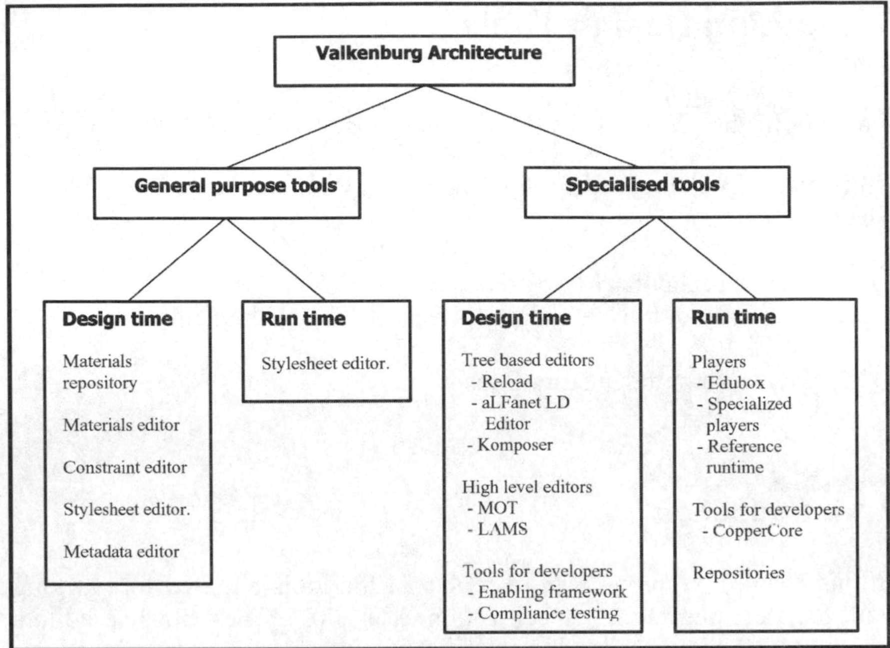

Fig. 7.1. Overview of LD tools

Indeed, the OUNL, which develops and delivers large numbers of EML courses to cohorts of learners, develops and manages its EML UOLs using Adobe Framemaker and other generic tools, and only the final delivery to the browser is through the specially developed Edubox server application (see Chap. 19). If LD is to be widely adopted, however, the process of creating and using UOLs has to be made much easier than can be achieved with generic tools.

7.2.1 Pieces of the Valkenburg Group Reference Architecture Which Do Not Require Special Tools

Since the establishment of the reference architecture there has been a tacit agreement among the members of the Valkenburg Group that the following pieces of architecture do not require the development of special tools:

- *Materials repository.* The learning materials used in a learning design, such as web pages, Acrobat documents, Flash documents, etc., do not have any LD specific characteristics, and so any generic materials repository may be used to store them. For example, DSpace (Lynch 2003) is a digital library system developed by MIT Libraries and Hewlett Packard, which is freely available and open source. Another alternative is Intralibrary, a Learning-Object Management System marketed by Intrallect.

- *Materials editor.* The choice of editor depends on the format used in the materials. No special LD features are required, and any of the popular authoring tools may be used, such as OpenOffice, Microsoft Word, Adobe Acrobat, Macromedia Dreamweaver, etc.
- *Constraint editor.* In order to limit the range of learning designs produced by an institution or group of users the base LD schema can be constrained. This both simplifies the authoring process and ensures pedagogic consistency. This task will typically be carried out infrequently by expert users. Consequently specialist tools have not been considered necessary, as expert users are familiar with standard tools which have the required functionality, such as XMLspy produced by ALTOVA.
- *Stylesheet editor.* A runtime player will typically use stylesheets to control the appearance of UOLs. These may be edited by expert users using generic tools such as XML Spy. Alternatively a simpler interface could be provided as part of the player. In either case there is no need to develop a special Learning Design Stylesheet Editor.
- *Metadata editor.* LD metadata is handled by the LOM specification (LOM 2002) using the IMS XML binding for LOM. A number of tools are already available to work with LOM, such as RELOAD, the Aloha editor, or any SCORM editor.

With the above functionalities being met by generic tools, the focus of LD tooling has been on those pieces of the architecture where the development of specific LD tools is seen to be essential if the development and delivery of UOLs is to be a viable option for learning professionals and institutions. These elements are

- Runtime player
- Reference runtime
- Learning Design Editor
- Learning Design Repository.

Before moving on to a discussion of these applications, we first provide an overview of user roles, and reflect on the various tools which they require.

7.2.2 User Roles

At a high level of description we identify five basic user roles for LD tools (there are of course others, such as educational administrators, technical support and systems administrators). These roles are not exclusive, and users may shift between two or three roles at various times, depending on the authoring workflow and the pedagogy being used. The roles are outlined below, with a brief discussion of the types of tools which they require.

1) *Learners and teachers participating in educational activities*
Learners need to be able to access the learning activities and resources which are appropriate to their role and their progress within the learning design. Services such as conference systems and questionnaires also need to be provided, and learners should normally also be able to access their own learning record and administrative information. Teachers need to be able to launch activities, monitor the progress of the learners, and intervene in the educational process as required by the UOL and the dynamics of the learner interactions.

Learners and teachers in this role interact with an application called a *player*. This accepts an LD-compliant XML file as an input, and generates the corresponding learning activities. At the appropriate times it provides access to the specified learning objects, tests, tools, etc., and coordinates the learners' interactions throughout the duration of the activity.

Players may be specialized in various ways. For example, if they are intended to be used in a clearly defined and constrained pedagogic context they may only need to implement a subset of LD,

The interface and appearance of players may need to be specialized for particular pedagogies and learner groups in order to maximize usability.

2) *Staff who set up UOLs to be run with learners*
Each time a UOL is used with learners it needs to be set up for a new *run.* To do this a member of staff has to enter the learner information for the new cohort, and set a date when the run will commence. This does not change the UOL itself, and the required functionality is provided by the player application. These staff members may also need to find appropriate UOLs to run with a certain cohort of learners, and they will do this by using a repository.

3) *Adaptors and assemblers of UOLs*
Users in this role are teachers who carry out high-level editing to adapt UOLs to their learners' needs, or to assemble them from high-level components. They need to be able to

- search for suitable learning designs which are close to their requirements
- incorporate new learning resources which they have found or created into the existing UOL structure.
- edit the activities to be carried out.

Users in this role use a repository to find suitable UOLs and components of UOLs.

If they are adapting an existing UOL then they need to be able to edit a subset of the LD elements which compose that UOL. In practice this will generally involve modifying a template, which enables them to edit certain exposed elements: for example, the learning resources used in a UOL. This approach is useful if an institution wants to maintain a consistent pedagogic approach in classes taught by different teachers, or across subject areas.

Another possible approach is to assemble a sequence of predefined learning activities which are at a lower level of granularity than an entire UOL, such as “discussion group”, “comment on a text”, or “negotiation activity”. These activities would be composed of a number of LD elements, for example a role part, an activity, an environment and a service, but would appear to the user as single editable object. For an example of this assembly approach see the section on LAMS below (note, however, that LAMS is not at present LD compliant). This approach is valuable when it is desirable to give the teacher substantial autonomy in defining the pedagogy which she or he wishes to use.

When the new or adapted UOL is ready, the user then needs to be able to preview it in a player, or in a preview component incorporated into the editor.

4) *Designers of UOLs*
These users, who may be pedagogic experts, course planners, and learning or instructional designers, need to be able to define roles, resources and the flow of activities together with the various branching conditions, either for use as a single design or as a template or component.

These users need access to repositories of learning designs where they can find parts of learning designs which they can reuse. They also require an editor which enables them to define the entire range of LD elements. Depending on the tasks which they have to carry out, they may also need a tool for creating the templates and components for assembly described in point 3 above. Depending on the workflow used in the design process, tools for specific parts of the authoring process may be valuable, for example activity authoring. Finally tools that support particular learning approaches and pedagogies will be needed. The LD specification enables a pedagogical scenario which is usually described in terms which do not have a precise and agreed definition (such as "constructivist", "problem-solving", or "drill and test") to be represented without ambiguity in a form which supports reuse and facilitates the use of technology. This also means, however, that any given learning design may be understood in different ways by different users, who participate in different discourses, and may need to describe it in different ways in order to understand it, and edit it. They may also want specialized tools which provide them with easy ways to author the structures which are typically used within their pedagogy. To some extent these needs may be met by templates, but they may also require more general editors which use particular metaphors and editing techniques and procedures.

5) *Developers of tools for LD*
Developers also have their own tooling needs. These include software for testing that the code produced by editing tools complies with the specification, a reference runtime implementation to ensure consistent interpretation of the specification when creating runtime systems, and engines and libraries to assist in the development process."

7.3 A Framework for Situating Learning Design Authoring Tools

We now focus on authoring tools and situate them along to axes, according how closely their interface follows the specification, and their degree of specialized focus.

7.3.1 Higher- vs Lower-Level Tools

The tools described for the five categories of user above vary greatly in the degree to which they require users to be knowledgeable about the specification. As mentioned in the section on general purpose tools above, UOLs are sometimes created with a general purpose XML editor. An author working with such a tool has to have a detailed knowledge of the elements of LD and their function in order to create a UOL, and has to provide both the LD elements and their values. Such an author is working at a low level, as close as possible to the specification. This is not, however a typical situation for an LD author. The XML binding for LD was created as an interoperable machine-readable format, and when it was proposed it was not envisaged that people would author UOLs directly with the XML.[1] Authoring tools need to represent authors' work with the specification in a way which is appropriate to the user. This applies to both experts in the specification and those who know nothing about it, but the interfaces and support which they require vary greatly.

XML experts will be helped in authoring LD documents by having access to tools which enable them to easily access the parts of an LD document on which they want to work, avoid them having to enter repetitive text, and to have their document checked for integrity. The ability to work close to the specification may be particularly valuable in debugging UOLs. The users of these low-level tools include professional producers of educational resources, and technical support staff within educational institutions.

Other authors will find the structures and terminology of LD incomprehensible, and need high-level tools which have vocabularies and representations that they recognize. Thus teachers, designers, etc., are familiar with terms such as lesson, curriculum, and so on, and need to be able to specify and visualize their designs in these terms, which do not necessarily have a direct equivalent in LD. For instance, while the everyday concept of learner has a formal equivalent in LD, the same is not true of the concept of homework. It will greatly help users who are not technical experts if the authoring tools can give assistance in mapping such concepts onto the formal language of LD. Thus a spectrum of tools may be established, going from those which are presented in terms and structures which remain close to the specification, and those which are presented in non-formal colloquial terms which are distant from the specification and use a hidden mapping between the users' interactions and the LD document which is being edited – for a discussion (in Spanish) of this issue in relation to QTI see Sayago et al. (2004). Similarly a variety of interfaces which are distant from the specification may be required to represent the learning design within the concepts and terminology which are accepted within a particular pedagogic practice.

7.3.2 General Purpose vs. Specific Purpose Tools

As has been observed above in the section on user roles, not all users need access to the whole specification. In a context where a users' role in a workflow means that they only have to perform certain kinds of action the complexity of tools can be greatly reduced by only presenting users with the functionality which they need. Similarly in institutions with a clearly defined pedagogic approach more tightly focused tools guiding authors towards a particular type of UOL are appropriate. This can be achieved

[1] Bill Olivier, one of the authors of the specification; personal communication.

using constrained schemas, or templates, or environments where UOLs can be constructed out of predefined components. On the other hand some authors require access to the whole of LD. Pedagogy specialists and experts in areas of knowledge who create new UOLs fall into this category, as do specialists in the technical aspects of UOL authoring and delivery.

These two axes create a quadrant within which tools may be situated, as shown in Fig. 7.2.

The need for tools in all four quadrants depends on the context within which LD is to be implemented, and the perspectives one has of the purpose and application of LD. As has been explained in Chap. 2, LD emerged from EML, and was developed by a large-scale distance learning provider, where UOLs are produced by large teams of experts. In this environment the production of courses (both traditional and e-learning) usually involves a large budget, and the involvement of teams of professionals, including experts in the subject area, pedagogy, design and technical issues. This team-based workflow, for example, is current practice in the development of EML-based courses at OUNL, the only institution which has so far produced EML or LD courses on a large scale, and it is carried out with general purpose tools which are close to the specification.

While LD was developed in the context of large-scale institutional development, however, it also has the potential to be applied in other contexts indeed this was part of the intent in providing it as a general use specification. In particular LD is significant in the potential it has for representing the range of teachers' practice. Previous e-learning standards have often been seen by teachers as forcing learning designers to adopt the "conduit" metaphor for learning. This metaphor is identified by Lakoff and Johnson (1980) as being: Ideas (or meanings) are objects, linguistic expressions are containers, communication is sending, and focuses on the role of content while it marginalizes or constricts the actions of the teacher. This was the case in the Prometeus Conference 2002 in Paris, where the education professionals who participated saw standards as vital, but also controversial and dangerous. Particular concerns were raised about the restrictions imposed by the standards, the bias inherent in the tools used to implement them, and the idea that e-learning standards make it possible to carry out education without teachers in the same way that the Jacard loom made weavers redundant (Griffiths et al. 2002, p 29).

In contrast one of the great strengths of LD is that it can be used to capture teachers' practice, and make it available to learners and other teachers in a standard and machine-readable way. The enthusiasm which many teachers had for sharing their practice was shown some years ago by the very much more informal repositories set up using Apple's Unit of Practice methodology, described by Debra Rein (2000). From this perspective a general purpose authoring tool for non-experts is clearly important.

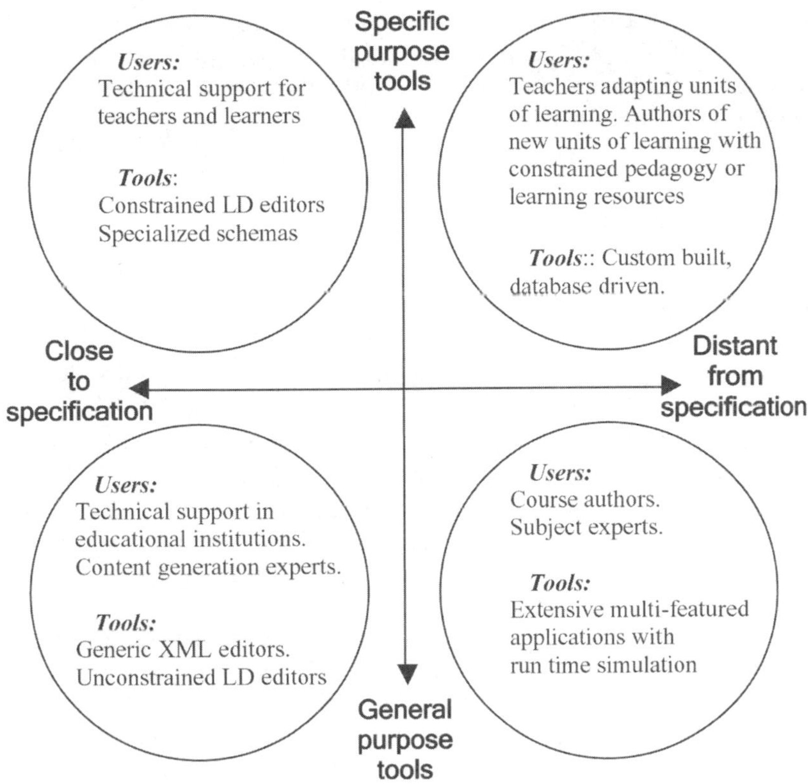

Fig. 7.2. Two dimensions of LD tool design

Such a tool would have potential application even outside the context of e-learning, as there is at present no standard way of describing teaching practice or planning for learning activities, and LD is well placed to meet this need, as discussed by McAndrew and Weller in Chap. 17 of this volume. Thus there may be a use for such tools even if the learning designs produced are never run in a player for learners, or are processed to generate printed lesson plans and handouts.

The contrast between these perspectives serves to remind us that tools are not neutral, and that they both emerge from and, in turn, modify the socio-cultural context in which they are developed and used – this interaction has been illuminated by Activity Theory, particularly by Engeström (1987). Consequently it is to be expected that a number of different approaches to LD tooling will emerge, and indeed the first indications of such distinctions may already be discerned in the developments described in this chapter. This spectrum is not unique to LD, and the same is true, for example, of HTML tools. Indeed that precedent suggests that the easiest tools to create, and the earliest to be produced, are those which correspond closely to the specification, while it takes an intense design effort and several iterations to produce a tool which is effective for the non-technical user and which produces well-formed code.

7.4 Design Time Tools

7.4.1 Tree-Based Editors

A tree-based editor presents the elements of LD as a branching tree. An interface is provided to enable the author to navigate through the tree, and to enter values for the elements. A good example of an editor of this type is the Perot LD Editor (see Chap. 21). This was the first tool to be designed to edit EML, the specification which it currently supports, but it has not been marketed. It was designed as a tool for expert users who handled the technical aspects of UOL authoring, while others were responsible for pedagogic design and resource authoring.

LD does not stand alone, it builds on and integrates other IMS specifications, notably Content Packaging (CP 2003), but also Meta-Data (MD 2001), Question and Test Interoperability (QTI 2003), and Simple Sequencing (SS 2003). Tree-based editors are often used for these specifications, and so it is natural to extend this approach to LD. There is a particularly strong link between LD and CP, and this is made clear in paragraph 2.2.3 of the LD Information Model (LD 2003) which states that “The primary use of LD is to model UOLs by including an LD in a CP”. In some respects this association is more of a marriage of convenience than a structural relationship, as is discussed by other authors in this volume, but nevertheless, this has led to the design of tools which enable users to author both specifications. As CP is both simpler than LD and also of wider application, it is a natural choice to take a tagging tool which works for CP, and then add LD functionality. This has been the approach taken by both RELOAD and GTK Komposer.

Both these applications provide users with access to the elements of CP, and enable them to navigate through a tree structure which directly reflects the specification, adding parameters and resources. To this extent they are “close to the specification”, but they are some distance away from the base line. RELOAD does not require the user to edit any XML code, simply to drag resources into a tree structure, leaving the application to generate all the code to represent the tree. Moreover RELOAD inspects the resources included by the author and manages all the references to the components of those resources. For example, if an HTML resource is used, all the references to image files will be identified and handled transparently, without the author having to be aware of it. This is a good solution for CP, as the specification is relatively simple. In adding LD to a "close to the specification" CP editor, however, as is planned for RELOAD, or in creating a new editor using the same principle, such as aLFanet, the increase in complexity is considerable, as is made clear in paragraph 2.3 of the LD Information Model:

> A 'unit of learning' represents more than just a collection of ordered resources to learn, it includes a variety of prescribed activities (problem solving activities, search activities, discussion activities, peer assessment activities, etcetera), assessments, services and support facilities provided by teachers, trainers and other staff members. Which activities, which resources, which roles and which workflow is dependent on the learning design in the unit of learning.

Less expert users can cope with the relatively simple structures of CP, in part because the process of building a content package is analogous to the familiar task of building an index, and a tree is an intuitive representation of this. LD structures are much more complex, the trees are correspondingly extensive, and their relationship with the end product more obscure. In LD, moreover, the creation of properties and conditions falls outside the scope of the tree metaphor, and as a result tree-based editors are much less intuitive. These users may be lost when confronted by the much more complex LD structures.

Because of these circumstances the aLFanet LD Editor, which uses a tree-based interface, is intended for users who already know the LD specification in detail. Like Komposer, this editor is embedded in another application which provides it with services, but in contrast to the Microsoft Word and web services solution used by Komposer, aLFanet is built on top of the Groove peer-to-peer application.

Given this degree of complexity, the designers of such tree-based tool interfaces for LD need to consider how they can maximize the support for authors in understanding the specification and the editing actions which they are being invited to perform. This may be through templates, automatic completion of elements with default values, dropdown menus, or in terms of changing the vocabulary from that used in the specification to one which is more familiar to their working context. The aLFanet Editor provides basic support for authors by ensuring that any file which it generates is valid by filling in the non-optional fields with defaults. RELOAD will provide additional support by presenting the interface for authoring in a series of modules. The screen layout for the Play/Act/Role-part editor is shown in Fig. 7.3.

Komposer, under development at the time of writing, establishes a quite different trade off between power and ease of use.

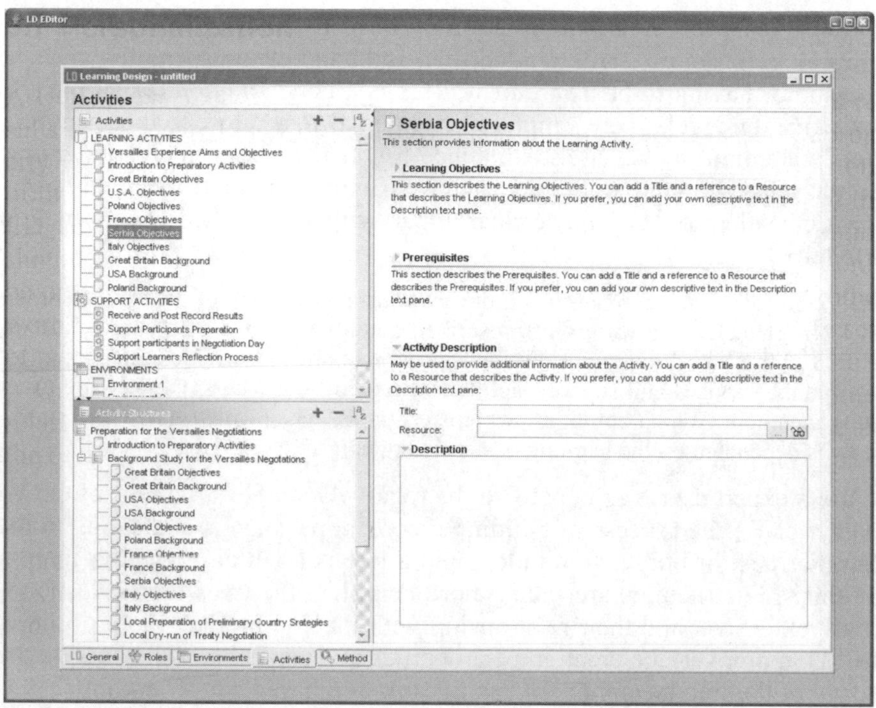

Fig. 7.3. RELOAD activity editor (under development)

The strength of this approach is that it is strongly focused on the needs of a particular user group: teachers and other content creators with limited technological skills. It supports them by offering them predefined pedagogic activities, and a workflow which takes them from authoring to delivery.

In the Komposer Authoring Platform, which is a tree-based editor, the complexity of the task facing the author is reduced by restricting UOLs to one role and a single path, and using a interface which is familiar from another context for authoring.

In creating web-based learning resources, authors often format their content to provide the look and feel they see as appropriate (Bartz 2002), and Komposer builds on this familiarity with the use of styles for web resources. Microsoft Word is used as the authoring platform as it presents a WYSIWYG front end to the authors, and provides familiar formatting tools to minimize the training effort which may be foreseen when users start to adopt the system. Within this familiar context a UOL template is provided using Word styles, which constrains the complexity (and expressive power) presented to the author by restricting UOLs to one role and a single learning path. Several generic Word templates (DOT files) are provided in the Authoring Platform so that the users can work within the LD structures given in the templates. Users familiar with the LD Learning Activity Structure may develop their own templates for the writers.

Figure 7.4 shows how this approach results in a template structure which is a great deal more approachable for a non-expert content than is a full featured editor such as RELOAD or the aLFanet LD Editor.

Support for users of the Authoring Platform is also provided by situating the LD authoring process within the wider Komposer workflow. This guides authors to (i) prepare their manuscripts in Word; (ii) use the "Styling"function to disaggregate the documents into smaller modules and to provide the look and feel of the course; and (iii) use the "Insert"function to aggregate other external and web resources. When the course document is completed, the CP-Generator of the Authoring Platform, the Komposer® Suite, converts the Word document into a set of XHTML files according to the styles provided in the document. A manifest is generated at the same time, and the organization structure is defined in accordance with the layout used in the Word document. The location of the resulting resource files is listed in the manifest. A CP Editor is provided to edit the metadata, the organization structure of the manifest, and to add and delete the resources files. A player will be included in the tool to play any CP-compliant packages.

7.4.2 Higher-Level General Purpose Editors

For some purposes tree-based editors will not be satisfactory, however much support is provided for the user, and an interface will be required which is further from the specification. One of the reasons for this is that the LD specification addresses real-world problems of learning and teaching, and seeks to resolve them by harnessing the power of a formal language. Thus a pedagogical scenario which is usually described in terms which do not have a precise and agreed definition (such as "constructivist", "problem solving", or "drill and test") can be represented without ambiguity in a form which supports reuse and facilitates the use of technology. This also means, however, that any given learning design may be understood in different ways by different users, who may want to describe it in different ways. Consequently there is a need for high-level tools which enable authors to define learning designs in terms of their own pedagogic skills and experience.

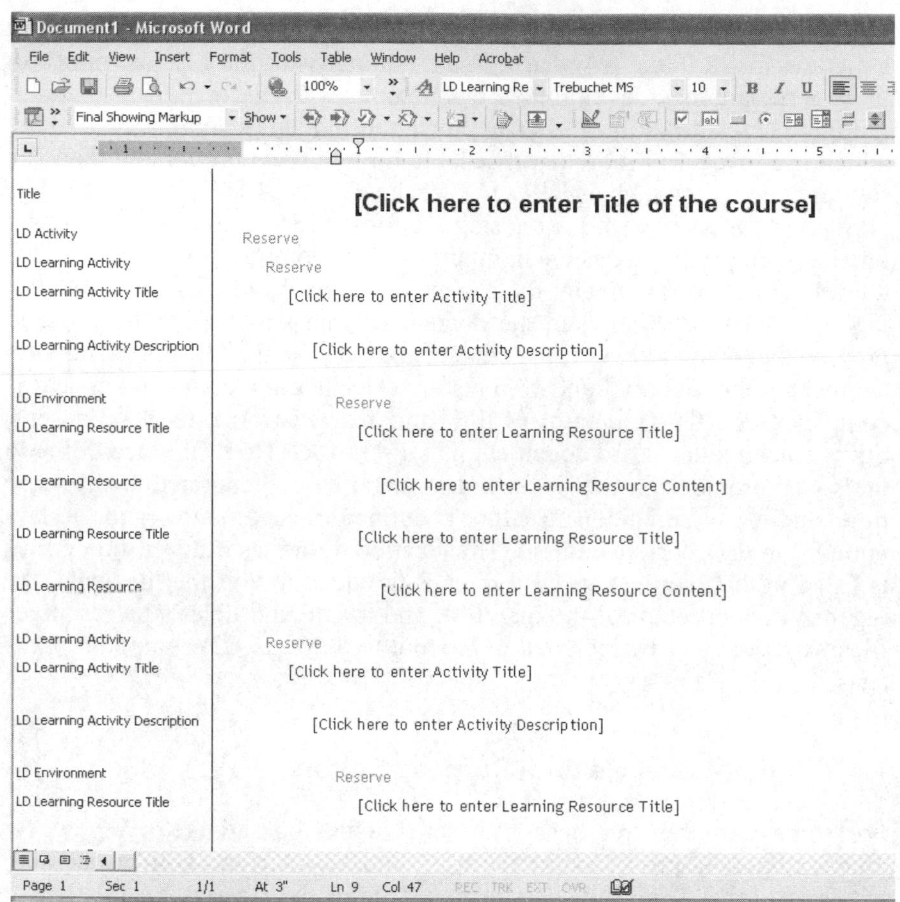

Fig. 7.4. The Komposer Authoring Platform

These can be either general editors, which give authors access to the full power of the specification (with the accompanying complexity which this brings), or editors for specific purposes or constrained pedagogic approaches. Such tools typically reveal the structure of a UOL in graphical terms, so that designers (and particularly non-expert designers) can obtain an overview, and navigate to the parts which they want to edit. The nature of this representation, and the forms which it might take, is one of the most interesting issues around the design of tools for LD authors. One possible solution is the use of UML as an authoring tool, as this is already used in best practice in designing UOLs. This is, however, unlikely to be a universal solution. First, it requires users to learn UML, and, second, because authors conceive of UOLs in many different ways, a variety of graphical representations will be needed to support these different approaches to teaching and learning.

A particularly interesting example of a general purpose high-level editor is the MOT+ system described by Paquette et al. in Chap. 9 they describe how the high-level graphical editor MOT+ can configured as an LD editor, and the learning designs created within MOT+ can be exported as LD XML files. As their chapter provides a detailed description of the system, we do not discuss it in depth here. It should be noted, however, that their work is significant, not only because it provides an example of a powerful and expressive high-level LD editor, but also because the structures of LD are mapped onto a graphical language which appears to be very remote from the specification. Indeed the graphical language used was established some years prior to the publication of the LD specification, as the fruit of many years of practice in defining instructional design structures. The ability to produce valid learning designs from this system clearly demonstrates that the metaphors and structures used to define UOLs can be quite distinct from the terms and structures used in the specification. This authoring system is therefore distant from the specification in the terms we have described. In Chap. 9, Paquette et al. provide a specific example of this, showing how the Versailles Negotiation in the LD Best Practice Guide can be represented in MOT+. The challenge to be addressed by tools developers is to identify the metaphors and procedures which are most appropriate for the various user groups, in terms of both their skills and understanding LD, but more importantly their traditions of educational practice.

Specialized High-Level Editors

MOT+, described above, provides a powerful graphical language which aims to provide learning designers with the tools which they require to define any structure which they may need. There is, however, an irreducible level of complexity in editing LD documents, in part because of the wide range of structures and properties, and in part because of the formality of a learning design. Some authors will prefer to have a more constrained editor which meets their needs without providing them with access to the whole of LD. This is the role of specialized high-level editors.

Templates for Learning Designs

For teachers who simply want to be to be able to teach with on-line resources, using one of a few basic pedagogic models, it is very helpful to have templates which provide a range of pedagogical structures which teachers can populate with resources and learners. It is to be hoped that a range of LD templates will develop as the specification becomes more widely adopted, and that these will cluster around particular communities of teachers and learners.

The first tool which provides explicit support for templates is EduploneLearningSequence, an open-source authoring and runtime player application released under the GNU General Public License. In the work-flow established by the application, the topics required in a learning environment are identified, and then templates which define the pedagogic models to be used by the learner are added. This makes it easy to produce multiple ways of sequencing the same learning resources (a similar approach was taken in the SCOPE project, see Chap. 21). The learning strategies supported range from guided tours of the resources, to more explorative strategies, and are based on the vocabulary of didactic metadata in Webdidactics, which has been adopted by the developers. *Webdidaktik* was developed by Norbert Meder (now: University of Duisburg–Essen) and his team during the project "L3 - Lebenslanges Lernen", a major research project funded by the German Ministry of Education and Research. Webdidaktik combines theoretical approaches of educational theory, media theory and knowledge organization. A multidimensional ontology of didactical metadata is used for organizing learning resources. For some of the core concepts see: http://www.eduplone.net/concepts/webdidaktik/. Within Eduplone these strategies can be altered, and new strategies added, by scripting in the Python language. The results are intended to be delivered to the learner through an Eduplone server, which functions as a specialized LD player. Both authoring tools and runtime are delivered through a web interface. The UOLs which are created by the system can, however, be exported as standard LD XML files, and can be run on any compatible player.

To support this functionality the developers have used Python to implement a subset of LD. The system is built on the Plone content management system, which in turn uses the Zope server infrastructure.

Similarly elive Learning Design, a German-based company, in cooperation with cogito GmbH, has released an integrated LD toolset for the design, documentation and optimization of didactic scenarios, called "elive LD-Suite". The documentation for this suite states that it also makes use of pre-modeled methodical structures, templates and pedagogic patterns, while enabling the user to extend the existing repository and interchange effective patterns and scenarios.

LAMS

LAMS (Learning Activity Management System) is also a specialized high level editor, but unlike EduploneLearningSequence it takes as its starting point the sequencing of a set of preset activities, rather than the application of pedagogic templates to content. LAMS is produced by WebMCQ and Macquarie E-learning Centre of Excellence (MELCOE), Macquarie University, Australia. It does not at present produce or run LD code, but is explicitly inspired by LD, and is designed to illustrate examples of the approach taken by the specification, as discussed in Dalziel (2003). LAMS has a full runtime system and learner administration facilities, but as it is not a compliant system much of the detail is not relevant to this chapter. The component for teacher authoring/adaptation of sequences is, however, a valuable example of how a specialized high-level LD editor could function. The author can drag and drop items onto a flow chart. In LAMS these items are called "activities", but the word is used differently from the same term in LD, and so avoided here. The items include synchronous discussion (chat), web polls, students posting material and structured debates. Learning resources can be added, and a series of on-line lessons can be planned and run. The components which can be used are fixed, but these cover many of the basic activities carried out in the classroom. This use of familiar elements makes the application easy for teachers to comprehend, as this is the way that conventional lessons are planned.

Thus the LAMS authoring application (Fig. 7.5) is specialized in the sense that it offers a set menu of learning activities which can be sequenced. If the proposed LD compliance were added, then it would be an appropriate tool for the assemblers of UOLs described in the section on user roles above. Some of the items assembled in LAMS would, if implemented in LD, require the combination of, for example, an environment and a service in a single entity which to a higher-level user appears to be a single object. Indeed one of the valuable contributions of LAMS has been to make clear the need for a lower-level tool for the creation of these reusable items.

7.4.3 Tools Which Are Standards Compliant, but Not Standards Oriented

It may that if teachers are to work effectively with high-level tools, then they will need to manipulate LD in combination with other specifications. For example, it may be useful to have a reusable item which combines an evaluation activity using QTI integrated with the use of a learning resource. This functionality should be transparent to teachers who adapt and reuse components, who should not need to know that at one point they are generating QTI and at another LD.

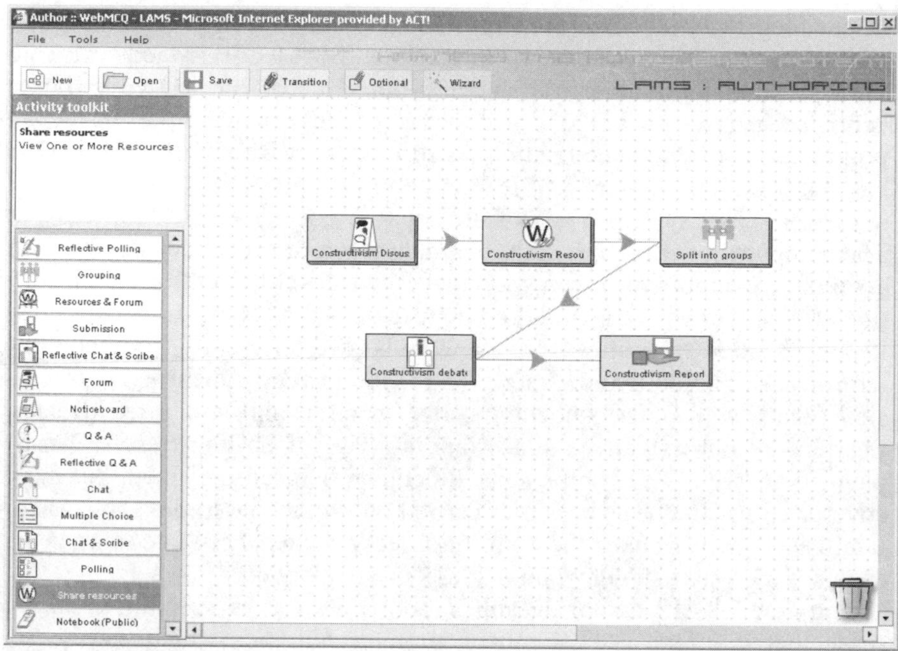

Fig. 7.5. The LAMS authoring component

In other words, for many purposes tools for the end user (teacher or learner) should be standards compliant (in their outputs), but not standards oriented (in their interface). Such tools should be designed in terms of the tasks which they carry out, rather than being structured according to the enabling technology, in this case the IMS suite of e-learning standards. The development of tools which can create reusable components which make use of a number of complementary specifications is clearly a significant challenge.

7.4.4 An Enabling Framework for Editor Development

The creation of an all-encompassing LD Editor is a major development project, which may be beyond the capabilities of a single organization. The Valkenburg Group Reference Architecture documentation also discusses the way that this problem may be overcome, by creating an LD editor "framework"in which the various components of an editor can be "plugged in". It is proposed that there should be two frameworks: one that controls the underlying data model of the LD instance, and another that handles the management of the user interface. The data model layer is also a logical point at which to enforce constraints, either embedded within the application by incorporating XML Schema checking, or through delegation to an external constraint handling service.

Plug-in tools provide controllers and views that fit into the presentation layer framework, and access the instance data model through the LD model framework. This architecture is shown in Fig. 7.6.

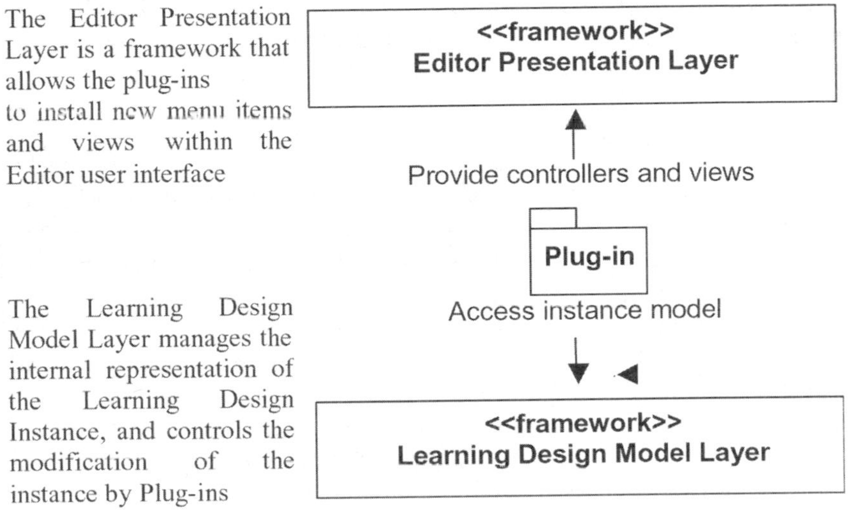

The Editor Presentation Layer is a framework that allows the plug-ins to install new menu items and views within the Editor user interface

<<framework>>
Editor Presentation Layer

Provide controllers and views

Plug-in

Access instance model

The Learning Design Model Layer manages the internal representation of the Learning Design Instance, and controls the modification of the instance by Plug-ins

<<framework>>
Learning Design Model Layer

Fig. 7.6. Plug-in framework for an LD Editor

Each plug-in can provide a particular kind of authoring capability, such as managing roles, activities or environment, while variations on the same authoring task can also be provided for different levels of user. For expert users, the editor could also have a "Raw LD" plug-in that simply allowed direct editing access to the underlying XML representation. Other types of plug-in might include a package that provides import and export of SCORM files, and a package to support access to the Learning Designs Repository and Materials Repository.

In actual deployment the two frameworks can be placed behind a single interface or façade to assist plug-in development. The end result is a toolset for developers which enables them to avoid handling all the underlying processes involved in manipulating LD structures, and to focus on the user interface of the editing tool which they are creating. This greatly facilitates the creation of editing tools for a wide range of different users, with varying metaphors, pedagogies, scope, terminology, etc.

Open-Source Java Libraries for Developers

A number of libraries and engines have been developed which can be used as the basis of the Learning Design Model Layer. The simplest approach is to hard-code the data model, and make it available to programmers, and this was how the open-source LD libraries created by the Interactive Technologies Group of Universitat Pompeu Fabra were produced.[2] This has the advantage of simplicity but may be hard to maintain and not easily extendable.

The RELOAD Approach

The RELOAD project (Fig. 7.7) takes a more complex approach. This responds to the need to allow for specializations of the schemas to be used for authoring specific UOL templates, and to respond to possible changes to the specification which will be reflected in the XML Schema files. If the XML Schema has been hard coded, or tied Java class bindings used, then the code will also have to be in these circumstances. A more generic and maintainable approach is to use the IMS Schema as the driving data model document. In RELOAD reusability and general application are enhanced by reading, parsing and modeling a schema as a Document Object Model (DOM). This schema DOM is used to generate an editable instance DOM which can hold the entries made by the user.

The advantage of this approach is that a framework is provided which can be applied to the whole range of IMS specifications, providing a framework which maximizes ease of development and maintenance of editors for LD and other IMS specifications.

7.5 Runtime Tools

7.5.1 Learning Design Players: Delivering the Unit of Learning to the Learner

Users in the learner role interact with an LD player, described in point 3 of Sect. 7.2.2 above. Players may be standalone applications, or a component of a more extensive environment, and the output to the learner is typically a web page.

---

[2] This work was carried out in the context of the SCOPE project, funded by the European Community. For further information see www.tecn.upf.es/scope.

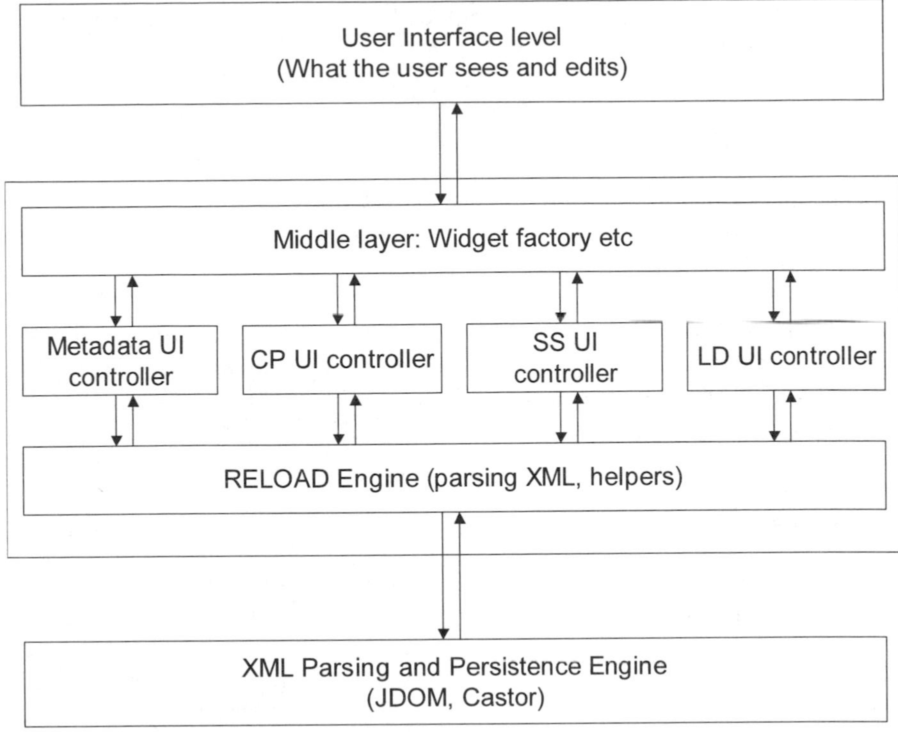

Fig. 7.7. The RELOAD architecture

At the time of writing the only full player available is Edubox, produced by Perot for the Open University of the Netherlands, which works with EML and does not accept LD input. This situation may change in the future, as Blackboard Inc. has signed a strategic alliance with OUNL with the aim of incorporating Edubox into Blackboard products, and to supporting LD.

Edubox is the delivery system used by the OUNL in all its on-line courses, This player has been important in the development of LD as it has demonstrated that the concepts underlying EML and LD are valid, and that their use as a solution for a large-scale education institution is effective. Edubox is a solution developed to meet the needs of a large institution, and has to cope with a large number of courses and users. Consequently it is a robust and scalable system built to industrial standards using IBM's WebSphere platform. Edubox is not available on the open market, as Perot Systems Netherlands is principally a solutions provider rather than a software vendor, but the system can be made available to its clients. It should be noted that the company is confident that it would not be a major development task to adapt the system to run with LD, using an XSLT stylesheet transformation.

7.5.2 Specialized Players

As mentioned above, it is possible to create players for specific purposes which do not implement the whole of LD. Indeed, the division of LD into three parts, A, B and C, is specifically intended to make it possible to implement the core functionality in A without necessarily incorporating the additional features in Levels B and C. The EduploneLearningSequence player is an example of a specialized player, only implementing those parts of LD which are required to run designs produced by the pedagogic templates in the editor (see below).

7.5.3 Learning Design Reference Runtime

Learners and staff are not the only users of LD players. When an author is creating a learning design it is not easy to envisage how this will appear to a learner when it is run by a player. This is not only because the XML code which makes up a UOL is hard to understand. If this were the case a simple preview function in the editor (as used in HTML editors) would resolve the problem. The problem is that the interactions between learners, and with the UOL, create many properties and states which are not explicitly stated in the learning design, but are the product of contingencies when the UOL is run. These have to be tracked in runtime, as is well explained in Chap. 6. There, the example of the "completion" status of a particular user at a particular time is given as a property which is not present in the UOL, and has to be generated by the player. An author clearly needs an understanding of how these properties will be handled by the runtime system, and this is the function of a reference runtime player. This provides LD authors with a simple and authoritative view of how their design will behave, and provides a benchmark for LD players, which should produce the same basic output, though they may present it in many different ways. There is no reference runtime player available for LD at the time of writing, but the CopperCore engine (see Chap. 6) provides an ideal platform for constructing one. This is a high priority in the development of LD tooling.

7.6 Repositories

One of the fundamental goals of LD is to support interoperability, reuse and sharing of learning resources. If this is to be achieved then users need an infrastructure which enables them to identify and exchange UOLs, and this is the role played by repositories. To ensure that reuse and sharing can contribute to effective educational practice, it is also essential that users can easily find UOLs which are appropriate to their needs, and repositories can facilitate this process.

There are many repositories which can store UOLs, together with the metadata which describes them, which can then be searched by potential users. A simple first step in creating an LD repository would be to reach agreement on how to identify a UOL within the metadata, and so enable users to search specifically for them. In addition, a repository which can parse the structure of a content package will have the potential to identify UOLs within searches. This is an elegant way of finding UOLs, but is a less general solution, as it is only applicable to learning designs which have been packaged using CP, and is not applicable to fragments such as acts.

These approaches are sufficient for many purposes, but there are also good reasons for building LD awareness into repositories themselves.

1. An LD-aware repository could provide a number of specialized services. For example, it could provide an ontology of LD by using templates and good practice examples, or offer searches for UOLs that have been used with a certain kind of content. It would also be possible to add a degree of intelligence to the repository, so that it could it could be used to search for UOLs with a similar pedagogy, or for content that has been used in similar learning designs
2. If a user wants to retrieve a fragment of a UOL so as to incorporate it into his or her own learning design, then the repository needs to understand the structure of LD in order to provide the elements which make up that fragment. For example, if the searcher wants to retrieve an act, then the repository needs to deliver all the elements of which it is composed, such as learning resources and roles. This awareness would also be required if an author wants to point at an act using an XML inclusion, as proposed by W3C (W3C 2004a), and so include it in a UOL at runtime.
3. An LD-aware repository can also provide information to the user on how learning resources have been used in other UOLs, giving a valuable perspective on the nature of those resources.

4. The repository could also store metadata provided by users, on what UOLs have been used for and how successful they were, as this is very valuable information for both learners and teachers.

The *Repository to Reality* project, funded by the National Research Council of Canada, is making a contribution to these issues, and in one of its lines of action Dr. Tom Carey, University of Waterloo, is developing a controlled vocabulary for the description of UOLs. This is an important first step towards the implementation of repositories for LD.

Desirable additional functionality includes natural language processing capability, so that users can search for UOLs which are in a language which they do not understand. Not only may they want to obtain a translation of the UOL, or use it with learners who do understand it, but also may be able to reuse fragments of the UOL as it stands. In the medium term the development of the semantic web will no doubt open up many new possibilities for LD repositories.

7.7 Tools for Developers

7.7.1 CopperCore: a Learning Design Engine

The development of an LD player is complex, because the application has to handle activity scheduling, and keep track of the states of the various learners and activities over time. Developers need to be relieved of the burden of dealing with these complex issues if they are to be freed so they can concentrate on the creation of innovative interfaces of a user player. To meet this need CopperCore (discussed in the previous chapter), was developed by the Open University of the Netherlands. CopperCore is an open-source reference implementation of the complex core of a player. This is described in detail in Chap. 6, and so only an overview is provided here.

CopperCore is not itself a player, since all user interface aspects are explicitly excluded from its scope. Rather, it implements what experience at OUNL has shown to be the biggest hurdle to development of LD-aware software – the runtime maintenance of individuals' activity lists in both single user and multi-role, multi-user situations and as time limits expire, acts and activities complete, properties are changed and their consequences propagated through conditions, etc.

CopperCore is best viewed as a running software process which takes a UOL as a content package as input and then responds to queries posed it to according to a published API. The engine can, for example, return the "activity tree" for a given individual in a given role at a given point in the lifetime of a run of a UOL. Data is returned as XML, allowing freedom to transform the results using XSLT into any number of user interfaces. A first implementation of CopperCore supporting LD Level A was made available in February 2004, level B and C support became available later that year. The software is written in Java™ and makes use of the open source J2EE™ Application Server JBoss and the open source database PostgreSQL. During 2005 also a core open source authoring environment will be included in the CopperCore suite to further help developers to create a complete LD learning management system or to include LD into an existing application.

7.7.2 Compliance Testing

An important tool for developers is an application which certifies compliance with the specification. This enables them to test the output of editor applications and ensure that it conforms to the same criterion for compliance as that used by other developers, thus greatly improving the prospects for effective interoperability.

The TelCert project (see http://www.opengroup.org/telcert/), funded by the IST programme of the European Commission, is developing a testing and conformance system which will include LD.

7.8 Conclusion

In our discussion of LD tooling we have sought to present the range and variety of tools which will be required as the specification becomes widely adopted. The list of available tools Table 7.1 on the other hand, shows that at the time of writing the tool set is still rather restricted.

Returning to the two dimensions of tool design identified in Fig. 7.2 above, the authoring tools from Table 7.1 may be classified as shown in Fig. 7.8.

As may be seen from Table 7.1, at the time of writing editing tools were more advanced than players, with a number of systems being demonstrated or in the late stages of development, and this is in part a reflection of the greater complexity involved in developing a player. It is, of course, of critical importance that effective players are available so that the power of LD can be demonstrated. In this respect the Learning Design Engine is of particular significance, as it provides an open-source platform for the rapid development of multiple players.

Table 7.1. Learning Design tool set available or under development at the time of writing

Name	Application	Type	Ownership	Spec. supported
Edubox	Player	General player	Proprietary	EML
Edubox	Editor	Customization of Adobe Framemaker	Proprietary	EML
Perot LD Editor	Editor	Close to spec. general purpose tree editor	Proprietary	EML
aLFanet	Editor	Close to spec. general purpose tree, editor	Open source	LD A
aLFanet	Player	Integrates .LRN with CopperCore	Open source	LD C
GTK Press Komposer	Editor	Close to spec. tree editor, linked to high-level Word-based resource authoring.	Proprietary	LD A Single role, single path
RELOAD	Editor	Close to spec., general purpose tree editor, with runtime preview.	Open source	LD, Levels A, B and C
MOT+	Editor	Distant from spec. general purpose graphical editor		LD Levels A, B and C
LAMS	Example of activity sequencer, inspired by LD	Distant from spec. specialized editor with graphical interface	Proprietary, parts may become open source	Non-compliant
elive	Editor	Distant from spec. specialized editor	Proprietary	LD Levels A and B
Chronotech editor	Editor	Also suitable for Edubox (EML support)	Proprietary	EML and LD Level A
Eduplone Learning Sequence	Integrated editor and player	Distant from spec. specialized editor, template based	Open source	LD Level A
CopperCore	Engine	Core of Learning Design player	Open source	LD Levels A, B and C
CopperCore	Editor	Basic LD editor	Open source	Level A
SCOPE Learning Design Library	Library	Java library	Open source	LD Level A

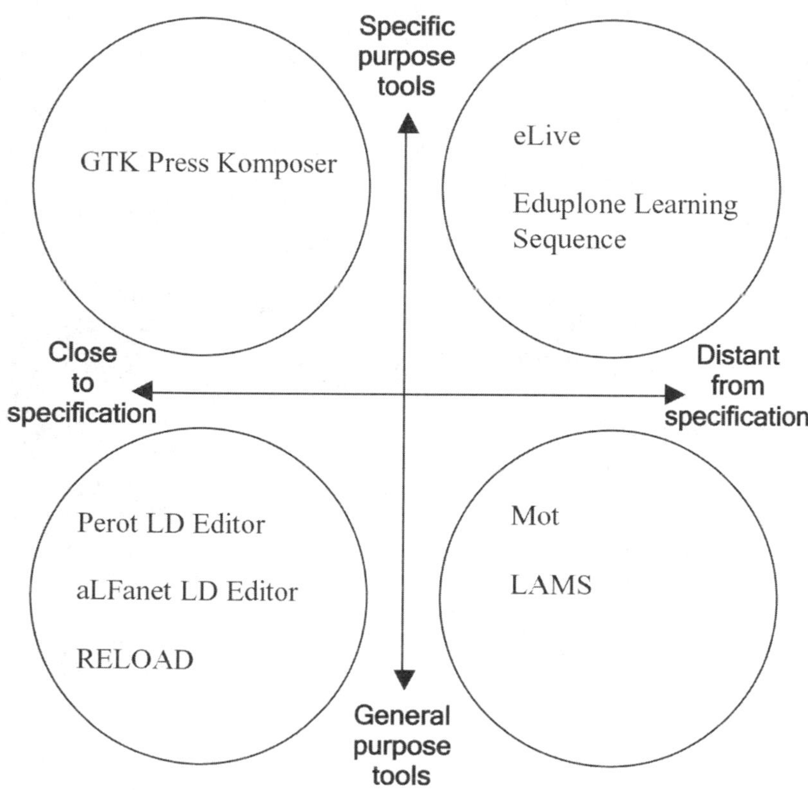

Fig. 7.8. Classification of LD editing tools

The effort involved in adapting existing repositories to provide LD awareness is relatively small compared with that of developing editing tools and players, and it is to be expected that repositories will emerge as the specification becomes more widely used, and large numbers of UOLs are stored.

Given the time which is required for the development of tools, the limited progress described in this chapter is impressive rather than a cause for pessimism. There is a strong group of developers, both within the Valkenburg Group and beyond, and progress is being made on all aspects of tooling.

Part II

DESIGNING E-LEARNING COURSES

Part II of the book contains eight chapters that provide an overview of the process of design and implementation of e-learning courses using the LD specification. The first chapter sets the scene by presenting a generic process for learning design. The second chapter introduces an instructional engineering method and modelling tools to design e-learning courses.

The next five chapters deal with specific topics relevant for the learning designer: how to integrate assessment into e-learning courses, how to design collaborative learning, how to design adaptive learning environments, how to design educational games and how to design learning networks for lifelong learners. The final chapter provides an overview of the implementation issues to be addressed by educational institutions when delivering e-learning courses using LD.

8 Basic Design Procedures for E-learning Courses

Peter Sloep[1], Hans Hummel[2], Jocelyn Manderveld[2]

[1] Educational Technology Expertise Centre,
Open University of the Netherlands, Heerlen, The Netherlands and
Fontys University of Professional Education, Eindhoven, The Netherlands

[2] Educational Technology Expertise Centre,
Open University of the Netherlands, Heerlen, The Netherlands

8.1 Introduction

Designing and developing instruction and learning is a complex process. Analysis of the behaviour of expert designers shows that it cannot be divided up into a simple, linearly ordered sequence of steps that, if duly followed, will inevitably lead to sound instruction (Kirschner et al. 2003). However, even if each expert has his or her own way of designing and developing instruction, we can still discern a number of phases that are an idealisation of the Instructional System Development (ISD) process. The five phases one often distinguishes are *analysis*, *design*, *development*, *implementation*, and *evaluation* (e.g. Reigeluth 1999; Morrison et al. 2004). Each phase concludes with a product. The evaluation phase, for example, typically results in an evaluation report that records the success, or lack thereof, of the entire design and development process, but often also serves as input for the next design and development cycle. Furthermore, each phase often involves using tools that improve the quality of the end product, or enhance efficiency or efficacy of the process. These tools may vary from checklists and manuals to software.

We start this chapter with a brief discussion of the five ISD phases, setting the stage for our main subject: a discussion of how the Learning Design specification (LD 2003) can assist and inform the Instructional Design (ID) process proper. The ID process focuses purely on the analysis and design phases of ISD and it is with respect to the analysis, design and development phases that the LD specification is particularly useful.

Two preliminary comments are in order here. First, in attempting to describe what it is that students are exposed to, designers design, developers develop, and teachers act upon, we have found it rather difficult to identify a term that does not evoke all kinds of associations with existing learning and instruction paradigms or philosophies. The term 'instruction' suggests a preference for teacher-led education, and the term 'learning material' a significant role for content. There is no easy way to avoid seeming to subscribe to a particular educational philosophy to the exclusion of others. Yet, this is necessary in the present context because we want to explore the various ways in which LD may be utilised. We will therefore adopt the following terminological convention: 'Instruction' will be used both to denote the ensemble of 'stimuli' (documents, messages, discussions, etc.) that evoke learning experiences in students and support experiences in teachers. In addition, we will also use 'instruction' to denote the collective of learning and support experiences themselves. We will therefore deliberately confound the process of having experiences with the products that elicit those experiences. This simplifies our discussion without leading to confusion in the present context.

Secondly, the chapter is essentially about a procedure for bringing order to the process of designing instruction and for formally describing the resulting designs. Questions of project planning and proper staffing are involved, but their discussion will be left to Chap. 15. Similarly, there are various tooling issues; these are dealt with in Chap. 7.

8.2 An Overview of the Five ISD Phases

According to the ISD model, the entire instructional design and development process can be broken down into five phases. We will discuss these to point out how LD relates to them. Table 8.1 reviews these phases; the table also shows the structure of the chapter by relating the phases to LD-based products, a stepwise design procedure and some specific examples.

Table 8.1. Relationship between ISD phases, LD-based products, a stepwise procedure for designing instruction and a specific case; see text for further explanation

Phase/subsection		Products	Steps	Case
1	Analysis (Instructional problem) Sect. 8.4.1	Narrative; simple, non-formal diagrams	-	Box 8.1
2	Design (Instructional scenario) Sect. 8.4.2	XML instance documents; semi-formal templates (e.g. UML activity diagram)	-	Figs. 8.1, 8.2 and 8.3
2.1	Learning flow	Activity table	1-7	Tables 8.3 and 8.4
2.2	XML coding	XML instance document (filled-out template)	8-10	Appendix
3	Development (Resources) Sect. 8 4.3	XML instance document (filled-out template)	11-12	Appendix
4	Implementation (Publication and run of UoL)	Instantiation for specific group and virtual learning environment	-	-
5	Evaluation	Evaluation report; adjusted narrative	-	-

The *analysis* phase involves analysing a specific educational problem. Various tools may be used to conduct the analysis, from a simple checklist to more sophisticated tools. At least the following questions will have to be answered:

1. Who is the instruction for and how would you characterise the learners?
2. What is it that they should learn, and how should their learning experiences affect them?
3. Is there a particular strategy that allows them to learn most effectively and efficiently, and that they find the most attractive?
4. How do we know that the strategy and actual learning experiences together have led these learners to achieve their learning objectives?

Usually, one works with more elaborate lists of questions. Morrison et al. (2004), for example, uses a list of nine questions, while Visscher-Voerman (1999) uses a list of 16. Kirschner et al. (2003, Table 6.1) review the lists recommended by a variety of authors. Also, in an academic environment, the analysis is likely to be conducted differently than in a business setting. However, the differences are in emphasis, not in the substance.

The phase starts by holding discussions with the various stakeholders or by surveying available documents, enabling the designers to find out what the instruction should accomplish (needs and task analysis). The analysis results in a narrative description of the subject matter (What should be learnt?) and a description of the instructional method (How should it be learnt?). The narrative is particularly important from the perspective of LD, and may contain simple, non-formal diagrams for illustrative purposes. It should, however, allow one to separate information about the subject matter from a description of the instructional method.

In the *design* phase, one creates a coherent view how the instructional aspect of the educational problem described by the narrative may be solved. The solution is expressed in the form of an instructional design, devoid of any content. LD requires two issues are distinguished: how the narrative may be translated into a particular instructional strategy, and how the design can be fleshed out with instructional materials. The chosen strategy must be described with sufficient precision to allow it to be expressed in LD's XML code.

Various tools may be used to ease the design process. Van Merriënboer (1997) and co-workers (De Croock et al. 2002a), for example, have developed a method that offers the best support to the 4C/ID model of instruction. Indeed, tools are often specific to a particular class of instructional models. Within the context of LD, though, the design may be better served by tools that are pedagogically non-committal yet sufficiently powerful to be able to represent any instructional scenario. Such tools can be used in any design process. UML activity diagrams (Rumbaugh et al. 1999) fit the bill. Gilbert Paquette and co-workers have developed a similarly general tool (MOT+), which has the added benefit of having been developed specifically with an educational application in mind (see Chap. 9). The XML code itself may be created with a plain text editor, although the ability to validate XML makes an XML-editor more suitable. Ideally, editors should be adapted to make them more suitable for editing LD XML (see Chap. 7).

In the *development* phase the instruction's content is developed. The instructional strategy developed in the design phase acts as a mould for the instruction. In this chapter, we will illustrate how the development of the instructional material fits in with the instructional design. After the development phase, a complete piece of instructional material is available for implementation. This requires a software environment or system that is able to parse the XML code, render it in a user interface, and keep track of the state changes of the system, either user or system generated (see Chap. 6).

This chapter, then, provides LD-related guidelines for the analysis, design and development phases, with an emphasis on the design phase. We will use a particular case of problem-based learning in medical training as an example to inform and illustrate the discussion (Sect. 8.4). But first we will briefly examine the LD specification (see also Chap. 2); a working knowledge of the specification is an absolute prerequisite for the discussion.

8.3 The Learning Design Specification

Our discussion will be couched in terms of the LD Information Model, often even its XML binding (we will not always strictly distinguish an element as it appears in the information model from its formal representation in XML).

Chap. 2 provided a detailed introduction to and review of the LD specification. We will not repeat that discussion here, with the exception of a small number of elements that play a major role in the design process. Table 8.2 lists those elements. Knowing their names and hierarchical relationships is a prerequisite for reading this chapter. Note also that our discussion pertains to Level C of the LD specification; it thus includes properties, conditions and notifications.

As Table 8.2 and Fig. 8.1 make clear, the most prominent elements in LD are the `components` and `method` elements because they have the largest number of sub-elements. The `method` element plays out the theatre metaphor: it contains a nested structure of `play`, `act`, and `role-part` elements. The `play` element usually occurs only once; it may contain one or more `act` elements. Every act consists of one or more role-parts. Acts run in sequence, each one being triggered by the completion of the preceding one. Note that each transition between two adjacent acts thus forms a synchronization point for all the subordinate role-parts: all the role-parts within some act must be completed before the subsequent act can begin. A play is therefore only complete when its final act has been completed. Also note that role-parts within the same act always run in parallel. The relation between role-part completion and act completion is a complex one. It is up to the designer to decide what this relationship is. For example, an act may be completed only if all its role-parts have been completed, if only one has been completed, etc.

Figure 8.2 focuses on the components part of Table 8.2. It shows in a graphical way that a `role-part` *refers* to the elements `role` and `activity`, and that an activity in turn *refers* to an `environment` element. The `role-part` element acts as a bridge connecting the `method` and `components` elements to each other. A `role-part` refers to one or more `activity` elements (in the latter case grouped in `activity-structures`) and one role only. Each activity (or `activity-structure`) refers to one or more `environment` elements.

As introduced in Chap. 1, likening a learning design to a theatrical play allows us to conceive of activities as parts of the scripts for the different roles that will be on stage together in the same act. Since role-parts run in parallel, different roles may do different things at the same time. That means that learners and staff (teachers) may be given different activities to carry out within the same time-frame (act). But different tasks may also be allotted to different subsets of learners, by discerning more learner roles.

Table 8.2. The major elements of the LD specification, in hierarchical order. Indentation denotes nesting. All elements are nested under the `learning-design` root element, the `components` element has a number of sub-elements, such as `roles`, which in turn has learners and staff as it members etc. An asterisk * means that an element may occur more than once; thus there may be more than one learner role, or more than one learning-activity. Further restrictions may apply, but are not indicated here

```
learning-design
      title
learning-objectives
      prerequisites
      components
            roles
                  learner*
                  staff*
            activities
                  learning-activity*
                        environment-ref*
                        activity-description
                  support-activity*
                        environment-ref*
                        activity-description
                  activity-structure*
                        environment-ref*
            environments
                  environment*
                        learning objects*
                        services*
                        environment-ref*
      method
            play*
                  act*
                        role-parts*
                              role-ref
                              activity-ref
      metadata
```

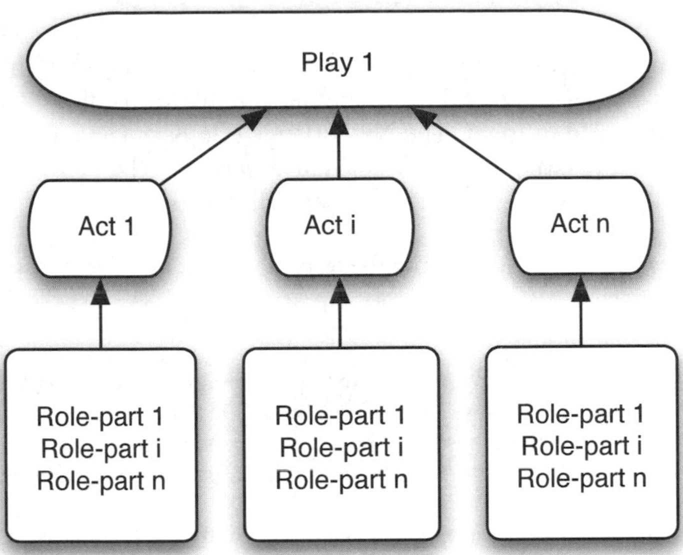

Fig. 8.1. A diagram of the relations between the major elements in the method part. The arrows indicate a part-of relation. Thus a `play` consists of one or more `act` elements, each `act` of one or more `role-part` elements; the `acts` furthermore exhaust the `play` and so do the `role-parts` with respect to the `acts`. See text for further explanation

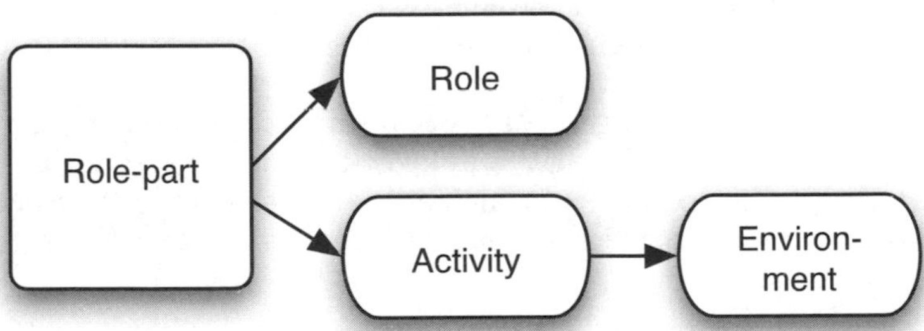

Fig. 8.2. A diagram of the referral mechanism in `role-parts`. As in Fig. 8.1, the arrows represent an association. So each `role-part` is linked to at least one `role` and at least one `activity`, and an `activity` may be linked to one or more `environment` elements. See text for further explanation

8.4 Designing Instruction with Learning Design

This section makes frequent reference to an actual case, described in Box 8.1. It contains excerpts from a third-year course book for medical students at the University of Maastricht, The Netherlands (De Krom and Antheunis 2002: Blok 3.2 *Uitvalsverschijnselen en functieverlies*). The text has been translated and edited slightly to better suit our discussion.

Box 8.1. The narrative: case description neuropathology course for medical students

---

The module *Disabilities* treats ailments of the sense organs and the nervous system. It is a follow-up of modules 1.3, 2.1. 2.2, and 2.7, that covered the normal structure and function of these systems. It is recommended to re-examine these modules, so as to be able successfully to build on the knowledge acquired there in this module.

The subject matter presented in this module, specifically the neurology, has the reputation of being difficult. In day-to-day practice this gives rise to the following argument:

This patient has a neurological problem.
Neurology is a difficult subject.
It is therefore best to consult a neurologist.

Clearly, this is not a recommendable practice; it minimally reflects a serious lack of opportunities for the non-neurologist. This module attempts to present the subject matter in such a way that structures and functions that are related to the pathophysiology of the sensory organs and the nervous system become clear. In the end, the students are expected to be able to arrive at a differential diagnosis as well as a diagnostic and therapeutic plan on the basis of a medical history and a physical examination.

This module covers ailments that either occur very frequently or are very serious. This way, the future physician acquires knowledge of symptomatology, diagnostics and therapy. The module furthermore moves from peripheral to central, an important issue in the topographical diagnosis of ailments of both the sense organs and the nervous system.

[*A discussion follows of the topics that are to be covered in the 6 weeks the course lasts.*]

The module aims to discuss the pathophysiology of ailments of the nervous system from the perspective of various disciplines. Integration of these view points will lead to a better understanding of the complexity of the sense organs and the nervous system.

[*A discussion follows of subjects not treated.*]

Clinical seven step method
The cases in this module may best be approached via the so-called clinical seven step method:

step 1 Discuss what body part or organ the case is about, and make an inventory of what the group knows about its normal structure and function.
step 2 Discuss what additional information needs to be acquired - through anamnesis or additional inquiry - to obtain a full picture of the patient's problem; collect it.
step 3 Combine the results of step 1 and 2.
step 4 Formulate a causal explanation for the combined results; what factors are risk factors for the patient in question?
step 5 On the basis of step 4 make a differential diagnosis ordered according to a decrease in likelihood.
step 6 Discuss how a more certain diagnosis may be arrived at.
step 7 Develop a therapy in the form of a plan.

[...]

Case 2-A, part 1 description
A 48 year old language teacher has decided to pay his GP a visit. He has been experiencing hearing problems for some time. In his classes it has become increasingly difficult to hear what his pupils are saying, and at the end of each day he returns home exhausted. Last week, he felt as if he was coming down with the flu. Although that feeling has gone, his hearing impairment even seems to have worsened. He does not suffer from dizziness or disturbances of equilibrium. A general examination also does not reveal anything in particular. In tonometer examinations, the test of Rinne shows a bilateral positive result, Weber's test lateralizes to the right. The othoscopy reveals that on both sides the middle ear contains air. The patient is worried and you decide to make a screening audiogram. The air conductivity threshold is about 45 dB for both ears.

[...]

Case 2-A, part 1 excerpt from the tutor instruction

Learning goals

- Hearing loss with an emphasis on perceptual and neural aspects
- Distinguish conductive and perceptive aspects
- Opportunities for treatment and revalidation
- Rekindle knowledge on tonometer test in skills lab
- Etc.

Medical history

- How did the complaint arise? Over time (not acutely)
- What kind of complaint is it? Problems hearing what people say in the presence of background noise (class) because of subjectively deteriorating hearing (both sides), on the right side more than on the left side. Hearing problem causes rapid fatigue and diminished capacity to work
- When did the complaint arise? First signs of it about 1.5 years ago
- Etc.

8.4.1 Analysis

The description in Box 8.1 is a typical example of a problem-based learning case for medical students (cf. Barrows and Tamblin 1980). It contains the *narrative*, i.e. highly informal information about the educational problem, provided as a description in natural language. The narrative addresses the instructionally relevant issues. With a view to the LD specification, the narrative should address at least the following questions:

i. What are the (learning) *objectives* and what *prerequisites*, if any, should the learners comply with at the start?
ii. What instructional strategy or *method* do we want to use?
iii. In view of the objectives and instructional strategy, what (learning) *activities* should the learners carry out and what the (support) *activities* should the staff perform to support them?
iv. What resources (learning *environment*) should be made available to both learners and staff, in the form either of learning *objects* or interactive *services*?

The narrative of Box 8.1 points to both the module's goals and prerequisites (question i). The goals are: to avoid simplistic arguments of the kind given, to be able to arrive at a differential diagnosis and a diagnostic and therapeutic plan, and to be capable of adopting an interdisciplinary perspective. Being up to speed on the preceding modules is a prerequisite. The instructional strategy (question ii) is discussed explicitly, the clinical variant of the seven-step method for problem-based learning. Although problem-based learning itself is not mentioned, it is implied: the medical school at the University of Maastricht uses it throughout its curriculum. The final three parts of the narrative of Box 8.1 contain excerpts from texts in the course book. These contain the actual subject matter of the case and thus provide material with which questions iii and iv may be answered.

8.4.2 Design

As discussed, the design phase only concerns the instructional method, i.e. question ii in the previous section. We will return to the remaining three questions later, when we discuss the development phase (Sect. 8.4.3). The design phase can be broken down into two sub-phases. The first sub-phase results in a description of the scenario's learning flow, that is, the temporal order in which the various learning activities unfold. Our description will be provided in a table, and accompanied by a UML activity diagram. Once the table has been completed, sub-phase 2 commences. In it, the actual

XML coding will take place. It is assumed throughout the discussion that we are dealing with one play only. If we had wanted to work with several plays, we would have followed the same procedure, with one exception: we would consider how the components (roles, properties, activities, environments) can be reused across the different plays.

The process of creating the activity table consists of a number of steps which all amount to filling in the columns of the table (see Table 8.3). It is best to work from the inside out; that is, to begin by focusing on the role-parts and the role, activities and environments associated with them first, and then look at how the various role-parts can be aggregated to form activity-structures and acts. The sequence is reflected in the order of the columns in Table 8.3. Table 8.4 (below) is the completed version of Table 8.3, and should be consulted throughout our discussion.

Step 1 Describe Role-parts. Describe the various role-parts in the sequential order in which they occur. The order may not always be obvious as, by their very nature, different role-parts may run in parallel. Nevertheless, begin with what seems to be the first activity and the role that carries it out, then move on to the next, and so on. Mark whether the activity is a learning activity or a support activity.

The seven steps of the clinical method in Box 8.1 correspond to the activities the students are supposed to carry out. These activities need to be supplemented by facilitator and evaluator activities, and it is customary to appoint a chairperson as well. Only the chairperson has been added, in order to illustrate how this role may influence the learning flow. See the Appendix for an elaboration of these roles and their activities in a generalised version of a problem-based learning scenario.

Table 8.3. An empty activity table. The text in the cells indicates the steps which are to be filled in.

Role	Activity	Environment	Activity completion	Property/ notification
step 1	step 1	step 2	step 3	step 4

Act	Act completion	Activity-structure	Activity-type
step 5	step 6	step 7	step 7

Step 2 Describe Environments. If an activity requires particular resources or perhaps a service, e.g. an electronic conference, describe this in the environment column.

Although Box 8.1 does not indicate this explicitly, a conferencing service and a 'resource centre' have been added in our example to allow students to obtain information and discuss their findings.

Step 3 Indicate Completion of Activities. Indicate for each activity how it will be completed. Various mechanisms are available, ranging from 'leave it up to the user' (user-choice), via a time limit that may be exceeded, to a property that needs to acquire a particular value. If this column remains empty, the activity's status is set to 'completed' by default.

In our example we have used user-choice throughout, but for all the student activities a time limit could also have been used.

Step 4 Set Properties or Notifications. Completing an activity may trigger various events, such as the provision of feedback. More interestingly, it may trigger the setting of a property or the sending of a notification (for instance, by email). If completing an activity is supposed to affect future events, a relevant property should be set or changed. Notifications are routinely used to move the flow of learning and support activities from one role to another. In this way the persons in that role are triggered to start moving.

This is indicated in Table 8.4. In the same vein, it is the chairperson who makes the therapy available to all participants.

Table 8.4 shows the activity table for the example given in Box 8.1. Note that a good understanding of the LD Information Model very much helps to fill out the table properly. In case of doubt one should always consult the LD Information Model to check for the validity of particular constructions. (Note that we are not referring here to validity in terms of the XML *syntax* – say, every opening `<element>` needs a closing `</element>` – but to validity with respect to the LD *semantics*.)

Table 8.4. Activity table for example in Box 8.1

Role	Activity	Environment	Activity completion	Property/ notification	Act	Act completion	Activity-structure	Type
Student	Discuss what body part or organ the case is about (step 1)	Synchronous conferencing service Resource centre	User choice		Act 1	When all students are done		
Student	Discuss necessary additional information (step 2)	Synchronous conferencing service Resource centre	User choice		Act 2	When all students are done		
Student	Combine results of both discussions (step 3)	Synchronous conferencing service	User choice		Act 3	When chairperson is done		
Chairperson	State problem	Synchronous conferencing service	User choice	Upload file	Act 3			
Student	Formulate causal explanation (step 4)	Synchronous conferencing service Resource centre	User choice		Act 4	When all students are done		
Student	Make a differential diagnosis (step 5)	Synchronous conferencing service	User choice		Act 5	When all students are done		
Student	Discuss how to obtain more certain diagnosis (step 6)	Synchronous conferencing service	User choice		Act 6	When all students are done		
Student	Develop a therapy (step 7)	Synchronous conferencing service Resource centre	User choice		Act 7	When chairperson is done		
Chairperson	State therapy		User choice	Upload file	Act 7			

Step 5 Look for Synchronisation Points. At this stage, all the role-parts should have been specified. Now the time has come to look for synchronisation points between activities; that is, to aggregate role-parts into acts. Consider a particular activity, A_n. Suppose analysis of the narrative and the activities defined thus far reveal that A_n may be initiated only if all the activities that precede A_n (A_1 through A_{n-1}) have been completed. In such a situation, activity A_n indicates a synchronisation point. The role-part associated with A_n should be the starting point for a new act, while the role-parts associated with the activities A_1 through A_{n-1} constitute the preceding act. (If some of the preceding role-parts have already been aggregated in an act, the rule applies to those preceding role-parts that have not yet been gathered under an act.) Creating acts amounts to partitioning the entire set of temporally ordered role-parts into subsets that do not overlap and follow on from one another: $\{A_1 \ldots A_{n-1}\}$, $\{A_n \ldots A_m\}$, etc.

Our example is rather uncommon in that most of the student activities constitute acts by themselves. In two cases, the combined student and chairperson activities constitute an act. In other designs, an act can easily consist of several activities.

Step 6 Determine Termination of Activities. Once a new act has been created, at least one of the role-part needs to be designated as the one that decides on the act's completion (if more than one role-part needs to be completed, all need to be completed). The chosen activity will usually, but not necessarily, be those whose completion is subject to user control, rather than activities that are completed by default. An act may furthermore be completed by exceeding a predetermined time limit. When deciding on what activity should be completed for act completion, recall that role-parts and hence activities may run in parallel. Where this is the case, it may be impossible to indicate the particular order in which activities may be completed. In our example, role-parts terminate activities, but a time limit could also have been used.

Step 7 Make Activity-structures. Once the sequential structure of acts is in place, look within the acts for role-parts that are carried out by the same role. Perhaps they need not be performed in the temporal order indicated, or perhaps not all need to be carried out. If so, the activities should be grouped in an activity-structure for which the relevant attributes have been set (sequence or selection, number of activities to select). The role-part in question now becomes linked to the activity-structure rather than to each of the activities within it. Another reason for creating activity-structures may be that one can link them, rather than its constituent activities, to an environment. This is simpler and more efficient than linking several activities all to the same environment. One may also associate some environment E_1 with the activity-structure that thus is common to all the activities in the structure, and still associate other environments (E_2 … E_n) with the activities that constitute the activity-structure. This allows for quite a sophisticated scheme of associated environments that can be well managed. Our example does not require activity-structures.

Table 8.4 is still incomplete in that no staff involvement has been planned. In the narrative of Box 8.1 staff involvement wasn't made explicit. However, to the extent that the instruction was implicitly designed according to the medical problem-based learning model, one may expect staff time to be allotted accordingly. Thus, we need three more roles: a coordinator who organises the module, a facilitator who tutors the group of students and appoints the chairperson, and an evaluator who assesses the students' performance. The Appendix provides a more elaborate table that also contains the roles of coordinator, facilitator and evaluator. It also provides a number of activity-structures (see step 7 above).

Now that the activity table has been filled in, we could also create an accompanying sketch or diagram. Figure 8.3 shows a UML activity diagram for Table 8.4 (see Chap. 9 of this volume for a similar MOT+ diagram.) Although the diagrams make it easier to complete the next subphase, coding the LD XML, neither is an absolute prerequisite. For more experienced users, the activity table is likely to suffice.

Sub-phase 2.2 also consists of a number of steps. For the sake of clarity, we use rank numbers that continue the sequence of steps in sub-phase 2.1. The steps in sub-phase 2.2 are all about the actual XML coding. The coding is carried out with the help of the activity table and, where available, the activity diagram. It is to be expected that in the not too distant future a graphical editor, perhaps one that uses an activity table or activity diagram as input, will generate the code. For now, however, one typically uses a generic XML editor that can validate the code on the basis of the LD XML binding. This will only be a syntactic validation, which prevents one from coding XML that is not well formed or does not conform to the semantics of the LD information model. The editor will not complain if one codes scenarios that are nonsensical from a pedagogical perspective, even if the scenario has an endless loop of activities.

We have decided not to illustrate the steps which follow with actual XML code. Although the activity table will allow us to do so, the text would rapidly become inaccessible. As an intermediary step, we provide what may be called XML pseudo-code, in the manner of Table 8.1. From this, one may easily obtain the actual XML code (the Appendix has XML code for the general case of problem-based learning).

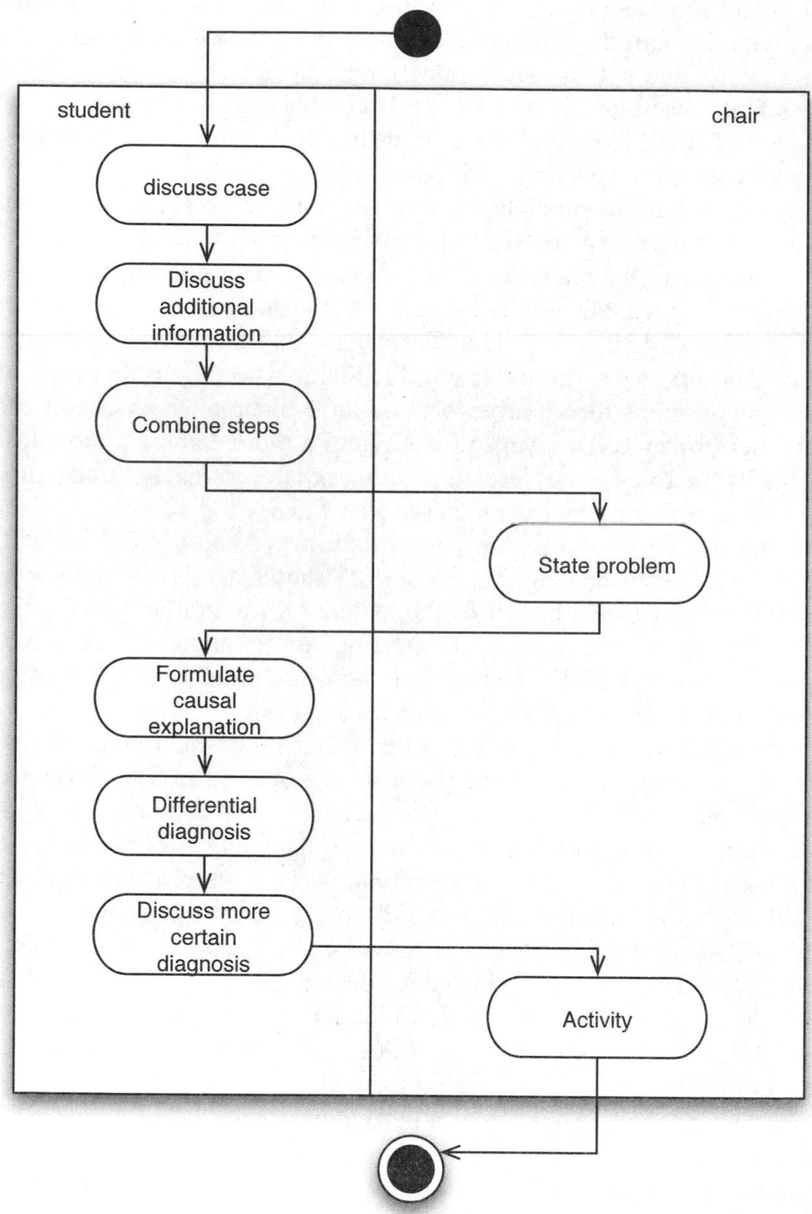

Fig. 8.3. A UML activity diagram for the case of Box 8.1. Compare with Table 8.4.

Step 8 Describe Components. First, focus on the components element. It should contain the sub-elements roles, properties, activities and environments, each with one or more role, property, activity, and environment elements. It may also contain one or more activity-structure elements. To be precise, roles are mandatory, properties, activities and environments are optional. However, any useful learning design will contain a few activities and environment elements. The first three columns and the last two columns of Table 8.4 contain information that helps to fill in the components element. Similar to Table 8.1, the case of Box 8.1 would result in the pseudo-XML of Table 8.5.

Table 8.5. Pseudo-XML for case of Box 8.1

```
components
      roles
            learner student
            learner chair-person
      activities
            learning-activity discuss relevant body part
                  environment-ref synchronous conference
                  environment-ref study-landscape
      learning-activity discuss additional information
                  environment-ref synchronous conference
                  environment-ref study-landscape
            learning-activity combine results
                  environment-ref synchronous conference
            learning-activity state problem
                  environment-ref synchronous conference
            learning-activity formulate causal explanation
                  environment-ref synchronous conference
                  environment-ref study-landscape
            learning-activity make differential diagnosis
                  environment-ref synchronous conference
                  learning-activity discuss more certainty
                  environment-ref synchronous conference
                  learning-activity develop therapy
                  environment-ref synchronous conference
                  environment-ref study-landscape
                  learning-activity state therapy
            support-activity (none)
            activity-structure (none)
      environments
                  environment
                        service synchronous conference
                  environment
                        learning object study-landscape
```

Step 9 Describe Method. Now focus on the method element. The method constitutes the learning flow in its most concise form. The 'role' and 'act' columns of Table 8.4 provide the relevant information; Table 8.6 provides the pseudo-XML for the method element.

Step 10 Describe Conditions. State the rules for completing activities and act, and fill in the `conditions` element. This is best done in the actual XML code. See the LD Information Model and Chap. 1 for an explanation of how the various modes of completion affect one another (LD 2003, Sect. 4.5 and Tables 3.1.7, 3.1.8 and 3.1.14).

Table 8.6. The pseudo-XML for the `method` element for the case of Box 8.1

```
method
    play
        act 1
            role-parts
             role-ref student
             activity-ref discuss relevant body part
         act 2
             role-parts
             role-ref student
             activity-ref discuss additional information
         act 3
             role-parts
             role-ref student
             activity-ref combine results
             role-ref chair-person
             activity-ref state problem
         act 4
             role-parts
             role-ref student
             activity-ref formulate causal explanation
         act 5
             role-parts
             role-ref student
             activity-ref make differential diagnosis
         act 6
             role-parts
             role-ref student
             activity-ref discuss more certainty
         act 7
             role-parts
             role-ref student
             activity-ref develop therapy
             role-ref chair-person
             activity-ref state therapy
```

Filling in the `components` and `method` elements requires meticulousness and a good understanding of the LD Information Model. The `conditions` element allows us to fine-tune the learning flow, and requires a basic understanding of programming logic in addition to the above. If one wants to work with the `conditions` element with any confidence, one must understand how conditional constructions are evaluated.

At this stage in the design process we have a document that contains valid XML and that describes the instructional design of the instructional problem we have analysed. To the extent that our problem represents a more general instructional problem, the document can act as a *design template* for that particular class of instructional problems. To be more specific, the instructional approach that underpins the case of Box 8.1 is problem-based learning. The design we have come up with at this particular stage exemplifies the problem-based learning approach. Obviously, activities would have to be described in more generic terms – a description such as 'discuss what body part the case is about' is hardly sufficiently generic – but that could easily be accomplished. In fact, that is precisely what has been done in the XML instance document in the Appendix. That document can therefore serve as a generic design template for problem-based learning.

8.4.3 Development

In the development phase the content is added to the instructional design. Strictly speaking, the development phase therefore is outside the scope of the present chapter. For the sake of completeness, however, we will look briefly at development here.

Let us assume that the content is available in a form similar to that provided in Box 8.1. The content now needs to be allotted to various recipient elements in the learning design (as content is often already available in some form or other, usually one will have to do some rewriting to tailor it to the design). The LD specification takes a generic approach to content by means of a two-step referral mechanism. It uses this mechanism primarily to comply with the Content Packaging specification (CP 2003; see also section 2.2.3 of the LD Information Model, LD 2003). As it happens this approach also fosters reuse of content and helps keep the XML instance document comprehensible.

The elements that may contain content are: the `learning-objectives` and `prerequisites` elements, and all components, i.e. the various sub-elements of each of the `roles`, `activities` and `environments` elements (cf. Table 8.1). Each one of these (elements or sub-elements) contains an `item` element. The `item` element also occurs in the Content Packaging specification. An `item` does not contain content itself, but points to a `resource` element. In this way resources may be used more often within a design (or content package). This is the first referral step. Contrary to what their name implies, resource elements do not themselves contain the physical resources. They point to them (the second referral step). All `resource` elements are grouped in the Content Packaging's `resources` element. The physical resources themselves may either be part of the content package (and thus come packaged with the design) or be located elsewhere (more on this appears in the Content Packaging specification). The Appendix shows how this arrangement works.

Step 11 Fill in Title, Learning Objectives, Prerequisites and Metadata. Fill in the learning scenario's `title`, `learning-objectives`, `prerequisites` and `metadata`. The subject of how best to fill out metadata deserves a chapter in itself. We will not go into that here but refer to the abundant literature on the subject (see, for example, JORUM+ (2004) and various chapters in McGreal 2004). Suffice it to say that metadata is of crucial importance for reuse, both in the instructional design itself and for the content embedded in it. Learning objectives and prerequisites are stored as resources. The `item` element inside the `learning-objectives` and `prerequisites` elements refers to a `resource` element that, in turn, refers to the physical resource that contains the learning objectives' or prerequisites' content.

Box 8.1 provides all sorts of relevant material. 'Deficit and loss of function, case 2-A' would be a suitable title. Lines such as 'At the end, the students are expected to be able to arrive at a differential diagnosis …' and 'The module aims to discuss the pathophysiology of ailments of the nervous system from the vantage point of various disciplines …' can be used to compile a list of learning objectives. (Note that the learning goals mentioned in case 2-A, part 1 are the goals the students themselves should formulate.) '[This module] is a follow-up of modules 1.3, 2.1, 2.2 and 2.7 …' indicates prerequisites.

Step 12 Fill in all Items (Resources). The final step is straightforward but labour intensive since the content that pertains to the learning experiences themselves is to be added. This content has been referenced by the various `item` elements within the component sub-elements. As discussed, referral starts with the `item` element, which refers to the `resource` element, which, in turn, refers to the physical resource.

The full text of the case contains a wealth of relevant information that should be placed into `item` elements for activity descriptions, etc. The case description ('A 48 year old language teacher … 45 dB for both ears') should be placed into an environment `item`. The tutor instruction–learning goals and anamnesis constitutes two environment items for support activities (not modelled in Table 8.4).

8.5 Summary and Conclusion

In this chapter we have described the steps that need to be taken to develop a design that conforms to the LD specification. We have done so, first of all, by grouping the various activities needed to arrive at such a document into the analysis, design and development phases of the Instructional System Development process. We then discussed the analysis phase, particularly with the aim of identifying to what conditions the ensuing narrative had to conform in order to be useful in the subsequent design process. We found that is was particularly important to be able to distinguish between elements that relate to the underlying instructional strategy and elements that contain the content that is needed to flesh out the design. The design phase, not surprisingly, builds on the first and the development phase on the second aspect of the narrative. To make the discussion more tangible, we then introduced a genuine educational problem.

A proper design, it was shown, is developed in two steps. First, we created a table in a series of seven steps detailing who (role) carries out what activities against which background (environment). The table also indicates whether activities should be grouped into activity structures and/or acts, and how activities and, where appropriate, acts are to be completed. Secondly, we created an XML instance document in three more steps with the help of our table. We pointed out in step 10 that we had arrived at a kind of design template for the instructional problem analysed. This template will easily acquire more generic value if the problem analysed has characteristics of general interest. If so, one would need only to ensure that the design template's descriptive terminology is sufficiently generic. Finally, we explained the slots of the design template into which actual content may be entered so as to arrive at a complete XML instance document. Such a document is complete in the sense that a runtime system capable of parsing and interpreting the XML document would be able to pose as a learning environment developed specifically for the educational problem analysed.

We realise that the details of the present discussion will become outdated as soon as LD-specific tooling is available. That will certainly be the case when an editor becomes available that is able to generate appropriate LD XML code from a graphical user interface. We nevertheless feel that this chapter still makes a significant contribution to our ability to work with the LD specification since the discussion identifies how, in our view, an LD-based design and development process should be carried out, and thereby helps to identify the functionalities of the tools that need be developed. We are convinced that the stepwise model presented here remains valid and valuable, irrespective of the tools that will become available in the future.

8.6 Acknowledgements

The authors are grateful for the comments that Solvig Norman provided; they have helped significantly to improve the chapter. The authors wish to thank M. de Krom, MD PhD, and L. Antheunis, PhD, and A. Scherpbier (director of the School of Education of the Medical Faculty of the University of Maastricht) for their permission to use excerpts from their work (Box 8.1) as well as Martin van Boxtel, MD PhD, for his help in translating the case from Dutch.

9 An Instructional Engineering Method and Tool for the Design of Units of Learning

Gilbert Paquette, Ileana de la Teja, Michel Léonard, Karin Lundgren-Cayrol, Olga Marino

CIRTA(LICEF) Research Centre, Télé-université, Montréal, Canada

9.1 Introduction

The fast evolution of learning technologies has multiplied the number of decisions one must take to create a distributed learning system (DLS). While it is true that a majority of the first web-based applications have been mostly used to distribute information, more and more educators have become aware of the need to go beyond simple uses of information and communication technologies. This context has generated a much-needed interest for pedagogical methods and, more generally, for the field of Instructional Design (Wiley 2002).

The term “Educational Modelling Language” (EML) was first introduced in 1998 by researchers at the Open University of the Netherlands (OUNL), as a response to Instructional Design and pedagogical concerns towards standardization and interoperability needs. The work on Educational Modelling Languages (Koper 2002), and the subsequent integration of a subset in the Learning Design specification (LD 2003), is the most important initiative to date, to integrate Instructional Design preoccupations into the international standards movement. In particular, it describes a formal way to represent the structure of a Unit of Learning and the concept of a pedagogical method specifying roles and activities that learners and support persons can play using learning objects.

The LD specification leaves open the choice of instructional methods and modelling tools that can support designers in the process of building learning design specification, especially for those aiming at distributed, networked or on-line education. Extensive research and development in the field of Instructional Design has led to a large body of methodologies. One of the approaches is described in the previous chapter. This chapter will elaborate on the work we did in Canada on the Instructional Engineering approach (Paquette 2001a) and the Learning Systems Engineering

Method (MISA)[1]. The approach is especially well suited to help designers build LD-compliant Units of Learning.

The chapter is structured into four sections. Section 9.2 presents the instructional engineering viewpoint on the LD specification. Section 9.3 outlines the MISA instructional engineering method and its relation to LD. Section 9.4 presents the MOT+ graphical representation language and situates MISA/MOT+ as embedding an educational modelling language with its XML machine-readable output. Section 9.5 presents a practical learning design case of a complex unit of learning.

9.2 Instructional Engineering Viewpoint on the LD Specification

Instructional Engineering can be defined as

> A method that supports the analysis, the design and the delivery planning of a learning system, integrating concepts, processes and principles of instructional design, software engineering and knowledge engineering. (Paquette 2003, p 56)

9.2.1 Defining Instructional Engineering

Located at the crossroads of instructional design, software engineering and knowledge engineering, from which it inherits most of its properties, Instructional Engineering is a particular systemic and systematic method in the field of educational problem solving. It is founded on the system sciences (Le Moigne 1995; Simon 1973) and defines the concept of a system as a series of units in dynamic interaction, organized in order to achieve specific goals.

The origin of *instructional design*[2] goes back to John Dewey (1900), who, a century ago, claimed the development of an "interlinked science" between learning theories and educational practices. Since the 1950s, the evolution of this new discipline has been carried by influential researchers such as B.F. Skinner (1974), Jerome Bruner (1966) and David Ausubel (1968). In the 1970s and 1980s, instructional theories blossomed through the work of researchers such as Gagné (1970), Scandura (1973), Merrill et

---

[1] MISA is the French acronym for Méthode d'ingénierie des systèmes d'apprentissage.

[2] In the American literature, this discipline is known as "Instructional Design (ID)", "Instructional System Design (ISD)" or "Instructional Science" (Reigeluth 1983; Merrill 1994) depending on theoretical inclination. In Europe, one of the pioneers of the field used the term "Scientific Pedagogy" (Montessori 1912).

al. (1979), Landa (1976), Reigeluth and Rodgers (1980), Collins and Stevens (1983), to name a few. These instructional design models and theories have been built on solid foundations and present an impressive body of work. However, today it seems necessary to renew the instructional design methods and tools to support the creation of Distributed Learning Systems (DLSs) that are heavily dependent on information and communication technologies.

Software engineering brings some interesting solutions to meet demands required by innovative technology used in a DLS. From a technical point of view, a Unit of Learning, and its distributed environment, is an information system consisting of a complex array of software tools, digital documents and communication services. This environment allows learners and facilitators to interact using information and communication technologies. By adapting software engineering principles to instructional design principles, Instructional Engineering proposes well-defined processes and principles that help produce deliverables, precisely described products of these processes. Moreover, multi-agent systems offer a good way to represent the enacted learning designs at delivery time as a set of agents, persons and digital objects, interacting to help some of the agents to learn and others to facilitate learning.

Knowledge engineering is a methodology developed in the field of expert systems and artificial intelligence over the last 30 years. Knowledge engineering focuses on identifying and structuring knowledge to explain it, using a symbolic or graphical language representation to facilitate its use by persons and/or computer systems. Knowledge engineering has been applied in education to build intelligent tutoring systems (Wenger 1987) and also as support systems for designers (Merrill 1994; Spector et al. 1993). Recently, the focus has shifted to machine-readable knowledge structures aiming at a new generation of the web (Berners-Lee et al. 2000). In an *instructional engineering* method, knowledge modelling processes or the workflow are at the forefront. The workflow model guides the designer in his or her tasks to define content and objectives using them as an orientation for the design of instructional scenarios, learning objects (or educational resources)[3], as well as the learning system delivery processes.

9.2.2 Relationship Between Instructional Engineering and the Learning Design Specification

Developing high-quality distance learning courses can be a difficult and expensive task. On-line course development faces two main challenges:

[3] We will use the terms learning object, educational resource or simply re-source as synonyms throughout this chapter.

viability and quality. A key concept has emerged as a response to the concern of viability, the concept of reusability. Basically, reusability means being able to use an educational resource or learning object (LO) in different educational contexts or courses, possibly supported by different independent or interoperated e-learning delivery systems, which demands a standard way of describing those learning objects. In the past few years, a vast movement towards international standards for learning objects has been initiated. Duval and Robson (2001) present a review of the evolution of standards and specifications starting with the Dublin Core meta-data initiative in 1995 up to the publication of the Learning Object Metadata (LOM) standard in 2002. A host of other specifications have been published since then.

But what about quality? High-quality learning objects are necessary but not sufficient to produce a high-quality course or unit of learning. When, how, for what and by whom will those LOs be used? The LD specification offers a standardized way to associate learning materials (learning objects), activities and actors in a learning scenario. Furthermore, having an XML format that can be read by any compliant delivery system, LD bridges the gap between the process of designing a course and that of delivering it. What is still needed, to ensure quality of a course, is to ensure the quality of the learning scenarios produced by the design process. Basically, instructional engineering methods like MISA, and tools like MOT+ and ADISA[4], guide and support course designer(s) through the process of designing high-quality learning systems and scenarios; in particular, by ensuring coherence through systematic documentation of all aspects of the design process and products, automatic propagation of many pieces of information as well as a systemic view of the process.

Figure 9.1 presents a general view of the relationship between instructional engineering methods and tools, and EML/LD specifications. The remaining part of this chapter focuses on a presentation of MISA as an instructional engineering method and MOT+ as a modelling tool to support this process. In Chap. 20, we discuss the DLS delivery process by analysing Explor@, an open system for learning and content delivery developed at Télé-université in Quebec.

[4] ADISA (Distributed Workshop for Learning Systems Engineering) is a tool developed at Télé-université. It is a web-based system that supports course designing teams in the elaboration and integration of the various elements of the MISA method.

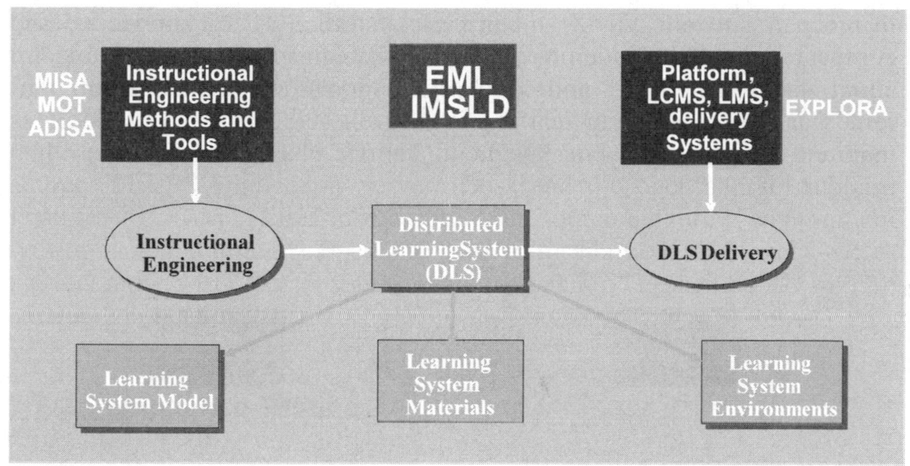

Fig. 9.1. Interrelations between MISA 4.0, LD Design and Explor@

9.3 An Instructional Engineering Method for Learning Design

9.3.1 Implementation

This section presents a synthesis of our work in Instructional Engineering at Télé-université in Quebec (Canada). We will present the main MISA 4.0 Instructional Engineering Method components and concepts, and then introduce a more detailed description of the design processes inherent to the instructional model, which in turn will assist instructional designers in producing LD-compliant Units of Learning.

9.3.2 The MISA 4.0 Instructional Engineering Method

A knowledge modelling approach is used to define the Instructional Engineering method itself, its concepts, processes and principles. This R&D initiative started in 1992 and has led to the MISA 4.0 version (Paquette 2001a; 2002a) and to its support tool, called ADISA (Paquette et al. 2001). The editor MOT+ is embedded in the ADISA system and accessible through a web browser from any workstation linked to the Internet.

MISA is based on a problem solving approach. The method starts by (1) identifying the educational problem, its context and constraints as well as general orientations, (2) defining preliminary solution, (3) building the learning system architecture including elaboration of the knowledge and competency model as well as the instructional model, (4) designing instructional materials, (5) modelling, producing and validating learning materials and (6) specifying learning system delivery model(s) as well as maintenance and quality management. The six phases in MISA are illustrated in Fig. 9.2.

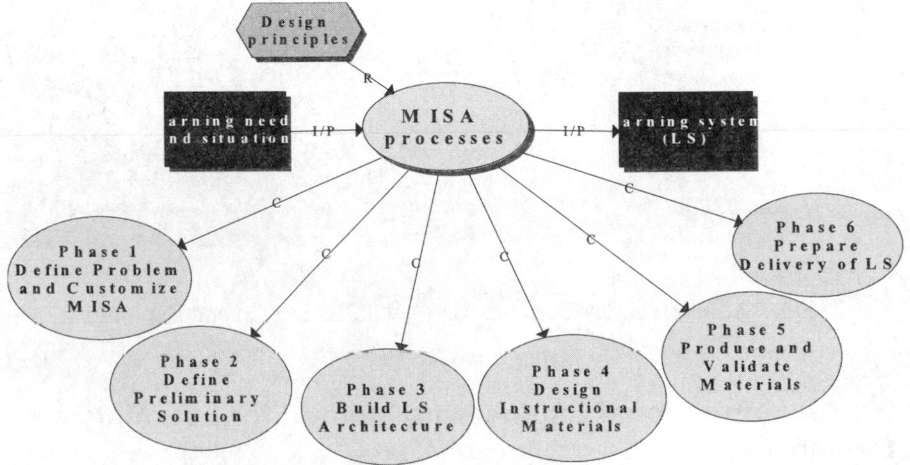

Fig. 9.2. The main MISA process and its six phases

The whole process is guided by a set of design principles that must be taken into account when building high-quality distance learning systems:

- *Self-management and meta-cognition principles*: Explicit association of a skill to a set of knowledge units, where the skill's generic process guides the design. Offer different learning paths and personalization options to be self-managed by learners. Promote self-management by introducing support tools like progress reports. Provide explicit meta-cognitive activities, such as for example individual and group product and process formative task evaluation.
- *Information processing principles*: Include rich and diversified static and dynamic information resources, clearly related to activities. Provide access to search, annotation and modelling tools to manipulate resources as well as production tools adapted to each task.
- *Collaboration principles*: Collaborative and individual activities must sustain one another. Adapt the modalities of collaboration to the generic process in which the collaboration is proposed. Allow for both synchronous and asynchronous interactions. Provide management tools for coordinating collaborative activities within the learning system.

- *Personalized assistance principles*: Encourage heuristic and methodological guidance rather than algorithmic assistance. Including multiple facilitators, both human and machine, to provide a flexible learning environment. Provide assistance mainly on the learner's initiative.

In each of the phases 2 to 6, MISA also proposes the development along four axes: knowledge, instructional, learning materials and delivery model.

The *Knowledge Model* centres on a graphical representation of the learning system's content domain. In this model, the domain's facts, concepts, procedures and principles are displayed and interrelated with precise links. Then target and prerequisite competencies are associated to units of knowledge, thus identifying prerequisites and learning objectives for the Instructional Model. Subsequently, knowledge units and competencies are attributed to learning units, instruments or resources used in the learning units.

The *Instructional Model* is essentially a network of learning events and units, to which knowledge and target competencies are associated. Each learning unit is described by a learning scenario specifying learning and support activities linked to resources in the environment. Resources holding content (called instruments) are associated with a subset of the knowledge model.

The *Learning Material Models* are useful to describe materials (learning objects), their media components, source documents and presentation principles as well as other specifications aimed at graphical designers and learning material producers.

Finally, *Delivery Models* are produced to show how and where actors use or provide the learning materials and resources such as tools, communication means, services and locations, used in the learning system. Each delivery model is a multi-user workflow, where actors use or produce resources, while assuming different roles. These processes correspond to organizational issues, such as group organization, staff assignments, technical help, resource delivery, and so on, which must be prepared to ensure smooth network-based or distance learning deployment.

The MISA Learning Engineering process produces specifications grouped in documentation called Design Elements (DEs), resulting from sub-tasks in the six phases presented in Fig 9.2. These DEs are also organized according to the four axes within each phase. Presently, MISA 4.0 comprises 35 basic sub-tasks, each producing one DE, numbered, as shown in Table 9.1, from 100 to 640. The first digit denotes the phase, the second, the axis or model, and the third, the sequence number within the axis.

The first task in each axis (shown in Table 9.1) aims to define orientation principles pertinent to the axis model and based on the general principles stated in the Problem Definition phase. These principles help define one or more graphical models (***bold italics*** in Table 9.1) built using the MOT+ knowledge representation technique and tool (Paquette 1999; 2002b). Graphical models are the basic DE in each axis, the backbone of the MISA method. Most of the other tasks, in MISA, describe properties of objects in these models (e.g., competencies, learning units, resources, roles) as well as their relationships. MISA also includes revision and validation tasks in phase 5, which allow the cyclic evolution of the learning system design and reduce the risk of costly errors. Phase 6 mainly serves to specify the deployment and delivery aspects of the learning system.

9.3.3 MISA Instructional Model

An Instructional Engineering method like MISA involves the interaction of many specialists such as content experts, instructional designers, media producers and training managers (see also Chap. 15). Each of these main actors is central to one of the four axes, but they all interact and intervene in all axes as well. We will now focus on the instructional model axis, where the instructional designer is the main actor.

In producing design element 220, the instructional designer will set a number of orientation principles, formulate a learning metaphor, identify the type of learning event network or course structure, specify types of learning scenarios, collaboration, content assessment (see Chap. 10), resources, documents, services, the degree to which activities can be customized and any other instructional principles, which could help construct the global learning design corresponding to the educational problem. Seventeen typologies have been thoroughly researched and integrated in the MISA method's support documentation as well as in ADISA.

Based on these principles, the instructional designer will proceed to design element 222, where he or she will construct the learning design's instructional model, called the Learning Event Network, which is a generic term to describe a module, a course, a training program, etc. In LD, it corresponds to the structure of the Method; that is, information on number of Plays, Acts and Activity-structures included in the Unit of Learning.

In MISA, a Learning Event Network is composed of learning events (LEs) and/or learning units (LUs) (which are terminal learning events), resources, links and rules. Composition links (C) are used to represent the hierarchy of nested learning events, also seen as the course structure. The precedence (P) link is used to indicate whether an LE/LU is a prerequisite to another. Resources are inputs (link I/P going in) to LEs/LUs or their products (link I/P going out). Rules express the conditions applied (link R) to LEs/LUs: for instance, a choice to be made between alternative LEs/LUs or a specification of the kind of evaluation, collaboration or adaptation that will take place during the LE/LU.

Table 9.1. MISA 4.0 Design Elements/tasks and products by axes

Problem Definition	
100 Organization's Training System 102 Training Objectives 104 Target Populations 106 Actual Situation 108 Reference Documents	
Knowledge Model	**Instructional Model**
210 Knowledge Model Orientation Principles ***212 Knowledge Model*** 214 Target Competencies ***310 Learning Unit Content*** ***410 Learning Instrument Content*** 610 Knowledge/Competency Management	220 Instructional Principles ***222 Learning Event Network*** 224 Learning Unit Properties ***320 Instructional Scenarios*** 322 Learning Activity Properties 420 Learning Instrument Properties 620 Actors and Group Management
Learning Materials Model	**Delivery Model**
230 Media Principles 330 Development Infrastructure 430 Learning Materials List ***432 Learning Material Models*** 434 Media Elements 436 Source Documents 630 Learning System/Resource Management	240 Delivery Principles 242 Cost-Benefit Analysis 340 Delivery Planning ***440 Delivery Models*** 442 Actors and User's Materials 444 Tools and Telecommunication 446 Services and Delivery Locations 540 Assessment Planning 542 Revision Decisions Log 640 Maintenance/Quality Management

Figure 9.3 shows an example structure of the Course: Equipment Maintenance, which is composed of five modules, where four are terminal LEs and thus called LUs, and one is an LE, decomposed into two LUs.

Each LU consists of one Instructional Scenario describing the relationship among actors (facilitators and learners), activities and resources,. The set of activities performed by learners is called the Learning Scenario. It includes all required and produced resources, links and rules. The set of activities performed by facilitators (e.g. tutors, teachers, evaluators, etc). is called the Assistance Scenario.

The next step is to build a learning scenario model for each LU, where the designer takes into account target and entry as well as prerequisite competencies, which were all defined in the Knowledge Model. Paquette (2001a) shows that it is possible to derive the learning scenario from a generic skill proposed in the target competency (or in a learning objective) for that LU.

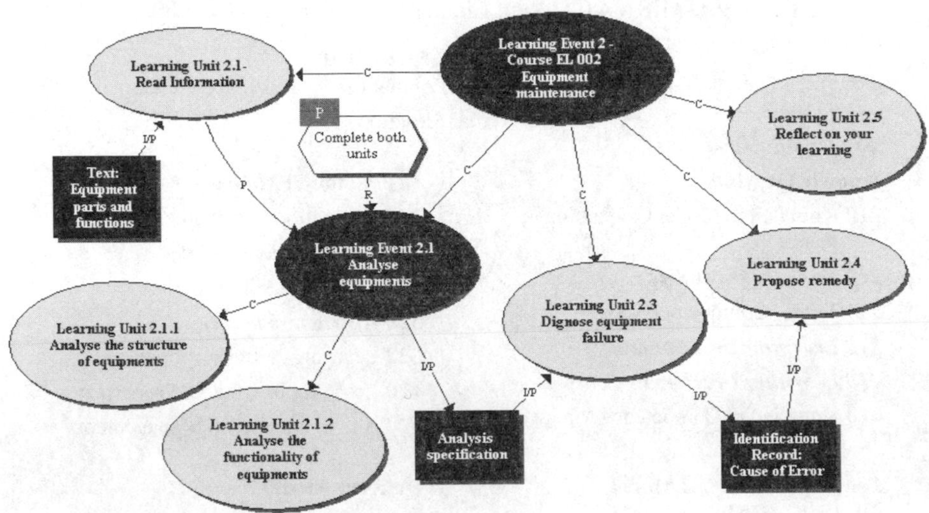

Fig. 9.3. Example of a MISA Learning Event Network

For example, if a target competency states that learners should learn to diagnose equipment failures, a generic diagnostic process will provide a workflow or task model composed of the individual diagnostic tasks including their inputs, products, and control principles[5].

An Assistance Scenario is created when the designer adds an instructional intervention strategy to this basic flow of tasks. For example, in an expository approach, an instructor will use the workflow model to present segments of the diagnostic process. In a constructivist approach, diagnostic problems concerning equipment failure will be proposed to the learners and the instructor will use the diagnostic workflow model to give advice to learners carrying out the tasks.

MOT+ graphical models use ovals to represent procedures. In instructional scenario models, they are used to represent activities that are performed by actor roles that are represented by small hexagons holding the letter L for learner or F for facilitator (equivalent to staff in LD). Rectangles represent resources in the environment, labelled I for instruments, T for tools, S for services and C for communication means. Unmarked resources are outcomes produced by the actor during an activity. White hexagons represent the four kinds of rules labelled P for progression, E for evaluation, C for collaboration and A for adaptation rules. R-links are used to relate actors to activities. For resources an I/P-link is used, ingo-

[5] This approach is similar to the KADS software engineering methodology (Breuker et al. 1999).

ing/outgoing to/from an activity. Activities can be linked to other activities by precedence links (P-link) expressing a sequence of activities. Rules found in the Learning Event Network model are also used in the Instructional Scenario model. Rules of progression, evaluation, collaboration and adaptation are represented by a hexagon and can be R-linked to activities.

Figure 9.4 illustrates a MISA instructional scenario representative of such a workflow model.

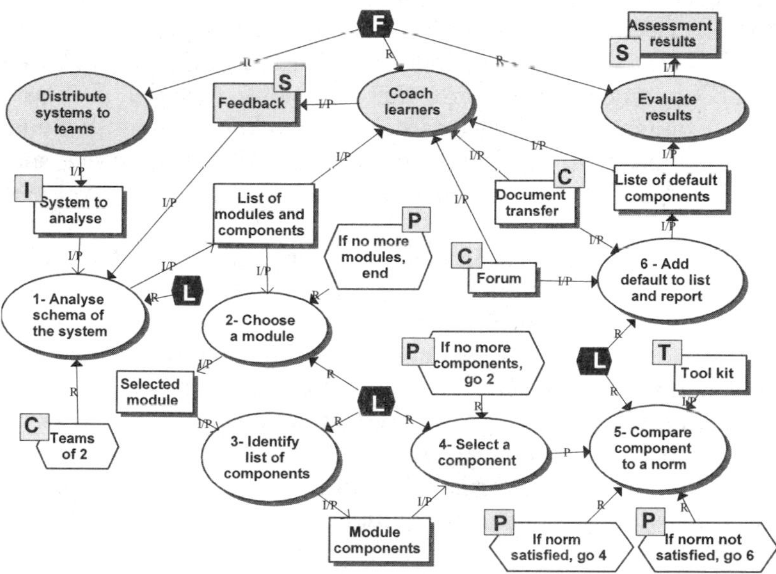

Fig. 9.4. An example of a MISA scenario for learning to diagnose equipment failures

In the learning scenario subset (white ovals), learners (label L) perform six activities, starting with the analysis of an electronic system for troubleshooting. A collaboration rule (label C) states that they work in teams of two. Progression rules (label P) define iterative cycles between activities until the complete electronic system has been analysed. Through these cycles, each team of learners uses learning objects (label I) as inputs and produces intermediate outcomes, which finally results in a list of default components. Using an assistance scenario (grey ovals), facilitators (label F) start by distributing the system to be analysed by the teams of learners, then providing feedback using a forum and document transfer, and finally providing assessment services to learners.

The instructional model encompasses five types of resources: instruments (documents/materials), tools/applications, services, locations (where learning is carried out) and communication means (such as "broadband", mail or face-to-face). These categories are expanded into sub-classes creating a complementary typology to the IEEE LOM Learning Resource typology[6]. In our definition, an instrument is the only type of resource that holds content. More precisely, they are associated to a sub-model in the Knowledge Model. We distinguish the "instrument" concept from the "learning materials" because they can, in general, be produced in different media formats. Usually, instruments are small pieces of information consulted or produced as a result of performing an activity and which, in turn, can be grouped and implemented in one or more media formats (to increase accessibility) to create a certain type of learning material, such as a tutorial, handbook, guide, etc. In particular, evaluation material, such as a questionnaire, exam or essay, is also associated to a knowledge sub-model and the target competencies are linked to the knowledge units in that sub-model. These competencies are the basis on which evaluation is developed and carried out.

The MISA method itself has been modelled using the MOT+ knowledge representation technique and tool. The relationship between MISA's tasks has been clearly and systematically represented using a process graph for each of the tasks. In the MISA documentation, this information is presented in the context table for each DE. Table 9.2 presents this type of contextual information for the task "Define the instructional scenarios", which produces the DE 320 – Instructional scenarios. The list of DE sources on the left includes some input information useful to the task that produces the DE 320; the list of DE sources to the right, uses information provided or produced in task 320.

To support the propagation of data from one design task to another, we have developed a web-based instructional engineering work-bench, ADISA (Distributed Workshop for Engineering Training/Learning Systems). For each DE, the contextual information table uses labels A (automatic), S (source), or I (informative) to indicate which data propagation type is used in ADISA. Propagation is automatic when the data is directly used and necessary to carry out the task in ADISA. Data is displayed in the designer's interface when he or she starts the task. Propagation is semi-automatic when the data from the source needs to be accepted by the designer beforehand. Informative propagation means that the designer may consult some data information that might influence decisions for the task at hand.

---

[6] See LOM (2002), Group Educational 5.2 Learning Resource type: exercise, simulation, questionnaire, diagram, figure, graph, index, slide, table, narrative text, exam, experiment, problem statement, self-assessment and lecture. Interested LD groups propose that this typology should be extended to include for example Unit of Learning and instructional methods.

The design documents of MISA can be edited in a flexible order, according to data propagation rules, and can be modified, published in several stages, stored in archives, displayed on screen or printed. The data in the design documents is translated into a unified XML structure, allowing both on-line and off-line work through an integrated web-based interface.

Table 9.2. A context model for an instructional design task in MISA

Source			→	*Target*		
104	Target Populations		320	222-3	Learning Event Network	
212	Knowledge Model			224-3	Learning Unit Properties	I
214	Target Competencies			230-3	Material Production Orientation Properties	
220	Instructional Model Orientation Principles			240-3	Delivery Orientation Principles	
222	Learning Event Network	A		322	Properties of Each Learning Activity	A
224	Learning Unit Properties			330	Development Infrastructure	
230	Material Production Orientation Properties			340	Delivery Planning	
240	Delivery Orientation Principles			410	Content of the Learning Instruments	A
310	Learning Unit Content			420	Properties of the Instructional Instruments and Guides	

It can be seen as a task map, allowing data propagation from one task interface to another, and also facilitating the information transfer to other systems. Other than supporting the data propagation between and among tasks and elements, ADISA supports the coordination of a group of experts, who plan and develop an instructional learning system, working both on- and off-line.

9.4 Graphical Modelling of Learning Designs

In this section, we situate MISA/MOT+ as an Educational Modelling Language, followed by a presentation of the graphical symbolism integrated into the MOT+ graphical editor. Instructional designers will use this graphical representation language to build an IMS-compliant learning design. Finally, we discuss the advantages of using the MOT+ graphical representation language and tool as well as new features to be added in order to become a fully compliant LD editor.

9.4.1 MISA/MOT+ as an Educational Modelling Language

In a study on educational modelling languages, Rawlings et al. (2002) give the following definition:

> An EML is a semantic information model and binding, describing the content and process within a 'unit-of-learning' from a pedagogical perspective in order to support reuse and interoperability.

According to this definition, MISA's specification of an Instructional Model is a kind of EML. The set of MOT+ models inherent in the Learning Event Network, plus the Instructional Scenarios of each Learning Unit, represented in a graphical way, can be directly compared to a semantic information model describing the content and processes of any unit-of-learning from an Instructional Engineering perspective. The translation of MOT+ models into XML files, automatically or by hand using an XML editor, makes possible interoperability and promotes reusability.

The MOT+ editor, which produces models like Figs. 9.3 and 9.4, has a built-in translator that produces an XML description of any such MOT+ graph. This translator has been used in the ADISA web-based support system to propagate information from one design element to another (Paquette et al. 2001). These XML files list the objects, links, sub-models, their properties and their interrelations. They do not constitute an LD XML binding, and a parser is under development to be added to the MOT+ tool, that can translate these XML structures into which standard machine-readable LD XML files.

9.4.2 A Graphical Language to Represent an LD Method Structure

When activating a Unit of Learning at runtime, the Method part of the XML file is central. This unique element and its sub-elements control the behaviour of the Unit of Learning as a whole, coordinating the activities of the actors in their various roles and their use of resources.

As presented in the previous chapters, and displayed in Fig. 9.5, the Method components, Plays, Acts and Role-parts, are all nested within each other. Plays are alternative scenarios run in parallel, while acts in a play are run in sequence. Within each act, role-parts are run in parallel, associating an actor's role to an activity (or to a more complex activity structure).

Method			
Play 1	Act 1	Role 1	Activity 1
		Role 2	Activity 2
		Role 3	Activity 3
	complete act requirements		
	Act 2	Role 1	Activity 5
		Role 4	Activity 6
	complete act requirements		
complete play requirements			
Play 2	Act 3	Role 1	Activity 9
		Role 3	Activity 10
		Role 4	Activity 11
	complete act requirements		
	Act 4	Role 1	Activity 3
		Role 2	Activity 1
		Role 3	Activity 2
	complete act requirements		
complete play requirements			
complete method (unit of learning) requirements			

Fig. 9.5. An LD Method

Because the MISA/MOT+ graphical representation system is generic, used for many kinds of models, such as representing domain ontologies or delivery process models, the MOT+ editor needs to be constrained in order to facilitate the modelling of LD-compliant Units of Learning. To accommodate all the LD components, a set of graphical conventions has been specified and an LD XML parser for MOT+ is under development. Figure 9.6 displays some of the symbolism used.

Within MOT+, some combinations of specific graphic symbols, labels and links can be used to describing all the LD components and to produce a compliant XML document.

With the MOT+ LD-adapted userinterface, the user will be presented with a Method model consisting of one Play, one Act and one Activity, which is the smallest possible structure for a Unit of Learning.

All procedures, such as the Method, Plays, Act, Activities or Activity structures, are represented as MOT+ procedures (ovals) and organized as a hierarchy using a composition link (C-link). To facilitate the interpretation and visualization of complex models, the activities in an act are embedded in a MOT+ sub-model, instead of being integrated into the main model as shown in Fig. 9.6. The precedence link, P-link, between acts illustrates a sequence of acts or activities. The absence of such links between activities denotes that they can be performed in any order (in parallel). Rules can be added at any level, using a white hexagon symbol, e.g. completion rules at any level.

At the activity (or activity structure) level, role-parts are represented as the combination of a role R-linked to an activity or an activity structure. A shadowed hexagon represents the role, associated by a responsibility R-link from the role to the activity or the activity structure. Icon-labels attached to the role symbol and on the activity symbol indicate whether it is a learner (black dot icon) or staff (white dot icon) role or learning or support activity.

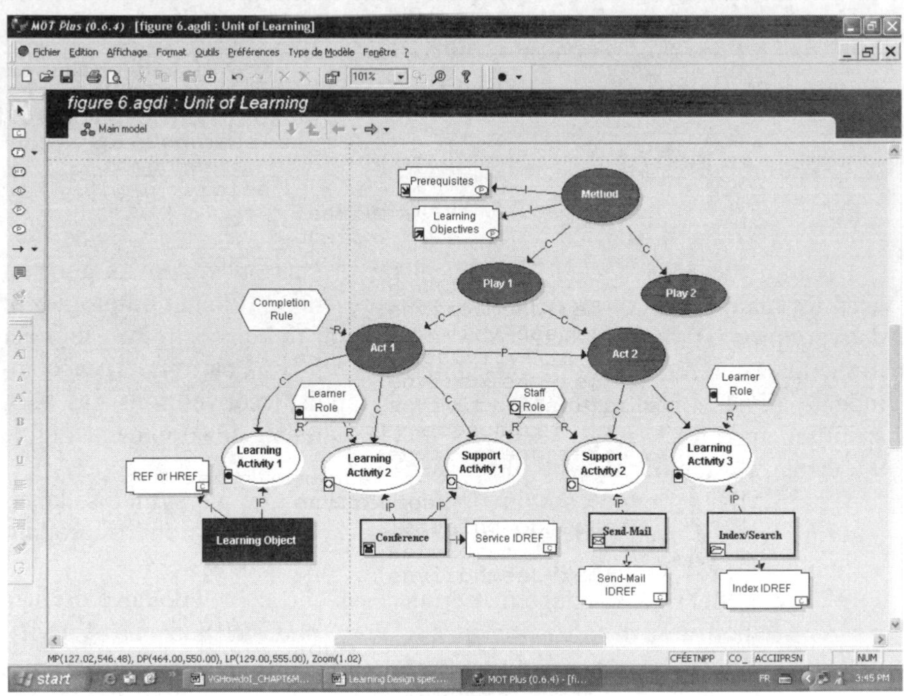

Fig. 9.6. An equivalent MISA/MOT+ model of an LD example

Environments containing learning objects and services are represented as concept objects (rectangles) and associated to activities through an input or product I/P-link, depending on whether they are used to carry out the activity (input), or produced (output) by performing the activity. Note that environments can be composed of many resources and services, which can be organized into a sub-model, using C-links to indicate relationships. Different icon-labels distinguish content resources (white squares) from the three kinds of LD services: conference (telephone icon), email (letter icon) and index-search (folder icon). An internal or external reference can be associated to any resource using an instantiation I-link from the resource to the reference. The reference item is represented by a fact symbol (rectangle with cut angles). Learning Objectives and Prerequisites are represented by a fact symbol bearing an icon-label in the-form-of-upward versus downward-pointing arrows, as shown in Fig. 9.6. To respect the IMS specifications, the designer can only attach these symbols to the Method or to a Learning Activity.

At all levels of the LD structure, time limit completion conditions can be defined using a white hexagon. If this symbol is absent, the parser interprets the completion condition as "user-choice".

9.4.3 Using an MOT+ Editor

Graphical representational techniques and tools will free instructional designers from using XML editors and viewers in order to consult either global or partial views of their design. Although well suited for software engineering purposes, UML graphs and diagrams, as proposed by the LD Best Practice and Implementation Guide, are not suited for instructional design, except maybe in very simple cases. Complex Units of Learning scenarios, especially those involving many actors, are not easily represented using UML graphs and activity diagrams. Moreover, it is important that all the LD components can be integrated using only one type of graphical model. This would greatly reduce the learning curve for designers to acquire a technique for constructing IMS-compatible Learning Designs, which in turn would increases the possibility of interoperability and reusability.

The advantage of a graphical editor as compared to an XML editor is that designs can be structured and easily modified in an iterative manner, which is common practice for instructional designers when developing training courses and programs. An XML editor obliges the designer to declare all components of a Unit of Learning (Roles, Resources and Activities), then to specify the Method structure and finally to list all resource references. In the MOT+ editor, the designer proceeds by constructing the course structure (Method, Plays, Acts, Activities and Activity Structures), then adding environments with their learning objects and services as well as rules for progression and completion in an cyclic fashion. In this way, preliminary designs and milestones can be presented and validated by team members and clients, avoiding both costly and time-consuming redesigns. Once consent is reached, the MOT+ editor allows the designer to save the Unit of Learning as a perfectly compliant LD XML document, ready to be used in a Content Packaging tool (e.g. RELOAD), yet to be developed, or to be instantiated for a run in a compatible Learning Content Management System, such as Explor@2 or ATutor[7].

Many years of modelling courses and programs, for both universities and companies, have shown the MOT+ strength and user-friendliness for non-computer professionals. Furthermore, the object-oriented paradigm (Paquette 1996; 1999), distinguishing objects that represent facts, concepts, procedures and principles related by a standard set of links, is rooted in Instructional Design theories as well as in Information Sciences, and thus provides a strong basis as a notational language for learning designs.

9.5 An LD Case Study

In this last section, we will use the Versailles Experience (LD 2003) to develop and build an LD-compliant Level A Unit of Learning using the MOT+ editor. We will then discuss the design method and tool used to build the model for this case.

9.5.1 The Versailles Narrative

The Versailles Experience (from LD 2003, Best Practice and Implementation Guide) is aimed at 14–16 year-old secondary school students. Participating schools organize students into six groups, one for each of the countries involved in negotiating the original Treaty of Versailles at the end of World War I: Great Britain, USA, Poland, France, Serbia and Italy. The design is based on collaborative learning and the duration is 4 to 6 weeks. The Unit of Learning has three main phases:

- *A preparatory phase* in which students explore the content to find out what their role is, the context of their adopted country and agree on priorities and strategies for the forthcoming negotiation. In this pre-negotiation period participants in each school are organized into the six national negotiating teams, where each participating school is given six passwords, one for each country. These give access to the appropriate materials and a discussion group (dedicated conference)

---

[7] Explor@2 demo at http://lice.teluq.uquebec.ca
and ATutor at http://www.atutor.ca/.

set up for each nation. Ahead of the actual negotiation, the tasks of the national teams are to:

- become familiar with their country's objectives,
- decide on their country's priorities – what they most want and what they can concede,
- become familiar with the objectives of the other countries,
- identify possible negotiating strategies and agree the favoured approach.

- *The negotiation itself.* For the Negotiation Day, there is a main negotiation forum with a conference Chair, but there are also 'side rooms' for each pair of countries to hold private discussions. These are set up as dedicated conferences with appropriate access provided for each team. When agreements are reached during negotiations, they are sent to a person playing the role of a Recorder who posts them on a 'Results Board'. Participants have access to the results at any time. Once the negotiations are completed, or at a given time towards the end of the day, participants are encouraged to review the outcomes of the day.
- *A post-negotiation period* offers the students the opportunity to disseminate what they have learned in the form of web-based materials presenting national perceptions of what the treaty meant to each of the participating nations. In this last phase, students reflect on what they have learned, writing it up from the point of view of what the outcomes mean for their adopted countries. This involves both face-to-face activities in each school as well as using the country team forums. These are then translated into web pages and posted under a preset page for each country. Students then review their collective postings.

9.5.2 An MOT+ Representation of the Versailles Case

We have built an MOT+ model of that learning unit, using the graphical conventions presented in the previous chapter. Because of the complexity of this learning situation, we need to use embedded activity structures (labelled by a bull's-eye icon) using MOT+ sub-models.

The main model presents the Unit of Learning structure, the LD Method. The method is composed of one play divided into eight sequential acts as shown in Fig. 9.7. Each act is described in a sub-model. Acts 1, 2, 4, 5, 7 and 8 are simple acts that are not decomposed further; that is, they do not contain embedded activity-structures, just simple role-plays where a role performs a single learning of staff activity.

Act 4 is an example of a simple act as shown in Fig. 9.8. This sub-model displays one central activity structure performed by two staff roles, a teacher and an expert. The activity structure is composed of six learners' roles and their corresponding learning activities, one for each country. Each national team (hexagon with Country Name) uses a private conference (rectangle with telephone label) to establish the country's negotiation strategy. Results can be accessed by all.

Figure 9.9 presents the main model for Act 6 covering the activities on the negotiation day between the six teams. At the centre, there is an activity structure, "Main_Negotiate", which uses an environment composed of a general conference in which there are two conference activities, actually indicating user-rights for the conference (see LD Information Model section 3.1.11): "moderate" played by a staff person called "Chair", and "participate" played by all learners, plus a teacher and an expert.

The central activity structure is further decomposed into eight other activity structures, all performed in parallel, shown by the absence of precedence (P) links. Six of them correspond to each national team of learners, associated to corresponding role-parts in the activity structure, each developed in a sub-model constituting a third level of models (this is shown by the little model icon on the upper left of the oval).

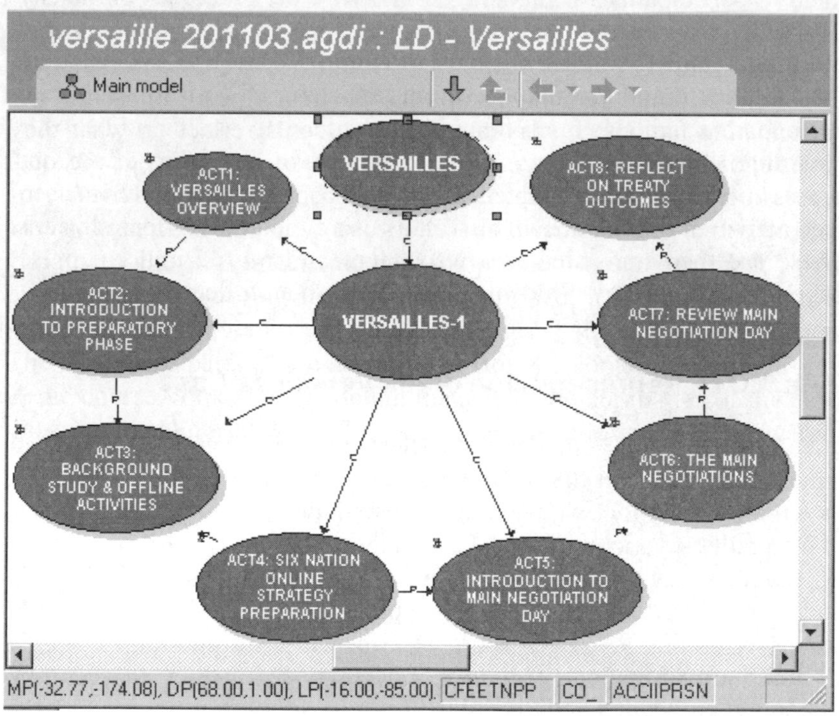

Fig. 9.7. The Versailles main model

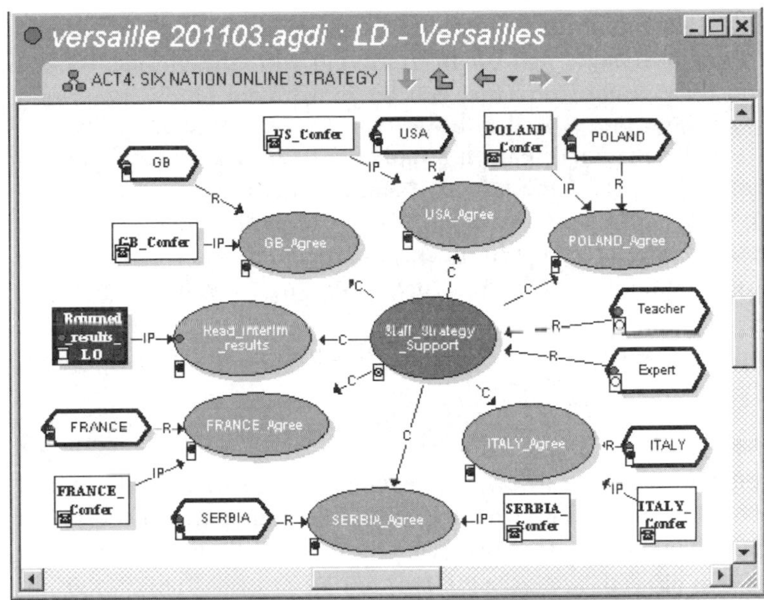

Fig. 9.8. A sub-model for Act 4: SIX NATION ON-LINE STRATEGY

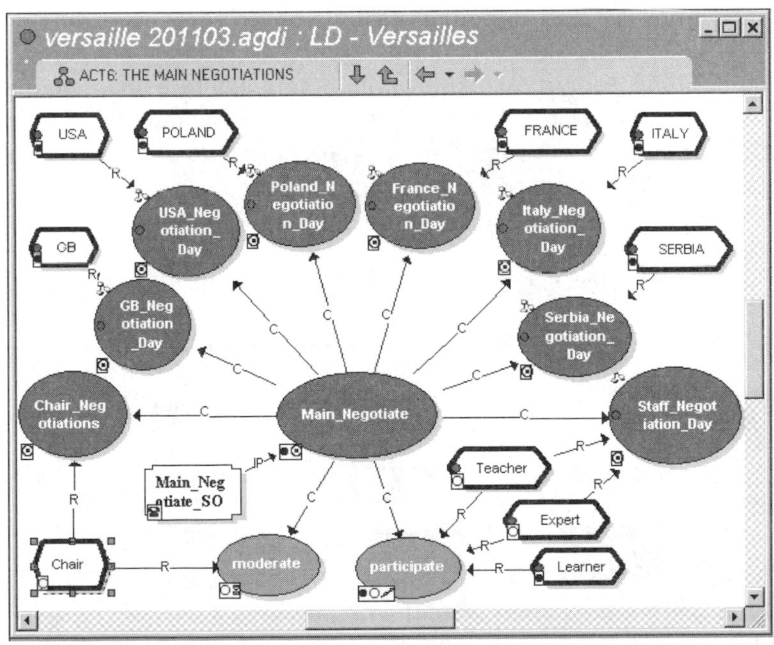

Fig. 9.9. A sub-model for Versailles' Act 6: THE MAIN NEGOTIATIONS

There are two more activity structures: "Chair_Negotiations" performed by the Chair role, and "Staff_Negotiation_Day" performed by Teacher and Expert roles.

Figure 9.10 presents one of the third-level activity structures, the one where the Great Britain (GB) team is involved. The lower part of the figure shows that it is decomposed into five learning activities where the GB team is involved in negotiations with each of the five other teams. For this, specialized conferences are open in the environment and each activity produces five corresponding agreements (the lower dark rectangles = products).

The upper part of the model in Fig. 9.10 illustrates the exchange of information between GB learners and staff.

There are three such learner activities: one where GB learners send the results of their negotiation using an email service, another one where a GB learner, taking the role of a Recorder, receives results in a mailbox and does some web editing, and a last one where this aggregated result is returned to GB learners and staff. Note that since GB learners are associated to the central activity structure, it is not necessary to repeat this association for the other learner activities. By default, it is inherited through the C-link.

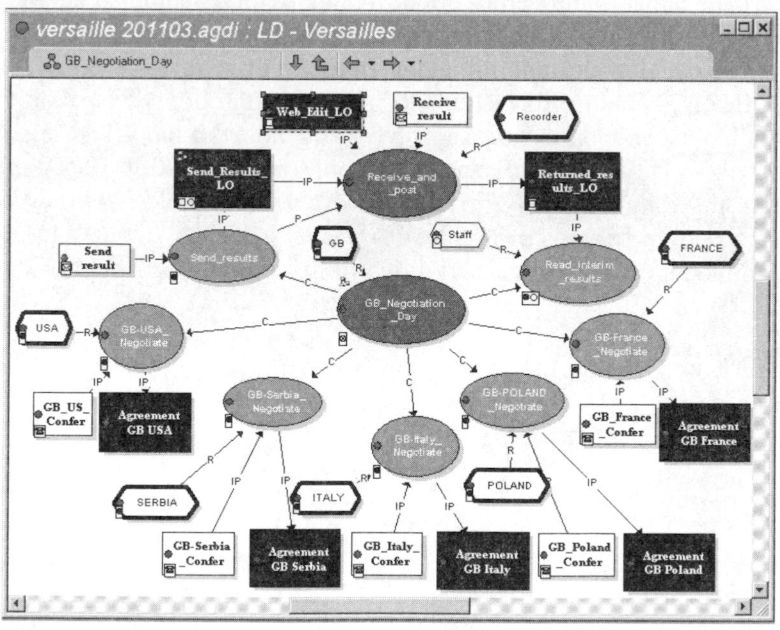

Fig. 9.10. A sub-sub-model for Activity structure: GB_NEGOTIATION_DAY

9.5.3 Discussion of the Case

This case is probably one of the most complex Unit of Learning scenarios that have been developed so far. In the classroom, a teacher would probably spend many hours explaining it to the learners. Collaborative scenarios like the Versailles example may have great learning benefits, but are difficult to implement in a classroom and even more so in network-based environments.

The advantage of providing a structural graphical model is that it can also serve as a task guide for both students and teachers, thus avoiding lengthy and repeated explanations.

The modelling of learning designs brings the greatest benefits, when the learning situations involve multiple roles, where the activities are not sequential, and where their results are reinvested in other activities. The process of building a model helps the designer to clarify his or her ideas and communicate them to the learners, whether in a class or acting as an on-line coach.

But there is more to it. If machine support is expected in a computerized networked environment, it is essential to formalize the flow of activities and precisely identify the actors, their roles as well as the resources used or produced in the environment. Once the graphical formalization is done, it can automatically be translated into LD XML machine-readable code, without direct intervention from the designer.

9.6 Conclusion

The adoption, at the end of 2002, by IMS of EML as the basis for a standard specification is great progress. It enables knowledge-based instructional engineering methods, like MISA, to produce learning designs that can potentially be read by any compliant LCMS, as is discussed in the following chapters describing case studies.

We have shown that the LD specification and the MISA method complement each other, by proposing an instructional engineering method in six phases, specifying four axes through the elaboration of a knowledge and competency model, a pedagogical model, as well as resulting learning material and delivery models. The LD specification provides a standardized formal and machine-readable representation of a learning design, whereas MISA proposes a systemic and systematic method to design and implement such learning designs. The MOT+ graphical editor, used to implement the MISA method, also appears as a promising alternative to UML modelling, mainly because it is rooted in instructional design theory and has been built with education and training applications in mind.

In 2004, we are completing the integration of LD-related tools in the eduSource[8] Suite of Tools application, which already contains an implementation of standards for learning objects, repository interoperability. In the five-year term of the LORNET[9] project, we will be working to extend the LD specification to more general function or workflow models (Paquette and Rosca 2002), and to adapt our Explor@2 delivery system to fully exploit the multi-actor concept claimed by the LD specification.

On a larger scale, we believe that international standardization efforts should focus on the very important question of the association of knowledge and competencies to the LD method components. In a semantic web perspective, this is an essential task where strong international collaboration is needed.

[8] eduSource is a large Canadian project that is implementing many IMS specifications and in which our group is responsible for the integration of the open-source software infrastructure (www.edusource.ca).
[9] LORNET is a new 5-year Canadian Research Network (www.lornet.org).

10 Integrating Assessment into E-learning Courses

Desirée Joosten-ten Brinke[1], Pierre Gorissen[2], Ignace Latour[3]

[1] Educational Technology Expertise Centre,
Open University of the Netherlands, Heerlen, The Netherlands

[2] Fontys University of Professional Education, Eindhoven,
The Netherlands

[3] CITO, Arnhem, The Netherlands

10.1 Introduction

Assessment is an integral part of learning, requiring learners to demonstrate the knowledge or skills they have acquired throughout the course. In this chapter, we focus not only on summative assessments, which are given at the end of a course, but also on formative assessments, that is to say, the use of assessments *throughout* the course whereby students are informed how to improve their learning by being given constructive feedback. The feedback in formative assessments is meant to guide students' learning. Also, their results can lead to a better understanding of personal educational needs.

The design of assessments should concur with the design of instruction and learning. Thus, the Learning Design specification (LD 2003) enables developers to formalize learning and the Question and Test Interoperability specification (QTI 2003) enables the formalization of testing.

The first part of this chapter will introduce assessment and its relation to learning design. Subsequently, the second part of the chapter presents the QTI specification and the structures and features it provides for describing assessments. Examples of how QTI and LD structures can be integrated will be shown and explained. Even though there is as yet no normative description of this integration available, the examples will clarify how both specifications enhance each other and how they interact. Their possibilities and impossibilities will be illustrated, using the two specifications in their current form, QTI version 2.0 and LD 1.0.

The last part considers a possible integration of LD and QTI with the four processes of assessment.

10.2 Assessment: an Integral Part of the Design of Learning and Instruction

In this chapter we will address the issue of how to integrate assessments into learning designs. Before reaching a solution, however, we will first discuss some developments in the field of assessment. Twenty years ago, considering assessment to be a part of learning was not that obvious. Before 1985 the "evaluation" and "measuring" tradition maintained that objectivity could only be achieved if the process of investigating the attainment of a student was kept separate from the instruction. On the other hand, the "mastery" tradition considered that the two were inseparable (Ewell 2003). At the time, assessment was the concluding activity of a study period. Once students passed the exam, they got a certificate or diploma and could continue to a following or a different course. Failing the exam often meant that the course had to be re-done in the same way. No personal feedback for future learning was given.

The word *assessment* was used separately for psychological tests and traditional assessment centres. In an educational context the word *testing* was most frequently used in the sense of measuring to see if students knew what they had learned. Later, assessment in the educational sense was introduced to distinguish between testing in traditional instructional models, on the one hand, and new 'student-centred' instructional models, like problem-based learning or competence-based learning, on the other. Traditional instructional models are based on (teacher-centred) knowledge transfer. Biggs (1999) describes the new learning as a system in which all activities, i.e. teaching, learning and assessment (formative as well as summative), interact. There must be an alignment between curriculum objectives, teaching and learning activities and assessment tasks.

This new mode of teaching also necessitates another way of testing. Segers et al. (2003) give a summary of the most important shifts in assessment:

- from atomic, objective tests towards more authentic, contextualized performance tests
- from simple marking to making a profile based on multiple measures
- from lower to higher levels of competence testing
- from testing only cognition to testing meta-cognition, affective and social dimensions

- from isolated assessment to assessment integrated into the learning process
- from teacher responsibility towards student responsibility in the learning and assessment process
- from assessment *of* learning towards assessment *for* learning.

The Assessment Reform Group (2002), a workgroup of the British Educational Research Association, explains this last point as a process of seeking and interpreting evidence for use by learners and their teachers in order to decide where learners are in their learning, where they need to go and how best to get there.

This new assessment paradigm implies assessment forms including performance assessment, authentic assessment, portfolio assessment, peer assessment, self-assessment, collaborative assessment. A good assessment covers a student's total competence and requires combinations of test forms. While such tools as interviews, learner reports and 360 degree feedback instruments are preferably used, multiple-choice questions and essay questions can also be used, e.g. in self-assessments or peer assessments.

In this chapter we use assessment for "all methods and models in which students have to perform tasks to determine information on their study process and progress, for themselves or others, for reasons of certification, placement or diagnosis, both in formative and in summative ways".

Assessment can be embedded in a learning design by having students perform tasks in which the performance gives evidence of their competence. These tasks are the basis for their learning activities. Initially, these tasks will be learning tasks, whereby students get support from a tutor or peer students. However, throughout the learning process the students must also perform the tasks on their own, as assessment tasks. This process can be described either in single-learner scenarios or multi-learner scenarios (Tattersall 2004a). Examples of the former include:

- checking learners' level of understanding before sending them down a particular learning path (intake assessment)
- checking whether a concept has been learned before allowing the learner to progress
- providing modules with a high level of feedback to keep motivation high
- ending courses with examinations.

Examples of multi-learner scenarios include:

- revealing individuals' answers to a group in order to promote discussion and learning

- arranging for peer assessment
- dividing a set of students into several groups of more or less equally able students
- dividing a group of students into sub-groups having people of differing levels of ability
- giving the best/worst performer in a group a particular role in a learning design.

The development of adequate assessments is a complex and expensive activity. However, the costs can be reduced by exchanging assessments, or parts of them, with colleagues in the same content domain. Assessment parts which are to be exchanged need to be described in a common format. Preferably, this would have to be an open, vendor-independent, standardized format. Various possibilities for this standardization will be outlined in the next section.

10.3 Standardisation of Assessments in Learning Design

There are two IMS specifications which are of particular concern for enabling the exchange of assessments: they are the LD specification and the QTI specification. Although there are other specifications and standards related to assessment, such as ePortfolio and Learner Information Package (LIP 2001), we will focus on the role LD and QTI play as formats for describing assessment integrated in a Unit of Learning (UOL).

LD supports the use of a wide range of pedagogical approaches in online learning, since it is a specification that enables the interoperability of learning designs. The specification is based on a social model, where different roles and activities are related. LD is used to model units of learning. A unit of learning is a delimited piece of education or training, such as a course, a module or a lesson. Such units consist of activities, assessments, services and support facilities provided by teachers, trainers and other staff members.

The predecessor of LD, the Educational Modelling Language (EML 2000), developed by the Open University of the Netherlands (OUNL), contains specific elements for assessments. Hermans et al. (2000) evaluated whether EML could support different forms of assessment. They made a subdivision in classical testing methods and alternative assessments. The authors concluded that EML could in fact model most of the classical item types (like multiple choice question, multiple response question, question answer and true–false question sequence question, matching question, short-answer question, prompt).

For assessment to be embedded in a unit of learning, it is not only the item types which must be modelled, but also the processes (like the ones described in the previous paragraph). Therefore, the study also looked at the possibilities of these formative assessments in which the processes in assessment are more important. Hermans et al. elaborated on an example of an assessment. The assessment process mentioned at the end of the previous paragraph can be modelled in EML (see Fig. 10.1).

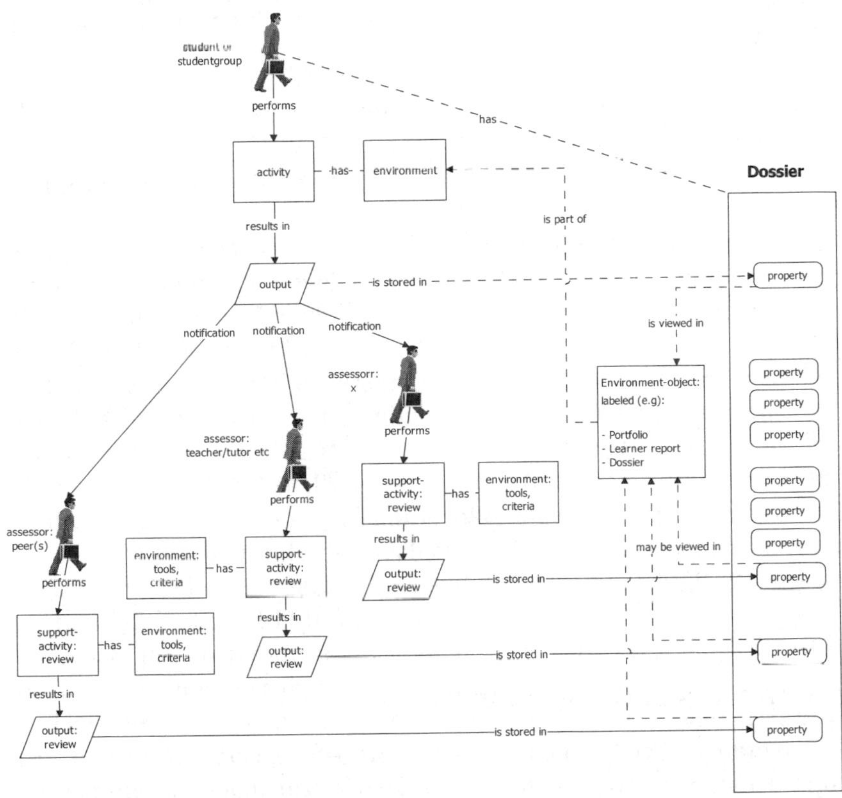

Fig. 10.1. Basic model of alternative assessment in EML

The language EML formed the basis for the LD specification; in 2002 the OUNL ceased further development of EML in favour of LD. A number of existing IMS specifications influenced the development of LD, notably the use of the Content Packaging specification as the container for the learning designs and the use of the QTI specification instead of the EML specific interaction types. Assessment, in LD, has no specific labelled elements, but is part of the environment of a learning activity. It is here that the elements of the QTI specification can be referenced.

In the next section we will first introduce the QTI specification before explaining how it can be integrated with the LD specification.

10.3.1 What Is QTI?

QTI is a specification that enables the exchange of questions (`assessmentItems`) and tests (`assessments`), including the results of these assessments. This exchange takes place between Learning Management Systems, as well as between Test Content Management Systems, tools to create tests, content authors and collections of test items.

QTI is designed to provide a well-documented content format for storing items independent of the authoring tool used to create them; to support the deployment of items and item banks across a wide range of learning and assessment delivery systems; and to provide systems with the ability to report results in a consistent manner.

The core data object within the QTI specification is the `assessmentItem` that contains the actual question, answer options, information about the correct answer, and scoring scenarios. An item is the smallest possible object in the QTI specification and cannot be nested, i.e. an item cannot contain another item. An *assessment* contains the collection of items used to determine the level of mastery that a participant has of a particular subject. Figure 10.2 gives this relation between `assessment` and `assessmentItem`.

10.3.2 Principles of QTI

Core Structures of QTI Version 2.0

All QTI version 2.0 (QTI 2004) items adhere to a specific core structure. Figure 10.3 shows the base elements available in that structure.

In the response declaration (`responseDeclaration`) section of the item, the response variables are declared so that its identifier, the cardinality and its base type are known. A response declaration may assign an optional *correctResponse*. This value indicates the correct value for the response of the candidate.

The outcome declaration (`outcomeDeclaration`) section contains the declarations for the outcomes (e.g. SCORE) returned for the question, including an optional default value for that outcome variable. The stem of the question and the possible interactions (e.g. the answer options of a multiple choice question) are located in the item body (`itemBody`).

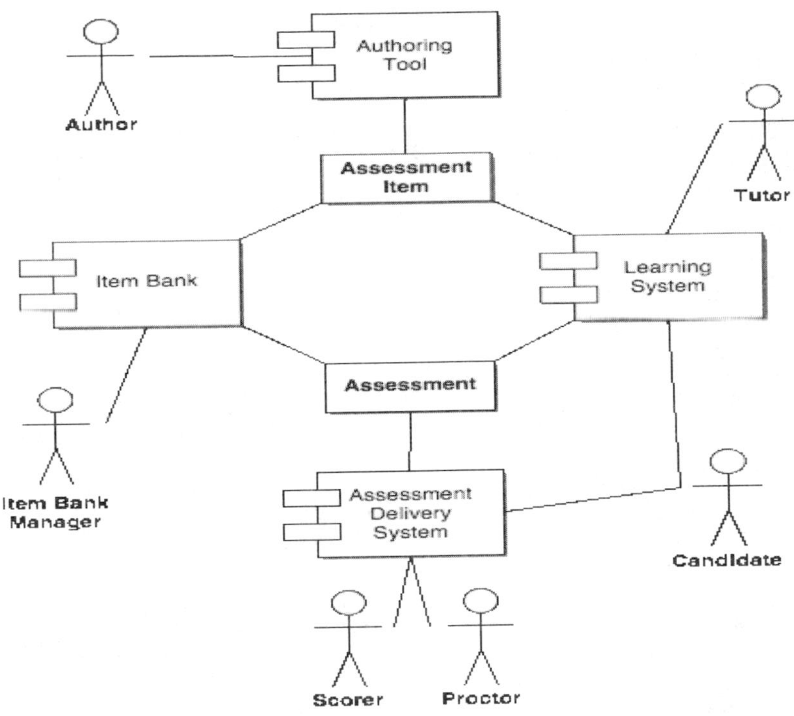

Fig. 10.2. Overview of the role of `assessment` and `assessmentItems` (QTI 2003)

When the candidate has selected one or more of the possible answer options to a question, the outcome variables are set by the rules in the response procession (`responseProcessing`) section of the item.

Version 2.0 of the QTI specification allows for advanced and complex response processing, as well as permitting the use of simple, built-in processing.

The XML code in example 10.1 contains all core elements of Fig. 10.3 and defines a complete multiple choice question (*What does the acronym LD stand for?*) with three answer options and the response processing. The example does not show feedback to the candidate. Readers familiar with the previous versions of QTI will recognize the improved clarity of the XML code. The example uses one of the default response processing options provided, which assigns the value 1 to the outcome variable SCORE, if the correct response (ChoiceB) is selected and assigns the value 0 to the outcome variable SCORE if one of the other choices has been selected. The use of templates eliminates any unnecessary duplication of XML code defining response processing.

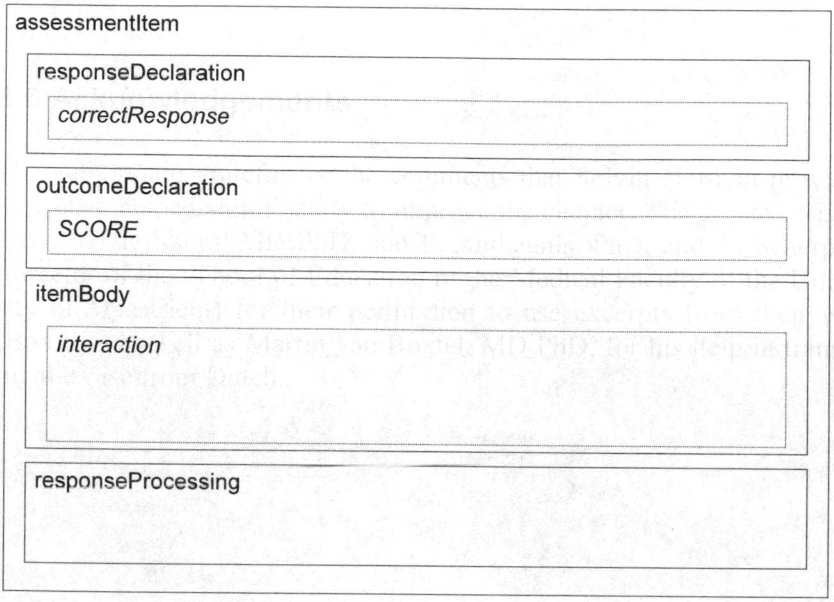

assessmentItem

responseDeclaration

correctResponse

outcomeDeclaration

SCORE

itemBody

interaction

responseProcessing

Fig. 10.3. Structure of an example of a single QTI version 2 `assessmentItem`

Example 10.1

```
<?xml version="1.0" encoding="UTF-8"?>
<assessmentItem identifier="choice" title="Simple LD ques-
tion" adaptive="false" timeDependent="false">
  <responseDeclaration identifier="RESPONSE" cardinal-
ity="single" baseType="identifier">
    <correctResponse>
      <value>ChoiceB</value>
    </correctResponse>
  </responseDeclaration>
  <outcomeDeclaration identifier="SCORE" cardinality="single"
baseType="integer">
    <defaultValue>
      <value>0</value>
    </defaultValue>
  </outcomeDeclaration>
  <itemBody>
    <choiceInteraction responseIdentifier="RESPONSE" shuf-
fle="true" maxChoices="1">
     <prompt>What does the acronym LD stand for?</prompt>
     <simpleChoice identifier="ChoiceA">Learning and Do-
ing</simpleChoice>
```

```
     <simpleChoice identifier="ChoiceB">Learning De-
sign</simpleChoice>
     <simpleChoice identifier="ChoiceC">Let's Do
it!</simpleChoice>
    </choiceInteraction>
  </itemBody>
  <responseProcessing tem-
plate="http://www.imsglobal.org/xml/imsqti_item_v2p0/rpMatchC
orrect" templateLocation="RPTemplates/rpMatchCorrect.xml"/>
  </assessmentItem>
```

Example 10.2 shows the XML code defining the response processing referenced in Example 10.1. If more complex response processing is needed, e.g. if partial credit for other answer options is to be rewarded, a custom response processing structure can be defined instead of the default template used in Example 10.1.

Example 10.2

```
<?xml version="1.0" encoding="UTF-8"?>
<responseProcessing>
<responseCondition>
 <responseIf>
  <match>
   <variable identifier="RESPONSE"/>
   <correct identifier="RESPONSE"/>
  </match>
  <setOutcomeValue identifier="SCORE">
   <baseValue baseType="integer">1</baseValue>
  </setOutcomeValue>
 </responseIf>
 <responseElse>
  <setOutcomeValue identifier="SCORE">
   <baseValue baseType="integer">0</baseValue>
  </setOutcomeValue>
 </responseElse>
</responseCondition>
</responseProcessing>
```

Rendering of QTI Items

Though the content model for QTI version 2 has been defined as XHTML code only, which no longer allows the use of, for example, RTF code, the QTI player still has a number of options for rendering questions. For example, the multiple choice question (Example 10.1) might be rendered as a list with radio buttons, as displayed in Fig. 10.4.

Another possibility is that these answer options can be selected by clicking on the answer, highlighting it, as shown by a screen print of the Canvas Learning Flash player for QTI (Fig. 10.5; Canvas Learning 2004).

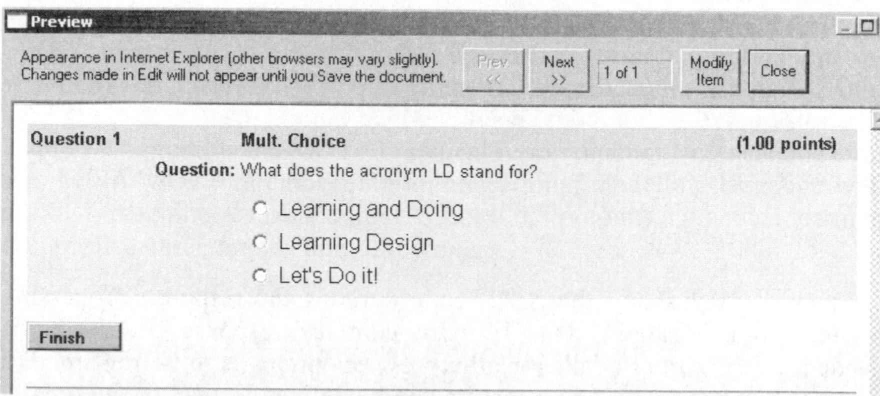

Fig. 10.4. The screen print of the question in the Respondus tool (2004)

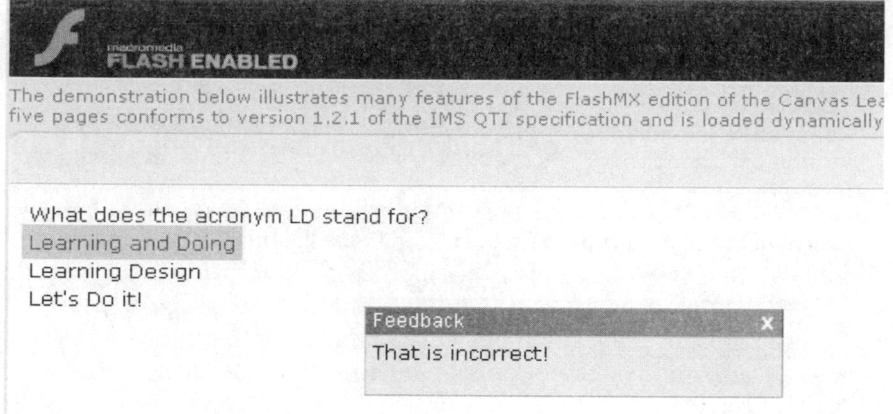

Fig. 10.5. A screen print of the Canvas Learning Flash player for QTI (Canvas Learning 2004)

Both are equally valid choices. This should be kept in mind while designing an QTI item; hints like *click on the radio button in front of the correct answer option* should be avoided. Instead, more neutral hints like *select the correct answer option* should be used.

Implementing QTI

The first official release of the QTI specification dates from May 2000. The most current release is version 2.0, which is a significant change from the previous 1.*x* versions. Because QTI has been around for a while and has reached a certain stability, there are an increasing number of tools which support the specification. These tools support both the creation of questions and tests as well as the actual testing process. While QTI has the reputation of being complex and somewhat difficult to implement, it is also regarded as an extensive specification.

As the level of support for previous versions of the specification differed, there was a lot of room for improvement. A quick scan of nine applications used within the Dutch Digital University (Gorissen 2003a) revealed that it is possible to construct a basic set of QTI version 1.2 questions, which can be imported by all the applications supporting QTI in one way or the other. However, as soon as more than just the basic elements of QTI version 1.2 were used, one or more of the applications failed to import correctly and/or interpret the QTI files. None of the applications had support for import/export of QTI version 1.2 sections, assessment or metadata.

Things are improving, however. A growing number of people are demanding QTI support and/or implementing better support for it. For example, the TOIA system (TOIA 2003) is completely based on QTI and the project has committed itself to build the optimal QTI import/export function into the system. The SToMP (Software Teaching of Modular Physics) project (SToMP 2004) developed a tool for teaching introductory-level undergraduate physics, extending QTI with a number of advanced variable processing features. CETIS (2002) is doing boundary testing of QTI, which will provide a good, yet not too elaborate, test set which can be used to test the QTI systems support. The Canvas Learning QTI player (Canvas Learning 2004) offers support for many of the things the other players were missing in the original quick scan (Gorissen 2003b).

Most importantly, though, QTI version 2.0, released in 2004, provides implementers, tool vendors and educational technologists with a specification that is simpler, still powerful, easier to implement and less ambiguous to interpret.

Integrating QTI and LD

As explained in the assessment section of this chapter, the LD specification does not have native elements for questions and tests. Instead, it relies on the integration of QTI. An example of this integration will be shown below (Tattersall 2004b).

The integration of LD and QTI revolves around properties and variables, and could be called a lexical integration. Essentially, when property identifiers and variable names are declared to be lexically identical at design time (i.e. in LD-based and QTI-based XML), they are considered to be a shared variable in runtime software environments which involve LD and QTI-based processes. Because properties are being used to store the values returned by the QTI item, the example implies units of learning at LD Level B or C. When multiple QTI items are used in combination with the same UOL, there may be a problem with duplicate variable names. More than one QTI item might use the variable SCORE to store the candidate's score for that question. The approach recommended by the QTI version 2 specification is to create compound identifiers for use as LD property names. This is done by combining the resource identifier, associated with the content package resource containing the QTI item, as a prefix to the variable name, using a period as separator. This approach is illustrated below.

In a typical example (Example 10.3), learning designers might create a property called SCORE to hold the result of the QTI test.

Example 10.3

```
<imsld:properties>
  <imsld:locpers-property identifier="Q_1.SCORE">
    <imsld:title>The result for the test</imsld:title>
    <imsld:datatype datatype="integer"/>
    <imsld:initial-value>0</imsld:initial-value>
  </imsld:locpers-property>
</imsld:properties>
```

In this example, a local personal LD property Q_1.SCORE, which has an initial value of 0, is being declared. This property is being used in the code shown in Example 10.4 to set the completion of a learning activity *LA-1*. If the value of Q_1.SCORE is 1, the status of the learning activity is set to completed. The property name Q_1.SCORE is formed by using the resource identifier of the content package resource which references the QTI item (Q_1, see also Example 10.6), together with the QTI variable name, separated by a period (SCORE, see Example 10.3).

Example 10.4

```
<imsld:learning-activity isvisible="true" identifier="LA-1">
     <imsld:title>Complete the question</imsld:title>
     <imsld:environment-ref ref="E-1"/>
     <imsld:activity-description>
       <imsld:title>Check your knowledge of LD</imsld:title>
       <imsld:item identifier="I-1" identifierref="R-1"/>
     </imsld:activity-description>
     <imsld:complete-activity>
       <imsld:when-property-value-is-set>
         <imsld:property-ref ref="Q_1.SCORE"/>
         <imsld:property-value>1</imsld:property-value>
       </imsld:when-property-value-is-set>
     </imsld:complete-activity>
   </imsld:learning-activity>
</imsld:complete-activity>
```

The question the candidate has to answer is referenced in the environment for the learning activity (Example 10.5).

Example 10.5
```
<imsld:environment identifier="E-1">
 <imsld:title>Simple Test</imsld:title>
     <imsld:learning-object identifier="LO-QTI-I1">
      <imsld:title>LD basic question</imsld:title>
      <imsld:item identifier="I-Q1" identifierref="Q_1"/>
     </imsld:learning-object>
</imsld:environment>
```

The environment does not contain the actual code of the QTI item, but references a resource in the resources section, which in turn points to the actual XML file (Example 10.6). In that file the response variable SCORE (see Example 10.1) is set to 1 when the correct answer is selected.

Example 10.6
```
<imscp:resource identifier="Q_1" type="imsqti_item_xmlv2p0">
 <imscp:file href="choice_01.xml"/>
 <imscp:file href="RPTemplates/rpMatchCorrect.xml"/>
</imscp:resource>
```

Multiple Rendering Engines

When QTI code is integrated or referenced from within a learning design, the QTI code also needs to be rendered in a form which can be displayed by a runtime environment, in most cases (X)HTML for use in an Internet browser. Figure 10.6 shows the rendering process. However, this functionality is not expected to be integrated into future LD rendering software. It makes (more) sense to have renderers for the different specifications used and have the runtime environment coordinate the rendering tasks by assigning the appropriate rendering engine for each content type.

In practice this should not make any difference to learning designers designing educational content, since the process should be hidden from them by the shared layer that renders the user interface (GUI layer). In general, however, it does mean users should be aware of the need for modular systems during initial design or of selection of their learning environments.

10.4 The Four Processes in Assessment

It is our view that a conceptual framework for assessment would be very helpful in finding solutions for the absent support for the integration of learning and assessment in a (blended) learning environment.

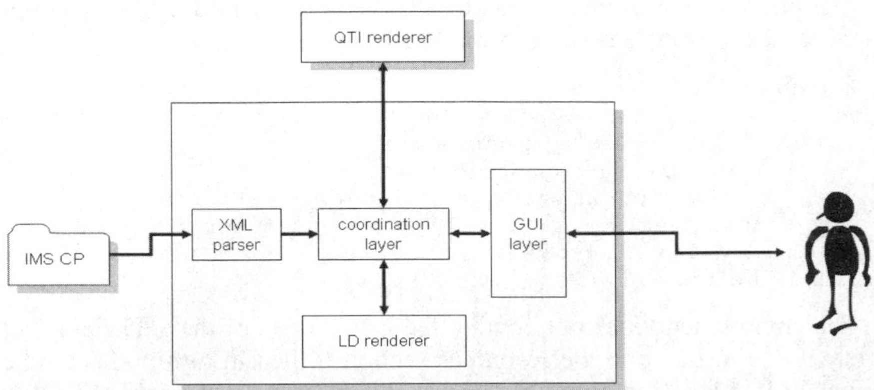

Fig. 10.6. The rendering process

The development of such a conceptual model is one step towards developing tools and practices and the next generation of specifications, in which the assessment and learning process descriptions are optimized to work together in an integrated way.

An underlying model of the testing process for the QTI specification is the Evidence-Centered Design Framework (ECD), employed by the Educational Testing Service (ETS) for developing educational assessments (Mislevy 2000; Almond et al. 2002). This model consists of four processes required for each assessment: "activity selection", "presentation", "response processing" and "summary scoring".

The ECD framework describes a process which begins by defining the decisions to be made based upon the results of an assessment. It then works backwards to develop tasks, delivery mechanisms, scoring procedures, and feedback mechanisms to provide evidence informing the predefined purpose of the assessment. The main processes and elements in the architecture are depicted in Fig. 10.7 (from Almond et al. 2002).

We take this framework to present a more general view of the total assessment process. Mislevy (2000) focuses on the delivery system taken in the assessment. As we have seen, there are also assessment types where an assessment delivery system is not (only) responsible. Many newer types, like performance assessments and portfolio assessments, are based on more human interaction – especially in the judging process.

Within this framework the word "task" is used instead of question or item. The activity selection process can take place in different ways and at different levels, either within the QTI code or from within LD.

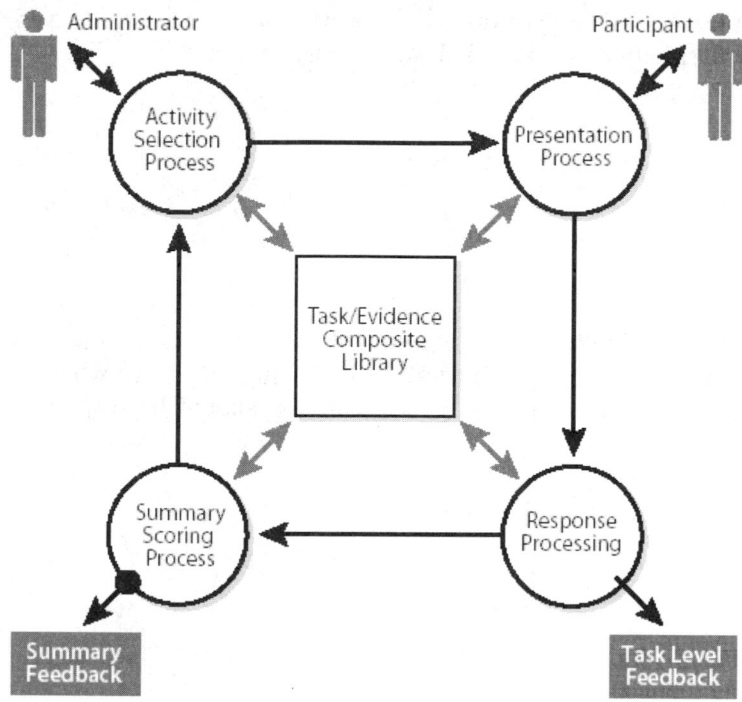

Fig. 10.7. The four principal processes in the assessment cycle

LD is designed as an integrative layer in which information expressed in other XML document types, such as QTI, can become part of the LD document by name spacing. Now that we are integrating QTI and LD we have to find out how information is expressed in one or both of these specifications. From the viewpoint of the four main processes of assessment we can distinguish different types of assessment and thus different expression types. In the next four scenarios we describe how we can use LD or QTI in relation to the ECD framework.

Scenario 1

In Scenario 1, students take a summative assessment at the end of a course (a Play), to decide which learning design they should continue with. In this scenario, the summative assessment is referenced from the environment of the learning design (Example 10.7). The assessment itself is expressed in QTI and returns one final score. This score is stored in an LD property, called A_1.SCORE (see Example 10.3), with the resource identifier for the assessment being A_1. The QTI document is part of the package and is referenced in the resources section as shown in Example 10.6.

Example 10.7

```
<imsld:environment identifier="E-1">
 <imsld:title>A Summative assessment</imsld:title>
     <imsld:learning-object identifier="LO-QTI-A1">
       <imsld:title>LD Assessment</imsld:title>
       <imsld:item identifier="I-A1" identifierref="A_1"/>
     </imsld:learning-object>
</imsld:environment>
```

The resulting A_1.SCORE for the assessment can then be used to decide whether the play can be set to completed (as in Example 10.4) or whether the next activity structure or rather a remedial step should be displayed (Example 10.8).

Example 10.8

```
<conditions>
<if>
   <greater-than>
     <property-ref ref="A_1.SCORE"/>
     <property-value>5</property-value>
   </greater-than>
  </if>
  <then>
   <show>
     <activity-structure-ref ref="AS-next-step"/>
   </show>
  </then>
  <else>
   <show>
     <activity-structure-ref ref="AS-remedial-step"/>
   </show>
  </else>
</conditions>
```

All four processes of the assessment cycle in this scenario are expressed in QTI (see also Mislevy 2000). The reference to the assessment and the conditions for the next step are expressed in LD, but the assessment itself, the items and responses and response processing, stays hidden from the LD designer.

Scenario 2

In a second scenario, students are offered tasks (implemented as QTI items) during the course, which are scored directly and which will give feedback in relation to their level of ability for the task.

In this scenario the reference to one or more tasks is expressed in LD, whereas the tasks themselves are expressed in QTI. From the assessment cycle the process of activity selection and summary scoring will not be implemented in QTI. The XML code for this scenario is very similar to the code for the first scenario, but now the sequencing, ordering and selection of the individual items are handled in the LD code and individual items are referenced as previously shown in Example 10.1. As in Scenario 1, the score resulting from the response processing is returned and stored in a local personal property. This scenario gives the LD designer more control over the assessment, but should only be used if really necessary, since it results in more complex LD code.

Scenario 3

The previous two scenarios both assumed that the response processing of the assessment and the individual items could be handled by the computer. That is of course not always the case. At the moment, for instance, essays or reports cannot be scored by the computer and need human intervention. This can be done by tutors, teachers or peers. The LD code can either reference complete assessments for the scenario (as in Scenario 1) or individual items (as in Scenario 2). Although the presentation process of the assessment cycle is still expressed in QTI, the response processing takes place within the context of the LD environment. The most important difference in this case is that it is not only the score which is returned, but also the response for those items requiring a human scorer. The content of the response can be simple text, a file reference or an object possibly containing a graphic or a drawing. The response, once received by LD, needs to be stored in a global personal attribute (Example 10.9), so that it can be made available to the human scorer.

Example 10.9

```
<globpers-property identifier="GP-RESPONSE-GUID">
     <global-definition uri="GP-RESPONSE-GUID">
       <title>My response to task 1</title>
       <datatype datatype="file"/>
     </global-definition>
</globpers-property>
```

Note that LD, much like QTI, has the `set-property` element which can be used for uploading files or for entry of text responses (Example 10.10). The advantage of using QTI in this case is that the tasks can also be used outside the LD context.

Example 10.10

```
<div class="C-Activity">
 <p>Please upload your task report here:</p>
```

```
  <ld:set-property ref="GP-RESPONSE-GUID"/>
</div>
```

Scenario 4

The fourth assessment scenario is one consisting of a combination of the assessment methods of the previous three scenarios, combined with a portfolio assessment at the end of a number of units of learning. During that portfolio assessment an assessor (possibly the tutor), together with the student, assess the portfolio of the student. This discussion will address individual results, as well as the process and the student's ability for self-reflection. Though part of this assessment scenario (e.g. the main criteria that will be taken into account) can be modelled and described using LD, there are no corresponding structures in QTI to model the assessment. In general, portfolio assessment, peer assessment, self-assessment and collaborative assessment are assessment forms which, at the moment, can only be described, not actually uniformly modelled.

10.5 Conclusion

This chapter describes how the LD specification and the QTI specification can be integrated. The first enables developers to formalize learning and the second enables the formalization of testing. Together they might formalize new forms of learning, integrating assessment in the learning design.

The chapter starts with the developments around assessments, indicating that more attention is now being focused on formative assessments. It is not only products which are assessed, but processes, too, which become more important in such new assessment forms like performance assessment or portfolio assessment.

QTI was not originally designed to facilitate these kinds of assessments. However, this chapter outlines four scenarios in which the possibilities of an integration of QTI and LD are explored.

11 Collaboration in Learning Design Using Peer-to-Peer Technologies

Michael J. Halm[1], Bill Olivier[2], Umer Farooq[1], Christopher Hoadley[1]

[1] Penn State University, USA

[2] Bolton Institute of Higher Education, Bolton, United Kingdom

11.1 Introduction

Two interesting sociological and technological phenomena have the potential for tremendous impact on the future architectures and delivery strategies to support Anytime, Anywhere Learning (AAL). The first is the ever-increasing nomadic and intermittently connected nature of learners illustrated by the growth of PDAs, mobile phones, tablet PCs and laptop and notebook computers. The second is the escalating use of instantaneous forms of one-to-one and group communication and collaboration as seen in the popularity of peer-to-peer (P2P) file sharing, SMS, Instant Messaging, Chat and Chat rooms, forums, etc. These technological and social trends require us to consider how the future of AAL will take place in this more decentralized environment and in the corresponding changes in architecture needed to support them. Furthermore, these trends will certainly have an impact on the implementation of future learning strategies.

This chapter explores how P2P technologies and architectures can potentially support these changing trends and how P2P technologies, particularly when hybridized with client/server technologies, can be applied to Learning Design, and how they can address the scalability issues faced by Learning Design systems.

11.2 The Evolution of Peer-to-Peer Environments for Learning

11.2.1 What Is P2P?

The popularity of file sharing and instant messaging (IM) applications on the Internet has raised the profile of P2P approaches, but distributed computing and IM are also part of the P2P paradigm. Simply put, P2P is a class of independent collaborating applications that take advantage of available resources such as distributed storage, processing power, available bandwidth, content, and human presence at the 'edge' of computer networks, due to the increasingly powerful, but largely unused, capacity of users' client systems. P2P on the Internet has grown remarkably, but what we have witnessed so far is only the beginning. Once thought of as nuisance, P2P will evolve into an indispensable tool for learning organizations.

A number of P2P architectures have evolved but this chapter investigates two models. The first model is the completely decentralized, pure P2P model, where each peer on the network is both a client and a server.

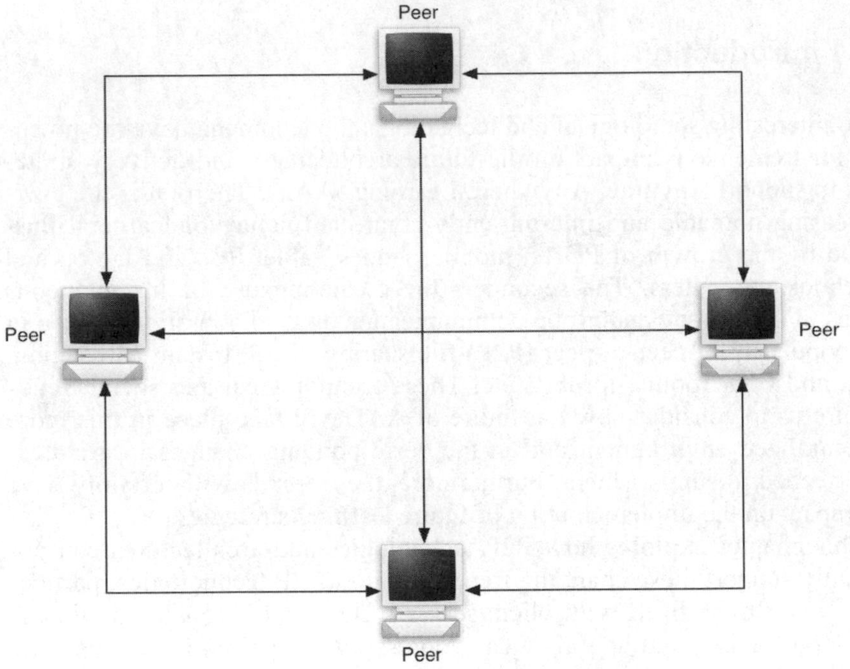

Fig. 11.1. The Gnutella model

This decentralized model, the Gnutella model, is illustrated in Fig. 11.1, – each peer is an equal member on the network. This type of network is somewhat fragile in the sense that when the peer application is not in operation, its resources cannot be discovered or shared, unless they are physically replicated across multiple peers. This model is likely to be most useful where learning communities do not have an institutional base, operating either across organizations or informally, as in an ad hoc group.

The second P2P topology is a hybrid model, the Napster model, as illustrated in Fig. 11.2.

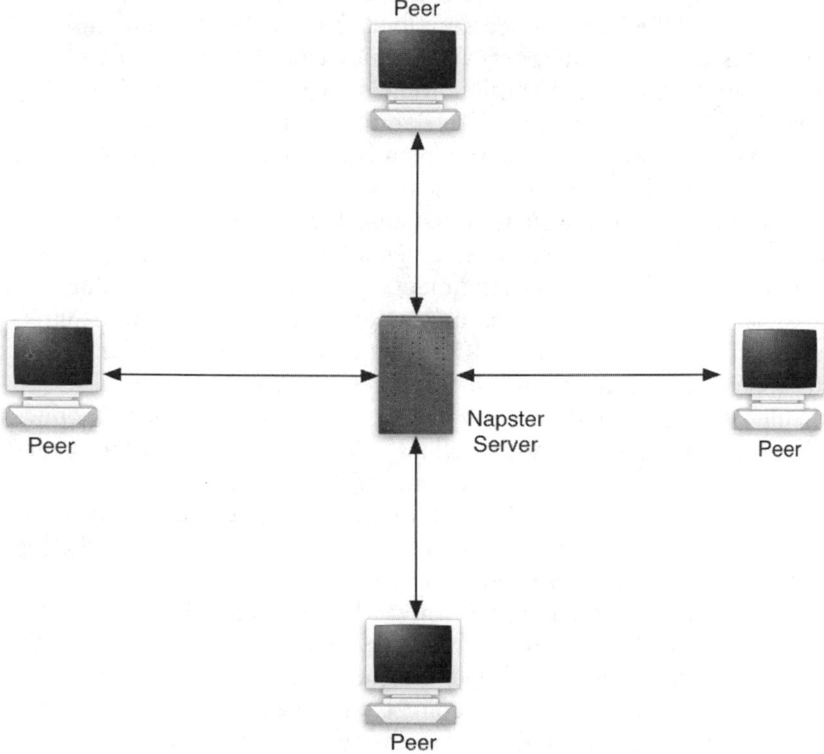

Fig. 11.2. The Napster model

This model represents a decentralized–centralized topology because a central server, or super peer, has been added to the traditional P2P network to provide a source for persistent services to the network where peers typically have intermittent connection. Persistence is achieved because the PeerServer is always available to store learning resources and activities even when the peer itself is unavailable.

11.2.2 P2P and Learning Design

Clearly the pure P2P architecture and the hybrid architecture provide different ways of supporting Learning Design (LD 2003) and in turn make different demands.

Both models support human presence, persistent and distributed storage, increase available bandwidth and time synchronization, but in different ways. They thus enable both collaborative activities and nomadic, intermittently connected use. Furthermore, when used to implement the Learning Design specification, they allow learning activities to be separated into smaller pieces and the heavy processing load they create can be completely or partially distributed to the peers. There they can be sequenced and presented independently of a Learning Management System (LMS). They thus can provide a solution to the scalability problem that sophisticated specifications like LD face when implemented on a single, centralised server. Moreover, P2P can facilitate a more learner-centred and learner-controlled model of learning such as that described in Chap. 14.

In the pure P2P model, each learner must have on their system a relatively complete LD runtime environment. This must not only be able to handle each individual's activities and resources within the multi-player structure of a Unit of Learning (UOL), but also be able to communicate with all other peers participating in the same instance or run of the UOL. In particular the events and property changes that control the synchronization of multiple players have to be reliably shared with all the other peers. There is also a potentially difficult issue of synchronizing clocks across peers for time-driven changes, although in practice this can probably be resolved by an implementation using an on-line time service such as the UK National Physical Laboratory's atomic clock.

Another problem that the pure P2P model has to address its the intermittently connected nature of many peers. Many users only have access to the Internet via a temporarily allocated Internet address. Often a presence server is provided where currently connected systems register their presence so that others can locate them, together with their temporary Internet address, and are then able to communicate with them directly. However, there is a problem when peers form and participate in a defined group and it is necessary for all messages to be reliably transferred to all members, as is the case when running an LD UOL. Peers have to track which others have received every message ensuring that it is sent to other peers as they reconnect. If the originating peer goes off-line and remains off-line when others come on, there can be potentially serious delays in message transmission. This can be handled by all peers in a group taking responsibility for ensuring that newly present peers are updated, but another route is to use a store-and-forward server, the route taken by the Jabber system. Similarly if a peer is the sole owner of a shared resource, it cannot be accessed by others when it is off-line. Again one solution is to distribute it among all current peers in a group, which can then update others, but another solution is to introduce a peer file server to ensure that shared files are always available regardless of the presence or absence of individual peers.

We thus find that the pure P2P model is often modified in favour of a hybrid model of peers operating through 'PeerServers' and services. However, the disadvantage of breaking the pure P2P model is that ad hoc groups typically have no means of setting up and maintaining shared servers and services, unless one of the group has a permanent Internet address that enables them to run services for the others. But the hybrid route is often preferred in an institutional or organizational context where IS services can support and maintain PeerServers on a 24/7 basis.

Turning to the hybrid, or 'Napster', model in Fig. 11.2, a 'PeerServer' pulls together one or more of the services that the peers would otherwise have to provide themselves. In terms of implementing LD, the most useful service it can provide is that of coordinating the different players participating in a single run of a UOL, while leaving the peers to handle each participant's interactions with their personal part of the UOL. To achieve this the UOL has first to be analysed and each individual's part extracted according to the roles they are playing in the UOL. To understand how a UOL can be split into a multi-player coordination part and a personal participation part it is necessary to review the structure of a UOL.

Figure 11.3, illustrating the learning design architecture, provides a conceptual overview of the LD specification.

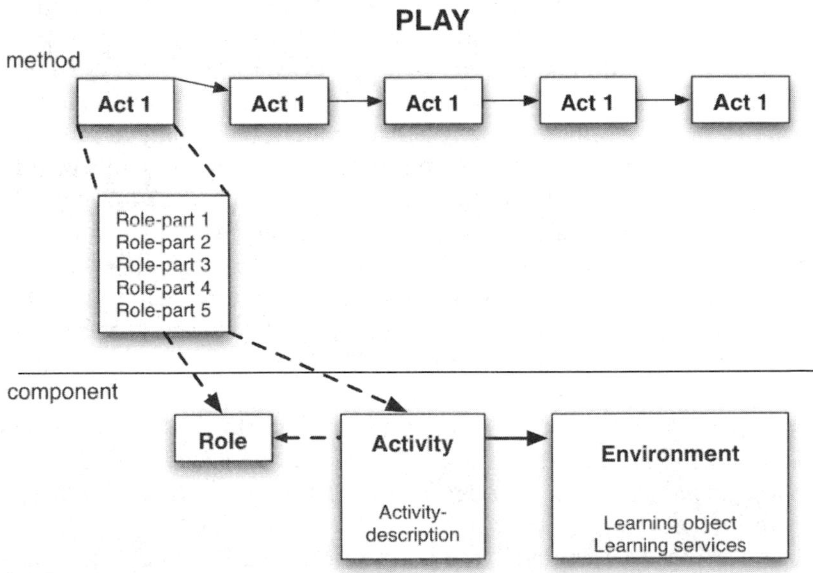

Fig. 11.3. The learning design architecture

This diagram is explained in Chap. 2 of this book.

The Play is performed by different players, according to the roles they are assigned, participating in a specific set of activities, where each activity has a defined environment containing a variety of specified learning resources (learning objects and services).

This enables a split to be made between the multi-player coordination part of a UOL, which embodies the Method, Play, Act and Role-part section, and the remaining parts of the UOL consisting of a personalized set of Activity structures, Activities, Environments and resources or links to resources. This then allows the coordination to be handled by a shared coordination service, or 'PeerServer', and the personalized parts to be distributed to peers.

This distributed model can then take advantage of the user's local computing power, storage, bandwidth, staged content and human presence in either the Napster-style or Gnutella-style P2P environment. This offloads a considerable burden from a centralized server and increases scalability as each new peer that is added also brings its own resources.

Consider the learning design architecture in Fig. 11.4, the LD for P2P. The PeerServer mediates communication between the peers (clients) and the learning design repository/course management system. This repository contains information of the Plays, Acts, and Roles to be used as part of pedagogical applications. A walkthrough scenario of this architecture could be as follows. The PeerServer retrieves an Act (Act 1, for example) from the learning design repository (Fig. 11.4A). This Act is parsed by Role as above and, according to the role each individual is playing, the Activity and its Environment are passed on to the peers that are connected to the PeerServer (Fig. 11.4B). Content can be downloaded to the peers if they wish to work temporarily in disconnected mode. After this point, the peers need not be connected to the PeerServer and, having retrieved their part, they can engage in it with relative autonomy, communicating with the PeerServer only as necessary, for example when they cause properties to change or need to be notified of properties' changes that affect their activity, and to send and receive LD notifications.

Where the peers are assigned a learning service, this has to be carried out on-line using the server assigned when the UOL was instantiated, unless this service also permits a degree of off-line working, as for example with an Internet email client.

Once an Activity is completed, the peers inform the PeerServer and pass any results of the Activity back to the PeerServer (Fig. 11.4C). This ensures persistent storage of Activity outcomes for future use.

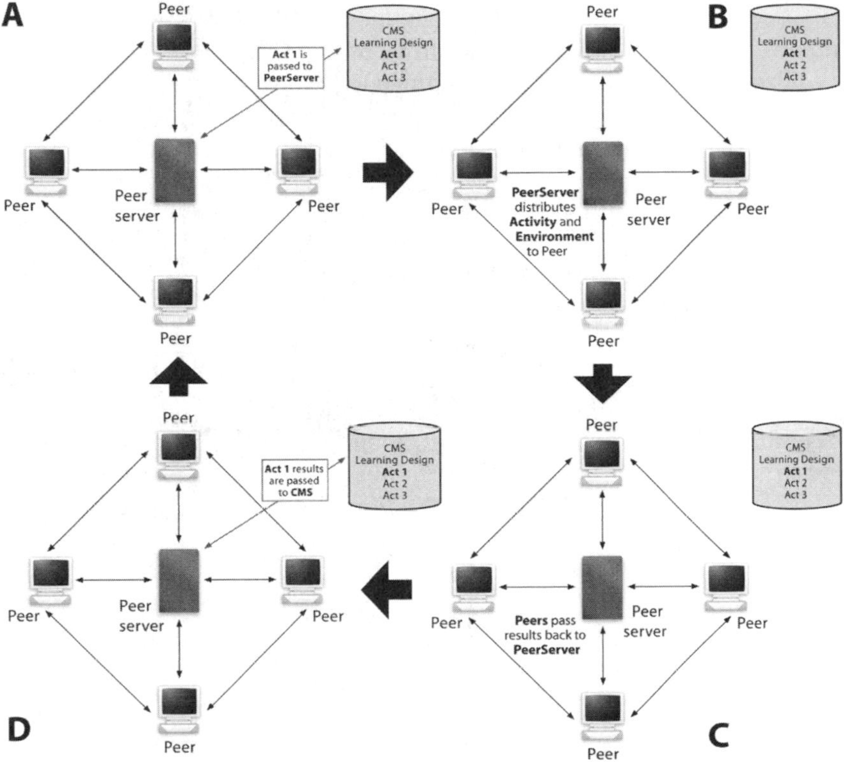

Fig. 11.4. Learning Design for P2P

In turn, the PeerServer routes these results back to the learning design repository for storage, and the process is started all over again (Fig. 11.4D).

Next we present a brief illustration of some of the further benefits of the hybrid model, starting with an expansion of the PeerServer model (Fig. 11.5). As mentioned, there are several different ways in which peers can use a server. In this version, all LD-related communication is being directed through the PeerServer, although LD email and conferencing services might be carried out directly between peers (not shown in the diagram), or could also be mediated via the PeerServer, where for example a recipient is currently not on-line.

This model can be adapted to enable a scalable centralized server architecture (Fig. 11.6). The personal LD engine becomes a session servlet, one for each logged-on participant. The servlets are coordinated through a separate coordination server, effectively the PeerServer, which remains unchanged. This separation of the LD coordination server from the personal LD engines has some interesting features.

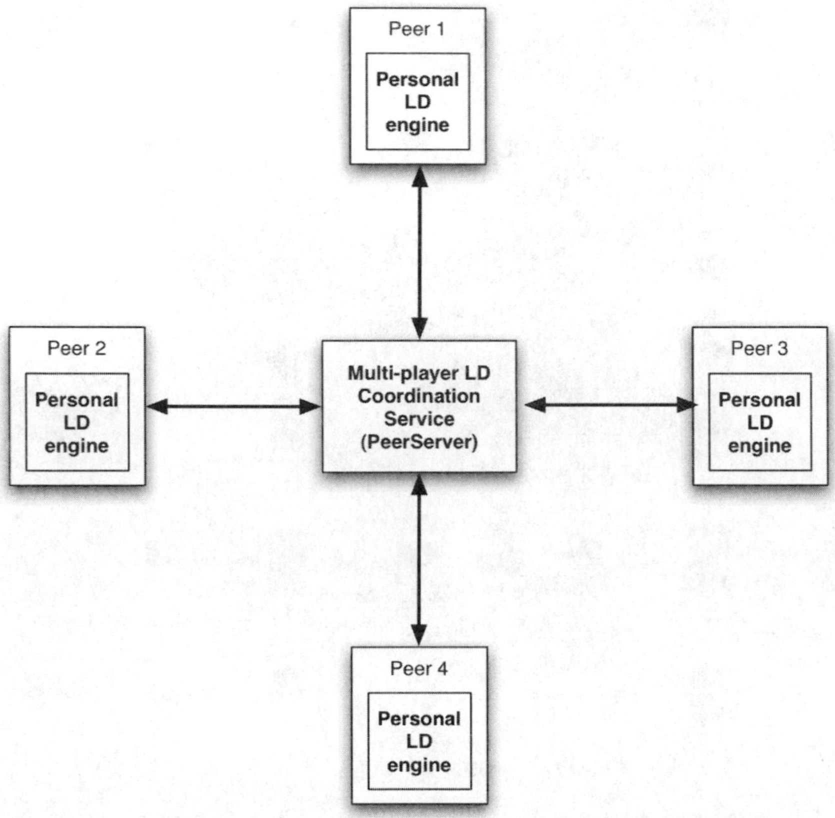

Fig. 11.5. Learning Design for P2P

1. It allows the server-based system to become scalable according to the number of users that need to be supported. Typically there would be many more than two per server as shown in the diagram, but it serves to illustrate how the architecture can be scaled by adding more servers.
2. By providing a separate coordination server, a UOL can be split across institutions and organizations, thus enabling shared courses to be supported.

Finally, the same structure can also support a combination of server-based and peer-based participants (Fig. 11.7). This supports both on-campus and off-campus students. It can also support a combination of students with and without their own portable systems.

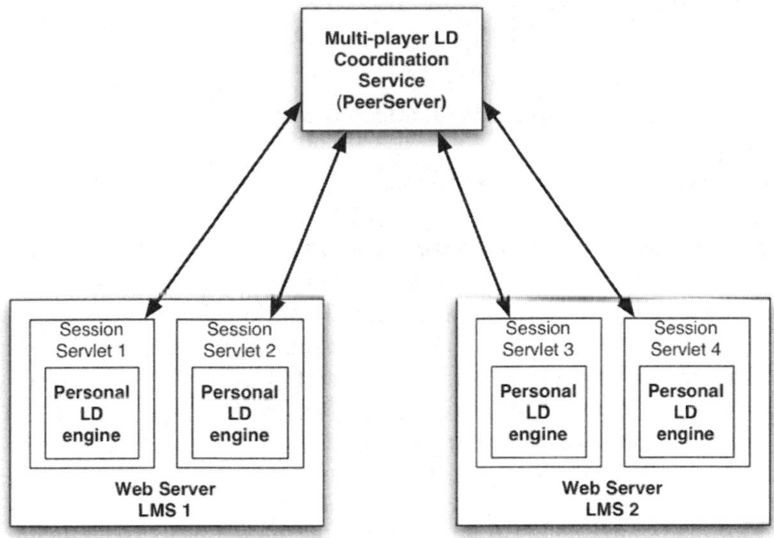

Fig. 11.6. P2P design adapted for scalable servers

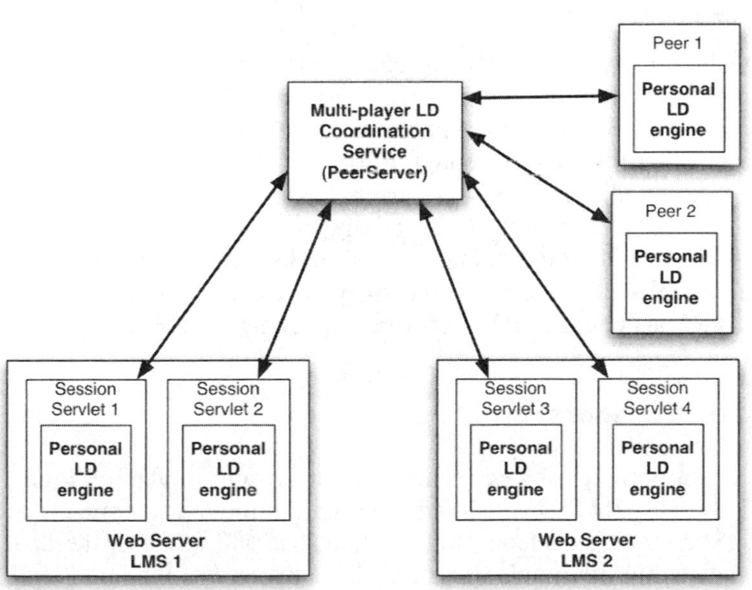

Fig. 11.7. P2P combination server *and* peer architecture

11.2.3 Challenges for P2P

Two challenges are:

- how to synchronize intermittently connected learning activity with the server
- the ability to provide secure transactions.

P2P learning environments must have a way to synchronize with client-server based LMS/VLE systems. While it is feasible for learning to migrate to the edge of the network, institutions will want to have evidence of competency and completion of assignments stored on centralized institutional infrastructure. There are a variety of ways to enable this synchronization but it is important to do it in a standardized way that guarantees interoperability between these different systems. There are three functional requirements necessary for this support:

1. the ability for the learner to select UOLs to be downloaded to the nomadic devices
2. the ability to download the selected UOL
3. the ability for the learner to reconnect to the central LMS to synchronize learner-generated data such as tracking information, test results and learner-generated content.

These ideally should have small standardised interfaces and formats to enable systems from different providers to work together.

Another area that will require considerable thought is the method to ensure that learning results and personal information are secure when a learner is disconnected. Projects are currently underway to develop a lightweight trust fabric that will allow locally produced certificates that will verify the identity of an individual who is publishing or retrieving materials from a central secure learning repository. These technologies promise secure transactions between P2P networks and central LMS/VLEs.

11.2.4 P2P and Collaboration

LionShare is a joint project of Penn State, Simon Fraser University, Internet2 and MIT to apply the P2P file sharing paradigm to an academic environment. LionShare is an academic P2P system that will assist in the distribution of academic materials through the university networks and beyond. The primary goal of LionShare is to provide a P2P network which has unlimited potential for collaboration among faculty, students, departments and even across multiple universities in a controlled way. This network will be accessed by a trust fabric built on emerging security standards such as Shibboleth, and has the potential to provide a method for secure transactions on the P2P network.

11.3 Conclusions

Recent trends suggest that P2P technologies have the potential to change the way learning systems operate from the current highly centralized environments toward a blended environment that allows for nomadic and intermittently connected learners on the edge of the network. Current e-learning community efforts to develop standards for interoperability to support meaningful, authentic learning activities suggest that it is now possible to exploit P2P in the instructional technology toolset. While P2P holds much promise, there are a few challenges that must be overcome before its true potential can be realised. This chapter provides a first overview of the implications of combining P2P technologies and LD with a view towards decentralising e-learning.

12 Designing Adaptive Learning Environments with Learning Design

Brendon Towle[1], Michael Halm[2]

[1] Thomson NETg, Naperville, USA

[2] Penn State University, USA

12.1 Introduction

12.1.1 Adaptive Learning: Background and Motivation

It has long been known that individual learners differ. Some learners need a picture before they are fully comfortable with their understanding, while others are more comfortable with streams of text. Some learners want detailed instructions before attempting a new task, while others want to jump right in and try on their own. Some learners are eager to offer the answer to any question, while others will participate only when asked (and perhaps even then only reticently).

Furthermore, if learners differ in the way they approach problems, it is not hard to recognize they would receive the maximum benefit from individualized instructions. Formally, this is known as an Aptitude–Treatment Interaction (ATI): the student's aptitude interacts with the way that the student is treated to produce varying results. The pioneering ATI research was done by Cronbach and Snow (1977). In the ensuing years, many different researchers have identified a variety of ways in which individual learners can be categorized (e.g., Gardner 1983; Kolb 1984; Martinez and Bunderson 2000). Further, many of these categorization schemes have had differing instructional schemes associated with them (e.g., Jonassen and Grabowski 1993), where each scheme describes how to treat learners in each category differently to best achieve particular instructional goals. This area continues to be an active area of research (e.g., Nokelainen et al. 2002; Sampson and Karagiannidis 2002; Sampson et al. 2002; Shute and Towle 2003).

While there are many technical hurdles to be overcome in successfully implementing e-learning, the importance of the learning experience is paramount. Learners must be able to form new mental models, or acquire new scripts or schemas to guide their actions in new situations. If individual learners indeed learn differently, the e-learning developer would be well advised to provide an environment in which the differing needs and talents of individual learners can best be focused on the learning process itself, resulting in the maximum benefit for all learners.

Previously, implementing adaptive learning on a wide scale was a relatively time-consuming process that required designing large portions of the infrastructure from scratch (the first author of this chapter had to do exactly that). Fortunately, the introduction of the Learning Design specification (LD 2003) provides learning designers with a specification that can be used to create many useful forms of adaptive learning without requiring that the learning designers build the infrastructure; the various technical capabilities provided in LD provide that infrastructure.

12.1.2 Remainder of this Chapter

This chapter will be devoted to examples of implementing adaptive learning using LD. Three relatively simple adaptive strategies, and the learner characteristics behind them, will be discussed and implemented in LD. Furthermore, the limitations of using LD to implement adaptive learning will be considered. Finally, some conclusions about the usefulness of implementing adaptive learning and enhancements to LD that will support easier implementation of adaptive learning will be examined.

12.2 Implementation Options for Adaptive Learning in LD

When one looks at a strategy for implementing adaptive learning in LD, there are at least two separate axes upon which that strategy can be described. One is in regards to the logic that implements the adaptive strategy: is it encapsulated within the Unit of Learning (UOL) itself, or is it external to the UOL? Another axis concerns what exactly is adapted: is it the contents of the UOL, or is it the interface to the UOL, or is it something else entirely? In Chap. 18, van Rosmalen and Boticario discuss a system where the adaptive logic is external to the UOL, and modifications are made to both the UOL and the interface. However, this chapter describes examples that take the opposite approach: implementing the adaptive logic completely within the UOL.

This also restricts what can be adapted. Within LD, there are at least four areas where a UOL could be tailored to individual learners based on their learning characteristics:

1. One could change the *environment* for different learners — providing different resources, or the same resources in a different order.

2. One could change the *method* for different learners.
3. One could slot different learners into different *roles*, or provide support from different roles for different learners.
4. Finally, one could change the *activities* given to different learners.

However, if the adaptive logic is to be implemented completely within the UOL, the logic must go within the *method.* Within the method, constructs are available to change a variety of things within the UOL; the environment, the activities, the play, etc. Because we limit our scope to adaptivity that can be completely contained within the UOL: all of the examples developed herein will have the adaptive logic within the method; for the sake of simplicity, they will also be restricted to option 1 above (changing elements within the environment). Later in the chapter, we will discuss the disadvantages of this approach, and detail alternative approaches.

12.3 Assumptions

All of the examples in this chapter assume the following:

12.3.1 LD Level B

All of the examples require a runtime system that implements at least LD Level B, since Level B introduces the *conditions* element, and the *conditions* element is required to implement the adaptive strategies.

12.3.2 Learner Profile Information

Since all examples are based on learner-characteristic adaptation, it is assumed a machine-readable record of learner characteristics has already been populated with the relevant information about the learner (such models are relatively commonplace, and public specifications are available for them—for example, Learner Information Package (LIP 2001)). Depending on the implementation, the system responsible for delivering the learning experience may or may not need prior knowledge of the contents of this learner profile. (It will certainly need prior knowledge of the *format* of the record, however.) Furthermore, the learner profile will have to be implemented in such a way that the delivery system can access this record while delivering the learning experience. The following examples assume that access to this profile is accomplished through the LD Level B *globpers-property* mechanism. The actual learner profile data could be modeled in

LD itself, or the *globpers-property* mechanism could have some sort of mapping to the native implementation of the system.

Note that the examples below are agnostic as to how the learner profile information is created. It could be that the learner interacts explicitly with some sort of profiling instrument; alternately, it could be that some sort of process observes the actions of the learner in the learning environment and generates the profile based on those observations. Also, note that in the long term, a learner's profile may not be static, but may change based on any of a number of factors; authors of UOLs should keep this in mind when appropriate.

12.3.3 Multiple Variants

Some of the examples require the existence of multiple variants of either content objects or services with which the learner interacts. While some adaptive strategies simply involve delivering activities to the student in a different order, others involve directing the student to a different activity; in these cases, the different activity must exist.

12.3.4 Instructor Variation

In some cases, proper implementation of the adaptive strategies will depend on how well instructors follow directions in presenting materials to different learners, or how learners might be coached differently.

12.4 Examples of Adaptive Learning in LD

The following are examples of how various sorts of adaptive learning might be implemented in LD. None of the examples claims to be the only way to implement a particular strategy; rather, they all show merely one way.

12.4.1 Synchronous vs. Asynchronous Interactions

Some research indicates (Jonassen and Grabowski 1993) that learners who are strongly introverted may be intimidated in synchronous interactions like chat rooms and instant messaging, and might derive greater benefit from asynchronous interactions like email and bulletin boards. Conversely, learners who are strongly extroverted might have greater benefit from synchronous interactions than asynchronous ones. Learners in the middle, while showing no inherent preference either way, might have the greatest benefit from whatever the learning designer believes to be the better of the two alternatives presented.

This simple adaptive strategy can easily be implemented in an LD environment.

First, there must be a *service* for each category of learner instantiated in the UOL. Each of these would be a *conference*; one would be synchronous and one would be asynchronous. (We'll call these "Synch Conference" and "Asynch Conference" respectively.) Initially, each of these services would be invisible (isvisible=false).

The adaptive strategy can be described quite simply as: *for each learner, only show the appropriate conference, depending on whether the learner is more extroverted than introverted, or vice versa.* Figure 12.1 depicts this strategy.

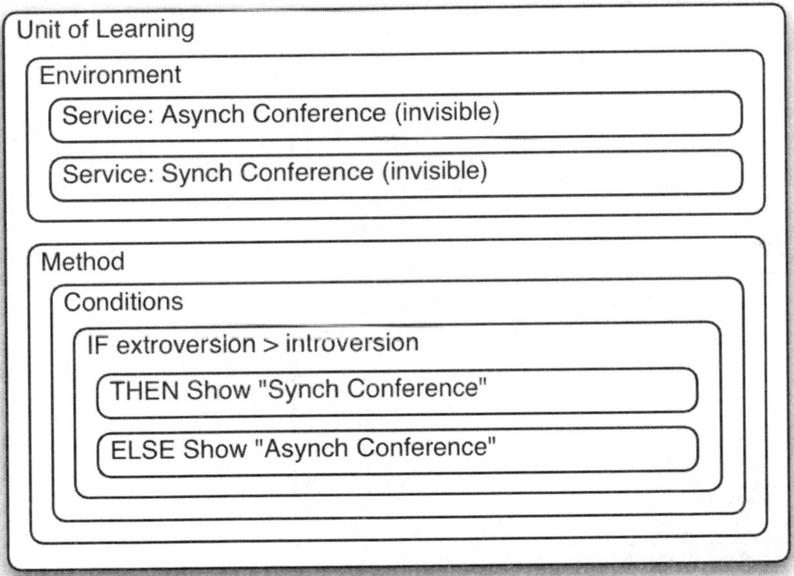

Fig. 12.1. Synchronous vs. asynchronous conference adaptation. Only the portions of the UOL relevant to the adaptive strategy are shown

12.4.2 Rule–Example vs. Example–Rule

Research also indicates (Shute 1993) that learners who exhibit more exploratory behavior may derive more benefit more from having examples presented before concepts, while learners who are less exploratory may benefit more from having the concepts presented before the examples.

This adaptive strategy can be implemented in LD as follows. First, at the location where the examples and content are to be presented, create two *items*, both with isvisible = "false". In the first (which we will call "inductiveContainer"), place a child item for the examples followed by a child item for the concepts; in the second (called "deductiveContainer"), place a child item for the concepts followed by a child item for the examples. In both containers, the child items should reference the same resource(s) to deliver the instruction; in this example, we're simply varying the order of presentation, and not the items that are actually presented. Finally, if the student's exploratory tendencies are greater than some threshold, show the inductiveContainer item; otherwise, show the deductiveContainer item. Figure 12.2 depicts this strategy.

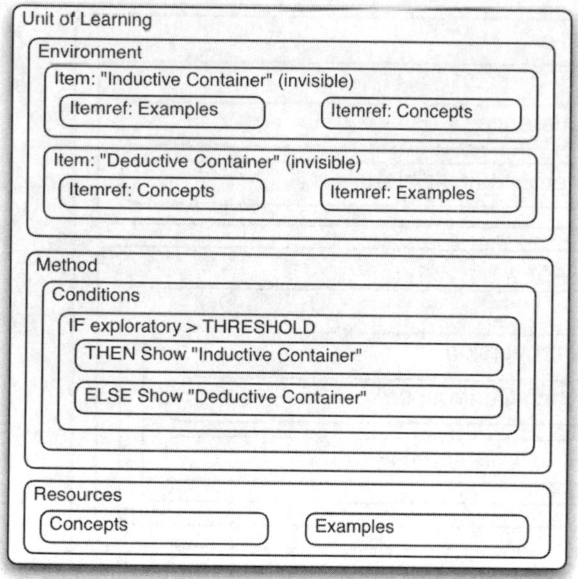

Fig. 12.2. Rule–Example vs. Example–Rule adaptation. Only the portions of the UOL relevant to the adaptive strategy are shown

12.4.3 Variations in Encouragement

Research by Margaret Martinez into learning orientation theory (e.g., Martinez 2001; Martinez and Bunderson 2000) has shown that individual learners approach learning differently in terms of their personal involvement and commitment to the learning process. Martinez characterizes these different types of learners as Resistant, Conforming, Performing, and Transforming. Because of differing levels of involvement and commitment, these learners require differing levels of encouragement and affirmation, and respond differently when they are provided. Resistant learners, for example, need substantial encouragement to continue with the learning process, while that sort of encouragement will be irritating or offensive to a Transforming learner. This implies a strategy where the feedback a learner receives is tailored to their learning orientation.

This adaptive strategy can also be easily implemented in an LD environment in a couple of ways.

A simple way is an adaptation of the previous container strategy. In the *feedback-description* of the appropriate *act*, four different sets of feedback are built (one for each level in the Martinez scale); all are hidden at first, and given a unique name. Then, in the method, show the appropriate material based on the characteristic value from the learner's profile. Figure 12.3 depicts this strategy.

An alternative strategy involves instructions to the support/teaching staff (if any exist in this particular UOL). If this strategy is used, four different sets of instructions to the teacher or tutor on how to give feedback are incorporated into the *support-activity* used by that role, and then showing the appropriate strategy as above. This strategy is not shown, but is conceptually very similar to the one shown below.

12.4.4 Other Uses

While all of the examples described above deal with adapting the learning process to accommodate the way that individual learners learn, there are other applications of this strategy. For example, UOLs could automatically be adapted to accommodate the accessibility needs of individual learners (i.e., larger type for visually impaired learners).

12.5 Limitations of Adaptive Learning in LD

While LD does provide an attractive environment for implementing some basic forms of learner-centered adaptive learning, it is not without its limitations. In this section, some of the more problematic limitations of implementing adaptive learning within LD will be discussed including: the difficulty of supporting multiple interactions, the lack of enforced ordering within the LD spec, and the "manifest-centered" representational scheme.

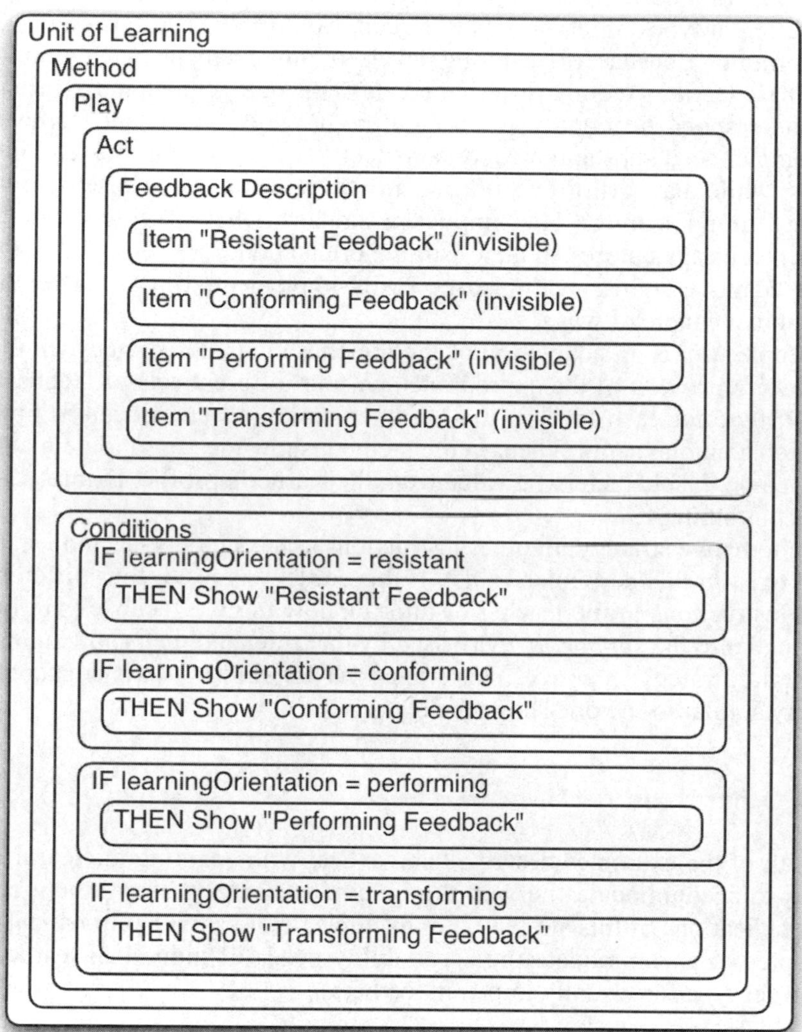

Fig. 12.3. Feedback adaptation. Only the portions of the UOL relevant to the adaptive strategy are shown

12.5.1 Multiple Rule Interactions

All of the above examples show adaptation based on a single characteristic of learners. While this is useful, individual learners have multiple characteristics; in many cases, designers will want to adapt based on more than one characteristic of any particular learner.

In cases where these interactions occur in different learning activities or at different stages in the same learning activity (such as the examples above concerning the type of feedback and synchronous vs. asynchronous conferencing), integration into the same UOL is a relatively trivial matter; the different adaptive strategies can simply be combined without interaction. In cases where the interactions overlap, however, the relatively large number of rules and rule interactions can be quite difficult to express within an LD Manifest.

For example, learners who are very practically oriented (or who lack patience with the learning process) may wish to see problems up front, so they know what benefit they will get from the course; other learners may wish to see the problems at the end. Further, learners who are confident in their own learning may do better if they are given the hard problems straight away, while learners with less confidence may do better with easier problems first. Imagine combining these two strategies with the Exploratory and Introversion strategies above. The LD Manifest required to simply set up the content, without accounting for the various conditions required for adaptivity, would look as shown in Figure 12.4. This is feasible, albeit somewhat clumsy. However, imagine that each learner was categorized on 10 or 15 dimensions, rather than just 4; it should quickly become apparent that the idea of extending this to several more interacting strategies is not likely to be feasible.

12.5.2 Lack of Enforced Ordering

Much of the current LD specification is relatively agnostic to the eventual user experience. For example, the hide and show actions as specified only remove items from a display list; the spec appears to be silent on the issue of whether or not those items can be accessed by other means, and is also silent on the issue of whether hidden (invisible) elements are experienced while the learner simply walks through the content by pushing the "next" button or its equivalent. While one can assume that hidden items would not be delivered to the learner under these circumstances, there is nothing in the spec to indicate one way or another, and some strategies require different delivery during a sequence than the items available during choice (see, for example, the use cases in the Best Practice and Implementation Guide of the LD specification).

This poses some problems for designers of adaptive learning. In most adaptive strategies, the designer wants to force the student to experience items in a certain order, or to not experience certain items at all.

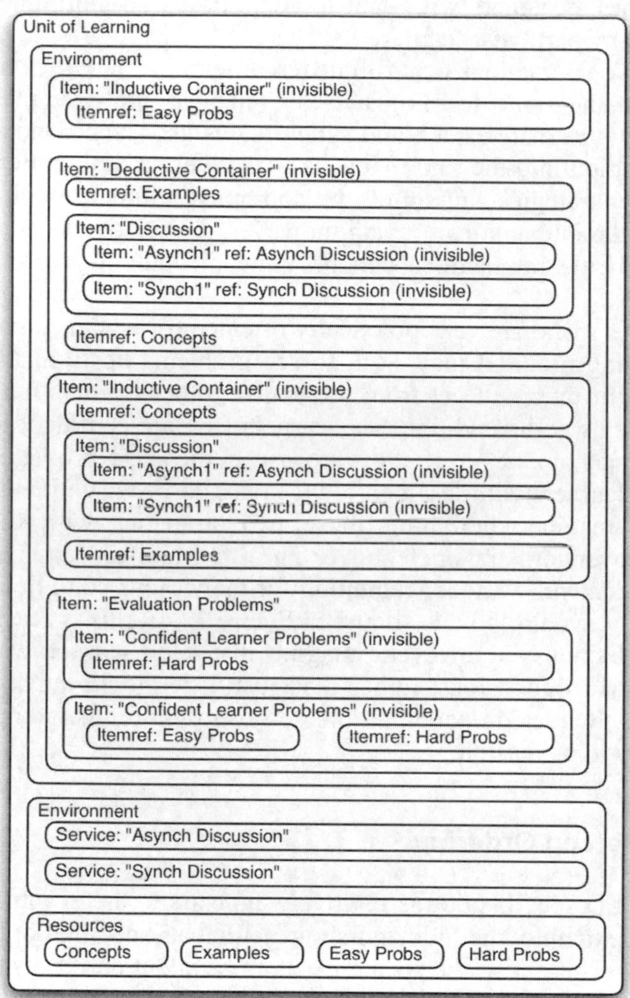

Fig. 12.4. Content necessary for complex interactions. Only the content is shown; the conditions necessary to adapt the content to individual learners are omitted

At this stage, it is probably best for designers to simply assume that students will not experience hidden items during a sequence; while this is less than satisfactory, the alternative appears to be to wait until the specification is revised.

12.5.3 Manifest-Centred vs. Server-Centred

LD is what we will call a "manifest-centred" or "manifest-based" representation: all of the information necessary to interact with a particular UOL is contained within the manifest for that UOL. While this is a good idea for many purposes, there are problems inherent in representing any adaptive learning strategy entirely in a manifest-based representational scheme. These include:

- The difficulties inherent with rule interactions for multiple characteristics (see above for more details).
- Once delivered, manifests cannot be changed to take advantage of new adaptive strategies.
- The same strategy is encoded in multiple manifests, causing redundancy in authoring and storage.
- The knowledge about learning objects is often embedded in the manifest, and not accessible through metadata for use in new or arbitrary strategies.

One solution to these problems is to move the adaptive logic outside of the manifest; this could be implemented roughly as follows (see Shute and Towle (2003) for more details). First, define a set of standard activities and/or content types, and provide metadata that maps from learning objects and activity structures to the standard activities and content types. Then, the LD player can take the role of a client of an adaptive server: the player sends the server information about what the learner has done, and the adaptive server sends back to the client the ID of the most appropriate next activity.

The important thing to note about this strategy is that the intelligence about the adaptive strategy is removed from the client and the manifest; the client neither knows nor cares what the adaptive strategy is, and nor does the manifest itself. This uncoupling of the adaptive strategy from the manifest (and thus from the knowledge about the learning objects and activities themselves) provides several advantages. It means that the adaptive strategy can be changed simply by tuning or adjusting the server (assuming that the metadata referenced above is always available, and that it does not require any changes as a result of the new model). Further, it means that the adaptive strategy is only defined once, rather than in every manifest.

This strategy does require that the pedagogical design of the UOL be such that it will be pedagogically effective regardless of what changes are made on-the-fly by the server. This is a bit of a departure from the typical LD approach, in which the "intelligence" of the UOL is hard-coded into the manifest; however, that departure is exactly the point.

12.6 Conclusion

Contemporary learning theory suggests that individual learners differ in the way they learn and that learning must be tailored to the individual learner. Consequently, learning environments must have the flexibility to adapt themselves for the individual learner. This chapter has discussed several different learner-characteristic, driven adaptive learning strategies and how these strategies can be completely implemented within the constraints of the existing LD specification. Adaptive strategies discussed include 1) Synchronous vs. Asynchronous, 2) Rule–Example vs. Example–Rule, and 3) Feedback adaptation. This chapter has also detailed some of the ways in which implementing adaptive strategies entirely within LD can prove insufficient, and suggested one way around these problems.

The LD specification is the first attempt to move existing e-learning interoperability efforts from first-generation products that have traditionally focused primarily on content toward more robust second-generation environments that support richer learning strategies. While LD does not offer all features necessary for implementing extremely complex forms of adaptive learning, it does provide a way to implement many simple adaptive learning strategies. Consequently, this is a positive step toward providing more robust infrastructure for adaptive learning. Thus, it must be viewed as a good first effort that will undoubtedly produce fruit and provide the catalyst for future specifications efforts in this area.

12.7 Acknowledgements

Griff Richards, Patrick McAndrew, and Peter van Rosmalen provided useful comments on early drafts of this chapter. Three anonymous reviewers provided further useful comments on a near-final draft.

13 Designing Educational Games

Griff Richards

British Columbia Institute of Technology and Simon Fraser University, Canada

13.1 Introduction

The goal of an educational mark-up language such as Learning Design (LD 2003) is to promote the reuse and sharing of instructional activities by using a meta-language to describe learning activities. The ideal meta-language would be easily readable by humans, encode the learning design separate from the content, and conform to a technical specification that would make it transportable among authoring tools and "player" software. With the promise of returning control of educational activities to the educators the recent release of version 1.0 of LD has sparked a great deal of interest in this area, and a number of prototypic tools are being developed as the concept is explored. A successful meta-language approach would be an ideal mechanism for expressing and altering instructional game strategies and thus promote their sharing, improvement and reuse in different contexts or with different content.

This chapter explores the use of LD to reference educational game activities. After examining ways in which existing games may be incorporated into units of instruction, the potential of LD to encode games as reusable activities will be discussed in light of the current trends for identifying game patterns, and with the "memory" game used as an example.

13.2 Overview of Games as Reusable Instructional Activities

One of the main drivers of the learning objects paradigm is the promise of reusability. Since complex interactive media elements are often costly to produce, there is an economic incentive to reuse good learning objects (South and Monson 2002). Essentially there are two ways in which reuse can take place. The first is to insert a learning object intact into a new instructional context and the second is to modify the learning object for the new setting. For example, an interactive diagram of the heart might be borrowed from biology for use in anatomy, but it might also be modified by changing the labels from English to French for use in a different language setting. In more radical reuse, the logic of the interactivity might be preserved but the content changed, e.g. replacing the heart with a diagram of the liver. In either case it is often more cost-effective to reuse and modify the heart object than build a completely new liver object.

The useful separation of a learning object's activity from its content is a key premise of LD. Once an object's learning design is extracted and documented, it is possible to repopulate the template with new content for use in a new instructional setting. When the new content in place, the LD XML can then be "played" and the new educational experience is available for learners. Educational games can also be considered as learning objects to be reused in a variety of ways. While some games could be reused without modifications, other games have been developed with the express purpose of being modified for new learning content or a different audience. For example, the SAVIE website[1] provides ready-made templates or "shells" for four different frame games into which instructors can load new content, and then save them for later use by their learners. Thus a template for a simple matching game like Memory can be used to generate several games, each a set of paired content for discrimination exercises. Similarly a variant of Tic Tac Toe can be set up to stimulate group interactions in a number of different settings. While SAVIE generously provides its frame games as a free service to educators, the games can only be used on the SAVIE web server.

The encoding of learning activities and content in a proprietary authoring system or computing system is a common barrier to the reusability of computer games. Despite the good intentions of sites such as SAVIE, the reusability of the game is constrained by the technology and the distribution models. Thus the fundamental structure and instructional strategy that comprise the game design are neither open nor modifiable.

13.3 Referencing Game Activities in Learning Design

LD is primarily a macro instructional design tool to help designers specify a path through a curriculum and to prescribe activities for a Unit of Learning (UOL). Its strength lies as a method for organizing curriculum into courses, and bringing learners together with learning opportunities. Figure 13.1 outlines the hierarchy of activities that can be encoded by LD. The most granular element is the "activity" and this is the level where educational games can be prescribed. As seen in the Versailles example of Chap.

[1] http://www.savie.qc.ca/CarrefourJeux/fr/Accueil/VisiteGuideePublique.htm

9, LD can orchestrate fairly complex collaborative activities and simulations into an interesting UOL.

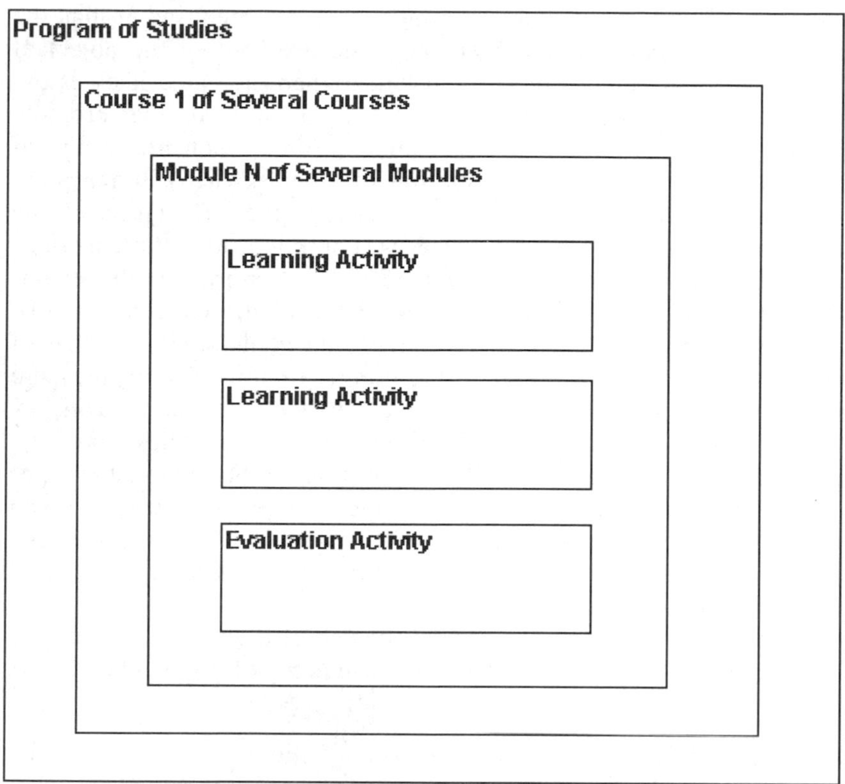

Fig. 13.1. The hierarchy of representations in LD

It is important to note that the level of granularity of learning activities that can be described in LD is not at the micro-design level. Unless a game activity was intentionally developed to be used in sub-components, LD does not provide a way of dismembering parts of an activity so they can be recombined anew. To do so would be akin to tinkering with the executable computer code in which the activity is encoded.

It is important to note that LD models are not computer code. They are abstractions that help specify relationships between participants, materials and sequences of events for learning. Given LD templates to serve as blueprints, a progression of tools including flowcharts, pseudo code and programming languages is required to add the increasing levels of detail needed to define and execute a computer-based game activity. Thus, it is easier to reference games as learning objects rather than to try to define and encode them in their entirety in LD. Game activities are probably best left as a sort of procedural call – the environment for the game is specified, learners are directed to engage in the game and, if necessary, parameters may be passed to the game and results of the interaction returned.

In general, an educational game is a medium for content rather than the content itself. For example, the Memory game itself is not the object of learning (other than perhaps the first instance when the game itself is explained). Memory is usually deployed with a set of cards that promote linked list learning – the sort of association formed when matching vocabulary terms with pictures or definitions of objects. The drill and practice that comes with Memory helps to reinforce the association of the terms. Memory could also be populated with simple arithmetic equations to be mentally solved before matching the results. A more complex example, the Versailles Game referred to in Chap. 9, is contrived as a means of engaging learners with content, perspectives and goals similar to that of countries in 1919. Once exposed to the corpus of information, they are placed into role-plays to attempt to negotiate a better treaty than the one arrived at in history. Presumably, the template for Versailles could be stripped and its content replaced with that from any other negotiation context. Thus the learning intent is not simply the situational content, but also the understanding of the negotiation process – the fundamental lesson being, as a recent advertisement for a negotiation course put it, "… you don't get what you deserve, you get what you negotiate".

LD can specify the conditions around the use of a game. For example, as diagrammed in Fig. 13.2, there can be a number of approaches to the use of a particular game within a learning unit:

- The game might be deployed first as a motivational tool, and then the learners can be debriefed in a conference where they reflect on what happened, why it happened, and what might be done to achieve a different outcome in the future.
- The game might follow a lesson or briefing session that sets up the characters and explains the rules.
- The game might be sandwiched between the briefing and the debriefing.
- The game might be used as a standalone individual learning activity where the learner prepares a report for marking by faculty.

Note from the "I/P" (Input or Product) arrow connecting the rectangular box that in all cases the game is included as a material input to the play activity. Both tutors and learners have roles to play, but not always in the same place and time. These examples are by no means the only ways to include faculty and learners in games; there could be a game where the faculty member plays a role in the game, or a staff person is required to support the game as an adversary or umpire.

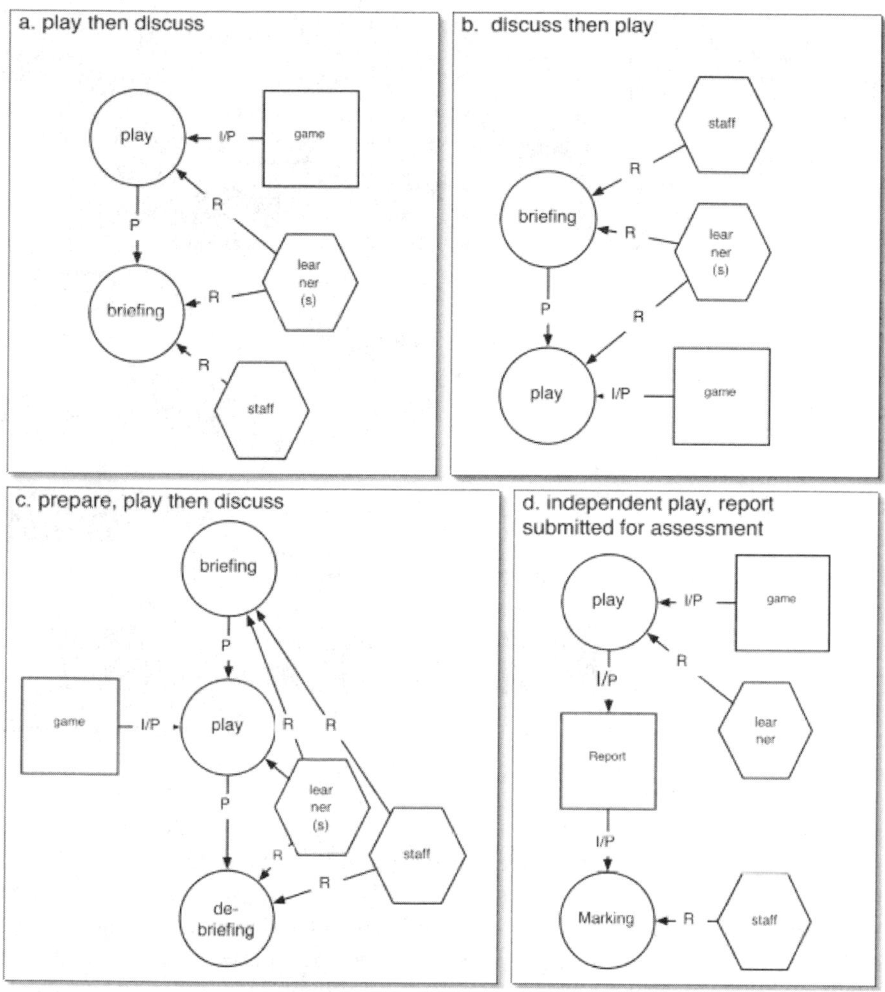

Fig. 13.2. Learning designs for inclusion of games as activities

The ability to define sub-roles for educational games and simulations is specifically mentioned in the LD specification (p 24). In examples c and d, the game activity is followed with some reflective activity.

In example c there is a group discussion and in example d a report is produced and input into the marking activity. As mentioned in the LD Best Practice Guide (p 8), in a Level C implementation of an LD system, the game or the marking activities might generate information which is returned automatically to either the student or to a student tracking system.

Contrast these simple learning designs with that of the role-play Versailles example in Fig. 13.3.

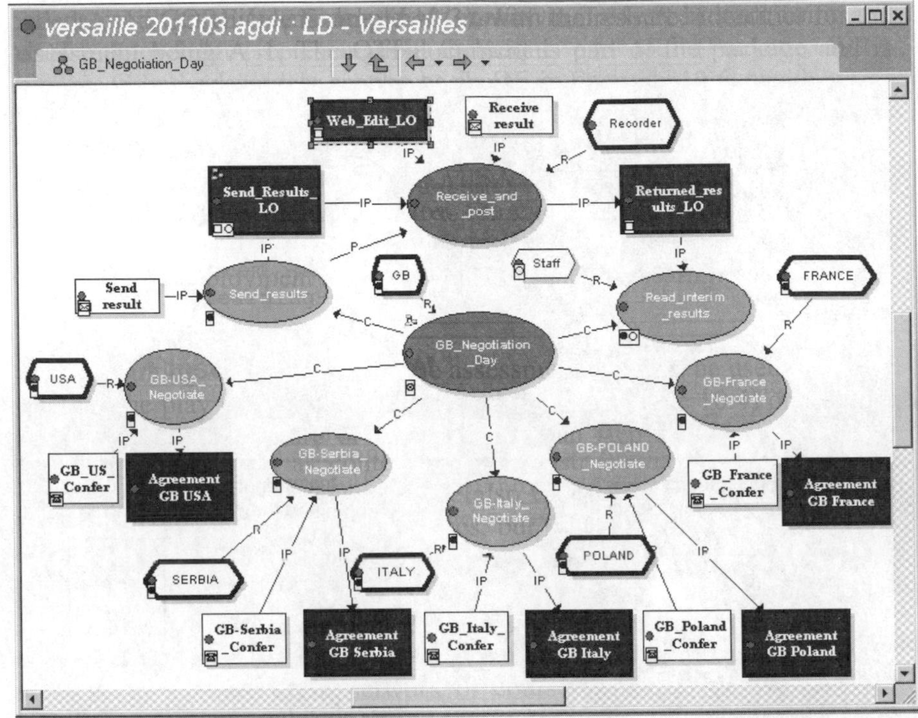

Fig. 13.3. Versailles expression in LD

When a game is referenced as a black box little information is known about its internal workings. When a game activity is encoded as in LD it can be inspected to see its organization and pedagogy within the context of the module. Moreover, the LD-encoded game is transportable; that is, as with any LD template it is playable on other LD players, and with other content. Might there be benefit in extending this level of detailed representation to all educational games and simulations? Perhaps, but the drawback is that even a simple simulation takes several views to represent fully. A complex game with intricate micro-design may be difficult to portray and the level of abstraction necessary for comparison between games might be lost in the programming code.

13.4 Game Representation: the Memory Example

In approaching the representation of a game activity in LD, it is important to consider the challenges of their depiction. Salen and Zimmerman (2004) propose Rules, Play and Culture as three schemas for describing games.

Rules are the formal schemas that define the game, Play the experiential and Culture the context of shared values that make game play meaningful. These schemas map nicely to the education world, where learning designs as the formalizations of learning activities yield different experiences to different learners based upon the human and content aspects of the activities, interpreted through the cultural context in which the learning activity takes place.

As an example, it is useful to consider the variety of ways a simple children's card game, Memory, might be represented. The *rules* provide the simplest description in natural language:

> Memory is a card game for two or more players. The cards are randomly placed face down on a flat surface. A player turns over first one card and then another. If the face values pair up, then the cards are removed to the player's score pile and the player takes another turn. If they do not match, the cards are turned face down and the play passes to the next player. Play continues until there are no more cards left. The player with the most cards is declared winner.

While brief, the rules provide sufficient information to set up and play the game. The rules tell us when to take turns, how to end the game, and how to determine the winner. The rules clearly identify in natural language a number of elements to encode in LD:

- There is a *role* in the game for two or more players. Note that one player might be a computer, another a student or a teacher.
- The *environment* includes
  - the *materials*:
    - cards
    - a flat surface capable of holding all the cards face down – in a very generic way – generic enough that the game can be played on the floor, on a field, or on a computer screen.
- The *activities* include
  - Preparation – randomize cards and deal face down on the surface.
  - Play – while there are cards
    - take a turn {flip two cards over, compare}:
      - if match remove and take another turn,
      - if not return cards and end turn.
  - Evaluation – compare piles; the one with the most wins.

Note how the rules are written for human understanding and are contextualized within our culture – it presumes we know what cards are, and that we have them available, that the players are capable of deciding which cards to turn over, and have the means to enact that operation. The *regulation* mechanism of taking turns is inherent in play, and the players have some means of comparing results to determine the winner. What is absent from the rules are other aspects of game playing such as conflict resolution – what do you do if someone insists on turning over all the cards at once? This is left to the players to interpret and enforce based upon their culture – if you violate the rules, then you are simply not playing the game, and if you don't quit cheating, your opponent will usually refuse to play with you or bash you on the head.

The rules are free of *content*, in this case the values of the cards. This means the game can be used with a large variety of content areas. In education it is common to build game shells so the content can be replaced quite readily. For mathematics the cards could contain equations to be solved mentally, or for biology, names to match with illustrated parts of the cell. No mention is made of *meta-content* that might be present but is not part of the game. For example, the cards might have a company logo printed on the back for advertising purposes, or the cards might have safety messages written on their faces so workers can be reminded of safe work practices while they play cards in their off hours.

The rules do not provide a game-playing *strategy*. Strategies are something experiential that players develop over time, and thus fall under Salen and Zimmerman's "Play" schema. In Memory a simple strategy most children learn is to pay attention and try to remember the cards flipped by other players. A poor strategy is to turn over a known card first because there is low probability that the next card will be a match. A better strategy is to work sequentially through the cards on the table. By turning over the next new card in a row, a player increases the number of known cards, since the second card turned over will either be a match (if the player's memory is good) or another new card.

Another possible representation of the game is a *visualization* such as a *picture* of the layout of the cards, which might help understand the preparation of the game, or a *flowchart* to chart the logic of the game.

Inevitably there may be *variations* on the game, depending on the culture. Local rules and handicaps might emerge to make the game easier for children. Games can have *progressive* levels of difficulty, or they can be *adaptive*, tracking the performance of each individual player and providing drill and practice in areas of non-mastery. There may also be variations in materials, in manipulation devices, in reward schemes, in timing, in the number of players, and the look and feel. All of these elements contribute to the complexity of designing and redeploying games.

As a game becomes more elaborate, it will take more time and effort to describe and document in any detail. The goal then is to come up with descriptions that are operationally sufficient. Games played face to face in a social setting will be easier to describe than those to be played on a computer. Indeed, while a set of rules might be adequate for the former, the latter will require scenarios, use cases, flowcharts, sequence charts and ultimately computer code. The prime questions are, "When dealing with the learning design of games, are there advantages in having a richer description language?" and if yes, "To meet practical constraints of documenting game algorithms, to what level of detail should it go?" "Is LD of itself sufficient to describe the rules, the play and the culture?".

Contrast the flowchart in Fig. 13.4 with the LD diagram in Fig. 13.5. These are different views of the same Memory game. While the familiar flowchart governs the flow of logic, the LD diagram depicts the relationships between roles, materials and activities. If computer games are ever to be successfully encoded in LD, the level of representation will have to match at least the level of logic of decision-making within each sub-activity. Perhaps the activity-structure feature of LD will need to be used to encode complex multi-path games, or games with adaptive rules that change with the maturity of the players.

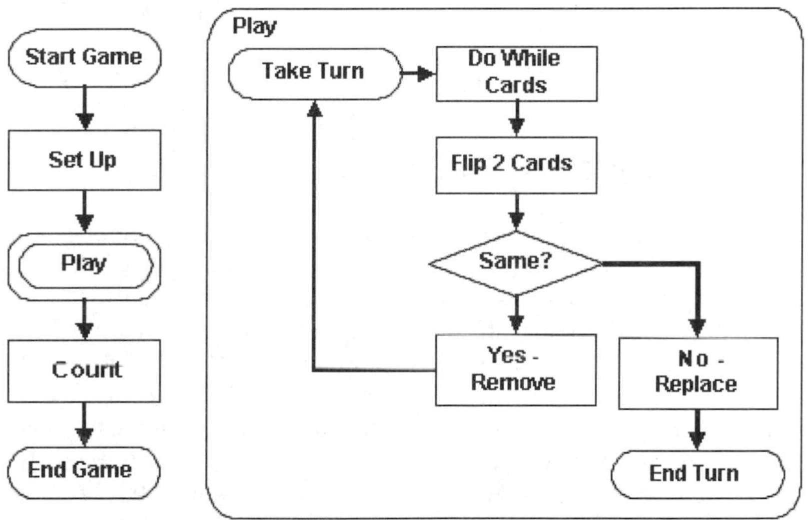

Fig. 13.4. Flowchart for Memory game

13.5 Discussion and Conclusions

Now that implementations of LD authoring tools and LD players have been delivered, it will be interesting to see the degree to which LD-Encoded games evolve and how game developers press for extensions to the current specification to facilitate detailing of game activities. The division between LD-encoded and LD-referenced templates is pragmatic.

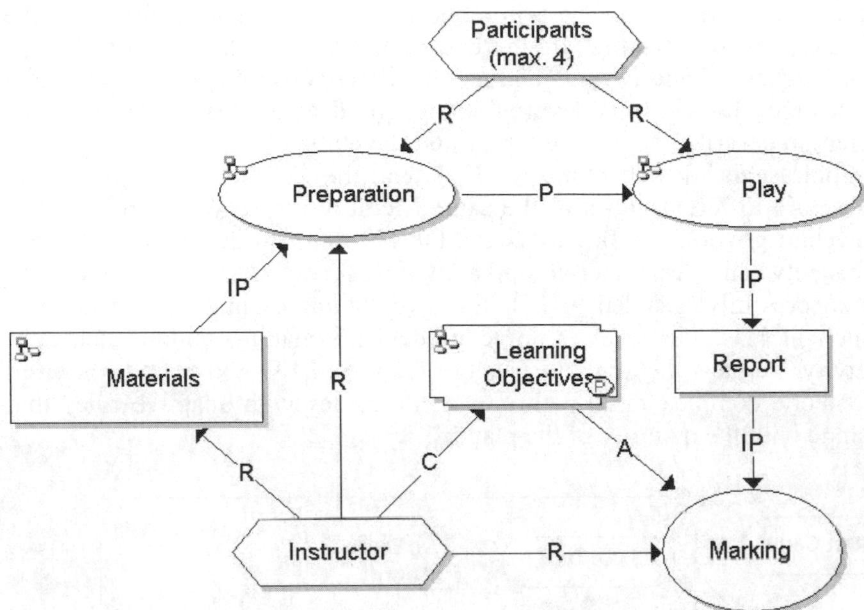

Fig. 13.5. LD graph of Memory game

Until we have more experience encoding games it may be more efficient to treat them as black boxes. Ideally it should be possible to have a library of interoperable game activity templates that could drawn upon to create the desired learning experience. It should be noted that the search for a game design meta-language is not new or unique to LD. Bjork et al. (2003) are in search of a game design pattern language somewhat akin to the pattern language proposed for architecture (Alexander 1977). However, pattern languages are essentially narratives of rules, and designs need to be semantically encoded in some ontology if they are to be effectively compared and recombined. This might be a possible role for a game meta-language variant of LD perhaps with extensions of the semantic-web variety that will allow a wider range of both representations and operations on those representations.

Should a library of LD-encoded game activities emerge we would then expect every LD player to interpret and reproduce every game experience. What is foreseeable is the evolution of a specialized LD game authoring tool which embeds the logic of several relevant game patterns, so that the author need merely choose the paths and decision points, and the resulting game could be reproduced on the generic LD player. An early example of a generic simulation authoring tool has been produced for emergency services training in the LogicProject (Key and Mundell 2004) where the author is free to link a variety of predefined presentation and response patterns to create a simulation case study that is playable through the web browser. While the range of simulation activities is limited to the templates available in the authoring system, there is no theoretical limit on the combinations and permutations that may be prescribed.

A repository containing examples of both LD-referenced and LD-encoded games that could be readily referenced by other lesson designers would be a useful starting point for encouraging the use of game activities in LD implementations and the adaptation of design templates to new instructional contexts. With time, the number and variety of examples and usage of both types of game inclusions can be expected to increase.

13.6 Acknowledgements

The author is grateful for discussions and comments of Olga Marino, Patrick McAndrew, and Peter Sloep, and to Bill Olivier and Gilbert Paquette for use of the Versailles simulation. Jim Bizzocchi provided valuable insights on game design.

This chapter was made possible through the Canarie e-Learning Program as part of the eduSource Canada Project. Partial funding for this work was received from the Social Sciences and Humanities Research Council through the SAGE (Simulation and Gaming in Education) Collaborative Research Initiative, and the Natural Sciences and Engineering Research Council through the LORNet Research Network.

14 Designing Learning Networks for Lifelong Learners

Rob Koper

Educational Technology Expertise Centre,
Open University of the Netherlands, Heerlen, The Netherlands

14.1 Introduction

As discussed in the preface of this book, Learning Design (LD 2003) can represent many different approaches to learning, such as competency-based learning, problem-based learning or collaborative learning. However, most current designers have some implicit assumptions underlying their designs that can be summarized as follows:

- E-learning courses are developed by teachers or expert developers
- Following development, the course is put into practice by enrolling students and assigning teachers
- Students take the course and the support is provided by the teacher
- Assessment is the responsibility of the teacher or an institutional or super-institutional entity
- The curriculum prescribes which courses a student has to take
- Students study primarily within the context of a single institution and with fellow students who also study within the same institution.

Given the current demand for more flexible, self-directed, informal and formal lifelong learning opportunities and the need for more efficient teaching scenarios, these assumptions provide an unnecessary restriction on the set of possible design solutions for a learning problem. In lifelong learning, roles are not fixed as implied above: students can be (co-)producers of course materials, can perform assessments (e.g. in peer and self-assessment), and can support other students. Similarly, teachers and experts can both teach and learn at the same time in a certain field of expertise. In the five-year RTD programme, called 'Learning Networks: connecting people, organizations, autonomous agents and learning resources to establish the emergence of effective lifelong learning' (Koper and Sloep 2003), we examine a form of education delivery that goes beyond course- and curriculum-centric models, and envisions a learner-

and curriculum-centric models, and envisions a learner-centred and learner-controlled model of lifelong learning where learners have the same capabilities as teachers and other staff members have in regular, less learner-centred educational approaches, but without increasing the workload for learners and staff members. Mechanisms responsible for this efficiency are the principles of self-organization (e.g. Hadeli et al. 2003; Maturana and Varela 1992; Varela et al. 1991) and software agents (Jennings et al. 1998) that provide support and feedback for people in performing their learning and support tasks in the learning and teaching process. It is expected that the application of self-organization principles will help empower learners to move beyond passive consumption of e-learning content towards active production (Fischer and Ostwald 2002). This shift of control aims to help relieve the burden on providers to predict needs, costs, expected use and income, and tilt the balance of responsibility for learning processes towards the learners themselves (see Tattersall et al. 2003).

We see a central role for LD in several aspects of realizing a Learning Network:

1. It provides a means to design courses that are modelled according to the lifelong learning perspectives discussed above (e.g. using peer assessment and peer support).
2. It formalizes the design in a semantic way, enabling automatic processing of software agents.
3. It facilitates pattern analysis of successful learning designs since the designs use a uniform specification language. These patterns can be used to help develop higher quality courses.
4. It enables the development of interoperable tools and content that can function in a distributed network and supports the sharing and reuse of learning objects.

This chapter presents a possible design for such a Learning Network, using LD.

14.2 Requirements of a Learning Network

Like any network, a Learning Network (LN) can be represented as a graph with nodes. An LN is a two-mode network, with the nodes being *LN members* and *Units of Learning* (UOLs). In the following sections we will aggregate the two modes into a single node, called an Activity Node (AN). An AN contains all the *runs* of all the versions of a UOL, including information about the members who are (or have been) active in it together with information the members have produced about it (e.g. feedback, completion data). Moreover, it contains a set of rules that govern its lifetime, specifically its 'fading out' and 'staying alive' behaviour. There are subtle but important differences between a UOL, a UOL run, and an AN. A UOL is the learning facility that is defined abstractly for any set of learners at any time. A UOL run is its instantiation for a specific set of learners in a certain time frame (e.g. a class, the actual run of a workshop). An AN is the set of all possible runs for different versions of the UOL.

The requirements for an LN are specified in Table 14.1 (from Koper et al. in press). These requirements can be elaborated in a 'use case model'. Use cases are abstractions of scenarios in which the concrete behaviour of persons within a system, or using a system, is described (Fowler 2000; Cockburn 2001). A use case model contains, among other things, use cases, actors and relationships. 'Use cases' (the ellipses in the diagrams in Fig. 14.1) are sequences of actions required of the LN to function properly. The 'actors' (the stick figures) are the persons or software agents that initiate the use cases, perform them or benefit from them. 'Relationships' (the lines in the diagrams) link two elements to show the interaction. The diagram in Fig. 14.1 is drawn according to the UML use case diagram specification (OMG-UML 2003; Booch et al. 1999). There is only one actor in an LN, the LN member. There are three types of LN members: lifelong learners (primary actors), providers and software agents, each of which can play roles in the management of the LN. Members can act individually or in groups. Groups can be formal (e.g. company employees) or informal. Software agents can, in principle, perform the same use cases as any of the human actors, but in most situations they will support a human member in performing a specific use case. Lifelong learners have specific expertise and competence in the discipline and these must be registered and updated in a learning dossier. The competence and expertise levels stored in the dossier must be standardized to be able to position a learner in an LN. A key notion in LNs is that lifelong learners can perform all the use cases, including those that are traditionally the responsibility of teachers. Control is expected to be distributed democratically using a set of agreed policies. The policies, the mechanism that provide feedback (usage patterns, monitor emergent properties and log tracks), and the reward system are the basic instruments to create self-organization in the system. Providers can be educational institutions, companies and libraries that provide lifelong learners (e.g. employees), the learning services (e.g. tutoring services) or the learning resources (e.g. books, CDs). LN members can perform a variety of primary use cases: for example, search an AN to plan a suitable learning route; get or access an AN; study an AN; or provide feedback about an AN.

Table 14.1. General Requirements for LNs

No.	*General Requirement*
R1	The objective of any LN is to offer long-lasting, evolving facilities for the members to improve and share their expertise and build the competencies needed in a disciplinary field.
R2	An LN should offer facilities for members to create, search, get/access and study LNs, ANs, UOLs and learning resources as a means of building expertise and competence.
R3	An LN should be governed by community policies that reflect the common goals and values of the membership. Instruments must be available to manage, change and apply the different policies (LN objectives and values, terms of use, standards and quality, reward systems, membership policies).
R4	An LN should have facilities to assign its members to specialized roles according to certain role policies. Roles are not fixed. Role change policies must be available.
R5	An LN should offer facilities to search for ANs and UOLs that match the members' needs and LNs, and should support flexible learning routes (positioning, logging of tracks of others and usage patterns).
R6	An LN should contain ANs and UOLs for different levels of expertise to serve a heterogeneous membership.
R7	An LN should offer ANs and UOLs in which learning designs are based on pedagogical models that are selected as suitable for the discipline, the membership and the learning objectives (e.g. problem-based and learner-centred, formative assessment, knowledge and community-centred).
R8	An LN should facilitate a high level of dialogue, interaction and collaboration within an LN and within ANs.
R9	An LN should support guidance/scaffolding, or more generally: support activities.
R10	An LN should support distributed control. LN managers are LN members with specific assigned management tasks (according to the change policies).
R11	An LN should provide first-order and second-order feedback to all members to support the optimization of organization and quality according to self-organization principles.
R12	An explicit exchange reward system which is consistent with self-organization principles should be available in LNs.
R13	An LN should have distributed, ubiquitous access.
R14	An LN should have facilities to provide automated support (software agents) for some members' tasks to make performance more efficient.

R15	An LN should use community standards for interoperability (e.g. UOLs, learner dossiers, learning/knowledge services and resources) and provide facilities to discuss and change these.
R16	An LN should find the right balance between usability for the participants and flexibility/complexity (information/training facilities, adaptable user interfaces, error-free technology).

Figure 14.1 shows the primary use cases as grey ellipses. The other use cases are specializations of a primary use case or are included in them.

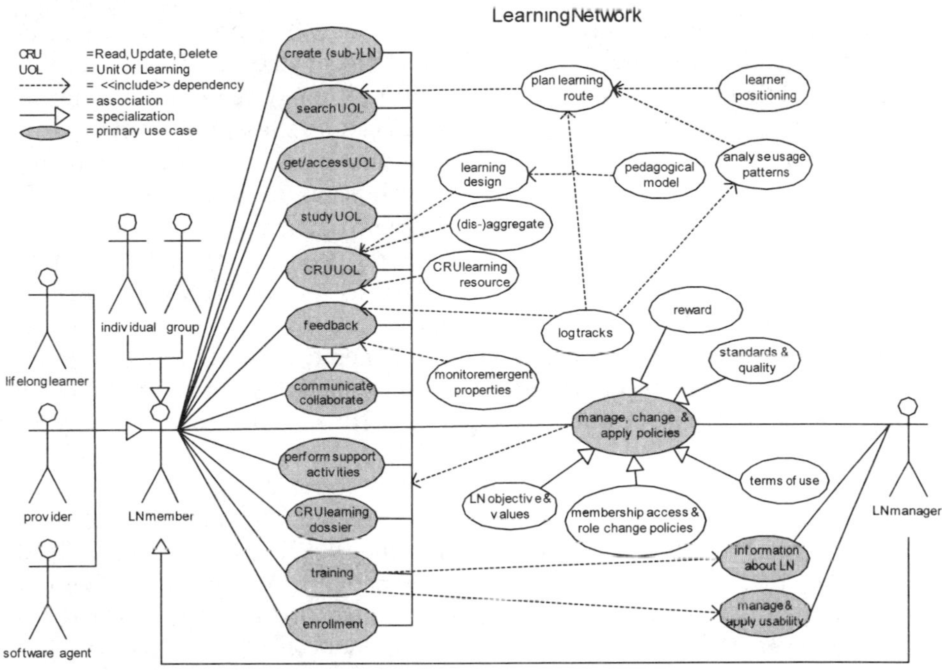

Fig. 14.1. Use case model for LNs

14.3 Formal Representation of a Learning Network

Using the AN concept, the formal structure of an LN can be represented as a graph in disciplinary domain D, with ANs as its nodes {a1, ...,*ai*} (Fig. 14.2). The nodes of the graph represent the available learning events, namely the ANs. An AN can be anything that is available to support learning, such as the different runs of a course, a workshop, a conference, a lesson, an Internet learning resource, etc. Providers and learners can create new ANs (and new runs within ANs), can adapt existing ANs or can delete ANs. In an LN, ANs are described with their metadata (title, objective, etc.) together with a link or reference to the actual AN.

An LN typically represents a large and ever-changing set of ANs that provide learning opportunities for lifelong learners (actors) from different providers, at different levels of expertise within the specific disciplinary domain.

When using the LN, actors travel from AN to AN. The path of ANs completed sequentially over time by an individual actor is called a learning track. A track represents the actual behaviour of actors. Paths through an LN that are planned beforehand are called routes (see Fig. 14.2). In traditional education, teachers or instructional designers are responsible for this route planning (e.g. curriculum planning). In lifelong learning, a different approach may be followed. Learning tracks can be shared between the participants in an LN. This can be a single track or an analysis of the aggregated, collective tracks from a set of participants to determine the most successful routes. This data is expected to help actors navigate in the LN.

Another concept in an LN is the learner's position in the LN (in Fig. 14.2, the set {a4, a8, a10}). This is defined as the set of ANs marked as completed in the LN, based on the actor's portfolio. This does not necessarily mean that the actor completed the concrete ANs, but covers situations in which the objectives associated with the ANs are already met by the actor (e.g. as a result of exemptions arising from previous study or work experience).

A target is any set of ANs that is sufficient to reach a particular level of competence or expertise in the domain (Fig. 14.2, the set {a1, …, a8}). These targets and their connected competency levels may be self-defined (e.g. step by step) or are predefined in the network. When creating an LN conforming to a predefined competency framework (e.g. European Language Levels (CEFRL 2001)), it is a requirement that every AN indicates its prerequisites and learning objectives in terms of the framework.

A target can be associated with one or more formal assessments to certify knowledge or a competency. This either can involve an additional, specific kind of AN, or can be integrated into one or more ANs. The difference between the set of target nodes and the set of position nodes defines the set of ANs that a learner has to perform to reach the target. Fig. 14.2 shows this to-do list as the set {a1, a2, a3, a5, a6, a7}. Given this list, a sequence of learning steps can be established, by deciding on the order in which the ANs are taken (e.g. first a3, then a1 and a5 simultaneously, then a2 and a7 simultaneously, and finally a6; see Figure 14.2). This decision can be based on the tracks of other successful and comparable learners in the LN. A learner can also follow a more exploratory route or can change routes on demand. Ultimately this will also create a track that can be shared.

position and target

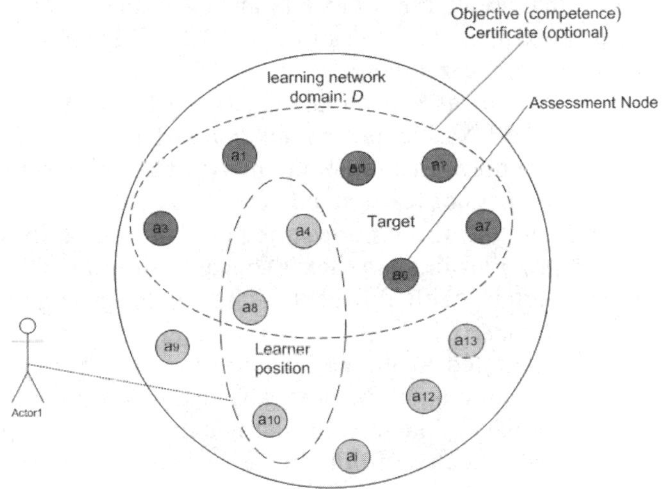

learning route

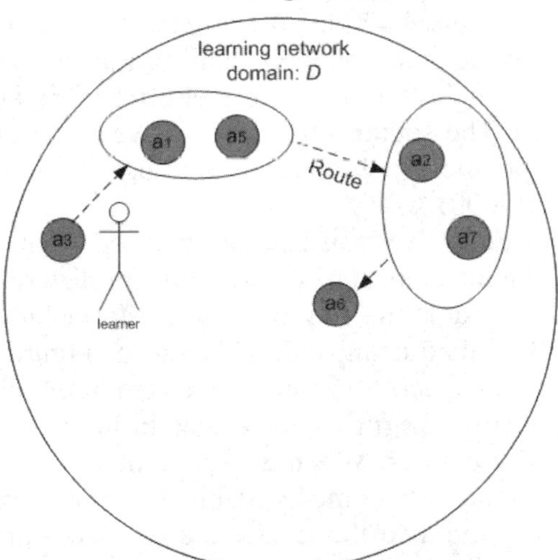

Fig. 14.2. LN in domain D with ANs {a1,…,a13}

14.4 The Architectural Structure of a Learning Network

Using the above requirements a model can be designed of the architectural structure of an LN (see Fig. 14.3). The model identifies the classes (the named boxes in Fig. 14.3) that are of importance in an LN and it specifies the relationships between the classes (the lines in Fig. 14.3). The main aspects of the architecture are summarized below.

The available LNs are listed in a web portal which can be freely accessed for information about the LNs. People can take on different roles in the LN according to certain policies in the community. Members can be learners, tutors, assessors, providers of learning content, etc.

The LNs themselves are not part of the portal: the portal only describes the LNs with metadata and provides links to them. This also allows for the establishment of different portals, with different views on the available LNs, running at different locations.

Software agents can be integrated in the architecture to support users, such as in providing recommendations on the next ANs to study, to search and filter information and knowledge sources in the network and to help users in performing certain tasks, such as filling in forms or using the system.

An *LN* lists the available *ANs* by the learning goals they can be used to attain. The behaviour of learners is logged and feedback and advice can be provided based on analysis of the behaviour of learners. ANs can be rated by learners or other reviewers to indicate their quality. For every person enrolled in an LN, a dossier, including a portable ePortfolio, is kept (together with some local data). The social interaction between the different participants is governed by policies, including terms of use, quality, membership policies, etc. (Preece 2000).

Three different aspects in every AN can be distinguished: 1) its design as available in the UOL 2) the different runs of the UOL for different users and different time schedules, and 3) the runtime resources (including services). The design can be described using LD. This part of Figure 14.3 is sketched in less detail (only roles, activities, etc.). To expand the diagram, the LD UML class diagram (Fig. 2.6 in Chap. 2) has to be merged with this diagram at the appropriate classes. When a UOL actually runs within an AN, additional runtime resources become available. Examples are email and conference contributions, and also the traces and resources produced during additional and non-described activities.

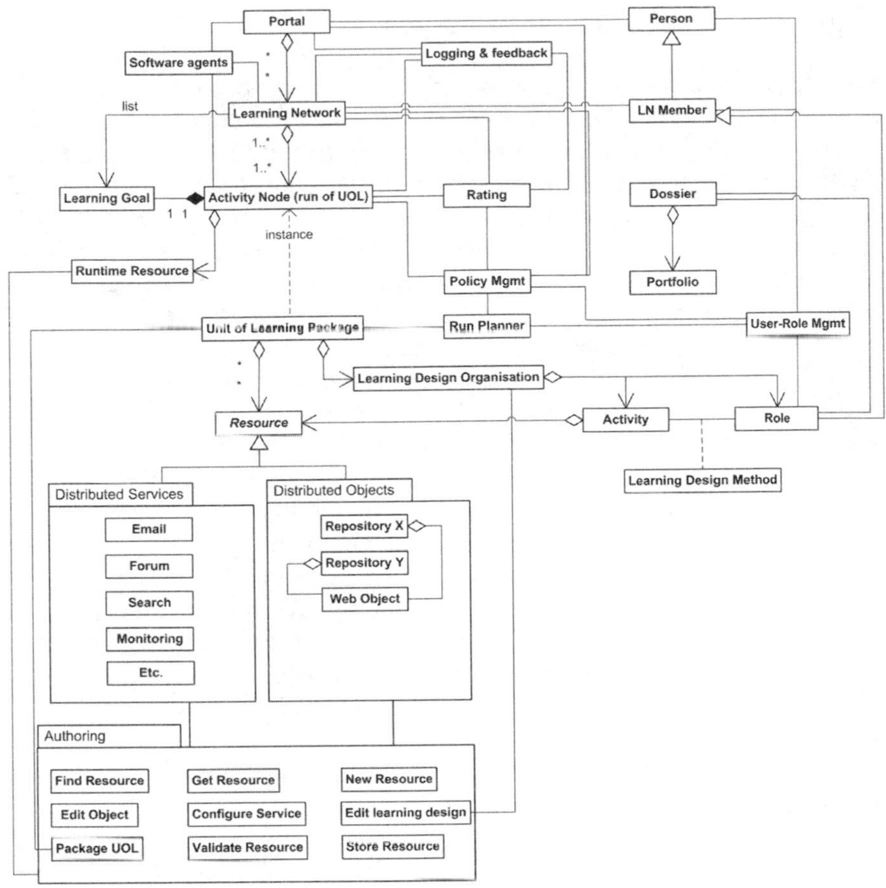

Fig. 14.3. Conceptual model of an LN's architecture

14.5 Implementations of a Learning Network

Two different prototypes were created based on the principles discussed above. The first prototype was created using Groove, a fairly easy to customize, peer-to-peer collaborative environment. The second, recent prototype was built with the experience we had using Groove, and is based on PHP Nuke and Moodle (see http://hdl.handle.net/1820/207).

14.5.1 The Groove-Based Prototype

Groove (groove.net) uses the concept of shared workspaces. A workspace can be created by any user (manager), who may then invite others to join the workspace in the role of manager, participant or guest (with different rights attached to each role). Users with the appropriate rights can add tools to the workspace from a predefined tool-set, such as discussion forums, shared files, collaborative writing, shared web navigation tools and shared calendars. Users may use the tools according to their roles. An important feature is that all users share the same tool-set. No user is privileged to access any special tools. This satisfies one of our major criteria for self-organized LNs. Policies can be communicated and implemented by setting user-rights. When setting up the Groove prototype, the logical model of LD was used, not its XML Schema binding. The test was primarily functional and not technical, i.e. interoperability issues, reuse and runs on multiple platforms were not supported in the prototype. Groove specifications indicate that the environment is highly programmable and uses XML for data storage. A subsequent implementation of the LD XML import and export should be possible in principle. In another project, the authoring part of the architecture has also been implemented in Groove in the context of the European Project aLFanet (see Chap. 18). This editor creates UOL packages in XML according to the LD specification (see manual at http://hdl.handle.net/1820/103).

The design of an LN described above was implemented as follows in Groove workspaces:

- An LN is a workspace with a name that starts with 'LN:', e.g. *LN: psychology*.
- An AN is a workspace with a name that starts with 'AN:', e.g. *AN: intervention-strategies*.
- Learning and support activities are modelled as records in a database with forms (using the Groove Form tool).
- Activity structures (sequences and selections) are created by organizing the sequence of the activities in a list and by providing extra textual information about the sequencing (see Fig. 14.4).
- Learning objects and services are links within the activity record with specific tools and resources in the environment.
- An environment is modelled as a labelled group of tools and services in Groove.
- Learning objects are contained in a files tool within the environment.
- Services, specifically discussion forums, sketchpads and outliners, are included in the environment as separate tools.

- Tracking and monitoring is implemented by asking learners to provide the necessary information in a form.
- Membership of the LNs and ANs is made visible by Groove (including on-line/off-line status and published profiles).
- Navigation is supported as follows: Groove provides a list of ANs to select from. The preferred route is modelled by listing each AN as a message in a discussion tool. The access files that Groove needs to access the ANs are attached to the messages. They are updated for every new AN that is developed.
- Communications and collaborations that are not related to specific LNs or ANs are supported by the standard communication facilities of Groove (e.g. chatting and setting up workspaces for sub-groups).

We conducted a study, reported in Koper et al. (in press), to determine to what extent the implementation met the criteria as stated in Table 14.1. The users were 25 participants with different levels of pre-knowledge who used Groove in a self-organized way to learn more about e-learning. Most of the participants created some ANs, and at the same time they studied other ANs of other participants. At the end of the sexperiment (6 month), 22 ANs were created and studied. Most of the basic use-cases were implemented like the search, study, get/access, etc. use-cases. To be more specific: the findings showed that we were able to implement most requirements except for R12 (reward system). It was not necessary to implement such a function in our rather closed situation, where one aspect of the community members' assigned activities was to participate in the LN. However, it seems to be a crucial function in more open, distributed, larger LNs. Issues such as internal/external motivation and financial versus other rewards (fulfilment of personal needs, reputation) have to be elaborated. Further, more generic economic principles such as exchange mechanisms in LNs need further study, specifically how to reward active participation and contributions of particular qualities in the LN. An analysis of the implications of theories such as the social exchange theory (Thibaut and Kelly 1959; Constant et al. 1994) for LNs is required.

Several requirements were only partially implemented, namely: R5 (flexible learning routes), R7 (pedagogical models), R11 (feedback), R13 (ubiquitous access), R15 (standards) and R16 (usability). To create flexible learning routes one needs to develop: a framework for the assessment of the learner's position in the LN; a method to define targets in it; a method to calculate learning routes; and a method to analyse usage patterns. We concluded that these topics should be further explored in future work. To support the use of adequate pedagogical models (R7), better design tools should be developed or selected. With respect to R11, a future system should include enough tracking data to be able to provide second-order feedback to stimulate self-organization. Ubiquitous access (R13) is another issue that should be elaborated. We envision that in a future LN, participants will be able to choose which tools to use in any situation (at home, at work, or 'on the road'), given compliance with certain standards. They may prefer their own email and chat systems to functions built into the LN application. Groove offers good facilities for off-line work, but at the price of using a specific client instead of the more common Internet browser. With respect to standards (R15), we need to address the issue of competence more than we did in this implementation. We had rather few ideas about a learner in the LN, and these ideas were not specific enough for us to measure progress. This should be improved. The last partially satisfied requirement was usability. We reported on learnability, technical problems and the lack of overview for navigation purposes. All these issues are related to the usability of Groove.

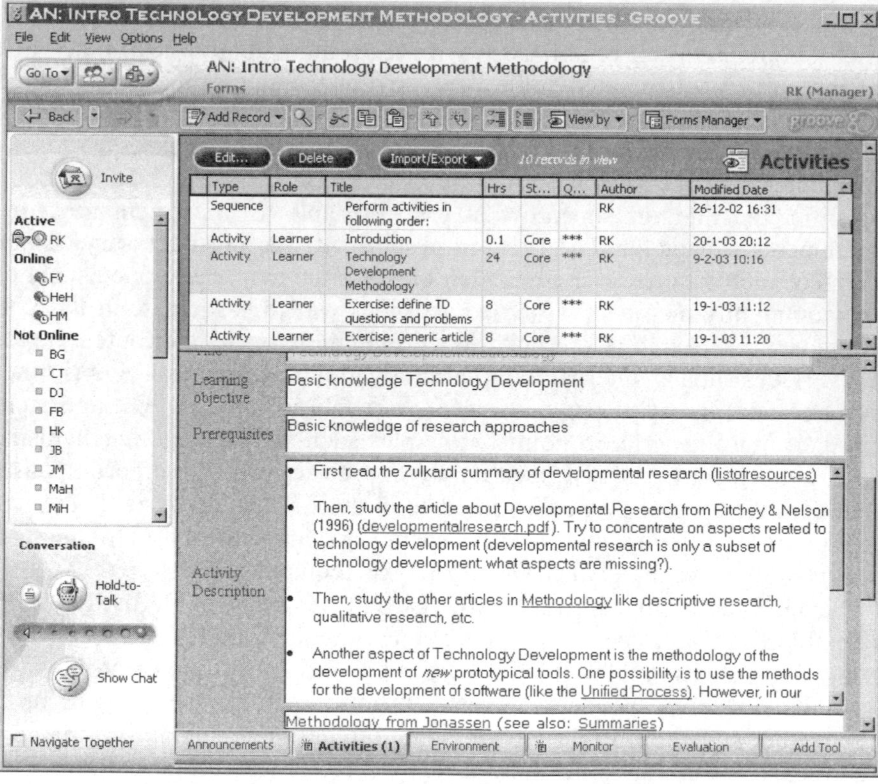

Fig. 14.4. Implementation of activities

14.5.2 PHP Nuke and Moodle

We evaluated the use of Groove as a platform, and although Groove provided us with the possibility of easily implementing some of the use cases from the LN framework, it was not without its disadvantages. In addition to the functional requirements, the main issues for selecting and developing tools for LNs are: technical stability; performance; sustainability; scalability; the use of open standards; and the use of commonly available tools such as email and webbrowsers. We decided that our next prototype would be based on open-source tools and components only. The LN component of the architecture is implemented in a package called PHP-Nuke (2004). It provides several views on the information about the different ANs available in the LN. The information *about* an AN is implemented as a PHP-Nuke item linking to the actual AN. The actual ANs can be any of a number of learning events – a face-to-face meeting or a course in a learning management system.

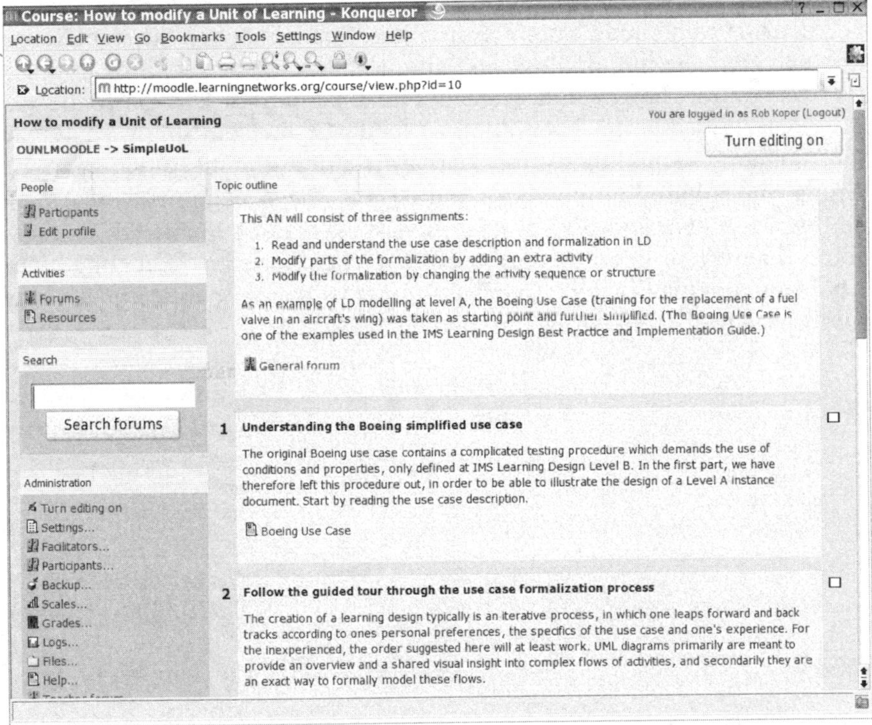

Fig. 14.5. The Moodle user nterface representing an AN within the LN for learning design

We selected Moodle (Dougiamas 2004), and an LD runtime system called CopperCore (see Chap. 6) to represent the ANs and UOLs. The idea is, however, that anyone can use his/her own systems that are integrated through the architecture. One of the first experiments created with this infrastructure is sponsored by the EU UNFOLD[1] project (UNFOLD 2003) and is establishing an LN for people who want to study learning design (see: ln4ld.learningnetworks.org). Figure 14.5 gives an overview of the userinterface of Moodle as it currently stands, just prior to the opening of the platform to the public.

14.6 Conclusion

We have presented a model for the design of a distributed network to support lifelong learning based on the use of LD. In order to explore implementation of the requirements, we created prototypes and used them in practice. The study of LNs is still in its exploratory phase. A great deal of work remains to be done to refine the framework, improve the implementation and evaluate the effectiveness and usability of the facilities in practice. LNs provide, however, a strong application area for LD. Currently we are working towards the integration of feedback mechanisms for navigational support, technologies for learner positioning, the calculation of learning routes based on positions and targets, the development of a suitable reward system and the use of software agents to support the primary actors. Interested readers may follow our progress at the site www.learningnetworks.org and view the publications at http://dspace.learningnetworks.org/handle/1820/11.

[1] UNFOLD (IST-2002-1_507835, January 2004 to December 2005) is funded under the European Union's Sixth Framework Programme. It is a Coordination Action within the Technology-enhanced learning and access to cultural heritage Action Line of the Information Society Technologies area.

15 How to Integrate Learning Design into Existing Practice

José Janssen, Henry Hermans

Educational Technology Expertise Centre,
Open University of the Netherlands, Heerlen, The Netherlands

15.1 Introduction

What does it take for an institution to adopt the Learning Design specification (LD 2003) for the design, development and delivery of its courses? What are the implications at an organizational level? These questions will be addressed in this chapter, drawing on the experiences gained at the Open University of the Netherlands (OUNL) with the deployment of EML. EML is the XML-based Educational Modelling Language developed at the Open University and later integrated in LD as the basis for the modelling of learning designs (EML 2000).

Although there are clear differences between the EML and LD specifications, which will be described in more detail in the next section, there are also many parallels. These parallels are sufficient enough to consider the process of adopting EML on a large scale as a valid frame of reference for deploying LD within an institution or organization.

The OUNL started using EML on a wide scale within its regular course development process in 2002. At present (March 2004) a total of nine courses are delivered to over 2000 users (students and staff) via the Internet, using Edubox. In addition, several other courses have already seen their life-cycle come to an end, including courses developed with external partners and hosted by the OUNL.

In terms of LD some of these courses represent Level B designs, but most of them include the use of notifications (Level C). The type of courses and the tools used in developing and delivering these courses will be described in greater detail below, in Sect. 15.3.

Having thus described the context and the extent of experiences relating to the use of EML within the OUNL, the remainder of this chapter will address several "how to?" questions, regarding the integration of an educational design specification. These "how to?" questions are presented in chronological order, following the stages in the course[1] development and delivery cycle: design, creation and delivery. The stage of analysis preceding the design stage is considered to have led to the decision to develop (part of) the course within LD and will not be dealt with separately.

Attention will be paid to what we perceive as a continuum between different approaches regarding the development of LD courses, with a "tailor-made" approach at one end of the scale and a "bulk" approach at the other. The variety of possible approaches in using LD and the consequences involved in choosing a certain approach will be considered throughout the chapter.

15.2 EML and LD

Is it justifiable to say that the experiences at the OUNL in adopting EML can serve as a model or guide for the integration of LD elsewhere? It is necessary to recognize that there are some differences between LD and EML, the most important being that:

- EML is a single, all-embracing approach to developing learning experiences, making it possible to model, for instance, all types of questions, whereas LD offers a framework which references other specifications in order to model questions, metadata, etc.
- EML contains a content model, allowing content to be modelled "in EML", whereas LD has no content model, leaving it open as to how (in what format) content is modelled, although XHTML is recommended.

In relation to the processes described in this chapter, these differences are not too significant. EML may be conceived of as an implementation of the LD framework, with specific choices regarding the content model and the use of metadata.

In general, the quality of design and creation tools determines to a large extent the efficiency of business processes and strongly influences the acceptance of learning technologies by teachers. As will become clear, tooling has been and still is a problem. However, this can be said to apply to EML as well as XHTML. So, these problems occur when working with EML as well as LD. However, although the availability of appropriate tools is an important issue with regard to the workflow and processes described in this chapter, we have aimed to consider and discuss this work-

---

[1] Courses are the smallest unit of delivery at the OUNL. However, courses may consist of more than one UOL. In some cases only parts of the course have been modelled in EML.

flow in terms of the underlying purposes and principles, regardless of specific tools. After all, tools can be expected to change and develop rapidly over time.

15.3 The OUNL Case

In the year 2000, after a two-year period of small-scale experiments, the OUNL launched a more ambitious experiment to explore the use of EML in the course development process as part of a strategy to become a Digital University. The so-called "Start projects" aimed to develop six demonstrable Units of Learning (UOLs) in EML within half a year. The ambitious nature of the project is evident from the fact that the staff involved in the development of those courses were trained on the job in working with EML. In addition, the experiences gained during the design and creation process were intended to result in a detailed description of the work processes involved. Prior to these Start projects only few educational specialists had gained any "hands-on" experience with the design and development of educational materials using EML. Now it was time to broaden the scope and see what it would entail to integrate EML in the organization, working with a team approach to course development, as is common with distance education institutions. Educational specialists, subject experts, editors and graphical designers received training and worked together to search for the most efficient ways to get the job done. The training involved both an introduction to EML and gathering hands-on experience with the tools used to create, edit and store EML documents: Framemaker+SGML and Microsoft's Visual SourceSafe. The tools used in the R&D phase were transferred, without finetuning, to the production environment. At this stage, a stronger division between design and creation appeared. Rather than having the educational specialist (incorporating EML expertise) doing all the "EML work", subject experts and support staff contributed as well.

Different teams developed different approaches. While some teams focused on the elaboration of a fully explicit pedagogical design before creating the corresponding structures in EML, others chose a more incremental approach. Some paid meticulous attention to the use of metadata, whereas others completely disregarded the issue of metadata. At the time, little integration within existing practices could be identified: the focus was on demonstrable products rather than courses to be delivered.

Meanwhile, several experimental implementations were also set up outside the OUNL. The development of a full curriculum at the Hotel Management School in Maastricht is particularly noteworthy. The separate modules of this curriculum were to be based on the pedagogical concept of competency learning. However, the lack of a common development approach and corresponding templates led to the production of a broad variety of learning designs. Time and money constraints forced the team to switch to a different development approach, in which design flexibility was restricted and a single design template was used to create the remaining courses. As a result of the conventions and rules underlying the (EML) template, the time required to create a concrete module design was reduced significantly.

Another noteworthy implementation is the Law-On-line project of the Digital University (DU), a consortium of universities and institutions for higher education in the Netherlands. The Law-On-line project aims for the joined development of on-line learning materials in a broad variety of law disciplines. These learning materials have a strong focus on self-assessment and are to be used within educational institutions using different delivery systems. Considering the collaborative development and the explicit purpose of reuse, this project has paid extensive attention to the use of metadata.

Back at the OUNL, from 2002 onwards, a step forward was made in the development of nine courses, modelled using EML. The courses were part of the regular curricula of several faculties. To support this major deployment a new version of the runtime system, Edubox, was developed by a software developer, based on specifications provided by the OUNL. In September 2003 the new player was put to use, delivering nine courses, to a total number of over 2000 students and staff members. Five of these courses include the use of notifications (LD Level C), whereas the other courses match LD Level B.

The integration of the EML/LD player into the existing virtual learning environment marks a shift in the functional use of the virtual learning environment. This shift may be characterized as a move from a predominantly supporting function, with a strong focus on information service, towards regulation of the primary educational process for both students and staff.

In conclusion we can say that the OUNL has moved from a pioneering stage towards a stage of consolidation. From all the different approaches and experiences gained hitherto, several recommendations have come to the fore, which will be discussed in the next sections. However, in our view the OUNL still has not reached a stage of full deployment/integration. In particular, authoring tools and processes need to be improved in order to gain more widespread acceptance within the organization and to be able to increase production efficiency. Nonetheless, the experiences gained in pioneering and experimenting offer a considerable empirical base from which guidelines may be derived regarding the adoption of LD within an organization.

15.4 How to Get Started

A major issue relating to the implementation of LD is the extent to which pedagogical flexibility is allowed within the (educational) organization concerned. If the organization is to allow the use of a broad variety of pedagogical concepts and models, this calls for a different approach and tools from an organization which wants to restrict the number of pedagogical models used.

The following scenarios illustrate the possible implications of both approaches, which may be taken to represent two extremes on a continuum.

In the "restricted" scenario the organization is likely to have a highly standardized approach to course development and delivery. Taken to its extreme, there is only one pedagogical model, e.g. problem-based education, and all courses are built in the same way: presenting a set of problems which need to be solved in several steps. Subject experts merely need to have a tool at their disposal whereby they can specify the problems and steps. Relevant materials and services can additionally be selected from a fixed set of resources, ranging from Internet sources to mail services. The tool presents a well-defined learning design, a form for completion, as it were, with a limited set of options to select from and 'blanks' to be filled by the subject expert. Subject experts can work relatively "undisturbed"; they need not know that "underneath" (in LD terms) the problem is an activity sequence and that each step represents a learning activity – nor need they consider other possible ways to model a problem-based approach.

At the opposite extreme of the continuum is the scenario resembling the "tailor-made" approach we have witnessed at the OUNL. Whereas in the first scenario a design can be considered to be integrated in the tool the subject expert uses, a tailor-made approach presupposes the flexibility to choose and develop an appropriate learning design. Experiences at the OUNL show that even in this scenario subject experts do not necessarily have to concern themselves with LD specification terminology or with XML authoring tools. Given the circumstances at the OUNL, and the need to work with XML tools in order to keep a wide variety of modelling options open, that side of things was left to the educational specialists, intermediaries trained in EML and the tools used to create it. Working according to this second scenario required considerable finetuning, which will be described in more detail in the following sections. This, of course, cannot necessarily be considered as a viable option in other contexts, where teachers work more individually and independently. A considerable challenge therefore lies in the development of authoring tools which support the design and development of a wide variety of models in a user-friendly way.

In order to get started, appropriate authoring tools, matching the necessary pedagogical flexibility and constraints, need to be chosen or created. Quite conceivably, the whole continuum of approaches needs to be supported. In this case the authoring tool(s) should allow the editing of "basic" LD files, on the one hand, and facilitate the creation of restricted templates, on the other hand (this approach is proposed by the architecture described in Chap. 3).

Once the relevant tools have been selected or created, staff involved will need to receive proper training regarding their use.

15.5 How to Design

During the design phase the outline of the course is planned. In the restricted scenario the design phase will involve matching course parts and content with predefined templates of courses or course-parts. For the tailor-made approach it is recommended that the course design is allowed to evolve in a number of iterative cycles, resulting from close cooperation between educational specialist and subject expert. First, a course outline is created, giving a "full picture" of all course components and the way they relate to one another. This outline is ideally represented schematically. Such a schematic representation ("educational architecture") could be a simple drawing in Word, a UML diagram, or some other, more sophisticated representation from, for instance, the MOT+ graphic editor described in Chap. 9. A schematic is created in order to facilitate communication and discussion between educational specialist and subject expert. It helps to establish whether all elements of the course are "in the picture" (e.g. different types of student and tutor tasks, different types of resources and services used). Although the educational specialist will already be analysing the course in terms of LD concepts, a schematic will describe the course in the terms used by the course itself. After all, it is intended to be a tool for communication between subject expert and educational specialist to establish whether they have a common understanding of the course and its constituent parts.

During the next step the educational specialist (EML/LD expert) translates the pedagogy and components of the course model to LD elements. The specific course model is mapped onto the pedagogical "meta model", which consists of abstract notions such as learning activities and learning objects. Figure 15.1 shows how a course can be considered as a specific example of a pedagogical model, which in turn is an illustration of the pedagogical meta model behind LD.

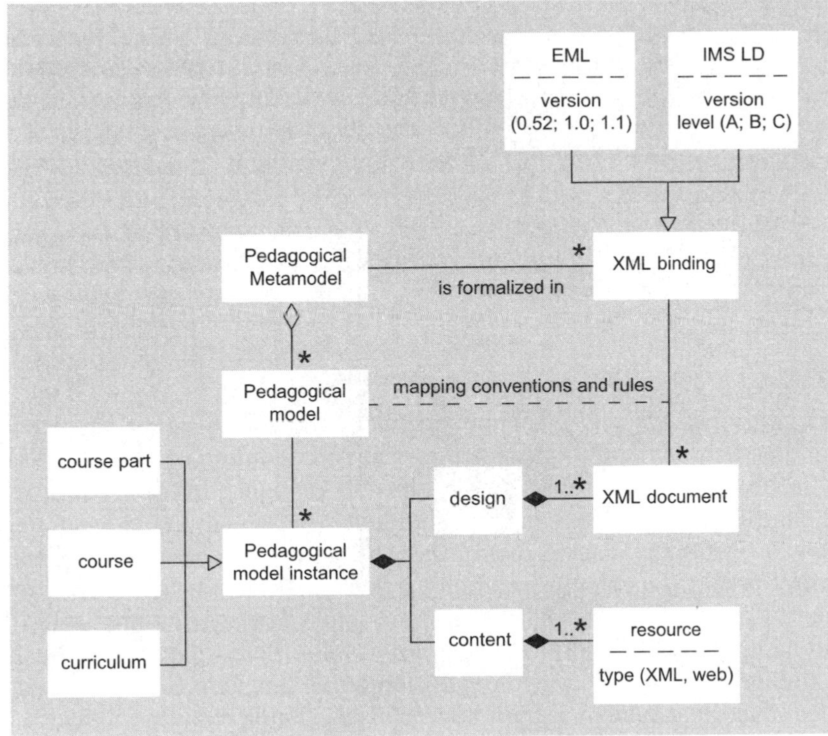

Fig. 15.1. A course as a pedagogical model instance

Figure 15.2 gives a more detailed description of the process of translating the course model to LD elements. First, the course is described in terms of roles, activities (and their inter-relatedness), tools and services. This is done separately for each role. Also, at this stage, decisions are made on the use of metadata, based on considerations regarding reusability: what metadata is needed on which levels? It is necessary to consider these issues at this stage as they may influence the way the course is modelled.

Once the schematic representation is agreed upon and the mapping of the course model to LD is finalized, a prototype can be created, which shows what the course will look like in practice for learners and staff. Thus, a better impression of the different roles within the UOL can be acquired by both the educational specialist and the subject expert.

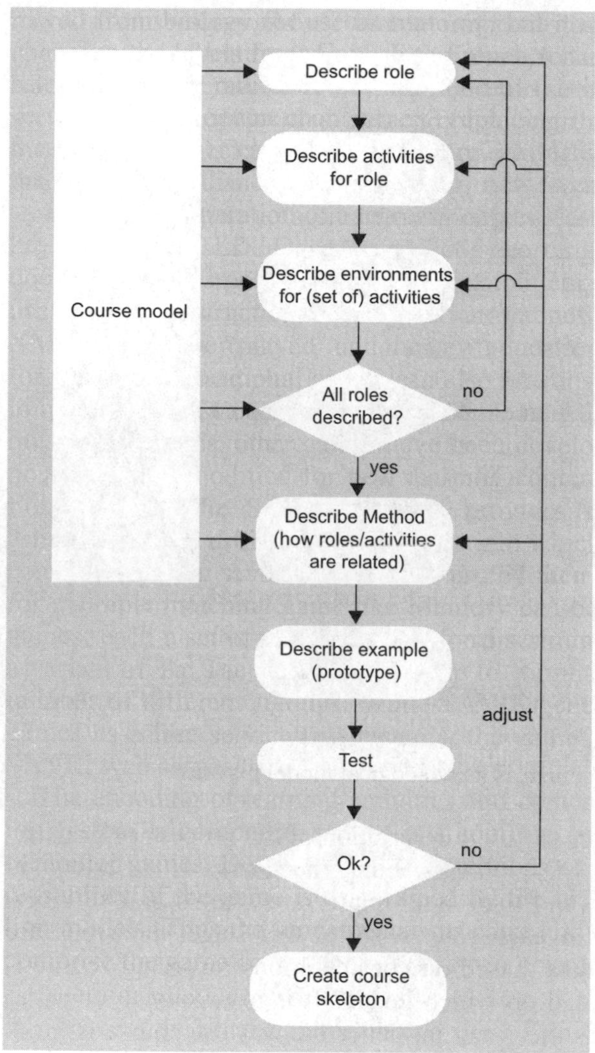

Fig. 15.2. The design process for the educational specialist in detail

So far, the design stage in the tailor-made scenario is a stage in which educational specialist and subject expert come to agree on an increasing level of detail in the design: creating a design is an iterative process, in which previous steps may require adjustments later on, when increased levels of detail may highlight omissions or misunderstandings. Several tools can be used (e.g. schemata, prototypes, etc.) to explain and discuss the design with colleagues who have no knowledge of LD and its concepts.

Once the design is agreed upon, i.e. the model and mapping as specified in the prototype are approved, and each component (e.g. "reading tasks", "exercises", etc.) of the specific course has been identified, it is possible to create the entire course structure in LD, along with templates for components such as learning activities and environments. We recommend that these templates are welldocumented with comments explaining how to use the template and what adjustments are necessary in order to create a new UOL or learning activity. The full skeleton of the course is thus created, which can then be "filled" with content and content-references. This process will be described in the next section. Figure 15.3 summarizes the workflow in the design phase.

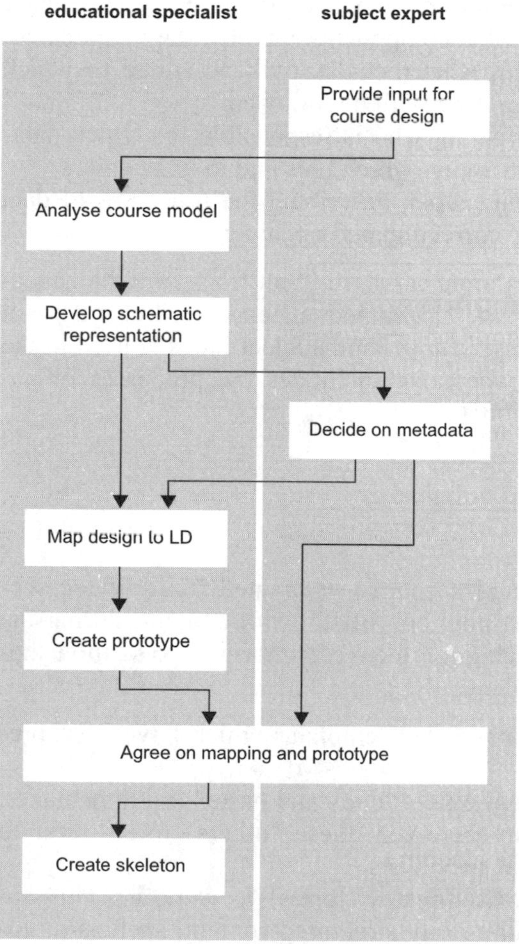

Fig. 15.3. Workflow in the design phase for educational specialist and subject expert

In addition to planning the course structure, arrangements need to be made regarding the storage of content and access to files. Decisions regarding the granularity, storage and management of content will have to be made right from the beginning of the design phase, when the issue of reuse is being addressed. By the time the full skeleton of the course is being created, a contentmanagement system of some kind must be available. However, the availability of a content-management system alone doesn't solve the problem of defining a proper content management strategy. A thorough content management strategy requires that attention is paid to:

1. The domain model, which describes which topics within the broader field of study are covered by what components and how they are related.
2. A metadata model, describing what metadata will be added to which components, and what logic or order will be followed.
3. An authorization model, describing who is responsible for which database files and/or authorized to access which files and to what extent.
4. A "life-cycle" or development model, describing the processes of data entry, publication and testing, correction and updating.

Obviously, this process involves input and agreement from both the educational specialist and subject expert. The subject expert contributes domain knowledge and expertise of classifications and subject indexes used in the field, whereas the educational specialist facilitates the processes of authorization, data entry, publication and testing.

15.6 How to Create

The templates selected (restricted scenario) or created (tailor-made scenario) in the design phase must now be "filled" with content, during the creation phase. Due to the lack of effective authoring tools, three approaches have been adopted at the OUNL:

1. Authors work directly in Framemaker templates which have been prepared for them.
2. Authors work in MS Word and others "copy and paste" to Framemaker. Depending on the complexity involved, these "others" might refer to supportive staff or educational specialists.
3. Authors are given MS Word templates (forms) to work in. This approach is appropriate only for strictly structured content, such as multiple-choice questions. The templates actually consist of EML structures which are hidden with only the relevant input fields (like "question", "correct answer") being visible to the author. This is comparable to the approach used in the Komposer tool described in Chap. 7, although the

approach described there is an alternative way of using word templates. After the form has been completed, the file is converted into an "EML file".

The third approach requires that all formatting (e.g. emphasis, lists, special characters, etc.) is added "manually" afterwards. In the first two approaches authors and data-entry typists receive instructions on the use of these formatting elements, should they have to be used. The approaches in which authors work either "freely" in MS Word or in MS Word templates entail more detailed planning, since extra handling by supportive staff or educational specialists is required. None of these methods of adding content to a design are either effective or satisfactory, illustrating the clear requirement for efficient and user-friendly authoring tools. Working with EML has meant that the OUNL has more or less been obliged to model content in the EML format, whereas LD (or rather Content Packaging) distinguishes between LD content and web content, making it possible, for instance, to simply add Word files. However, this doesn't mean that there are no problems regarding content-authoring in the context of LD. In all instances where content requires learners to produce some input, or where content must be presented in a uniform way (as specified through style sheets, for example) these resources must be created using XHTML, which is currently not supported by adequate, easy-to-use authoring tools.

Once content (including formatting elements) has been added to the design, either directly in EML or via templates, and has been validated, another cycle of evaluation takes place, in order to test the content. This particular stage of testing is comparable to the final editing of written materials and can be carried out by an editor, if they are sufficiently familiar with the content. Errors may result not only from spelling or typing mistakes, but also, for example, from putting a link covering a certain subject in the wrong place. If the editor is not sufficiently familiar with the subject, the testing will have to be undertaken by the author(s). Depending on the complexity of the design and the volume of content modelled this way, the iterative cycle of testing, editing and retesting may take a considerable amount of time, postponing the moment of completion of the course. Once testing has been finalized and any necessary adjustments have been made, the course is ready to be delivered to learners.

It should be highlighted that the process described above presupposes that content creation takes place "beforehand", in design time as opposed to runtime, when learners have already started studying the course. This approach does not necessarily need to be adopted in other contexts, although it is by and large the procedure used within the OUNL. Nevertheless, the delivery system used at the OUNL does allow content to be changed (updated) during delivery (runtime), although it does not allow alterations to the design, such as the addition of entirely new activities. It is important to note that this is simply how the system used by the OUNL is regulated, rather than being an inherent feature of EML or LD.

Figure 15.4 shows the workflow for the roles and tasks involved in the creation phase.

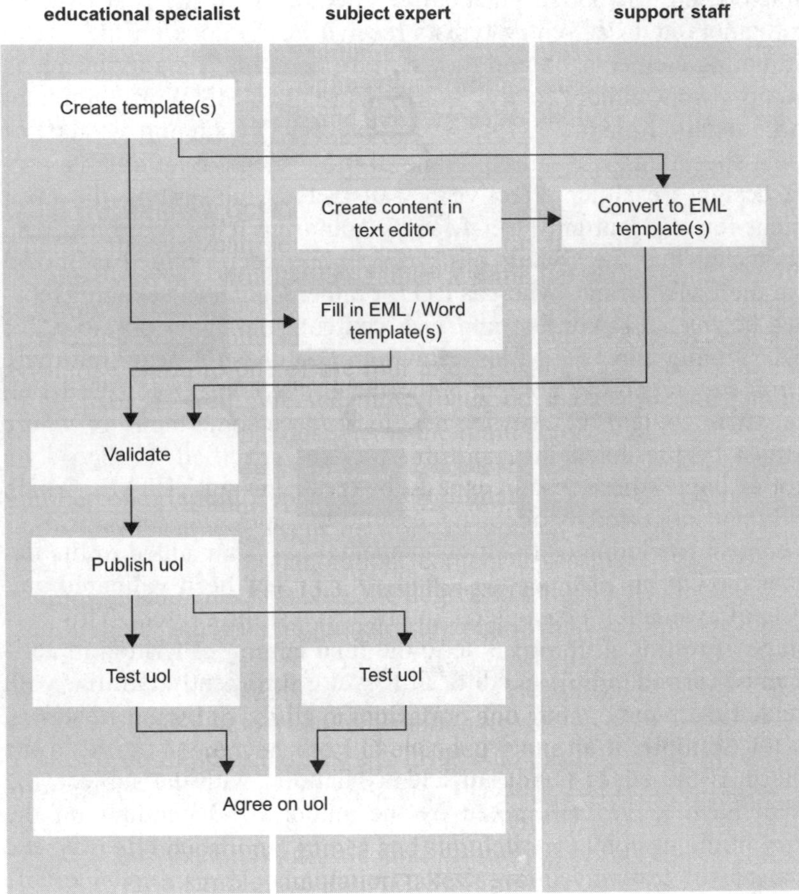

Fig. 15.4. Workflow in the creation phase

15.7 How to Deliver

LD courses at the OUNL are delivered via the web, using a delivery system called Edubox. In implementing a delivery system it is necessary to assess how it will be required to connect with other systems, for instance administrative systems. At the OUNL the delivery system is integrated with an electronic learning environment called Studienet and an interface has been created to connect to the student administration system. Within Studienet students have a personalized homepage; connecting the delivery system with the administrative system has made it possible to automatically add a link to a course delivered by Edubox to the homepages of students who have subscribed to that course. Students gain direct access to Edubox through a "sign-single on" capability, without needing to re-enter their user and password details. Other systems that could be integrated are services such as conferencing clients. However, these connections (interfaces), however relevant, primarily concern practical features of the production environment, rather than the core of the delivery process.

The process of course delivery typically involves a number of actions. The Edubox delivery system consists of two components: Edutool and the player. In order for a course to be made available to students and staff in the player, the course must first be published and users assigned to it. This involves several steps in Edutool:

1. Publication management: first the course must be published. This involves uploading all files and some technical "processing" to check references and materials. Publishing a course also requires a presentation format, which is specified using a style sheet, to be selected. In the player OUNL uses, activities and activity structures are presented in a frame that has the title "To Do". This could be modified depending on the pedagogical style and changed into, for example, "Tasks" or "Problems". It is also possible to provide different style options within a style sheet enabling the interface to be switched to another language.
2. Run management: publishing a course doesn't automatically make it available and visible. Students and staff have to be assigned to the course before it becomes accessible to them. This is done via so-called "runs". This is comparable to a face-to-face course being offered by an institution, where the course has been designed, materials prepared, but the classes have not yet started. Students and staff are 'scheduled' or assigned to the course through a run. Since several runs can be associated with a single version of a course, there is a "create once – use many times" situation. Runs offer a mechanism to spread a large number of students subscribed to the same course over several groups tutored by different members of staff or to organize students into groups according to the study centre they are related to. Run start and end dates can also be set. If a run has no end date specified and the course design or organization doesn't involve a particular grouping, newly enrolled students can simply be added to an existing run. As long as the course (the version) stays the same, it is sufficient to add new students to an existing run or to create new runs. (For more detail on the concept of "runs" see Chap. 4).

3. Role management: after runs have been created and staff and students have been allocated to specific runs, these staff members and students have to be assigned to the specific roles identified in the learning design. It is important to remember that while a course design must include at least one learner role, it may also include several additional learner and staff roles. At this stage of role management the *people* who have been assigned to a run are now assigned to the *role or roles* they will perform while taking or tutoring the course.

At present, at the OUNL, publication management, run management and role management are all coordinated by one person who is in charge of Edutool. However, one could, for instance, also authorize tutors to organize runs and manage roles, although this would require some instruction regarding the use of Edutool.

Other actions that may be necessary to enable the delivery of a course include:

1. Instruction of tutors: depending on the complexity of the design and the variations permitted by the style sheets it may be necessary for tutors to become familiar with the learning design as well as the interface.
2. Services required by the learning design, which the runtime system does not support, may have to be created/instantiated (e.g. communication services).
3. Content update: to the extent that content update may be needed in runtime, arrangements must be made regarding instruction and authorization of those responsible for the updates.
4. A helpdesk service should also be provided, for both students and staff. The need for helpdesk support is likely to vary depending on the scenarios in use. The experiences of the OUNL suggest that with tailor-made scenarios the helpdesk function may become quite complex. Filtering requests for help, in terms of identifying what the problem relates to (the student's computer, provider services, the OUNL learning environment, etc.), becomes more complex with LD, as the delivery system (interface and database operations) and the designs themselves may be potential sources of problems. Consequently, it is recommended that helpdesk staff should get back-up from the educational specialists involved in the design of the LD courses as well as from the staff responsible for Edubox.

15.8 Conclusion and Discussion

Integrating LD within an organization involves a considerable degree of planning, even if we take into account that in future many tasks will be facilitated by increasingly sophisticated and user-friendly tools. The need for additional organization stems from the fact that the deployment of LD introduces new tasks (e.g. related to the publication and authorization of courses), changes current tasks and the tools used to perform them (e.g. design, editing) and may even add to current tasks (e.g. helpdesk support).

In addition to providing staff with sufficient training in order to enable them to adjust to these alterations, the reason for these changes must also be carefully communicated. A notion not uncommon in the field of organizational change states: "As much as possible, necessary skills and favorable attitudes should be fostered *before* changes are introduced" (Johns 1996, p. 565). However, even though permutations on an organizational level may be justified, it may not always make similar sense on the individual level. This is why some level of reluctance or even resistance can be expected in bringing about these changes.

Favourable attitudes require efficient and user-friendly tools. Until these tools are available it is necessary to proceed with care. Even when highly efficient and user-friendly tools have become available, choosing a suitable deployment strategy will be an important first step. The choice between a tailor-made approach, a more restricted approach or a combination of both will also influence the selection of tools. Therefore, in answer to the question "How do you deploy LD within your organization?", our main recommendations are as follows:

1. Decide on the level of pedagogical flexibility/constraint required and choose tools accordingly. Other factors which should be considered include: the degree of (de)centralisation, level of specialization of staff, work processes, the need for runtime flexibility and cost-effectiveness. Generally speaking, allowing more pedagogical flexibility will produce higher expenses, due to the time needed to develop LD courses.
2. Following the guidelines provided in this chapter, consider the workflows involved and decide to what extent they either are supported by the tools chosen, or have been made redundant by increasingly sophisticated tools.
3. Communicate the rationale behind the deployment of LD, the consequences involved for staff and train staff to use the tools chosen.

Part III

EXPERIENCE

The final part of the book contains seven chapters presenting specific projects and initiatives that explore the use of LD within a specific context: company training, distance education, secondary level school and medical education. Since the LD specification was only released quite recently, most of the projects (also) deal with the development of tools as a condition for any experimentation in practice. The last chapter explores an example in some detail, examining both the LD code and interface used by learners.

16 Applying Learning Design to Self-Directed Learning

Martin Morrey, Charles Duncan, Peter Douglas

Intrallect, Linlithgow, Scotland

16.1 Introduction

In 2001 Intrallect Ltd was asked to deliver the first part of a large-scale programme of on-line learning for meteorologists. The customer, EUMETSAT, is a European agency responsible for the satellites that provide cloud images and derived data products to European meteorological services. EUMETSAT was about to launch its second generation of Meteosat satellites (MSG) and needed to train its customers how to use the new data.

Intrallect Ltd is a software company based in Linlithgow near Edinburgh, Scotland, which specialises in innovative e-learning solutions and learning object management. The company was spun out of the University of Edinburgh by the authors in 2000. Intrallect's three founders are all former atmospheric scientists, so they had good knowledge of the subject domain for this project. In their academic careers Intrallect's founders have been involved in several large-scale projects to deliver learning on the web. One of these, EuroMET (Gondouin 1996), was an EU-funded project which produced 4500 web pages of interactive learning content in each of four languages.

The scale of the EuroMET project led the team to develop a set of principles for e-learning development that they have applied in all their subsequent work:

- learning content should be as granular as possible (Duncan 2003)
- content should be separated from style and the delivery technology
- navigation of the granular materials should be defined externally, not embedded in the materials (Koper 2003b)
- most learning interactions can be expressed as an instance of generic interaction type.

The motivations for these principles are to maximise scalability, reusability and future proofing in the development of learning content. During EuroMET and related projects a kit of authoring tools and delivery tools was developed that applied these principles. The subsequent emergence of XML, and applications of it like the Educational Modelling Language (EML 2000), mean the above principles can be applied using readily available and widely used technologies. The authors were attracted to EML over other educational modelling languages (Rawlings et al. 2002) because it enables educators to define completely whole courses independently of the delivery technology, while potentially supporting a broad range of pedagogies.

This chapter aims to give the reader an impression of some of issues that may need to be considered in creating a practical implementation of Learning Design. The solution described does not use all the potential of Learning Design, because it was designed to satisfy the needs of independent learners, but it is a valuable example of how a profile of Learning Design can be developed to suit the needs of a particular project.

16.2 Requirements

The contract included requirements for a set of bespoke authoring and maintenance tools, and three initial "modules" of learning content. The Statement of Work stated that the solution should have the following general characteristics, among others:

- "Follow a structure based upon a library of modules."
- "Present clear learning objectives and follow a solid pedagogical scheme."
- "Different courses can be constructed from a common module library."
- "The structure will allow easy navigation (and location) throughout the material."
- "The contents should be structured to allow ease of translation into other languages."

The initial content was to be the seed of a library of reusable "units-of-study" which could be combined to create bespoke courses to suit particular institutions and study groups. The materials needed to be usable across a range of media, specifically the web and CD-ROM, so it was necessary to separate the learning content from the delivery technology. The target learners were weather forecasters in European meteorological organizations, considered to have a self-motivated and self-directed approach (Fischer and Scharff 1998) to their professional development.

A high frequency of formative interactions was required in the material, ideally at least one in each "knowledge object". The set of generic interactions that was agreed with the customer is listed in Table 16.1. The content of the questions and the content of the feedback for correct or incorrect answers could all contain images as well as text. Sequences of questions of the same type were displayed one after another.

Table 16.1. Agreed set of generic interactions

Interaction name	Description
Multiple choice question	One or more questions in which several choices are presented, one of which is the correct answer.
Multiple response question	One or more questions in which several choices are presented, one or more of which are the correct answer.
Matrix question	A series of questions in which the potential answers are all of the same type and presented in columns.
Image hotspot	An image is presented with a question whose solution is found by clicking on hidden areas in the image. Images may be multi-spectral, in which case the images are presented in a stack which can be viewed one image at a time.
Drag and drop	The question may include a background image and the interaction involves moving one or more text phrases or images to specified locations (for example, to form a list, or label a diagram). One draggable object may be located in multiple droppable locations.
Animation	A series of images are displayed and played as an animation. The controls available to the student include: start, stop, pause, step forward, step backward, play once, loop, swing, increase speed, decrease speed, show only every second image.
Slide show	A series of images is presented each with a text caption. The student can step backwards and forwards through the sequence.
Slide show combined with MCQ	Similar to Slide show but for each image in the sequence a multiple choice question can optionally be presented.
Special	Any valid code on a web page can be included using this option, which makes it easy, for example, to include Java applets.

The material was required initially in two languages, English and French, with the potential for translation into further languages later. A reference library was needed as part of the "environment" to give access to a significant collection of background material.

16.3 Application of Learning Design

16.3.1 Management of the Project

The high degree of flexibility required by the customer led the Intrallect team to choose EML to form the backbone of an effective solution. The activity model of EML was attractive because it allowed the pedagogical approach to be separated from the creation of the content. The built-in content model of EML allowed content to be written before the page design and interactivity mechanisms had been finalised. Translation of the text-based material was simplified because it was defined in a structured format. All of these activities could be progressed in parallel during the project.

16.3.2 EML and Learning Design

The original work was all completed before EML had been released through IMS as Learning Design (LD 2003). However, the use of the EML activity model described is equivalent to an implementation of LD. As described below, the Question and Test Interoperability Specification (QTI 2003) was used as the interaction model instead of EML's own interaction model, so this is highly relevant to an LD approach. Although the EML content model was used, it could easily be replaced by an alternative such as XHTML-Basic.

16.3.3 Navigation Model

The material was revealed to the learners as a set of "modules", which each required approximately 45 minutes of study time. The modules were viewed in an "Environment" which included a library of relevant reference material, links to communication tools, and a glossary of terms. Because the materials were designed for self-study, only the "learner" role was used. Modules were assembled from the units-of-study, in a branching path, including core material and optional sections.

In LD terms, each unit-of-study was a set of "knowledge objects" connected in a linear navigation scheme. The ordering of these knowledge objects into a unit-of-study was defined in a simple activity-sequence. At the next level in the hierarchy, units-of-study were combined in a parent unit-of-study which defines a module. The conditional paths between the child units-of-study were expressed as nested activity-structures. In order to provide a usable interface, it was necessary to limit the depth of nested activity-structures to three levels.

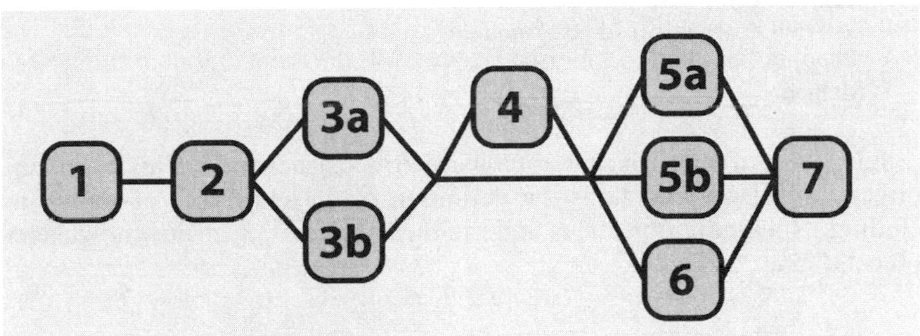

Fig. 16.1. Diagram showing the possible paths a learner could take through an example module. Each numbered square represents a unit-of-study. The expected movement is from left to right

An example of module structure is shown in Fig. 16.1. Learners were allowed to take any path through a module they chose, even jumping to the last unit-of-study or moving randomly through the units-of-study, but there was a notion of a recommended path which was defined in the EML "Method" for that module. An cxample of the "Method" part of the EML describing a parent (module-level) unit-of-study is given below. "Link-name" attributes have been removed for clarity.

```
<Method>
 <Activity-structure Default-visibility="Show" Id="module">
  <Activity-sequence>
  <Unit-of-study-ref Ref-worldwide-unique-id="1/struct.xml" />
  <Activity-selection Number-to-select="1">
   <Activity-sequence>
   <Unit-of-study-ref Ref-worldwide-unique-id="3a/struct.xml" />
   <Unit-of-study-ref Ref-worldwide-unique-id="3b/struct.xml" />
   </Activity-sequence>
   <Unit-of-study-ref Ref-worldwide-unique-id="3c/struct.xml" />
  </Activity-selection>
  <Activity-selection Number-to-select="0">
   <Unit-of-study-ref Ref-worldwide-unique-id="4/struct.xml" />
  </Activity-selection>
  <Activity-selection Number-to-select="2">
   <Unit-of-study-ref Ref-worldwide-unique-id="5a/struct.xml" />
```

```
  <Unit-of-study-ref Ref-worldwide-unique-id="5b/struct.xml" />
  <Unit-of-study-ref Ref-worldwide-unique-id="6/struct.xml" />
 </Activity-selection>
 <Unit-of-study-ref Ref-worldwide-unique-id="7/struct.xml" />
 </Activity-sequence>
</Activity-structure>
<Play>
<Role-ref Id-ref="learner"/>
<Activity-structure-ref Id-ref="module"/>
</Play>
</Method>
```

Each unit-of-study has a reference to a "struct.xml" file in a subdirectory. This file contains the definition of the child unit-of-study, including its learning objectives and the linear navigation of its knowledge-objects.

16.3.4 Extending the Interaction Model

The set of generic interactions agreed with EUMETSAT (Table 16.1) required a richer set of interactions than was available in EML 1.0. The obvious alternative was to use the QTI specification, which could support almost all the required interactions. After speaking to members of the OUNL team it became clear that it would be possible to replace the EML interaction model with QTI by inserting the QTI DTD into the modular version of the EML DTD.

In hindsight a better solution would have been to use XML namespaces to include QTI, but namespaces are not very compatible with XML defined in DTDs. At the time XML Schemas had only just emerged, and the EML and QTI specifications had not yet been given XML Schema bindings. If the project were being done again now, the most sensible approach would probably be to use XML namespaces to combine a pedagogy-defined LD with content described in XHTML-Basic and interactions in QTI.

16.4 Realisation

16.4.1 Design of Navigation Interface

One of the key challenges was to realise the "learning design" in a way that was easily comprehensible to the learners when they were navigating their way through the units-of-study. The Intrallect team came up with a "stepping-stone" metaphor for a unit-of-study. This made it possible to visualise a range of possible pathways through the units-of-study.

In the web realisation of this metaphor, colour was used to indicate completed, suggested and optional units-of-study. Learners were allowed to "jump" to any stepping-stone they wished, but a recommended path was always available. Figure 16.2 shows how the module structure described above was revealed to the learner.

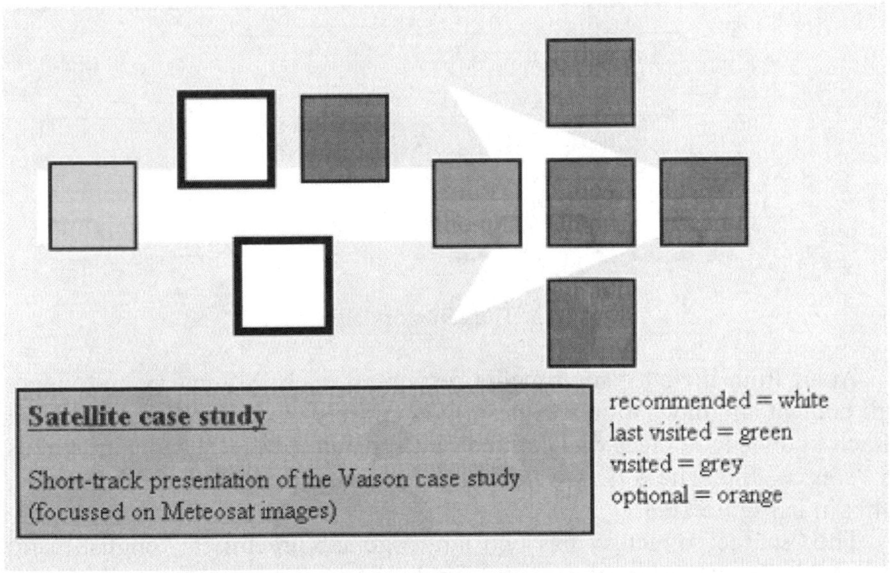

Fig. 16.2. Learners' view of the module structure

16.4.2 Structure of the Material

An XML editor applying the combined DTD was used by the content authors. A set of templates was provided to avoid having to create objects from scratch. Reusable and subject-specific media files are stored in separate sub-trees of the directory structure, shown in Fig. 16.3.

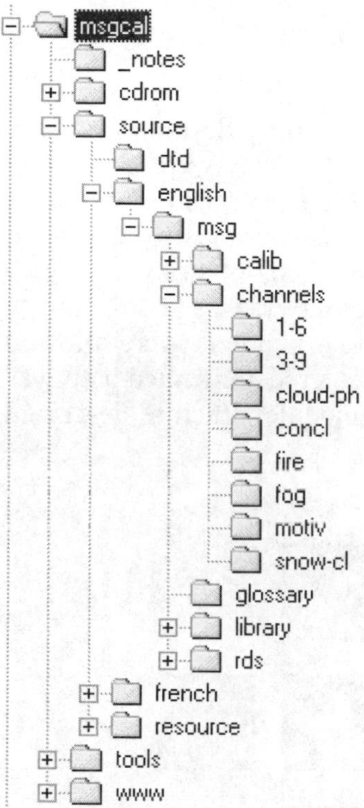

Fig. 16.3. The directory structure

Apart from included multimedia resources, such as imagery and video, all content and navigation was described entirely in XML (EML and QTI). Each knowledge object was defined in a separate EML/QTI file, known as a "source" file. These files were stored in a predefined directory structure, shown in Figure 16.3.

The "source" directory has two language subdirectories: "english" and "french". Translated copies of the English material were mapped into an identical structure in the "french" sibling directory. In this example the three modules are "calib", "channels" and "rds". Each of these modules contains its units-of-study as subdirectories. Each unit-of-study subdirectory contains the knowledge object files.

The same directory structure also holds the "www" files (i.e. the files containing the HTML that is generated by the transformation) and the "tools" required to transform the source files to HTML. Another directory, "cdrom", at the same level as "www", contains the files making up the

CD-ROM specific version of the modules. The multimedia resources for all modules and units of study are in the "resource" directory which has the same subdirectory structure.

16.4.3 Rendering of Pages

XML Stylesheet Language Transformations (XSLTs) were defined to turn the EML/QTI source into pages of Dynamic HTML for web or CD-ROM viewing. Figure 16.4 shows an example of how the HTML output looks when displayed in a web browser.

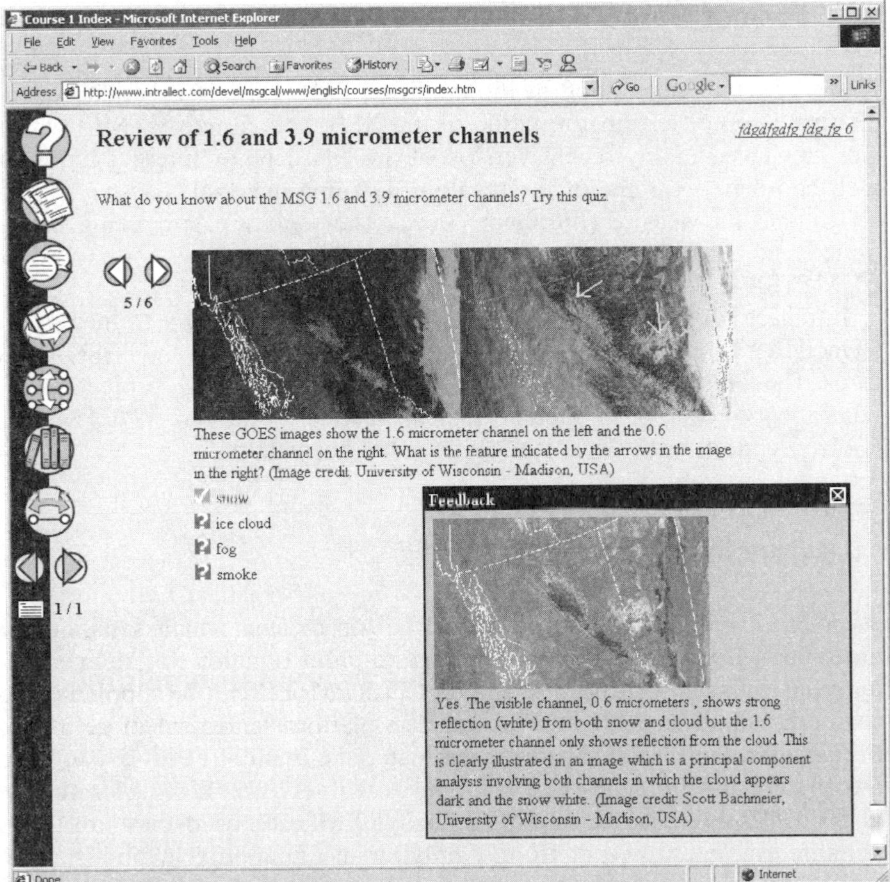

Fig. 16.4. A screenshot of a rendered page showing a multiple choice question with feedback box open

Access to the navigation interface and the rest of the environment is through the toolbar on the left-hand side.

Since this was a single-learner model and no summative assessment was included, no server component was required for the actual delivery of the learning. All generic interactions were realised in client-side DHMTL and JavaScript. EUMETSAT wanted to gather statistics on the use of the materials, so tracking of page access was required. This was achieved using a simple CGI script (Black et al. 1999), which wrote a record of each page access to a log file.

16.5 Project Outcomes

A working implementation of the modified EML DTD was produced, including a complete transformation of the XML source into HTML, which can be viewed in any recent version of the Netscape or Internct Explorer wcb browser. A sample of the resulting learning materials can be viewed on Intrallect's website (Intrallect 2002). The tools are still being maintained and updated by Intrallect as part of an ongoing contract with EUMETSAT.

Intrallect has since run four successful training courses for trainers from EUMETSAT and related organizations in how to apply the MSG-CAL tools. The tools have also been adopted by the EUMETCAL project, a collaboration of European meteorological services, and renamed "Meteo-CAL". Support for the Spanish language has been added.

16.6 Conclusions

A practical implementation of EML/LD was created which satisfied the customer's need for a flexible and future-proof solution for delivery of learning material over the web and on CD-ROM. LD can be supplemented with other models such as QTI to create a platform-independent definition of a set of highly interactive learning materials. It is not necessary to have a complete set of off-the-shelf solutions to do very useful things with LD. Users will sometimes be happy managing XML source if they are given suitable templates to work from. Applying an LD approach can also give significant advantages for the management of content-development projects.

17 Applying Learning Design to Supported Open Learning

Patrick McAndrew, Martin Weller

Institute of Educational Technology, The Open University, Milton Keynes, UK

17.1 Introduction

In this chapter we consider how Learning Design (LD 2003) can be applied to "distance education and in particular the model of open learning applied in our organization, The Open University. We do this by reflecting on the changes underway as more course are taught on-line, and looking at the lessons from applying LD to some activities from our courses. From this experience we believe that LD can apply to the design process as well as to course delivery and we expect to develop its use more fully as tools are developed.

The Open University in the UK has a well-established and successful approach to distance education. This approach has been termed Supported Open Learning (SOL) and is an holistic approach combining the use of different media with active support from tutors working with relatively small groups of learners. The roots of this approach are in the use of high-quality media in print, audio, video and broadcast television with students offered tutor support through day-schools, telephone and formative commenting on assessments. However, The Open University is now one of the largest providers of on-line education with over 200,000 learners on-line and single presentations of on-line courses that have exceeded 10,000 enrolments. This change in focus has been accompanied by adjustments in the models for participation in courses and in approaches to production. The Open University has recognised the need to review how it can adopt methods that capture the success of its experience, but also encourage sharing of models and closer working between pedagogic designers and those implementing the components used in on-line teaching.

LD is one candidate for the foundation for the representation of courses at the University. The LD specification offers an approach to representing course materials that captures the design of the activities and the roles expected of the learner and teacher. Once the application of LD moves beyond single courses to represent generic, sharable models for courses and for activities within courses, it can then offer an effective tool and take its place in the production process. It may then become the catalyst in the creation of a more open approach to supporting the community of learning technologists and academic teachers (Laurillard and McAndrew 2003).

LD, and the Educational Modelling Language that came before it, claim strengths in being neutral in their pedagogy. This is an important attribute of the approach as it allows all aspects to be represented; however, the overall goal is to represent and encourage "good" pedagogy. New technology in particular has shown (e.g. Butson 2003) that it can support bad pedagogies as well as good. Indeed it can appear to encourage less good practice by obscuring what was known before. In the experience of The Open University the introduction of on-line learning has meant that stages of production have become compressed, editing cycles have been carried out less thoroughly, and validation and testing of learner actions have been omitted. The result has been a running together of teaching materials with tools and resources that can be confusing to the students. The supported open learning approach, where a human tutor gives guidance, has proved a robust strategy for making up for weakness in course materials, but means that there is greater variation in student experience and those course materials that lack clarity can persist.

Improvements to this process will come from making the design of the learning more explicit; with the potential for validation either by checking before proceeding with implementation or by positive experience from other instances of the same structures (e.g. a similar activity on another course). Such designs are sharable and should improve and evolve. LD clearly offers the potential to help address these issues. The Open University has therefore carried out a partial review of LD to see how it can be used. In particular it has looked at some courses which can be considered to have positive attributes; they are highly rated by their students, they have modular or object-based structures, and an activity-based underpinning. The activities from such courses appear highly suitable for the application of LD and are considered as the initial test. It is important to recognise though that this is part of a wider plan to review the models for all courses across the University. Therefore as the process is adopted we will be examining ways to include more traditional course approaches. We are also left with further issues of:

- How can we determine the overall effectiveness of material?
- Can we use a theoretical framework (such as activity theory) to carry out pre-assessment of activity structures?

- At what granularity (course, block, activity, etc.) is it appropriate to apply LD?
- How stable is a design? Can making a small change in one line make a significant change to the overall experience?

17.2 Supported Open Learning and Learning Design

LD has potential for application at different scales. In The Open University we are particularly interested in whether it can be applied to the team-based approach to developing courses that is used for most of our courses.

17.2.1 The Open University Approach

In Supported Open Learning at The Open University in the UK a centralised course team is responsible for producing the course materials and an overall design for the student's learning experience. This will typically be described within a "course guide" that explains how the student is expected to study, accompanied with a timetable that sets out expected progress. On a typical course therefore a group of students are expected to act as a cohort, and this is enforced through the use of assessment in the form of Tutor Marked Assignments (TMAs) with tight deadlines. The student body is usually organized in groups of approximately 20 students who are assigned to an Associate Lecturer as their tutor. The tutor's role is to support the students through remote contact and in face-to-face tutorial meetings, and to give detailed feedback on the TMAs. This model has proved to be very successful in enabling students to study with the Open University and to allow variation in how students and tutors operate. However, while this approach still applies as a general description there are now many variations in the support model especially as applied in on-line learning. For example, there are now cases where the course guide and material supplied to the students has been reduced so that the emphasis is on working collaboratively in groups guided by their tutors, either using activities designed by the course team or related activities designed by the tutors. Conversely on some courses tutor involvement has been reduced with the on-line activities providing the primary guidance and opportunity for interaction in student peer groups with reduced back-up support from tutors who now have responsibility for 200 students rather than 20.

This new situation, with more variability across the courses, raises questions on the underlying model: Is more support needed or is less? How can the tutors be supported if they can now choose the activities their students carry out? Can cases of best practice, or poor practice, be recognised and disseminated? To answer questions such as these an important step is to know how to describe the designs of the course and activities. LD offers scope to do this; in particular if it can then demonstrate activity models with different roles and levels of support it will be valuable in many ways, such as for course team review and discussion and staff development. This would be the case even without full implementation and integration into an LD player. For example, the course planning process at The Open University requires media selection and specification at a very early stage, this would be assisted by being able to prepare or adopt designs before developing materials but would not need these to be supported by a full delivery system.

17.2.2 Course Models

The context for The Open University is a comprehensive review of its approach to courses with the aim of improving management of the costs associated with courses by increasing its understanding and use of models for the new courses that it produces. The course models review that has taken place has produced more than 30 recommendations across implementation, financial, development and educational issues.

LD can have an impact across the whole of the course models project, but some of the elements in the review can be seen to have a "top-down" rationale; for example, the initial breakdown of curriculum types is into five broad categories that are related to general approaches to the curriculum and teaching strategy. LD has a "bottom-up" impact on the course models as it allows particular structures to be described, and a process impact as it can change the decision points and production flow. The key elements that we see LD influencing can be categorised into the provision of descriptive tools and collections of designs, application of testing and validation of such a description and changes to production processes. The successful adoption of LD does not necessarily mean that it can meet all these needs. Early use of LD is more likely to be as a tool for describing course structures rather than a production route for course materials. Accordingly the initial trials looked at whether examples of good practice can be encoded in LD and reflected on the value of that process.

17.3 Applying Learning Design

An initial assessment of the value of LD was carried out by selecting a course (*Learning in the Connected Economy*) and converting short activities to LD format.

17.3.1 Learning Design Applied to a Simple Example

The content for the chosen course is already in the form of learning objects (using an approach described in Weller et al. 2003). The object chosen for this task was one entitled "Technology viewpoints". It was selected as it represented a middle-ground in terms of complexity. It contains two activities, a number of external links as well its own textual content. Thus it is more than simply text, but not as complex as a collaborative task that calls on external services such as synchronous collaboration tools.

LD was applied through the formal stages encouraged in the best practice guide. That is, a narrative was constructed, activity analysis carried out using UML representation, and an XML instantiation produced incorporating the method in the form of plays and acts. The chosen activity was found to match to Level A in LD; since there is no need for complex interaction, there was only one role, that of a student/learner; and with no need for synchronisation a single play and single act LD was produced.

17.3.2 Learning Design Applied to a Multi-Role Example

The simple example above demonstrated the steps and feasibility in converting material into LD, but the potential of LD was not demonstrated. This is seen far more with Levels B and C of the LD specification. Level B is probably an order of magnitude more complex than Level A and would be the real test when designing an LD implementation system. A more complex activity involving collaboration was then selected. The activity is a four-week debate, which involves the students in researching material, providing summaries of articles, discussing asynchronously, engaging in a synchronous debate with set roles and then writing a report. As such it is a very complex task to coordinate.

For this example there were six role: a tutor/support role and five distinct learner roles within the debate (Proposer, Opposer, Scribe, Technical reviewer, Interrogator). The debate in this example takes place first in an asynchronous and then in a synchronous format. Dealing with these together proved difficult and so activity diagrams were drawn for the separate activity parts. The role assignment for the synchronous debate is shown in Fig. 17.1 following the swimlane convention. The bold lines show a division into three acts as the selection of roles requires a synchronisation point as does completion and conclusion of the debate. Analysis of this relatively complex activity showed that LD is capable of representing such a process but also that it was time consuming, especially if the end point was to be a complete XML instantiation.

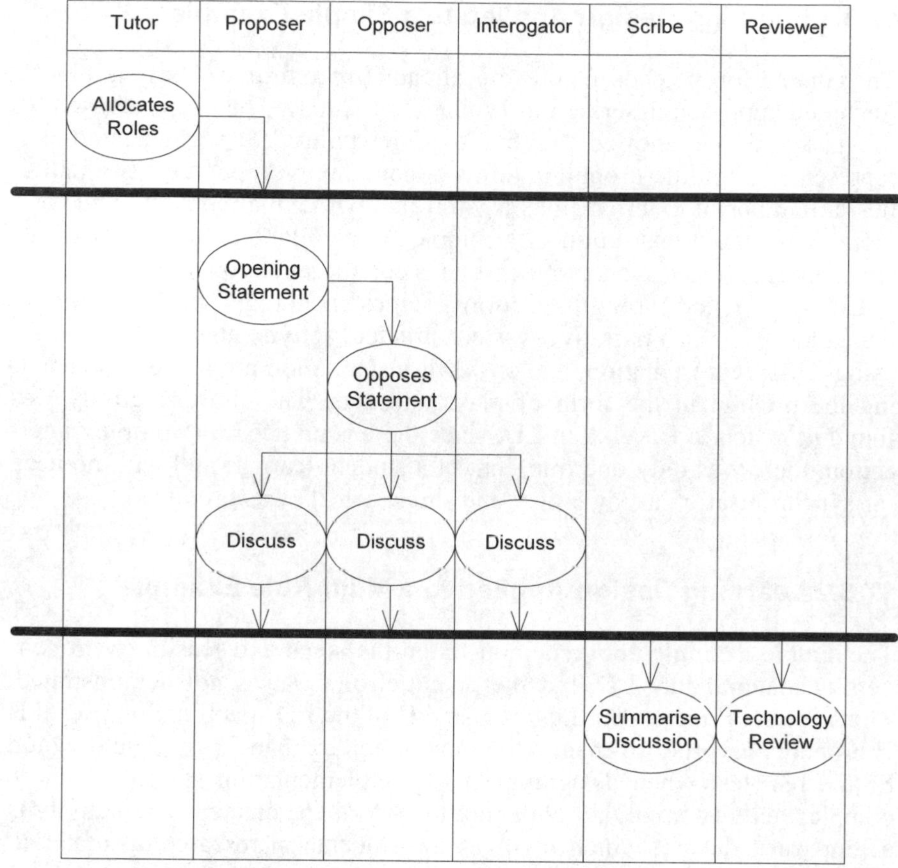

Fig. 17.1. UML activity diagram for synchronous debate showing tutor and learner roles

17.3.3 Learning Design as a Design Tool

In the previous examples LD was applied through the formal stages encouraged in the best practice guide. As discussed in Chap. 7, tools are being developed, but many of these stages have yet to be supported by authoring tools, validation and connection through to a runtime player. The motivation for some of the stages is therefore weak. However, the key process of producing a formal, or semi-formal, representation of the activity has shown itself to be revealing. This stage may well be the key for reuse of designs and the demonstration of explicit structure in courses.

A further course activity from a different course, *Application of Information Technology in Open and Distance Education*, was considered together with the use of the LD-inspired Learning Activity Management System (LAMS). LAMS (Dalziel 2003) offers a simple interface for constructing sequences of linked actions that may have conditions attached. It provides an integrated editor, group management system and a set of collaborative tools matched to particular consideration of roles. As such it is much less flexible than LD and, in its initial version, can only be used if its own collaboration tools are adopted. This set of conditions made it unsuitable for a complete implementation within our courses; there was mismatch between role descriptions and between the tools that can be used. However, as with LD, the value of the tool emerged during the design process. An activity (originally designed by one of the authors) in the course was chosen that has had problems in previous presentations. At the point in the course when they meet the activity students are expected to have experienced various approaches to collaboration and are presented with a task (evaluating and discussing examples of educational multimedia) that involves several stages. Breaking down the task into separate linked activities (shown in Fig. 17.2 using the LAMS design mode) revealed that the written activity description had missed out a collation action within the sequence presented to the students (see Fig. 17.2). This had not always been critical as tutor and peer support would often compensate but indicated a weakness in the design that generated uncertainty in the flow of the task and, in some cases, had caused the further stages to be poorly completed. This early realisation could then be represented in the construction of the LD representation of the play by introducing a new act that represented the task.

17.3.4 Discussion of Learning Design Examples

The complexity apparent in writing down these examples highlights an important issue associated with LD (and indeed all e-learning specifications), which is that they entail an increased overhead in the creation of educational content compared with a "normal" authoring approach, where some details are not recorded. To justify the overhead of LD we need to consider what the advantages are in comparison with an approach that does not correspond to any of the specifications (though it would also be valid to compare with other specifications such as Simple Sequencing (SS 2003). One of the main potential advantages is reusability. So, while the above example may be complex and time consuming to specify, once this has been done the design can be reused with different content. This is because LD separates to some degree the content and the pedagogy.

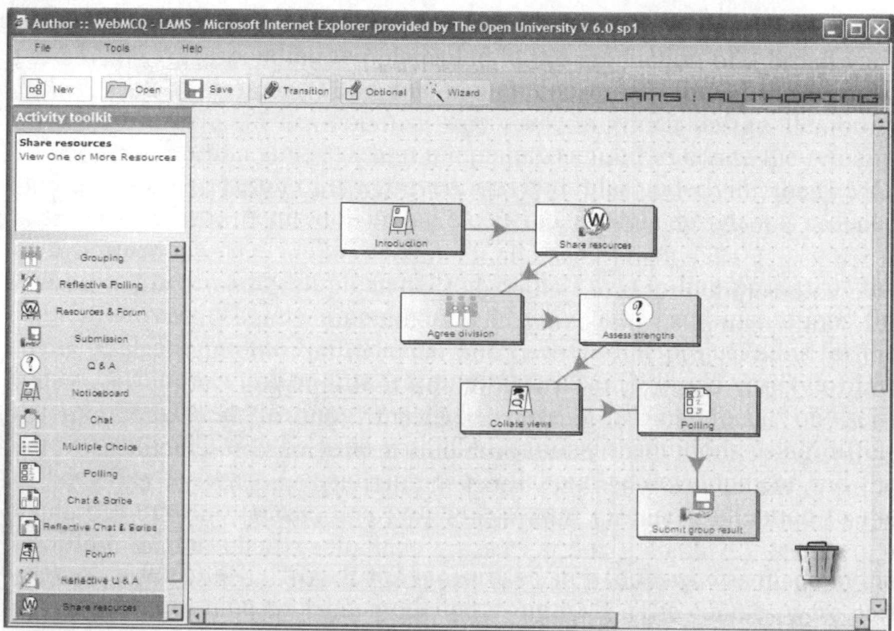

Fig. 17.2. LAMS activity structure showing new activity introduced for valid flow

Within most institutions, including The Open University, the number of different types of activities is actually quite limited. A good deal of the teaching can be accommodated within a single-user linear model involving one play and one act (as in the first example). Producing LD for a whole course such as *Learning in the Connected Economy* could furnish the University with designs applicable across many of its other courses. In particular it may be possible to operate at a finer granularity than the course level that is the initial focus of the course model review described above. It is at the level of individual activities that reuse could be accomplished, and these could be packaged together into many different types of courses. LD can also then be used to specify a whole course if that is needed.

Another issue about LD is the implied prescriptive nature of each design. There may be events or paths that are unforeseen by the learning designer and an LD approach might seem at odds with the flexible and dynamic nature of e-learning. Indeed, whether any specification can cover all the types and sequences of interaction that take place in learning is an unresolved question that will only be addressed by using LD in earnest. On the other hand, LD aids the educator in specifying what it is they want to happen, and thus can make it more likely that their educational goals will be achieved. It is worth stressing that LD does not remove the human educator from the system, but because the specification has been made more explicit, it does mean that the environment can be used to aid the educator.

For instance, many of the steps in the complex example could be automated or at least have associated prompts. Having such support can be particularly important when operating on a large scale in distance education.

17.4 Plans for Learning Design at The Open University

The initial work undertaken at The Open University has shown the use of LD as support for thinking through structures and reflecting on the different models or templates that we can support. However, development of an overall environment incorporating LD would bring further benefits and enable a path from design selection, through validation (technical and pedagogical), personalisation and presentation to the learners. The multiple role representation and synchronisation features in the full specification would extend this to flexible cohorts of students (this has been called "fill-up-and-go" presentation) and to assessment. This work is under development as shown by the work represented in other chapters of this book. The Open University has started work to adopt the CopperCore LD engine produced by the OUNL (see Chap. 6) and carry out a pilot integration within a flexible knowledge and content management system, the OU Knowledge Network. This will allow a user interface to be developed for the management and sharing of design templates, and instantiation with the tool sets that are available to the Knowledge Network. The first evaluation of this system will allow validation of designs and demonstration of their feasibility; as has been noted above, this in itself can help support greater pre-specification of course design. The second evaluation will seek to apply LD within staff development; this application has been selected as it brings challenges about roles and formation of student groups, while avoiding the need for the stringent quality assurance and scale requirements of student facing systems.

Beyond the pilot phase LD offers a way to formalise the activity structures that are used within our courses. This formalisation can allow research on key aspects of interest, for example:

- Analysis of the activity structures against theoretical positions, such as activity theory (Mwanza and Engeström 2003).
- Research in the stability of activity designs and the context in which they can apply.
- Methods to classify the effectiveness of designs and to share descriptions of best practice through the database and related case studies.
- Development of template collections for use within The Open University and support for staff development in how to use them.

- The support offered by LD for the analysis needed for the course models, implementation, such as the calculation of workload and identification of assessment.

17.5 Conclusion

LD is an exciting concept that enables us to engage with ways to describe educational design and material in a new way. The consequences of a full LD implementation could mean entirely new ways of working with separation of design, content and presentation with benefits for sharing and reuse. What the initial study at The Open University has shown is that even before such implementations are available the approach advocated by LD is allowing a fresh look at the structures and designs in use across the University and giving a practical way to implement reviews in a way that can support staff and potentially improve the student experience. LD can produce good descriptions of activities and in doing so reveal aspects that are unclear. It may be possible to break down courses informally into tasks and roles without using the full IMS specification, however, the formal approach taken by LD means that technical validation of materials can automate some of the checking and management of the designs. Forward plans to adopt LD can build on the significant community activity now taking place, both within the Valkenburg Group, supported by the UNFOLD project, and outside any formal support system. We expect that progress will be made on integrated players, the design of tools that can support specialised design aspects, sharing of designs, and research into pedagogic validation.

The work of The Open University in the UK is to make initial contributions to these developments and to look for ways to apply the tools as they are developed.

18 Using Learning Design to Support Design and Runtime Adaptation

Peter van Rosmalen[1], Jesús Boticario[2]

[1] Educational Technology Expertise Centre,
Open University of the Netherlands, Heerlen, The Netherlands

[2] aDeNu Research Group, Artificial Intelligence Department, Computer Science School, UNED, Spain

18.1 Introduction

One of the key challenges in e-learning is to allow for adaptation to learners' personal interests, characteristics and goals. E-learners require content and activities based on their preferences and prior knowledge, not just static, page-turning sequences. In this case study we describe the aLFanet project,[1] which intends to develop a learning environment that integrates new principles and tools in the field of learning design and artificial intelligence. The created environment is to offer intelligent personalization capabilities in order to support effective and flexible learning scenarios consistent with the demands of the knowledge society.

In the project we focus on two almost opposite approaches to adaptation, both common in e-learning. In the first approach, dominated by a strong tradition in instructional design, a team produces a detailed design of content, interaction and presentation. Within the design different options may be worked out for different learners, based on such user data as level, interest or learning style. The options for adaptation are prepared at design time and require limited, if any, interaction of tutors at runtime. The second approach relies on tutors having an active role. The author, and possibly also the tutor, designs the material. Subsequently, at runtime, the tutor adapts the course based on the learners' interactions (usage data), i.e. to what extent do learners succeed and which questions arise? Both of these

[1] The authors thank their colleagues at SAGE, EDP, KLETT, ACE-CASE, UNED and the Open University of the Netherlands for their contributions to the deliverables upon which this chapter builds. The authors' efforts were partly funded by the European Commission in aLFanet, active Learning For adaptive internet (IST-2001-33288). For more information see http://alfanet.ia.uned.es or http://www.learningnetworks.org.

approaches, however, tend to be (too) expensive as a result of high development costs or high delivery costs due to the required extensive support.

The approach is summarized in Figure 18.1 and represents the so-called open framework for aLFanet.

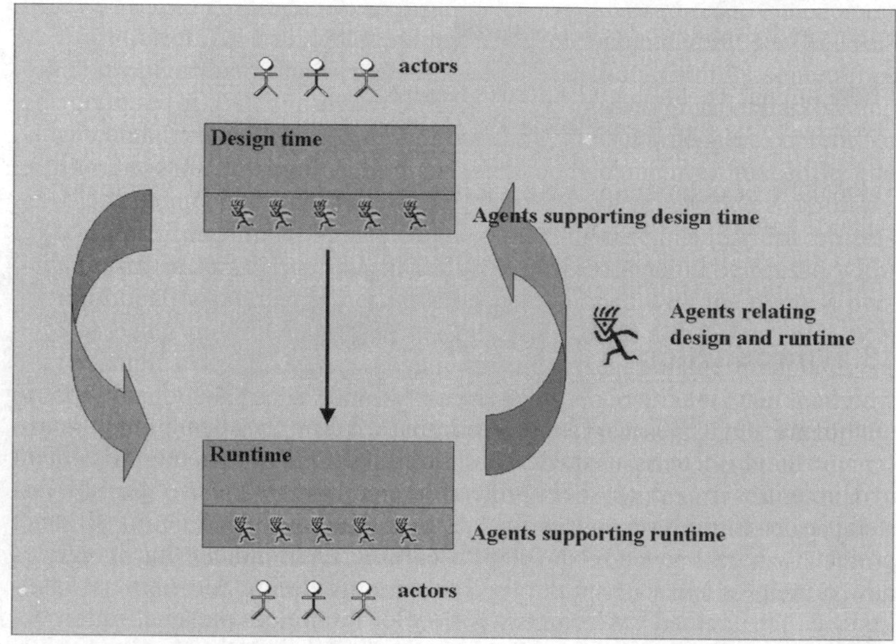

Fig. 18.1. Relating design and runtime adaptation

On top of the figure, the actors (authors) are designing courses using Learning Design (LD 2003), which are used in runtime by other actors (learners, tutors). There are three types of agents identified: agents that support the designers at design time, agents that support the learners and tutors at runtime and agents that relate the runtime with the design time. The latter type of agents warn for instance the designers when the learners and tutors in runtime behave different than the design prescribes, and warn the learners, and learners and tutors are warned when they behave different from the design intentions.

In this chapter we discuss this open framework developed in the aLFanet project. To enable the design of this framework, a study was conducted of tools, technologies and standards which allow for the outlined approaches and are able to support them in an efficient and effective manner. The section below first gives an overview of the results of this study and subsequently discusses the reason for selecting LD. Next, the first version of aLFanet is discussed. It describes the LD tools developed, an authoring tool and an engine, and the two ways in which LD is used. The first way, the 'classical' way, is to enable authors to create an explicit design of adaptive courses. The second way, specific to aLFanet, is to make communication and collaboration possible between authors, tutors and software agents, based on an explicit and machine-readable design in LD. The chapter closes with the current progress and conclusions.

18.2 Adaptive E-learning Systems and Technologies

The requirements for aLFanet can be summarized into three main categories:

1. To what extent does the framework support active and adaptive e-learning?
2. To what extent is the framework open to the use of different types of learning models, alternative learning scenarios and new components, such as agents?
3. To what extent does the framework support the user (author, student and tutor) efficiently?

A review of existing technologies and systems covering e-learning systems, including web-based Adaptive Educational Systems, agents and standards, was carried out to find solutions for meeting these requirements. The main findings of this review are summarized in the paragraphs below. Also, we discuss how using LD is expected to contribute to the first two categories and the use of agents to the last (for the complete review, see De Croock et al. 2002b; for a review of only e-learning systems, see Van der Klink et al. 2002).

Most e-learning systems (WebCT, Blackboard, TopClass, Ingenium, Docent, etc.) are not explicit about the didactical methods and models supported, nor is it possible to express them explicitly, as methods and content are intertwined. Adaptation tends to be offered in the shape of mere predefined settings requiring extensive customization. Web-based Adaptive Educational Systems follow a similar approach as Intelligent Tutoring Systems and hypermedia systems. Intelligent Tutoring Systems (Wenger 1987) use knowledge about the domain, the student and about teaching strategies to support flexible individualized learning. Adaptive hypermedia (Brusilovsky 2001) apply different forms of user models to adapt the content and the links to the user. However, there are only few examples which use standards or generic approaches, such as agent architectures (Paiva 1996), in order to improve adaptation to different settings.

It is important for aLFanet to build upon existing standards, in order to enable an open framework. This is why a wide range of standards was reviewed, though it must be noted that, in reality, most of them are specifications rather than formal standards (Van Es et al. 2003). The following learning technology specifications were identified to be relevant:

1. Learner Information Package (LIP 2001), for student-related data which needs to be exchanged between the different sub-systems.
2. Meta-Data (MD 2001), for content-related adaptation. The specification creates a uniform way of describing learning resources, so that they can be detected more easily and subsequently used.
3. Question and Test Interoperability (QTI 2003), for defining the structure of questions and tests.

The use of these specifications still left a piece missing in the jigsaw. aLFanet wants to offer a highly adaptive, personalized learning experience, including a variety of pedagogical methods. This requires the capability to model both structure and process, including the specification of roles and activities. LD offers this capability and allows for the integration of the other standards. Moreover, in-depth knowledge of LD is available and directly accessible in the aLFanet consortium.

Web-based technologies in conjunction with multi-agent methodology form a new trend in the modelling and development of learning environments. Multi-agent methodology has recently appeared as an alternative to conceive distributed learning applications (Webber et al. 2001). There are two main reasons for this: the evolution of multi-agent technology itself is one and the second is due to the fact that multi-agent methodology deals well with applications incorporating crucial issues, such as distance, cooperation among different entities and integration of different software components. Agents (Jennings et al. 1998; Wooldridge and Jennings 1995) have proven to be useful in many different types of applications, from email filters to traffic control or for guiding cooperation and communication among students/with lecturers (Boticario et al. 2000). A minimum requirement for agents is reactivity: that is to say, agents perceive their environment (which may be the physical world, a user via a graphical user interface, a collection of other agents, the Internet or all of these combined), and respond in a timely fashion to changes that occur in it.

LD can facilitate agents to perceive their environment. The events the student is involved in can be formally derived from the learning design (e.g. the activities, their resources, and the relations between the activities). In addition, the agent can query the general properties of the learning design (e.g. the completion status of an activity). Finally, dedicated sets of properties can be defined for use by a particular agent, describing an element of the learning design or the state of a user. As for the user, some sets are unique per individual, others for every individual for a specific course run and some sets are common between groups of persons in a particular role. Additionally, depending on the type of agent, LD can be used for task allocation and control by assigning a task to an agent, i.e. by substituting a staff role for an agent (e.g. an agent that automatically assigns a peer ready to join a collaborative task).

18.3 The First Version of aLFanet

The assumption underlying the use of LD in aLFanet is that it can be used to represent learning scenarios in a way that authors, tutors and agents can manage. Authors use LD to specify advanced pedagogical designs, including adaptation. They are provided with an authoring tool and templates for different learning scenarios, which allows them to create new courses easily. This approach guarantees optimal support for learners in the learning process. An LD engine (cf.. Chap. 6) translates and executes the learning design, using the set of learning objects and services available. However, not everything can be foreseen in the design process. Many unforeseen events can occur during the actual learning process and there may be a demand for additional support. Normally, tutors provide this additional support. In part, tutor support may have been designed, for instance, for marking an essay; another part of tutor support may become apparent during the course, e.g. when students ask questions on how to proceed or how to understand a certain topic.

In aLFanet, tutors are supported by agents which apply combinations of machine learning algorithms to the data gathered from the actual users' interactions. Thus, different types of adaptive features are provided, such as automatic sub-grouping of learners according to specific criteria, automatic message classification in forums, and supporting learners by recommending what to do next. Similarly, other agents provide meaningful reports to the authors of the course based on learner interactions. They compare the design and the expected results with the actual results and the time needed to achieve them. Each of the actors – author, tutor and agent – frame their actions on a pedagogical model explicitly defined in LD and the properties derived from it.

In order to validate the idea behind this approach, a minimal learning scenario (cf. Fig. 18.2) was designed, which involved the active participation of a tutor, two agents and a student.

LD is not explicit on how to integrate agents; in our case a choice was made to model the agents as having a staff role. The agents communicated with the other actors by sending a notification when they finished. The resulting Unit of Learning (UOL) was successfully tested in Edubox 2.0 (cf. Chap. 19), to which two dedicated agents had been added.

Method: Agents Supported Education			
Play 1:	Activity 1	Role 1: Student	• Read and answer a set of questions
	Activity 2	Role 2: Staff - agent to score assessment	• Monitor the assessment • Score the assessment • Notify the tutor
	Activity 3	Role 3: Staff Tutor	• Select topic area for student
	Activity 4	Role 4: Staff - agent to select a resource from an article database	• Monitor • Select an article for the article database based on (level, topic) • Notify the student
	Activity 5	Role 1: Student reads the introduction and the advised article	• Read the article

Fig. 18.2. The main design of the Unit of Learning

After the initial test a final architecture has been worked out. The architecture (Carrión et al. 2004) is a three-layer composition with an independent Authoring Tool to create the courses:

1. A Server layer is in charge of the user front-end, managing application security, showing the user interface and tracing user interactions.
2. A Services layer is a group of services which provide the application functionality and main logic. It contains, among other things, a Course Manager, an LD engine, agents and an Interaction Module, which contains the facilities for collaborative and user works tasks. The layer is open to include new (types of) services. Figure 18.3 shows how LD is positioned in relation to the Authoring Tool, the services and the user front-end (a further description is given in the remainder of this chapter).
3. A Data layer comprises the data management and storage.

18.3.1 Authoring, Publishing and Delivering LD

The Authoring Tool (cf. Fig.18.4) has been created in Groove (www.groove.net), a peer-to-peer collaborative environment which is, as such, particularly suitable for teams to create and share contents over the Internet. Users can add tools to a workspace from a predefined tool-set, such as forums, shared files and calendars.

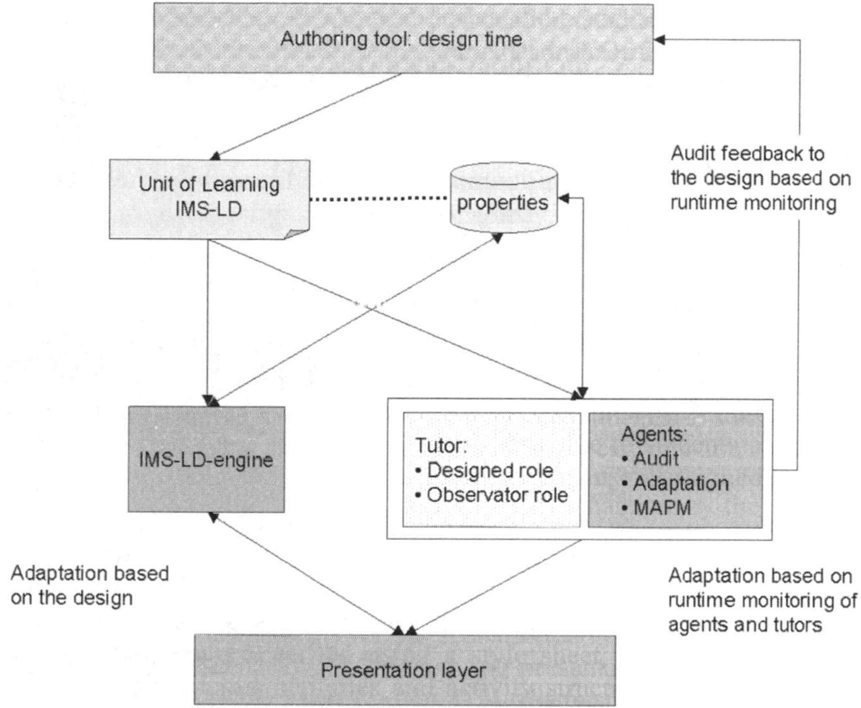

Fig. 18.3. The aLFanet framework: 'LD as communicator' in between the various services

Additionally, it is possible to integrate custom-made tools. The core part of the Authoring Tool is the LD Editor. This sub-module allows the user to create and edit courses in LD which are published in the aLFanet LMS. The LD Editor closely reflects the structure of the LD specification with some adaptations to enhance user-friendliness. It wraps the different concepts of the learning design in sub-structures in order to be more intuitive and conceptually organized to the user. Additionally, it makes sure that the user can save a valid LD file at intermediate stages, too. However, although the actual LD code is hidden, it still requires a solid understanding of LD and its interdependencies. As a final result, a UOL can be saved as a zip file following the CP specification (CP 2003).

Before a course can start, it needs to be populated with users (learners, staff, etc.). The Course Manager includes interfaces for user creation and deletion and for assignment to roles, runs and publications (see the previous chapters for an explanation of runs and publications). Additionally, it includes the possibility to validate the content package and provides interfaces to access properties.

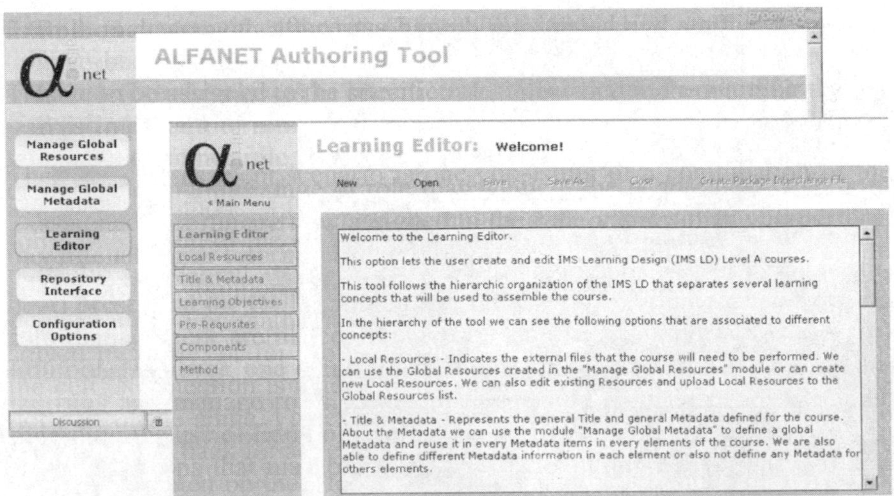

Fig. 18.4. The main menu of the Authoring Tool and, on top, the LD Editor (Learning Editor) opening screen

The LD engine, implemented using CopperCore (see Chap. 6), provides the business logic for the delivery of the course and ensures property values are maintained. The engine itself also uses a set of implicit properties, such as `activity_completed` and `activity_visible`, which are not explicitly declared by the author in the learning design, but which capture the progress of the user. Finally, the actual activity tree (see 'To Do' in Fig. 18.5), composed by the LD engine for a user, is based on the run and the role of a user, the status of the user and the status of other users.

18.3.2 Adaptation and Agents

In aLFanet, three different areas have been identified for adaptation to the users' preferences, habits, features, interests and needs. These areas are adaptation included in the instructional design, adaptation of the interaction and adaptation of the presentation. Additionally, there is another kind of adaptation area, which is advice to the author on adapting the original learning design. Each area is supported by an agent (or a collection of collaborating agents). The agents operate on the information available in the learning design, in particular the properties, and on information obtained by analysing user actions. At the moment, three agent modules are being designed and under development: Multi-Agent Pedagogical Models (MAPM), Adaptive Module (AM) and Audit. MAPM and AM support the first three areas of adaptation, Audit supports advice to the author.

Adaptation included in the Instructional Design provides different course contents, activities and services to the learner, depending on the specifications of the learning design by the author. MAPM support the author in selecting and applying an instructional model. Giving the complexity of this task, two generic pedagogical models have first been selected: concept understanding and forming complex cognitive skills (Leshin et al. 1992; Van Merriënboer 1997). A simplified version of these models was applied to an existing Spanish language course and expressed in LD. For each type of learner the adaptation was based on the assessment of three personal constructs: level of knowledge (absolute beginners, 'false' beginners – people who have studied the subject before), cognitive modalities (visual, auditory) and learning styles (thinkers, doers). The combination gives eight possible learning paths. The next step is to define how MAPM supports the author in applying these (and other) models and how it supports the author in defining a model in LD, e.g. with the help of wizard-based templates.

Adaptation of the Interaction enables adaptive interactions during a course. Thus, tutors and learners receive access to services, contents and activities to work with, users to contact, etc., as needed. The adaptation is provided by the AM and is based on learners' interactions.

Adaptation of the Presentation deals with presenting a different user interface to each learner, according to his/her user model. This adaptation is also provided by the AM. To provide the adaptation of the interaction and the presentation, a complex set of models has to be managed by the AM. There are models for three different entity types: users, groups and services. The AM combines information on the current learning context (for instance, 'which activities are available') and properties of the learner (such as background knowledge) with information obtained from user interactions. It does so by applying a combination of machine learning algorithms (e.g. an analysis of interaction data of the Interaction Module to distinguish between discussion leaders and readers). The AM has a multi-agent architecture which works autonomously to solve the set of adaptation tasks it has been designed for, such as:

1. select a moderator for a group of learners in a group task;
2. recommend the next activity to a learner.

Finally, Audit is responsible for a specific form of adaptation: that is to say, it supplies the authors with information on how effective (or efficient) their design has been in practice. This will help the authors to adapt their design if required. Audit analyses the extent to which the original design and the actual learning practice match, by collecting and analysing the relevant runtime data (see Table 18.1 for a simple example of the results of a certain activity). It then reports the results to the author.

Table 18.1. Runtime data associated with an activity

Field	Value
Event	
EventTimeStamp	5-11-2003 16:48:48
ActivityID	Act 4
PlayID	Ply 1
UOLID	UOL 2
LearnerID	Lrn 5
Result	3.2
RoleID	Rol 2

Audit starts with some simple reports, such as the number of study hours for a given learner and activity. The goal of these reports is to help to observe (part of) the progress of students or a particular student. An additional aim is to compile integrated reports on a course and report the results in relation to defined critical success factors. This helps authors to assess their design (they get the average score or average study time for an activity and can compare this to the expected score or study time).

18.3.3 Current Progress

ALFanet is built in three steps, each one increasing its functionality. Each step includes a validation round with students from different backgrounds, companies, private and university students, and in different domains, Internet technology, language and waste management. The validation will focus on authors, tutors and students and will include a full course cycle. This means it will look at how a course is developed, used and updated.

A ‘proof of concept’ of this approach (see the scenario in Fig. 18.2) was tested by using Edubox 2.0. Figure 18.5 gives a view of the current interface, after the first development step. One part, ‘Recommendations’, is of particular interest. It contains the suggestions automatically created by the agents in the system and those provided by the tutor for the learner. In the first step the validation of the system focused on usability, in particular from the perspective of the author. A special point of attention concerned the extent to which authors can successfully design courses which utilize the adaptive options in the system.

The main requirements to ensure this are that each course is expressed in LD and uses a minimum set of LIP and MD to supply the agents with onset information. The first results of this validation show that the role of MAPM is crucial for a common, non-LD-expert author. If presented with only the authoring tool, a non-LD-expert author is limited to creating only simple designs.

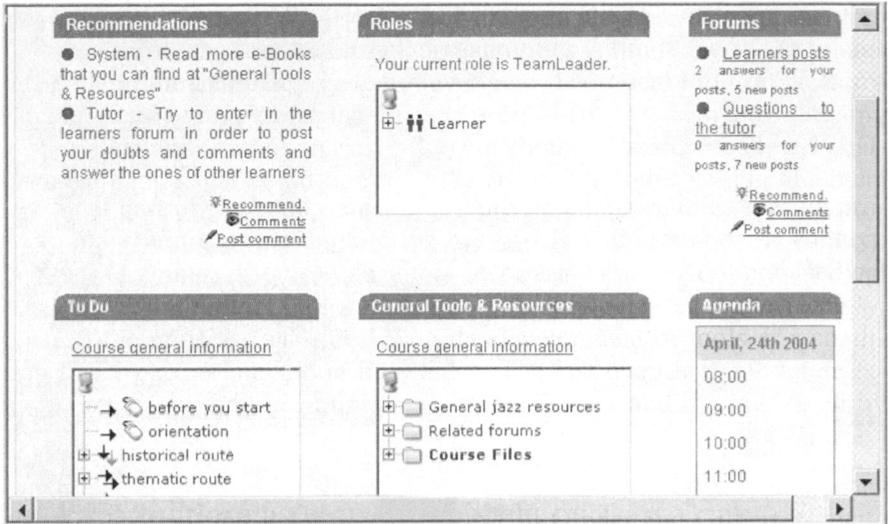

Fig. 18.5. A screenshot of the interface

For the next stages of development, the following issues need to be studied

1. How well do design and runtime adaptations combine; which types of intervention will be appreciated by the learner (and when); who is in control?
2. Is LD (combined with other standards) sufficient to enable and structure the communication between the different actors (in other words, is it necessary to have an additional, dedicated 'agents-LD' specification)?

18.4 Conclusions

The objective of this chapter was to outline the role of LD in a framework for an e-learning environment which integrates new methods and services for active and adaptive e-learning. LD enables the formal description of any learning design and can be used to communicate between the different actors (authors, tutors and agents) in the framework. The first version of the framework indicates that the approach taken is feasible and that the framework is well worth exploring further in the pursuit of a generic, standards-based framework for e-learning.

19 The Edubox Learning Design Player

Colin Tattersall, Hubert Vogten, Henry Hermans

Educational Technology Expertise Centre,
Open University of the Netherlands, Heerlen, The Netherlands

19.1 Introduction

Part of the mission of the Open University of the Netherlands (OUNL) is to innovate in higher education to improve the efficiency, effectiveness and attractiveness of learning. New educational technologies provide one means to this end, and the university is committed to technology development and the advancement of technological knowledge. Specifications form an important category of such knowledge, as highlighted by Gibbons (2000), and OUNL devotes resources to the development of educational technology specifications.

OUNL has offered on-line and blended courses for many years, and was quick to see the need to support a wide variety of pedagogical approaches and to liberate learning processes from the particular system(s) involved in their delivery. These needs led to investments in the development of specifications for describing the teaching–learning process, starting with the Educational Modelling Language (EML 2000), and continuing with the Learning Design specification (LD 2003).

EML's development was driven by a series of requirements, including the requirement for formalisation: "EML must be able to describe pedagogical models in a formal way, making them machine-readable so that automatic processing is possible". Here, automatic processing covers a variety of mechanisms, from simple validation exercises, such as checking whether the required learning resources are actually available, through to full execution of an instance of the generic, modelled learning process. In this latter case, we speak in terms of playing an instance of a Unit of Learning (UOL), using software known as a player.

The investment in specification development at OUNL has been mirrored by an associated investment in software development, with two central aims. First, to examine whether the requirement for formalisation has been met (i.e. is it possible to implement a player for the specification?) and second, to open the door for feedback on the player and specification, promoting iterative development of both.

Three generations of EML players have been developed, known collectively as Edubox and designed to interpret and execute educational scenarios and their content modelled using EML. These developments, which proceeded both internally and with commercial partners, culminated in a productionlevel system which is today used by thousands of students at OUNL.

This chapter traces the development of the players before describing the current version of Edubox in its broad production context, aiming to give insight into the ways in which educational modelling has been applied in a large production context.

19.2 The Historical Development of Edubox

The historical development of Edubox was driven by the development of EML (Koper and Manderveld 2004). Table 19.1 summarises the developments.

Table 19.1. The historical development of the Learning Design specifications and players

Year	Specification	Player
1998	(Q4) EML 0.5	
1999	(Q4) EML 0.9	(April) ELON ("Edubox 1.0")
2000	(December) EML 1.0 public release	(June) Edubox 2.0.0
2001		Incremental versions up to Edubox 2.0.6
2002	(January) EML 1.1	(September) Edubox 3.0
2003	(February) LD approved	(September) Edubox 3.7 in production

The Edubox players are used in the context shown in Fig. 19.1. Authors use tools to create UOLs which are stored in a repository. A UOL modelled in EML describes a class of possible instances of a learning process. This abstraction is instantiated by assigning individuals into the appropriate learner or staff roles. The specific instances are referred to as runs, which can be executed in a player so that learners and staff may participate in learning experiences (see Chap. 4 for an explanation of this process). The various sub-processes involved in moving from a UOL to a run are supported by run tooling, and make use of information on staff and learners.

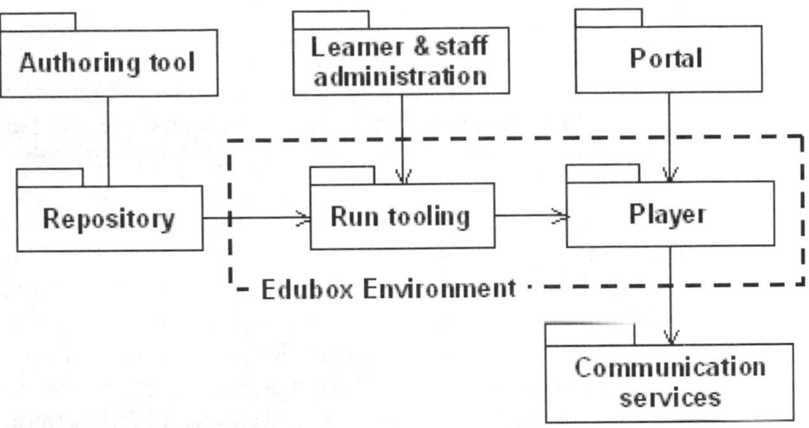

Fig. 19.1. The high-level system architecture in which a player operates

The learning process itself is supported by a player, which exploits communication services such as conference and mail systems to facilitate various modes of interaction in the learning process. Note that the player is a component of a wider "learning portal" or virtual learning environment, which handles interaction above the level of a UOL (e.g. information provision which is not course related).

In early evaluations, the first versions of EML were found to be specific to the modelling of competency-based learning. The step towards a pedagogical meta model (Koper 2002) resulted in EML 0.5. This version of EML was used as the basis for several courses delivered using a player known an ELON (ELO stands for *Electronische Leeromgeving*, or "electronic learning environment"; the 'N' stands for network).

Educational models and their associated educational material were described in EML 0.5 using the editor Framemaker+SGML together with an SGML-aware content management system (known as Information Manager). The manual authoring process was augmented by the conversion of a large amount of content, pre-structured in Microsoft Word using a specific set of styles, from Rich Text Format (RTF) to EML elements and attributes. Once authored, EML 0.5 files could be played by ELON.

ELON was an early prototype, although, as is often the case with a prototype, it was also used in production. Evaluations of the courses delivered using ELON revealed shortcomings in both the software and the modelling language, and led to the development of EML version 0.9. This was quickly followed by EML 1.0, which was applied across a much wider range of settings, and was released publicly at the end of 2000.

19.3 Edubox 2

Edubox 2, interpreting EML 1.0, was used in many pilots, including large-scale projects in both higher education and training situations. Issues identified during the pilots led to a series of incremental releases of Edubox 2 up to 2.0.6.

Again, Framemaker+SGML was used as the authoring tool for Edubox 2, allowing SGML/XML documents to be created and edited, then validated against the EML DTD. The repository became Microsoft's Visual SourceSafe, and software was written to integrate both authoring environment and repository. This hid much of the complexity of Visual SourceSafe, giving checking in and checking out of content, version management, scalability, and so on. Figure 19.2 shows a screenshot of Framemaker+SGML being used to author EML 1.0 content.

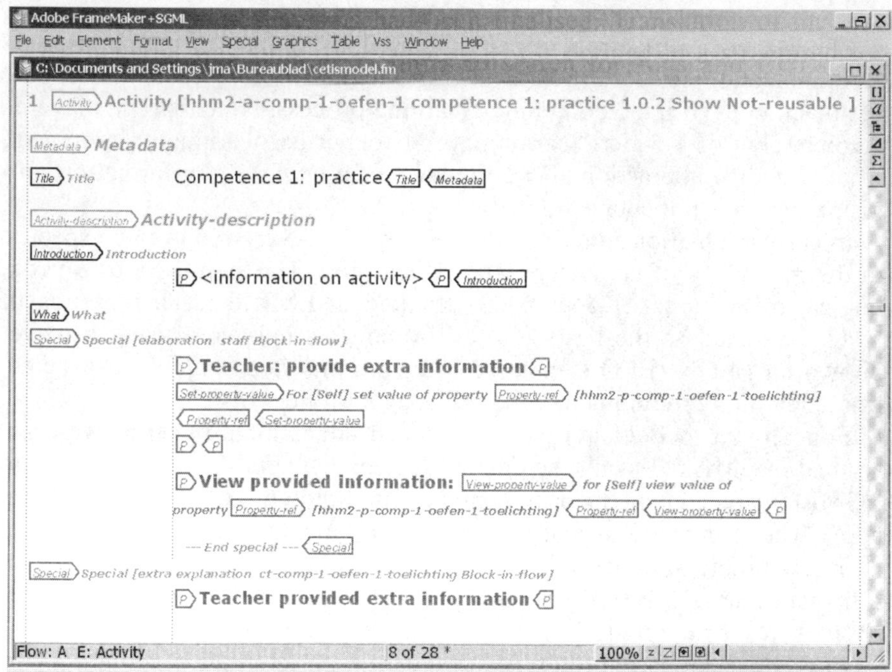

Fig. 19.2. Using Framemaker+SGML to author EML 1.0 content

Content experts experienced some difficulties working with Framemaker+SGML, and an alternative authoring process was developed whereby the content experts composed Microsoft Word files. These files were then sent to a separate group of people with both EML and Framemaker+SGML expertise, who copied and pasted the content into the appropriate format. This approach was further refined through the use of Microsoft Word templates containing hidden EML structures within which the content-experts worked, making the content more amenable to automatic conversion.

Several run tools were developed to facilitate the process of instantiating an abstract UOL. The packaging of a UOL was handled by a tool which linked the SGML file to the media-specific elements referenced within the UOL (e.g. images, sound and video files). This package was then transformed by another tool into a so-called "publication" which fixed the medium (e.g., print or web-based delivery, although only the latter was ever used in production), language (e.g. Dutch or English), style (fonts, colours, etc.) and creation date. Finally, a further tool supported the filling of student and teachers roles with user information, so that the learning process could be carried out.

Figure 19.3 shows the Edubox 2.0.6 player used by learners and staff.

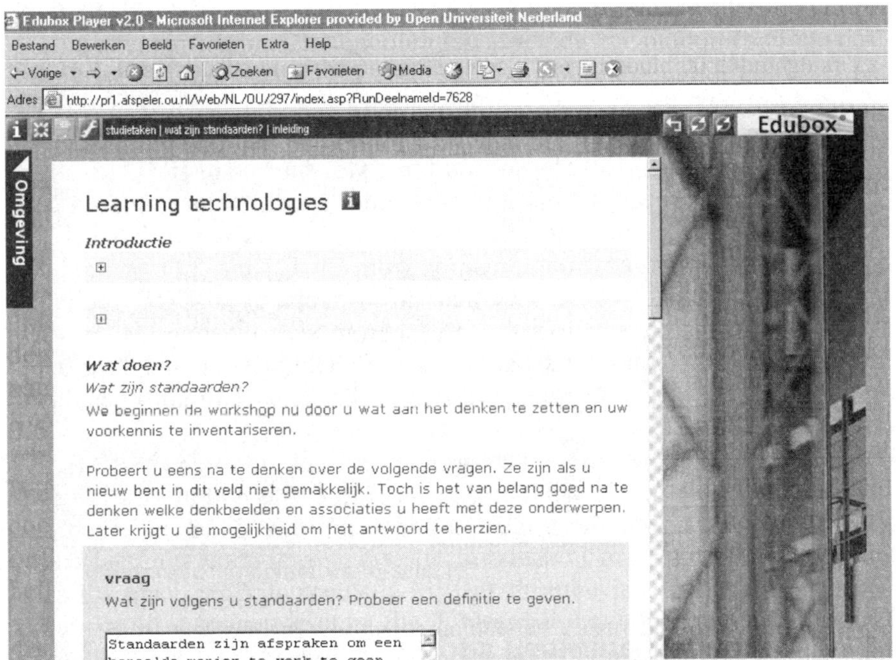

Fig. 19.3. The Edubox 2 player

The technologies used to implement Edubox 2 were centred on the Microsoft platform, and involved a wide range of products and languages, including SQL Server, Internet Information Server, ADO, ASP, Delphi, Visual C++, JavaScript and Omnimark.

Edubox 2 was piloted in a number of situations, with feedback being elicited from learners, tutors, authors, help desk staff and several other parties.

The pilot feedback spanned a wide range of areas, from confirmation of Edubox's beneficial role as an integrator for e-learning processes and content, to concerns on the quality of the player software in terms of non-functional requirements, and the need to manage expectations of the costs involved in building effective e-learning content. Although much of the feedback concerned the wider implications of using EML and Edubox, those aspects which related to the player were used to improve the software incrementally.

19.4 Edubox 3

Two forces influenced the development of Edubox 3. First, OUNL took the decision to pursue educational modelling as part of its e-learning strategy. Although Edubox 2 had been used in production settings with hundreds of learners, the move to bigger scales of delivery implied by this decision brought with it new requirements in terms of scalability, reliability, performance and security. The second force was the use of EML 1.0 as the basis for the LD specification. Although both specifications share a conceptual background, there are differences in their respective XML bindings. More fundamentally, the transition from EML 1.0 to LD entailed dissecting the former—which specified all aspects of a UOL including learning content, assessments, etc.—to accommodate existing IMS specifications, including Content Packaging (CP 2003), Question and Test Interoperability (QTI 2003), Learner Information Package (LIP 2001), and others.

EML 1.1 anticipated the arrival of LD and sits between the EML 1.0 and LD specifications. It embraces, for example, the notion of a (zipped) content package containing a manifest and employs items and resources. However, in contrast to LD, EML 1.1 also defines a content model which consists of XHTML mixed with EML 1.1 global elements, and which is interpreted in a specific way by the Edubox player—questions (test-items) are a subset of those global elements. EML 1.1 also allows for "web content", referring to various kinds of content which may be handled by a browser without special interpretation.

Edubox 3 was developed to be able to play EML 1.1 to a set of non-functional requirements identified during pilots with Edubox 2. Its development was put to tender and the contract was awarded to Perot Systems. This third generation of Edubox was built on a different set of technologies, including J2EE, JavaScript, CSS, XSLT and SOAP. Figure 19.4 shows the web player in use.

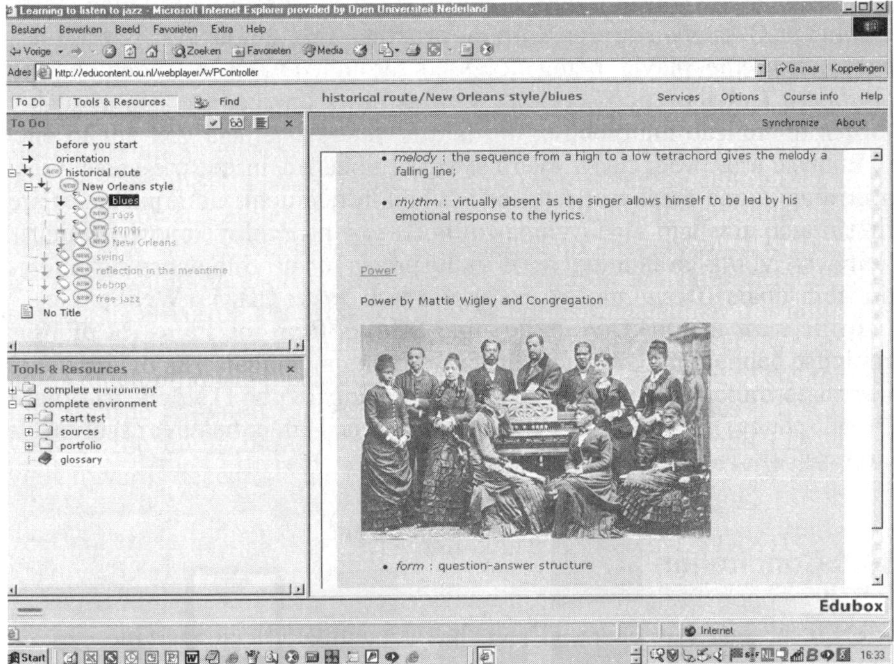

Fig. 19.4. The Edubox 3 Web Player

The authoring aspects of the context essentially remained unchanged between Edubox 2 and 3. The nature of EML 1.1 opened the door to automatic conversion from EML 1.0, and a converter was written to perform the transformation. This meant that prior investments in content could be preserved, and that the existing authoring processes and software could be retained, avoiding the need for new software and author retraining. Other authoring avenues are available, though, and any XML editor can be used to create EML 1.1 for packaging as a UOL.

Note that the door is also open to convert between LD and EML 1.1, making Edubox 3 an LD-aware player. However, no converter has yet been written given the current EML-based authoring processes at OUNL. Moreover, the task is more complex than the corresponding EML 1.0 to 1.1 conversion due to the (likely) use of several specifications in an IMS-based context.

The series of tools required to move from an abstract UOL to a running learning experience were bundled into a single sub-system known as Edutool. Edutool allows authorised users to upload zipped packages, arrange the styling of a UOL, enrol learners, manage multiple runs of a UOL, and perform various other administrative functions.

The Edubox 3.0 web player is a server-based system with which learners and staff interact in the learning process. This interaction is browser-based, with the player being accessed through OUNL's student portal, *Studienet*. Collaboration services, such as news groups, are also available for use in the learning process.

Edubox is a production-level system, embedded in mature system administration and deployment processes and infrastructure. All packages are first tested in a shadow environment before being deployed in the production servers, which is a high-end multi-processor machine running a relational database (from Oracle) and application server (IBM's WebSphere).

In September 2003, nine e-learning courses from the Faculties of Psychology, Law and Business Administration, modelled using EML 1.1, were launched, with over 2000 students using Edubox 3.7. In line with OUNL policy, the courses were of a competency-based nature, involving a large self-study component.

19.5 Conclusion

Over the last few years, OUNL has accumulated considerable experience in educational modelling, both from a theoretical perspective and in educational delivery practice. Thousands of students today use a player in the course of their education and there is worldwide interest in the specifications and software products developed by and with OUNL, together with the lessons the university has learned in putting educational modelling technology into practice.

This pioneering transition has not always been plain sailing, but the innovation has been adopted and would not have been possible without the three generations of the Edubox player.

During the innovation process, much attention has been given at all levels of the university to the specifications and the players. As a result, they have achieved a prominence which is perhaps disproportionate with their role as mere enabling technologies in the educational process—both are, after all, silent on the educational quality of a learning process, allowing both good and bad approaches to learning to be modelled and played. EML's successor, LD, broadens the reach of the approaches, stimulates the market for tools, and helps the enabling technologies to fade into the background of the educational process, allowing educators to focus on identifying effective, efficient and attractive approaches to learning.

20 Delivery of Learning Design: the Explor@ System's Case

Gilbert Paquette, Olga Marino, Ileana de la Teja, Michel Léonard, Karin Lundgren-Cayrol

CIRTA(LICEF) Research Centre, Télé-université, Montréal, Canada

20.1 Introduction

The Learning Design specification (LD 2003) presents new challenges to learning delivery systems. To comply with this specification, delivery platforms must understand different learning strategies and course structures, must manage multi-actor environments, must allow for standard learning object integration, must deal with conditions and rules to be validated at runtime and must support notifications.

In this chapter, we take a look at these requirements from the viewpoint of an open delivery system, Explor@-2. Explor@-2 is the result of a research stream that started a decade ago at Télé-université's LICEF research centre. Explor@ has focused, right from the beginning, on a resource (or learning object) management orientation, making it possible to assemble a set of educational support tools, documents and services to be shared across all programs, courses or activities delivered by an organization. The chapter presents Explor@-2's basic LD information model and analyses how Explor@-2 can deal with LD-compliant courses – how it can deliver units of learning modelled either with the LD Level A specification or with the LD Level B or C specifications. The chapter ends with some conclusions on future research and development to be done in order to build a fully LD-compliant delivery system as well as on some promising directions for developing powerful and adaptive distance learning environments.

In an earlier chapter, we described a methodology, MISA, for designing and developing learning systems as well as two software tools, MOT and ADISA, developed to support this methodology. The relationship between the design products of the methodology and the LD specification has also been shown. In this chapter, we look at the LD specification from a delivery viewpoint by presenting the Explor@-2 delivery system (Paquette 1999; 2001b). As Explor@-2 delivers courses designed using the MISA methodology or another method, it must represent the four models: knowledge model, instructional model, media model and delivery model.

This chapter is divided into four sections. Section 20.2 provides a general presentation of Explor@: its evolution and current global architecture. Focusing on the instructional model, section 20.3 presents a UML model of the Explor@-2 LD information model as well as its instructional activity structure editor. Section 20.4 shows how we can use this editor to build a representation of an LD method that can be delivered using Explor@-2. Further, the components of Explor@-2 that correspond to the LD specification will be presented. Although integrating LD Level B and C in Explor@-2 should be straightforward, we propose in Sect. 20.5 an alternative approach to deal with personalization, advising and notification, which suggests further interesting studies on how to design and integrate external global applications (advisors, managers, helping systems, intelligent tutors, etc.) to the LD specification. The conclusion gives some hints on where to go next and on how to handle the inherent complexity of powerful, flexible distance learning systems.

20.2 Explor@-2 General Presentation

Explor@-2 is the result of a research stream that started a decade ago at Télé-université's LICEF research canter. The initial research efforts (Paquette 1995) focused on a Virtual Learning Campus (VLC) model, architecture and prototypes. To build the VLC model, object-oriented modelling techniques were applied such as Jacobson's use cases methodology (Jacobson 1992) and the Object Modeling Technique, OMT (Rumbaugh et al. 1991), to identify sets of actions that different actors would do while interacting within a virtual campus. Five actor types were identified then: the learner, the trainer, the content expert (informer), the designer, and the manager. Sixty-three roles that can be played by these various actor types were defined.

Right from the beginning, the ambition was to build a distance learning operating system capable of supporting a variety of roles within a variety of delivery models such as High-tech Distributed Classroom, web/multimedia self-training, On-line training, Community of Practice or Performance Support Systems. From 1995 to 1999, we have conducted various research and development projects supported by the Québec Information Highway Fund and the Canadian Telelearning Network of Centers of Excellence (TL-NCE). This work has lead to the implementation of our Virtual Learning Campus (VLC) architecture using web-based technology. In 1999, the Explor@-1 implementation of our VLC model was completed and a number of distance learning courses were developed and delivered through it, mainly at the Télé-université, but also in pilot applications at Hydro-Québec and in professional associations.

The Explor@-1 system had a set of innovative features that are still pioneering.

- Contrary to the general authoring system paradigm, Explor@-1 focused on a resource (or learning object) based learning management, making it possible to assemble a set of educational support tools and resources to be shared across programs, courses or activities delivered by an organization.
- The system had more flexibility compared to the traditional learner–trainer-manager trio, enabling the definition of any set of actors.
- Each course could be designed to meet different needs implementing different pedagogical approaches, by using a variety of proprietary or third-party tools, made available to learners, course designers and other facilitators, such as instructors, content experts (informers), training program administrators, etc.
- An Advisor Editor enabled the designers to build a set of rules that would trigger help/assistance in various forms (questions, messages, visual cues) when certain conditions were met by values in the user properties tracked by the system.
- The Explor@-1 system was designed to support the integration of existing web courses without changing their format or assistance structure, thus allowing an organization to transform its training/learning methods progressively.
- Finally, the open modular structure of the system made it possible to significantly reduce design time, speeding up the implementation and allowing periodic updates by the design team or the on-line tutor. Environment maintenance also became much easier. Once the first course was implemented, each additional course integrated into Explor@ could be limited to a few web pages and hyperlinks to existing documents.

From 1999 to fall 2002, we conducted a third major R&D effort within Technologies Cogigraph, a spin-off from Télé-université research centre. The Explor@-2 system was developed and implemented at Télé-université and at Canal Savoir[1] for its SavoirNet delivery infrastructure.

Figure 20.1 presents a conceptual view of the core architecture of the Explor@-2 system. It deals with four types of objects: actors (or roles), learning objects (or resources), knowledge and competency (or content), and operations structures (or functions).

---

[1] Canal Savoir is Québec's university television channel grouping most universities in Québec and some colleges. It has started to diversify its educational system to support different combinations of web and TV delivery models.

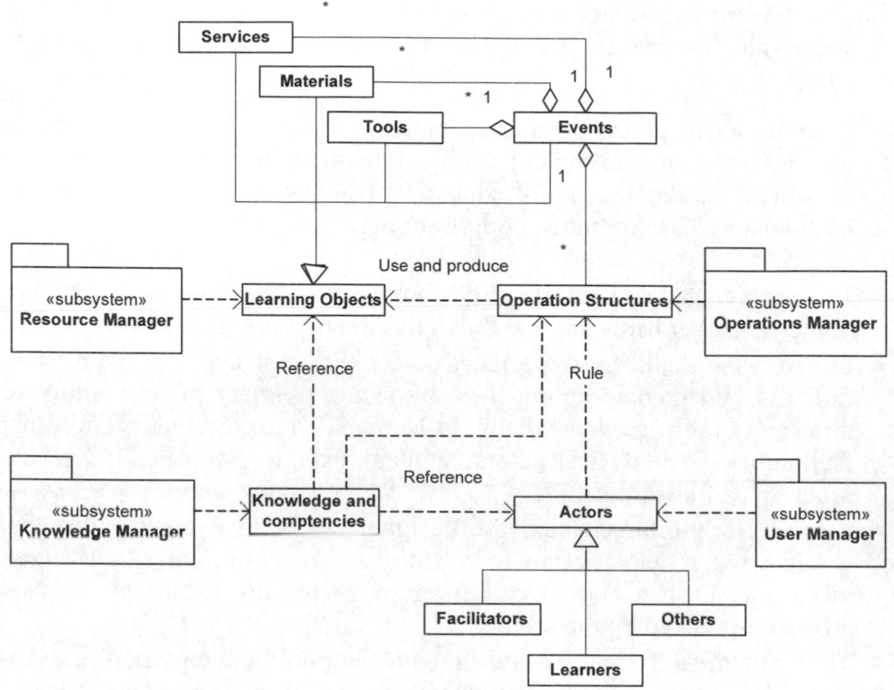

Fig. 20.1. High-level architecture of the Explor@-2 system

Actors operate functions composed of operations (or activities) where learning objects are used or produced. Knowledge and competencies describe the information owned, produced or processed by actors, processed in operations or contained in resources. Four corresponding managers store and retrieve information in a database, construct information structures and display information to users.

As was stated before, Explor@ has a resource management orientation allowing for the integration of learning objects and services in a learning scenario. The resource manager shown in Fig. 20.2 (Paquette et al., in press) is the Explor@-2 component in charge of this management. The two upper components, Learning Object Aggregator and Learning Object Launcher, operate on the learning objects themselves found in one or more repositories, located on servers somewhere on the web. The six other components all relate to metadata management services. Locally, Learning Object Metadata (LOM 2002) records referencing the resources are stored by the Explor@-2 resource manager in a relational/XML database.

The Explor@-2 system provides designers with three main ways to aggregate learning objects into larger resources.

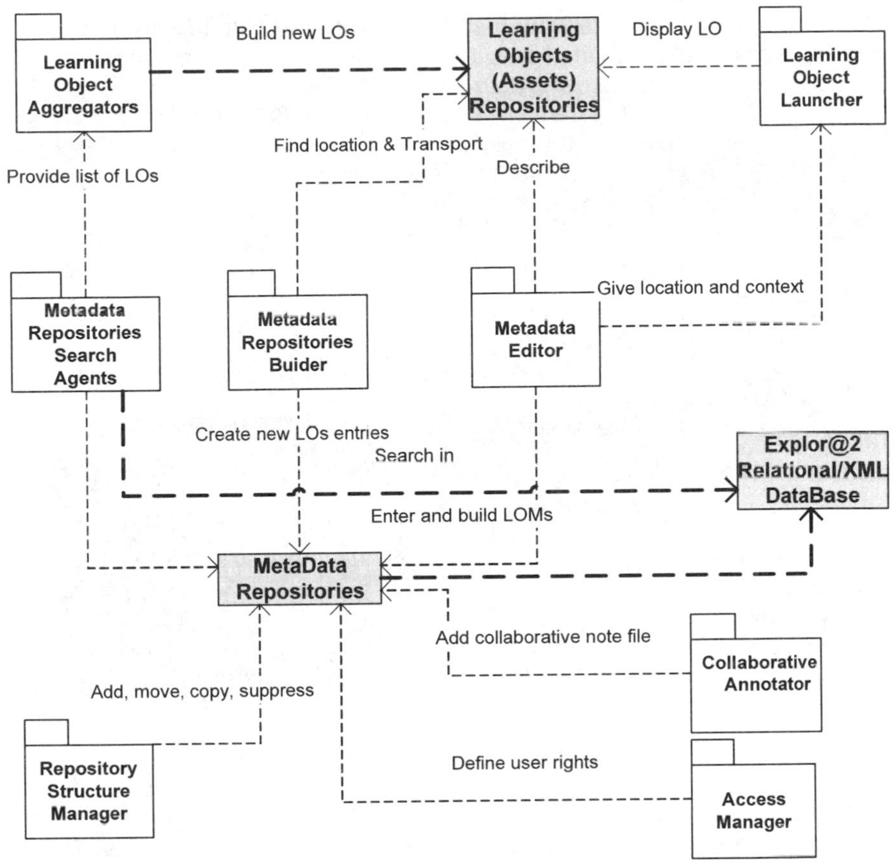

Fig. 20.2. Main components of the Explor@-2 resource manager

The corresponding designer's tools are the Resource Aggregator, the Role Environment Editor and the Instructional Structure Editor. The Resource Aggregator is a simple tool to build web pages filled with hyperlinks to resources found using the metadata repositories, search agents. The Role Environment Editor aggregates resources into an environment according to the roles of an actor. Using this editor, a designer identifies the different roles an actor has to play in a course or a Learning Event, and defines it indirectly by creating an environment made of spaces (menus) grouping resources assisting an actor to carry out its various roles.

The most important aggregation tool is the Explor@-2 Instructional Structure Editor. It enables a designer to import or build a tree structure describing a Learning Event (or a course scenario) grouping activities where resources are used or produced by a role. This editor is the Explor@-2 version of an LD editor. It helps designers to construct a runtime learning model. During runtime, a progression tool shows students their progression through the learning event based on the structure produced by the designer with the activity editor.

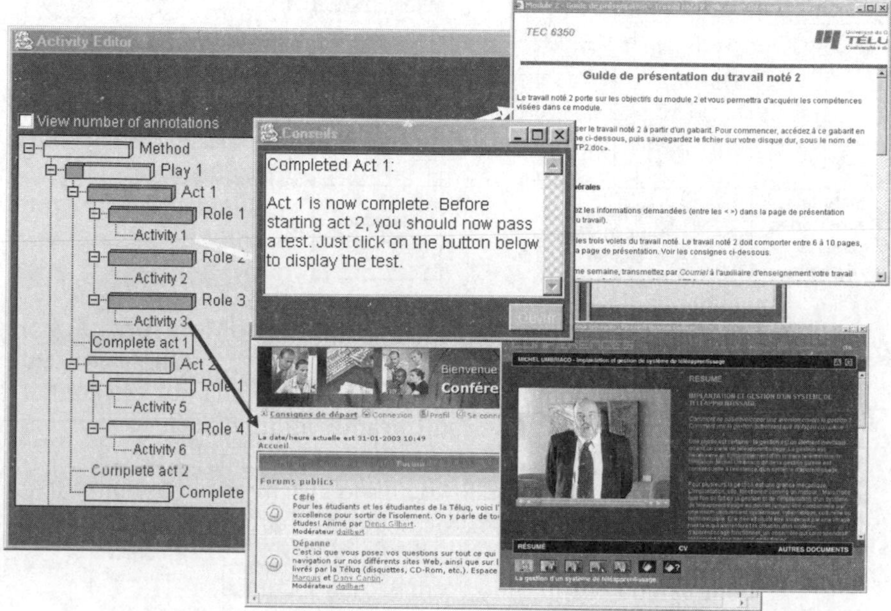

Fig. 20.3. Screen display of a student delivery environment

The left-hand window in Figure 20.3 presents the resulting Instructional Structure corresponding to the LD Method, Play, Act, Activities and Role parts displayed in the Explor@-2 progression tool and produced by the Explor@-2 editor.

For each node and leaf, the user (learner or staff) can access services and learning objects (tools, documents and services) pertinent to the play, the act or the activity by double-clicking on the corresponding title. Three such resources are shown:

- A direct link to an on-line conference (forum) service.
- A video lecture, which can be viewed in segments or as a whole, accompanied by a PowerPoint presentation and other pertinent resources to enhance subject comprehension.
- An exercise guide matched to Act, 1 Activity 1.

The “Completed Act 1” window, at the centre, is where feedback is provided to the user when Act 1 is completed, either because the learner clicks a box or when the time limit set by the designer is exceeded. The progress bar shows whether or not the user has completed the act. As a user progresses from one activity to another, the completion level is calculated for the Play level as well as the Method level, all according to rules set forth by the course designer in the Explor@-2 Instructional Structure Editor.

20.3 The Explor@ Learning Design Information Model

Explor@-2 provides designers with a set of tools to build a UOL and support learner and staff using web-based instances of it. In Explor@-2, using the Instructional Structure Editor, a designer can import (from ADISA, MOT, or any useful XML tree structure editor) an instructional structure or build it from scratch, associate resources to the structure, describe time, collaboration and evaluation rules, associate knowledge and competencies, add advice and assessment questions, specify a progress/completion mechanism and, finally, describe advisor/assistant rules governing actions in the environment.

The Instructional Structure in Explor@-2 starts with a root representing the main Learning Event: a program, a course, a module, etc. (the method element in LD). The second level is composed of smaller Learning Events nodes (plays in LD) that can be decomposed (through LD acts and activity structures) at any number of levels until we reach terminal nodes corresponding to Learning Units (activity structures in LD with no sub-activity structures). Below are terminal nodes that correspond to activities (learning or staff single activities in LD) in the MISA instructional scenario. Finally, below these terminal nodes there are the input and output resources from an activity (the environment in LD).

A corresponding conceptual model is shown in Fig. 20.4. Tree leaves are special kinds of nodes. Any node may have associated resources, advice and assessment questions. It can also hold a progression rule that specifies if the sub-nodes are to be processed in sequence or in parallel, possibly with options, such as do two out of four nodes. The completion of sub-nodes will affects the progression level of a parent node, according to the progression rule associated to the parent node.

Additional elements can be associated to the leaves of the Instructional Structure, corresponding to properties such as required completion time, collaboration time and type, assessment tag and weight (percentage of the evaluation). The system adds these elements, values and propagates the cumulative value to the all upper levels of the Instructional Structure corresponding to Learning Units and Learning Events.[2]

Besides the Instructional Structure, the designer can build a knowledge and competency tree structure and assign knowledge and competencies to activities that are regrouped upward and assigned to larger activity struc-

---

[2] See Chap. 9 for the correspondence between MISA and LD terminology.

tures. This association informs the learner about which learning events, learning units, and/or activities will correspond to certain knowledge and competencies. An alternative way to associate knowledge is to use the Instructional Structure Editor to add a text description of the competencies to any node or leaf of the structure or to recover a learning object describing the knowledge from a learning object repository.

Figure 20.4 also displays the actor's environment concept (produced with the Role Environment Editor presented above). Any environment in the learning system groups the resources for each actor into one or more spaces like self-management, information, resource production, collaboration or assistance. Figure 20.4 also indicates rules that can be assigned to any node to build an advisory system for the users. This important aspect corresponds to LD Levels B and C and will be discussed later.

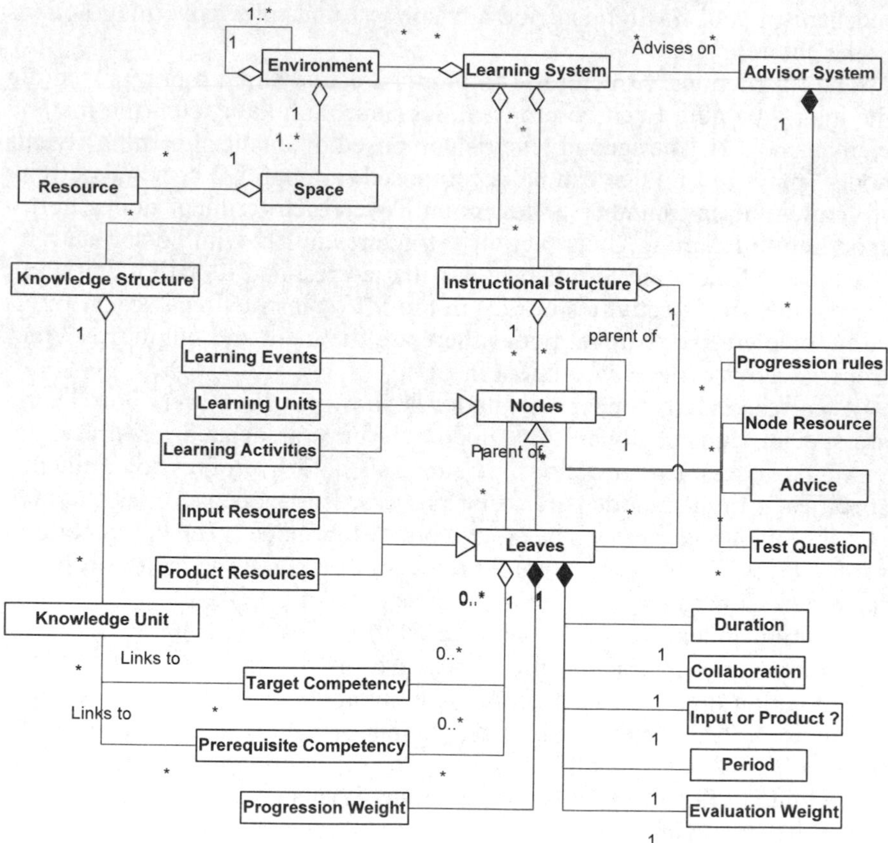

Fig. 20.4. The Instructional Structure of Explor@-2

20.4 Integrating the LD (Level A) Specification in Explor@-2

We will now focus on the Instructional Structure Editor presented in Fig. 20.5. On the bottom left side of the window, we see functions to add or suppress nodes and leaves of the Instructional Structure (Add node, Add leaf, Remove). It is also possible to import an XML structure built with the MOT+ Editor embedded or not in the ADISA instructional design support system to MISA (see Chap. 9).

Selecting any node, a designer can assign progression rules on how to proceed within the corresponding event, unit or activity, in sequence, in parallel or with options. Designers can also use the editor to assign other node and leaf attributes such as duration, evaluation weight, assignment, advice, annotation capability. They can also associate to nodes in the Instructional Structure learning object pointers stored as LOM records, to be launched at runtime.

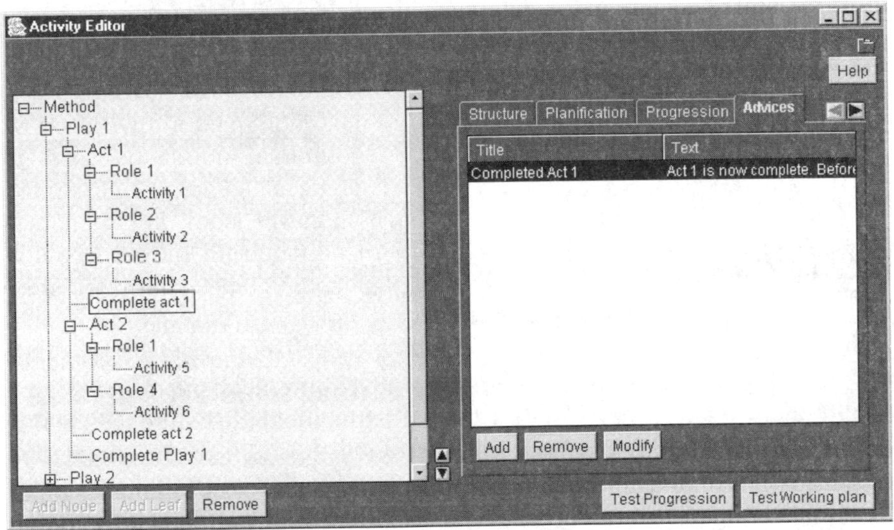

Fig. 20.5. The Instructional Activity Structure Editor

Using this editor it is possible to build a representation of an LD Method and an Explor@-2 user progression as the one displayed in Fig. 20.3. Figure 20.6 presents a concrete instantiation of the activities of that structure. Here, the Method corresponds to a Learning Unit called Module C and the plays present two alternative course delivery models from which a learner has to choose one: web delivery (play 1) or classroom delivery (play 2). Play 1 consists of two acts in sequence. In the first act, learners prepare a seminar by consulting resources, participate in a discussion forum and produce a presentation; tutors animate the forum; experts provide advice to learners in and outside the forum. In the second act, learners deliver the presentation while assessors take notes to produce an evaluation report (this activity could figure in a third act). Figure 20.6 shows that two of the three role-parts in Act 1 have been completed; one of the learners has still to produce a text. If the learner clicks the check box of this activity, the system displays a validation question with two possible answers, each triggering advice on what to do next.

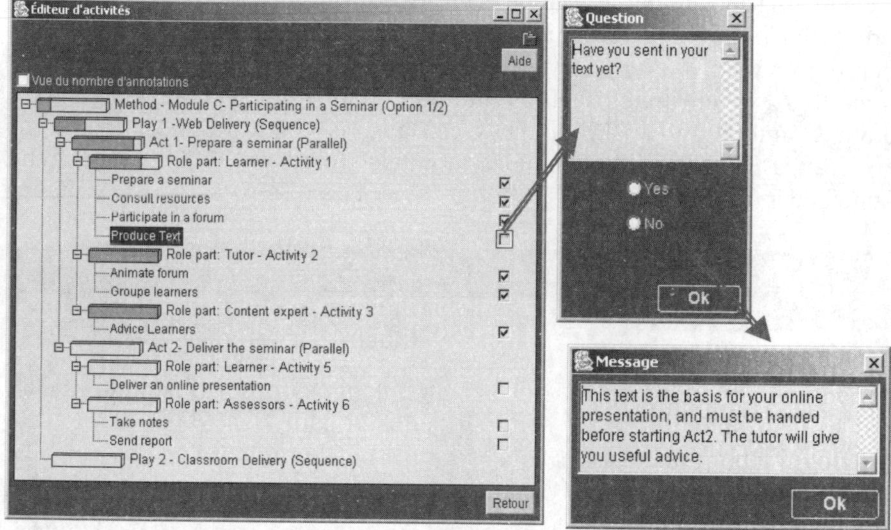

Fig. 20.6. The Instructional Activity Structure at runtime

Explor@-2 has a built-in bottom-up propagation mechanism to assign a progression level to each node of the Instructional Structure calculated from its leaves, which can be used to provide feedback using completion requirements for acts, plays or the method as specified in LD.

When the user selects a leaf of the tree structure, he/she can declare it completed. If the designer has prepared an assessment question, only a right answer will turn on the completed requirement flag; if there is no question, the flag will be on by default or after a certain time limit selected by the designer. If all the role-parts in an act are completed, in whatever order, the act is completed. If all the acts are completed in the specified sequence, the play is completed. If the required number of plays is completed, the method is completed. When an act, a play or a method is completed, a feedback message can be displayed.[3]

This example can be generalized to any method, showing that the Instructional Structure in Explor@-2 is generic enough to build any unit of learning modelled with the LD specification. In practice the corresponding XML files could be produced either by an MOT model or a slightly modified activity editor, and read into the Instructional Structure.

Actually, in Explor@-2, each actor or role has its own activity structure (which is not multi-role) and its own resource environment, so additional functionalities will have to be built to exploit the multi-actor capabilities of the LD specification. These include synchronization mechanisms when the completion of an act requires verifying that all or some other roles have also completed the act. We will then provide an LD activity editor as an option, generate role environments automatically and activity structures for each type of actor, and provide contextual alternate views to help an actor situate the activities within a play. A way to do this using the concept of a function model has been presented in Paquette and Rosca (2002).

On the other hand, Explor@ can produce and deliver instructional structures that are more complex than an LD Method since it is possible, at any level, to assign to any node a progression mode specifying that the subnodes are to be completed in sequence, in parallel or with options. This might pose certain problems when we want to translate an Explor@ Instructional Structure into an LD specification to increase reusability and interoperability with other delivery systems. This problem will need further investigation.

20.5 Integrating Level B and C Specifications in Explor@-2 or Taking an Epiphyte Approach

The LD Levels B and C give additional possibilities to a simple feedback produced by completed parts of a method. On the other hand, they are minimally required to provide adaptation and role coordination capacities in a distributed learning environment. As we see in the LD best practices document (LD 2003), conditions and properties allow for the personalization of pedagogical treatments. Instructional designers may, for example, personalize the activities a student has to do, as a result of his/her profile and pre-test scores (examples 2.1 and 2.3 from the best practices docu-

[3] In the actual version of Explor@-2, that message is entered by the designer in the assignment attribute of a node and is displayed only if the user asks for it. In a previous version such a message could be displayed at the initiative of the system; this functionality will be reintroduced in the next version.

ment) or previous experience (example 2.7) or as a result of recognizing particular learners' needs (example 2.10: obtaining learners' profile from a human resources database), the resources to be used in a particular activity (example 2.2: the systems find adapted resources according to the student cultural group), the composition of groups, taking into account students' profiles (example 2.2) or the selection and sequencing of activities (example 2.14). This personalization is achieved by inserting actions (show, hide, notify and change property) into the learning structure, which are to be triggered when conditions on properties are met. Those conditions are inserted in different parts of the LD, at the Method, Play and Act level.

It might be worthwhile to look at another possibility which would be to leave the design free of conditions and actions and to have an external advising agent monitoring it and eventually taking control when needed. This is the approach taken in Epitalk (Paquette et al. 1996), which has been applied both to support instructional engineering in MISA (Paquette and Tchounikine 2002) and to assist learners using Explor@ (Girard et al. 1999; Lundgren et al. 2001).

This approach is based on an external advisory system, a set of software agents that can be grafted onto an existing host system. As was shown in these articles, Epitalk has many advantages over the more traditional "branching-like" approach where conditions are wired in the host system. The following principles guide this type of system:

- the actions giving advices or adapting the environment can be added to an existing host system without having to change its code;
- the actions and the conditions are based on a model of the host system constructed by the designers using a terminology that he/she chooses for some intended purpose (this aspect is accessible to an instructional designer without programming skills);
- an advisory editor can be built to support instructional designers in the difficult task of building an adaptive assistance system: to build an instructional model and assign conditions and actions to the model;
- since the assistance is mediated by a model constructed by the designer, it enables him/her to address assistance issues from different viewpoints; for example, one agent could manage the resources proposed to the learner, while another one would assist on the coherence of a tutor's interventions.

Epitalk can in principle be applied to activity models for any actor or sets of actors, thus making it possible to address the multi-actor aspects of an LD Method. In Explor@-1 (Girard et al. 1999) and ExploraGraph (Dufresne 2001), Advisor Editors made it possible to build a model of the host system and to use it to maintain a user model and define rules triggering actions when certain conditions were met. We are now in the process of re-introducing such functionalities into the actual Explor@-2 system.

As shown above, the Explor@-2 advisory component of the activity editor actually includes a simpler advisory system than in Explor@-1 focused on student progression in the learning design. It has two components: the Advice Editor and the Student Advisor. The Advice Editor allows the designer to tie to each node in the learning design: its weight of importance; its type of progression (sequential, modular, parallel or optional); pop-up advice and assessment questions. The Student Advisor in Explor@-2 actually supports three functions:

- It displays diagnostic questions and pop-up advice while navigating in the course site (proactive advisor – dynamic advice).
- It makes available contextual advice in an assistance space of the user environment where the user can trigger pieces of advice (passive advisor – static advice).
- It displays viewers, for example a progress bar showing the student's progression in both the Instructional Structure and the cognitive structure (student self-monitoring).

To give dynamic advice and to display the student progress bar, the advisory system dynamically builds a simple student model, tracing student interaction, both with the learning system and the advisor. Rules in the Advisor Editor are actually specialized: their conditions involve properties on the user's progression, navigation and answers to the diagnostic questions; their actions are mainly to trigger advice or a question, and to update progression viewers.

In spite of this specialization, those rules already have the structure required to implement in Explor@-2 Levels B and C of the LD specification. Indeed, triggering advices could be transformed into sending a message by including email names and addresses. Showing and hiding is already possible. Property modification could be made by generalizing the modification of the progress bar to other properties, as was the case in Explor@-1.

From an implementation method point of view, this discussion leads us to propose that a next version of the LD specification should consider an approach similar to Epitalk, basically a multi-level design allowing grafting of the advisory system onto the host system instead of including it. This could be done either by changing the XML binding to address multi-level designs, or alternatively, by limiting LD to its actual Level A and adding a new companion specification for an assistance system that can be grafted onto a learning design of Level A.

20.6 Conclusion – Where to Go Next ...and Further

Educational modelling languages and the LD specification bring important innovations to the e-learning toolset and present new technical challenges. The next step, on our part, will be to analyse the specification from a delivery point of view to adapt our Explor@-2 system so that it can fully process all three levels of the LD specification. Within the eduSource[4] project, we will also define generic services that any delivery system should provide to fully exploit this specification.

Looking further ahead, we believe that a new era of more powerful and flexible distance learning systems is starting. LD is a cornerstone in this direction. Its proposed model of a method leads directly to delivery models of a distributed learning system seen as a set of multi-actor process models. Pushing this idea further, our knowledge, delivery and assistance models are also basically process models in the sense that they describe and relate activities, objects and actors. In Paquette and Rosca (2002) we have developed this idea under the name of function models. Function models are models that aggregates resources used or produced by users with operations that these users perform and possibly other functionalities such as assistance services. Function models are promising components to describe, model and manipulate the different processes that take place in a distance learning course and their relations. They allow for the description, not only of the anatomy of a learning system, but also of its physiology, as a dynamic set of interactions.

In the LORNET project[5] we intend to develop and to tool the concept of function models to provide a solution to the inherent complexity of a distance learning system and to encourage the evolution of the delivery systems towards greater flexibility. As part of the project, we will build a collection of learning designs integrated to learning object repositories and we will provide different ways to aggregate these learning designs with knowledge objects and with assistance objects in a unified way through function models implemented as multi-actor coordination interfaces. These goals correspond well to the research agenda set forth by Duval and Hodgins (2003), where they outline that authoring by aggregation and design for

[4] The eduSource project, an ambitious Canadian project that aims to implement a functional network of learning object repositories, based on international standards and providing a software suite of tools to find, reference and use learning objects in educational applications.

[5] LORNET (Learning Object Repositories Networks) is a major five-years research network heavily funded by the Canadian government to address these questions in a semantic web and knowledge management perspective. It groups five of the major Canadian laboratories in the field, headed by Télé-université's LICEF research center.

content reuse are research issues that must be addressed in the near future, if reusability and interoperability among learning resources are to be attained. Furthermore, by allowing function models to mutate, change and evolve, we expect to be able to produce flexible, personalized, evolving and even emerging learning situations.

21 Challenges in the Wider Adoption of Learning Design: Two Exploratory Case Studies

David Griffiths, Josep Blat, Francisco Casado, Rocío García, Juanjo Martínez, Sergio Sayago

Interactive Technologies Group, Universitat Pompeu Fabra, Barcelona, Spain

21.1 Introduction

This case study presents the conclusions drawn from the creation and evaluation of three Units of Learning (UOLs) by the Interactive Technologies Group[1] of Universitat Pompeu Fabra. They were developed using the Education Modelling Language (EML 2000), the successor of Learning Design (LD 2003), and trialled in both distance and blended learning. The focus of the work reported was on evaluation of EML as a possible solution for two contexts: a distance education course, and on-line support for face-to-face education. While our conclusions address the suitability of EML for this purpose, we are very much aware that this is determined to a substantial degree by the tools used to create and deliver the UOLs. Consequently we report extensively on this aspect of our evaluation.

We provide a brief description of the purpose of the UOLs and the development process, and then focus on our reflections on the outcomes, drawing on usability studies and feedback from learners. In particular we discuss the constraints which limited the adoption of the solutions, principally the difficulty of the authoring process. We conclude with reflections on the need for tools which can support users in making use of the wide range of opportunities opened up by the EML/LD specifications.

21.2 The Units of Learning Developed

Three UOLs were developed and are described in the following sections.

[1] www.tecn.upf.es/gti.

21.2.1 The Two SCOPE Units Of Learning

The two SCOPE UOLs constituted the prototype for a distance learning, continuous education training course for medical specialists, created within the SCOPE Project (SCOPE 2003) and funded by the eContent programme of the EC. We acknowledge the essential contribution made by our partners, particularly the publisher DOYMA and the Hospital Clínic Barcelona, and the technical support generously provided by Perot Systems, the Netherlands. The SCOPE Project took content from a medical journal and repurposed it for web delivery, establishing the G&H Continuada service.

The *aim* of the SCOPE UOLs was to add further value by reusing these resources in educational activities, and they constituted the prototype for an on-line continuing education course for medical specialists.

The *objective* was to demonstrate reuse of resources in different contexts by separating educational resources from pedagogic structure, assessing the effort involved, and carrying out a small-scale evaluation of the end-users' responses.

The *work carried out* included the creation of two parallel UOLs with two pedagogic approaches: the traditional "read and test", and "problem-based learning" (PBL). This chapter assumes a basic understanding of PBL in the sense used by Barrows and Tamblyn (1980) in a medical setting, and by Waters and McCracken (1996) in a computer science environment. Both UOLs used the same learning resources, to demonstrate that the UOLs could function as pedagogic templates for use with learning resources. The development process was evaluated, and small scale trials were carried out with users.

21.2.2 The Interface Design Unit Of Learning

The Interface Design UOL was designed for a contrasting environment: an on-line complement to a face-to-face second-year degree course in Interface Design at Universitat Pompeu Fabra. Many teachers have questioned the added value of Learning Management Systems (LMSs) as a support to presential learning, over and above that provided by the web. This trial UOL was prompted by the perception that EML and LD might have value in this respect, as they are fundamentally oriented towards pedagogy. It constitutes an initial cost-benefit analysis of the advantages and effort involved in using LD for supporting face-to-face classes. The authors are aware that the EML specification was not developed for this purpose, but wanted to explore its potential contribution, in line with Raymond's aphorism "Any tool should be useful in the expected way, but a truly great tool lends itself to uses you never expected" (Raymond 2000, p 16).

The *aim* of the Interface Design UOL was to test the quality and usability of existing tools, and the cost required for learning and using them compared to the benefits for teachers and learners.

The *objective* was to blend a small portion of a typical subject with an on-line UOL, assess the effort involved, and carry out a small-scale evaluation of the end-users' responses.

The *work carried out* included creation of an EML UOL to support face-to-face teaching of a topic in a face-to-face course in interface design for undergraduates. This was used with a cohort of students, and a questionnaire administered.

21.3 Developing the Units Of Learning

All three UOLs were created using the LD Editor and delivered using Edubox, and we thank Perot Systems Netherlands for providing us with free access to these tools, and technical support. The UOLs were created using EML, because the LD specification had not been published when development started (November 2002). The pedagogic framework for the SCOPE UOLs was established following discussions with experts in the field from the Hospital Clinic. The UOLs were designed taking into account our target users, final year students and professionals in hepatology and gastroenterology. The UOLs offered two learning paths: problem-based learning (PBL), and a traditional "read and test" approach. Both paths were designed for single-learner interaction.

The course was designed in such a way that the first action of the user was to select one of the learning paths. The traditional approach consisted of the completion of questionnaires and consulting scientific articles. The PBL path consisted of the completion of several stages, each of which presented the user with a specific problem and a number of possible solutions. Both diagnostic and therapeutic competencies, were tested in the PBL path.

Metadata was added for each piece of information inside the EML, in order to support the definition of reusable learning objects in a range of granularity, as described by Duncan (2003). This was done for the whole course, the different learning paths, the scientific articles and every individual question and questionnaire. Each of these items was considered potentially reusable for e-learning in the context of a medical publishing company. The scientific articles were reused from the electronic medical journal service provided by the publisher. As a first step towards promoting reusability these articles were disaggregated from the journal, and each in turn disaggregated in three types of resources: the article itself, the bibliographic references and key related issues, as discussed by Koper

(2003b). The UOLs were duplicated in HTML, which provided the opportunity for early user feedback, on the interface and its look and feel, before access to the player was available.

21.4 Reflections on the Development Process

21.4.1 The Editing Environment

The three UOLs were implemented by technical staff using a beta version of the Perot LD Editor[2] which was kindly made available by Perot Systems Netherlands. This tool presents the structure of an EML document to the author, who can edit the various elements directly, facilitating navigation through the document, and helping to produce valid EML. Two usability evaluations of this tool were carried out: a semi-structured interview with two EML editor users and a heuristic evaluation, following the method established by Nielsen (Nielsen 1992; 1994; Mack and Nielsen 1994). The conclusions coincided in indicating that the chief determinant of the usability of the application is the way in which it closely reflects the specification itself. The interface is designed using the same terminology as the standard and the relationships between EML elements are directly mapped in the interface. This makes the interface demanding to use for two reasons.[3]

- the user must have a extensive knowledge of the specification, in terminology and structure, before starting;
- there is no way of conceptualizing a course or UOL design independently of the specification.

While these issues may not be a problem for the LD Editors' target users, who are technical experts, they mean that a tool of this type is not appropriate for the content experts and authors, such as those who in the preferred workflow for the SCOPE course would have authored the UOLs which we produced. If such users are to be able to use authoring tools, then the terminology used in the application should not depend on that used in the standard. At the same time the underlying structure of the concepts should be maintained, so that the system is effective for both novices and

[2] The Perot Editor generates EML code, but is called an "LD Editor" because it is planned to provide the capability to convert EML to LD.

[3] It should be stressed that a beta version of the LD Editor was used.

experts (who will recognize the concepts underlying the day-to-day vocabulary).

These design principles were applied within SCOPE in the development of QAed,[4] an open-source tool for the authoring of tests and questionnaires using the Question and Test Interoperability Lite specification (QTI-Lite 2001). This tool is centred on the practice of creating tests rather than on the structure of the specification. It provides support for the usual workflow of the teachers when performing this type of task; the specification details, and how the support to the standards is performed, are hidden from the user by means of offering a comprehensible terminology which is closer to the users, and mapping into the user interface the structure of the specification. The QTI specification (QTI 2003) is much less complex than LD, but the application provides a simple case which shows the approach which we recommend for the development of LD tooling addressed to non-technical users. Our experience in developing QAed indicates that developers should consider if the focus of an editing tool is a specification or rather the teachers' and learners' workflow. This might involve a combination of different specifications, but the author need not be aware of the fact. The QTI and LD specifications are not designed for teacher- and learner-centred approaches to course development, and so their suitability for this purpose is not a criterion for their success. Nevertheless, we believe that this context is important for authoring tools working with these specifications. Even in content publishing contexts, such approaches could be useful for promoting participatory design jointly with teachers and learners while content authors are developing learning scenarios.

The expert users of the LD Editor identified some additional features that would have assisted them in their task, and which may be generalizable to other editors which work close to the specification:

- Feedback indicating what information will appear in the player would be valuable, for example by distinguishing visually between elements which will appear in the rendered UOL, and those which will not be rendered, but are required to enable the system to work. Similarly the user interface should distinguish between mandatory and non-mandatory elements.
- The authors requested access to an HTML editor during the design process, so as to avoid entering HTML by hand, and so creating the possibility for errors. In the Valkenburg Group Reference Architecture (see Chap. 3) a separate materials editor is foreseen, so the solution would appear to be an integration of the materials editor and the LD Editor.

[4] QAed is available for download at http://www.tecn.upf.es/gti/leteos/newnavs/qaed.html.

- Even for expert users, if all the navigation related to the creation of activities, environment, roles, etc., is located in the same menu, then the learning curve may be steep. A modular approach is an alternative possibility.
- As a general principle for such applications, all authoring actions which can be carried out automatically, such as keywords or identifiers, should be automatic, so as to reduce the cognitive load on the user. Similarly the user interface should indicate to users how to fill in the fields, for example by offering default values.
- The UOL authors found that there was a lack of support in Edubox for the representation of the specialized symbols required by mathematics and scientific subjects. This was resolved by the use of images inserted in the text, but a better solution would be the use of a widely recognized specification, such as the W3C recommendation MathML.[5] Developers of players should be aware of the need to incorporate such functionality.

21.4.2 Delivery and Evaluation of the Units of Learning

All three UOLs were delivered using Edubox,[6] which is described in Chap. 19 of this volume. Support for Spanish was added to the Edubox system through the creation of an XSLT stylesheet, demonstrating its extensibility.

Evaluation of the SCOPE UOLs consisted of four sessions with individual physicians, some of them post-graduate students, who had extensive knowledge of the subject matter covered by the UOLs. As the UOLs were intended for continuing education for medical professionals, these users were a close match to the intended learners. The focus of the evaluation was on the usability of the course user interface and the UOL designs. Questionnaires were designed and administered to users before and after the trials, gathering information on the background of the users (pre-test) and their impressions after using Edubox and the UOLs (post-test).

In addition to the questionnaires a "talk-through" evaluation was also carried out. A list of tasks to be carried out by trial users was prepared, which were typical of learner actions when using the UOLs. The users were asked to "think aloud" while following the requests of the evaluation monitor, and were video recorded for subsequent analysis. For example, the protocol for one task was:

---

[5] For more details about MathML, see http://www.w3.org/Math/.

[6] Again provided by kind permission of Perot Systems Netherlands. The SCOPE UOLs are currently available at: ouserv3.perot.nl/edutool/EduToolController (Edubox version), www.tecn.upf.es/gh/ (HTML version).

- The first step is to select one of the two learning paths. Could you tell me if you understand what these two learning paths are about?
- Please try to complete the first level of the problem-based learning.
- Do you understand the relationship between the "tools and resources" and the "to do" panel?
- Are the icons comprehensible? To what extent?

The Interface Design UOL (Fig. 21.1) was used with a group of students who all attended a face-to-face class which covered the same material as that in the UOL. During the class they used the UOL for half an hour, and were then asked to fill in a questionnaire. The responses of the teacher and the UOL editor were also evaluated. The following sections discuss the outcomes of the evaluations.

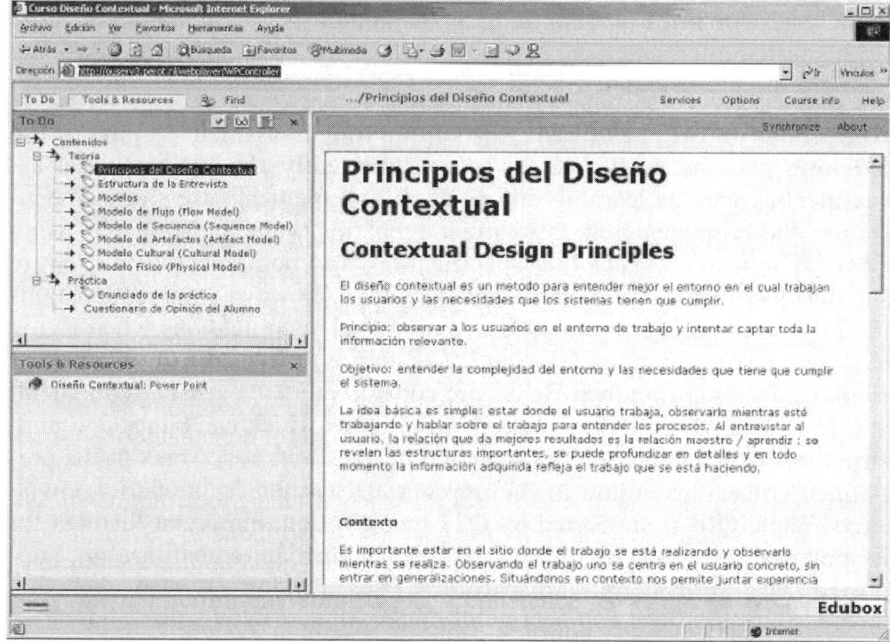

Fig. 21.1. The Interface Design UOL opening screen in Edubox

Reflections on Unit of Learning Delivery

In both the SCOPE and Interface Design UOLs the interface of Edubox was usable, in that it did not constitute a barrier to use of the application, but certain issues were, however, identified, as follows.

Terminology and choice of learning routes. The response to the organization of the two learning routes in the SCOPE UOLs was positive (suggesting that pedagogic flexibility is valued by the users). They chose the traditional read and test methodology learning itinerary, rather than the problem-based learning itinerary for skills development. The reason for this was a salutary reminder for course authors: the learners reported that they did not really understand what "modelo para el desarrollo de competencias" (skills development) was, and so they stayed with the more familiar sounding "modelo instruccional tradicional" (traditional instructional model).

This underlines at the level of the user the need to avoid technical language and terminology which we also identify at the authoring level. This is an especially difficult issue at the European level, as, for example, the concepts of competencies and skills would be more familiar to learners in some other countries.[7] It also reminds the author that the adoption of more sophisticated e-learning pedagogies is not simply a technological issue, but also one of culture and practice.

Reflections on the use of EML for supporting assessment as part of the learning process. EML proved to be sufficiently flexible to model assessment as well as learning processes. In the medical case study, for instance, the corresponding assessment scenarios were implemented using EML as well as the QTI Lite specification, and both specifications were satisfactory. In the other implemented UOLs, however, our conclusions identify shortcomings in the QTI-Lite and QTI specifications when trying to describe some common assessment scenarios such as the Question Item Bank (QIB). Question Item Banks are considered in the sense used by Bull and Dalziel (2003): that is, a collection of items which can be used to construct assessments through the selection of questions based on various predefined criteria according to the appropriate assessment scenarios envisaged. While QIB is supported by QTI specification, important features for its practical use, such as the overlap exclusion requirement, are not supported, as described by García-Robles et al. (2004). Overlap exclusion means, in simple terms, enabling some questions to force the removal of other questions. As stated in Chap. 10, there are also other advanced assessment scenarios such as peer-to-peer, self-assessment or groupwork

[7] This may in part be a problem of translation, and in later versions of the UOL the Spanish equivalent for skills development was changed to "actualización/revision de conocimientos". Nevertheless it highlights the problem of translating some educational concepts, which can hinder the reuse of UOLs across cultures. The issue of multilingual educational terminology is being addressed by CEN ISS. This is valuable, but does not resolve the differences in practice and concepts which underlie the differences in terminology.

which are not supported by the QTI and QTI-Lite specifications, but LD can be used if the assessment is to be integrated into the overall learning process.

Representing activities and resources. One open question identified by users was the best way to represent activities and resources. In the SCOPE UOLs there were many scientific articles associated for each learning activity. Edubox show these articles as a list, and uses icons to distinguish between the different states which they are in at any time (such as "consulted", "passed", "pending", etc.). Users suggested that they would prefer to see the activities which they need, at any moment, and not the whole set of activities. For example, at the beginning of the course only the main activities could be shown (activity structure, choice activities…) and subsequently, only the activities related to the main activity selected, etc. It seems that in this case the more information which they were shown, the less useful it was.

If UOLs are to be reusable, they should be created independently of how the player will represent the course. However, if these suggestions were to be implemented, and a variety of possible player renderings of the same UOLs were available, it would raise the issue of how the UOL author could predict the interface on different systems. This is why a reference runtime player will be of significant importance to the implementation of LD. Working within Edubox, the author of a UOL has the responsibility for modelling the learning process in such a way that this overload is avoided.

Similarly users suggested that the resources associated with each activity could be classified using folders which were related to one question (which is the meaning of… according to the study of X and Y), questionnaire, or activity, It was also requested that content which had become available as the learner progressed should be flagged. One possible approach to this request would be to use nested environments.

There is probably no single best way to represent activities and resources, but we note this issue as one which should be borne in mind in authoring and rendering UOLs. To provide flexibility in this respect it might be advantageous to provide preferences which could be set by the learner, or by the course administrator.

The meaning of icons and menu items. In the Interface Design UOL about half the students who answered the questionnaire stated that the Edubox icons were understandable, if not at first glance, then with the help of the contextual help (text which appears when the cursor is placed above the icon), but the majority of the users felt that the meaning of the icons could be clearer. Similar results were obtained from the four "talk-through" trials of the SCOPE UOLs.

The students in trials of all UOLs were generally in agreement that the functionality of the modules was clear, but they again commented that the terminology used was not always immediately clear, and could be improved. In the "talk-through" sessions for the SCOPE UOLs one interface feature relating to this issue was identified: in the menus "Actividades" (Activities) and "Herramientas y recursos" (Tools and resources) the items shown in the latter depend on the activity selected in the former, and this was not immediately apparent to users. Once the evaluation monitor had helped them grasp this idea the use of the menus presented no problems.

It should be added that the responsiveness of the UOLs in all trials was rather low, which was a function of the performance and connectivity of the server, rather than the software used. This may have raised doubt in the mind of the user as to whether they have chosen the correct action.

General reflections. These results suggest that both the software used and the particular UOLs which we developed could be improved in various respects. We conclude, however, that the questions identified in the evaluation of delivery of the UOL all reflect the same underlying issue: it is hard to represent LD structures to learners in a way that is immediately comprehensible. There is no reason to suppose that this is the result of a structural problem in EML or LD. Rather it is a function of the lack of an established body of practice and feedback from users. LD has been developed to encode the essential elements of a pedagogic approach in an iterative process lasting a number of years, and we believe that a similar iterative process will be required to develop the best approaches to representing this encoded model both to learners and to teachers, and the applications which make this possible.

The HTML version of the SCOPE UOLs closely followed the look and feel of the G&H Continuada journal which provided the learning resources used. It did not prove possible to reproduce exactly the HTML version in the Edubox version. A particular limitation was that the frames are not resizable and do not have a scroll bar. This would not be a problem for many implementations, but in the context of SCOPE this was significant, because the publishing partner wanted to extend the look and feel of the journal to the continuing education course which is based on it.[8]

21.5 The Effectiveness of the Solutions Developed

The conclusions regarding the effectiveness of these two prototype applications were essentially the same: the effort involved in creating the UOLs

[8] Screen shots from the two applications are available at www.tecn.upf.es/scope/showcase/training_course.htm.

in this context, and with the current tool set, is too great to justify the benefits which come from the use of EML. This similarity, however, masks substantial difference between the two contexts, both of which make use of different subsets of the functionality offered by EML.

In the SCOPE UOLs, the learner interactions required by the system are relatively straightforward. There is a single learner completing a series of learning tasks, and being evaluated with a multiple choice test. There are no services being called, and there is no collaborative learning. In these circumstances something similar could be created using a simpler standard for which more mature authoring tools are available. In this context the added value of EML is limited, mainly being the ability to adapt to a more flexible pedagogic structure if that should be required. In practice, however, changes are likely to be infrequent, because pedagogic decisions are not taken by teachers, but for the entire programme. Similarly, the business model for resource sharing is primarily envisaged as taking place within a single publishing company.

For EML/LD to be a viable solution within this context, tools would be required which simplified the task of producing pedagogic templates for a relatively unchanging set of UOLs, and, more importantly, for editing those templates to include new learning resources, etc. A tool for editing the smallest possible effective subset of metadata descriptors would also be necessary.[9] At present such tools are not available off the shelf, and although producing the templates would be possible using present tooling (as the SCOPE UOLs showed), the maintenance tools would have to be created specifically for this purpose at considerable cost, or a technical expert would be required to carry out this function on a regular basis.

The limitations mentioned above on the presentation of the course in Edubox (the only player available) were also a significant factor for the publisher. This could no doubt be adjusted in the Edubox application, but again would cost money, which cannot be justified by the benefits of using EML/LD. In the current state of tooling, therefore, EML/LD was not a cost-effective solution for the SCOPE prototype, given that the project did not need to use many of the more sophisticated features of the specification.

The teacher involved in the trial of the User Interface Design UOL was enthusiastic about the technology when it was first explained to him. However, this enthusiasm turned to scepticism when the effort involved in creating the UOL became clear, requiring lengthy work by a team of experts. In particular the features which offer a clear advantage (such as learner tracking, and communication tools) are those which are most time consum-

[9] The increasing demand for tools for editing the smallest possible effective subset of metadata descriptors was one of the conclusions of the POOL project (www.edusplash.net/) in Canada.

ing (and hence expensive) to implement, and which can be substituted in a face-to-face environment by direct contact with learners. Moreover the aspects of reuse, and interoperability of content, are also expensive in terms of both planning and implementation, and are outside the traditional role of the teacher in the face-to-face university environment. We conclude that at present work with EML and LD has to be carried out with the support of specialized centres, which cushion users from the difficulties. The high cost of such a service could be balanced against other strategic factors to make the use of EML/LD in a blended environment an attractive option.

The existing traditional teaching context constrains the use of the technology just as much as the technology constrains teaching practice. In our case this was fundamentally a lecture and practical work with on-line documentation, and for this purpose the learners noticed little change with the introduction of a UOL. To explore the wider potential of LD teaching practice would have to change, along with the role of the technology within it, and this is not an easy task. The evolution of mixed presential and on-line learning programmes might well enhance the cost-effectiveness of EML/LD within traditional education, as would tools which are easier to use, by an order of magnitude. In this case the valuable focus on flexible pedagogy, and the ability to support multiple users, would become convincing features.

21.6 Conclusions

The SCOPE UOLs achieved their objective of demonstrating reuse of resources in different contexts, with the educational resources separated from the pedagogic structure, confirming the suitability of EML (and by extension LD) for this purpose. The UOLs constituted a template for the creation of the continuing education course, which facilitated the aim of reusing published resources in educational activities. This was not developed and tested in a full-scale implementation because of the lack of suitable tooling. The essential tool required for the specific needs of SCOPE was a specialized editor, enabling teachers to adapt UOLs within the predefined pedagogic framework without the assistance of technical experts. A desirable tool for this publishing context is a specialized player, which preserves the look and feel of the G&H Continuada service, and meets the needs and preferences of a specific learner group.

The objectives of the Interface Design UOL were also met, and the UOL was used successfully with a cohort of learners as support for a face-to-face course. In our particular case the added value provided by the use of EML as opposed to HTML was not significant, but the result may not be generalizable to other pedagogies. The effort involved in developing the trial UOL was considerable, and prohibitively expensive for providing support for courses developed by individual teachers. This is no doubt why EML in the past, and now LD, have not been used beyond the context for which they were designed: distance learning institutions which have a clear need to exploit its ability to model a wide range of pedagogic approaches, or to use its capability to coordinate multiple learners. Our small-scale study suggests that the use of LD in blended learning will not be possible unless, firstly, new tools are provided which teachers can use without the help of technical experts, and, secondly, the pedagogic context adapts in order make use of the capabilities of the new technology. Now that more flexible and varied tooling for LD is becoming available the first of these conditions may soon be met. The second condition may be more intractable and is likely to be the subject of extensive future debate and research.

22 A Learning Design Worked Example

Pierre Gorissen[1], Colin Tattersall[2]

[1] Fontys University of Professional Education, Eindhoven, The Netherlands

[2] Educational Technology Expertise Centre, Open University of the Netherlands, Heerlen, The Netherlands

22.1 Introduction

This chapter takes the reader through an educational scenario to illustrate the modelling of a Unit of Learning (UOL) using Learning Design (LD 2003). In addition to examining the XML code, the chapter shows screen-shots from a player application running the scenario to help the reader in understanding the runtime consequences of design-time decisions.

The example used in the chapter is a simplified version of parts of the use case described by Dalziel (2003). The approach taken to modelling essentially follows that described in the Best Practices and Implementation Guide of the LD specification.

22.2 The scenario

The narrative of the scenario can be condensed into the following aspects:

- *Title*: What is greatness?
- *Pedagogy/type of learning*: Individual and group-based learning.
- *Roles*: Learner, Tutor.
- *Types of learning content involved*: On-line forms to enter thoughts and responses.
- *Types of learning services/facilities/tools involved*: The Monitor service.
- *Learning activity workflow*:
  - Learners are asked to think about the question: “what is greatness?”.
  - They then record a few sentences of initial thoughts.
  - This process is monitored and ended by the tutor.
  - Learners see the responses of other learners.

- Each learner then enters personal reflections on all responses (not made public).
- The tutor receives all responses and personal reflections once they have been entered.
- The tutor gives feedback on the responses and reflections and finishes the learning activity on a per-learner basis.

The UML Activity Diagram corresponding to the learning flow is show in Fig. 22.1

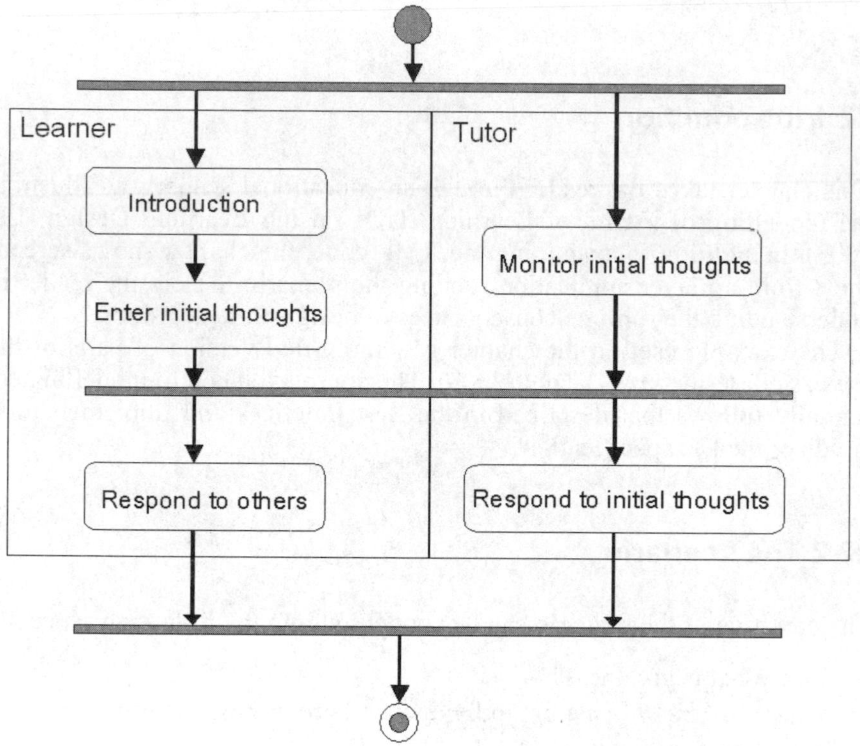

Fig. 22.1. The UML Activity Diagram for the scenario

22.3 Running the Scenario in a Player

In the following sections, the five activities in the scenario are described, screenshots of a run of the scenario in the Edubox player (see Chap. 19 for a description) are shown and some specifics of the underlying XML structures are explained. The LD code implementing the scenario is covered in more detail in the next section.

22.3.1 Introduction (Learner)

At the start of the scenario, the learner is presented with an activity-structure and an environment containing general resources which will be made available throughout the whole scenario. The `structure-type` of the activity-structure is `sequence`. This means that the activities within the structure are displayed in sequence and the learner has to complete an activity before being able to proceed to the next one.

The first learning-activity is an introduction to "what is greatness?" Figure 22.2 shows the activity in Edubox.

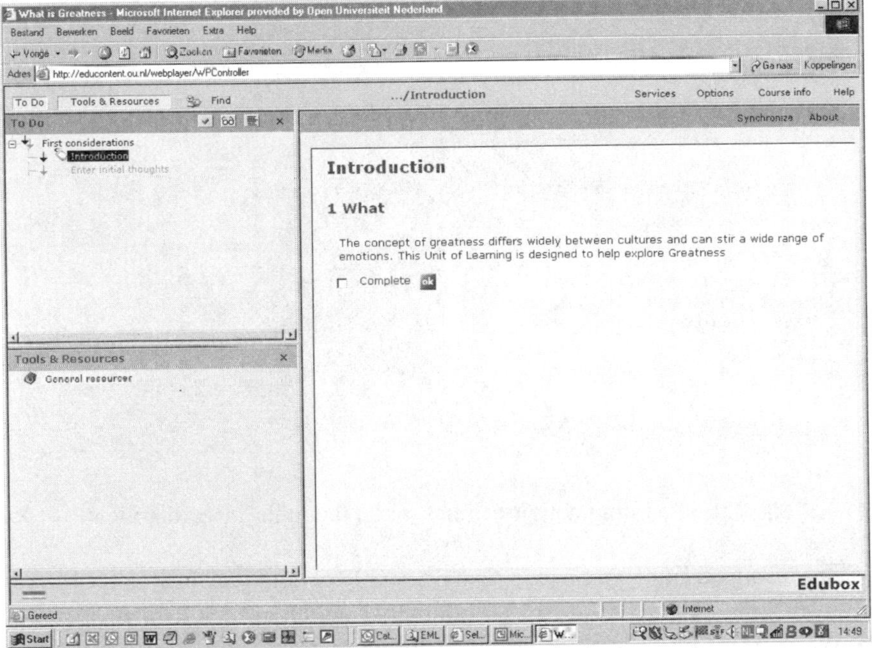

Fig. 22.2. Learning-activity "Introduction" (learner view)

The LD offers some general resources which are available during all activities by clicking on the General resources environment link. This first activity can be completed by selecting the checkbox, which is rendered by the player based on the <complete-activity> information. Note that the checkbox shown in the user interface is generated as a result of the player interpreting the LD, rather than having been explicitly coded using XHTML.

22.3.2 Enter Initial Thoughts (Learner)

After completing the first activity, the second activity in the sequence is made available to the learner. Here, learners can enter their initial thoughts in a text area on a page. Unlike the previous activity, there is no option for the learners to set the status of the activity to completed. Instead, the tutor indicates when the activity is complete. This is arranged for in the LD by making the completion of the activity dependent on a property value which can only be set by the tutor.

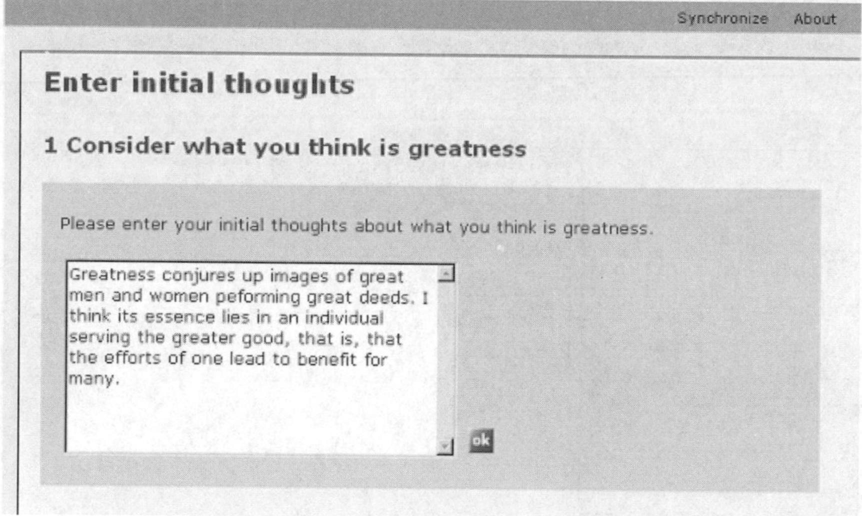

Fig. 22.3. Learning-activity “Enter initial thoughts” (learner view)

The resource file (type `imsldcontent`) for this learning-activity contains an LD `<set-property>` element, which refers to a property of datatype “text”. As a result, the player renders a text box automatically, as a result of the interpretation of the XML.

22.3.3 Monitor the Initial Thoughts (Tutor)

While the learners are involved with the first two learning-activities, the tutor monitors their progress and decides when to end the second activity, and as a result, the first act. This is achieved using a so-called Monitor service, allowing the tutor to view certain specified properties. Figure 22.4 shows the tutor's view.

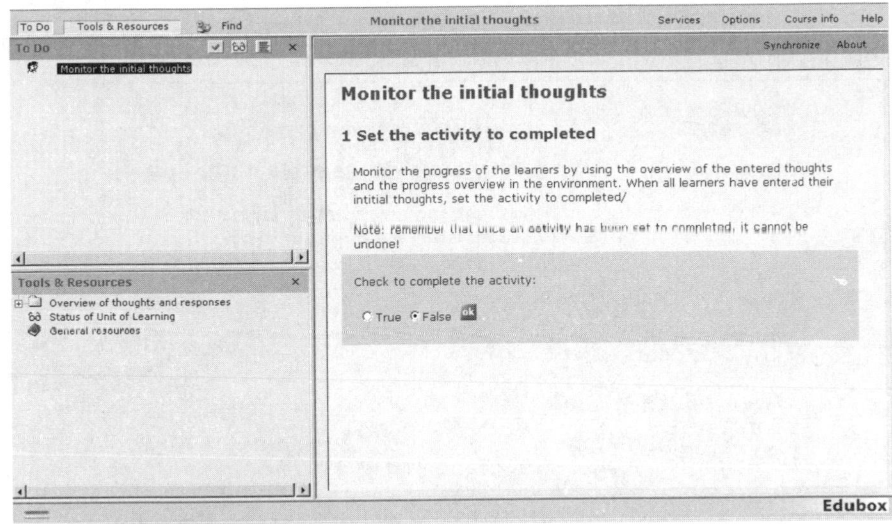

Fig. 22.4. Support-activity "Monitor the initial thoughts" (tutor view)

The Monitor service "Initial Thoughts" is part of the Overview of thoughts and responses in the Environment (Tools and Resources), as in Fig. 22.5.

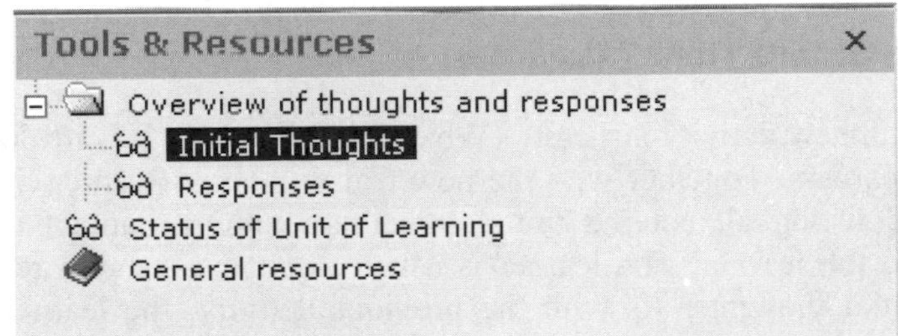

Fig. 22.5. Resources and services available to the tutor

The service shows a list of usernames and the entries for the second activity enabling the tutor to monitor the progress of the learners, as shown in Fig. 22.6. When the tutor decides to set the activity to completed, he or she sets the property using the select box which can be seen in Fig. 22.4.

This has the consequence of displaying the next `activity-structure` to the learner (What do others think?), displaying the next `support-activity` to the tutor and making various aspects of the interface associated with the first act read-only.

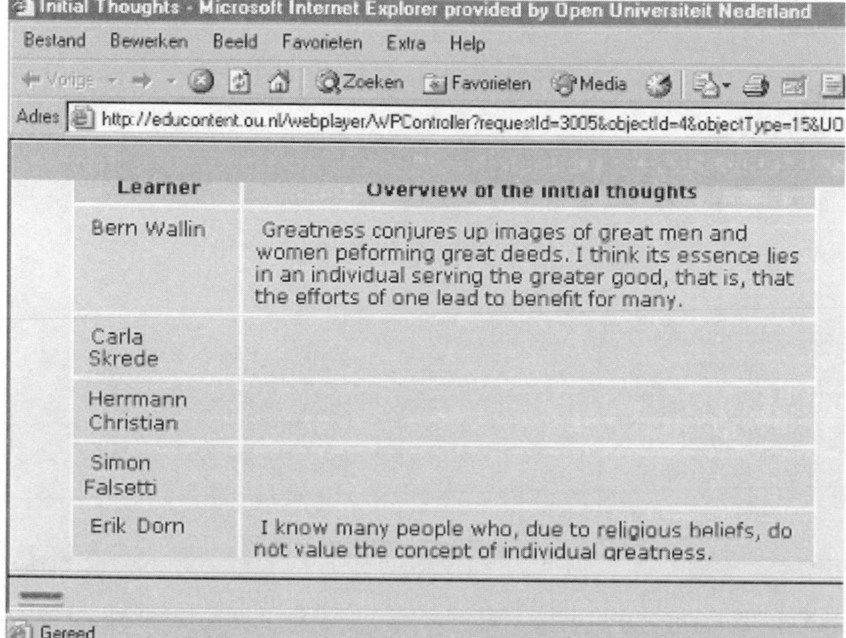

Fig. 22.6. Overview of initial thoughts (tutor-view)

Interaction now moves on to the second act.

22.3.4 What Do Others Think? (Learner)

In the second act, a new activity-structure (What do others think?) is made available to the learners. Together with the new learning-activity an environment resource listing all entered initial thoughts (without names) is made available to the learner. The learner is asked to enter a general response to the initial thoughts. As with the previous activity, the learner cannot set this activity to completed. That is done by the tutor on a per-user basis. The environment resource with the feedback by the tutor is initially hidden, but is made visible by the player once the tutor has entered feedback for this specific learner. This is based on the conditions in the LD code.

Figure 22.7 shows the learner view at the start of the second act. Learners are able to examine others' responses by using a monitor service, rather like the one made available to tutors. However, the design excludes the names of other learners (see Fig. 22.8).

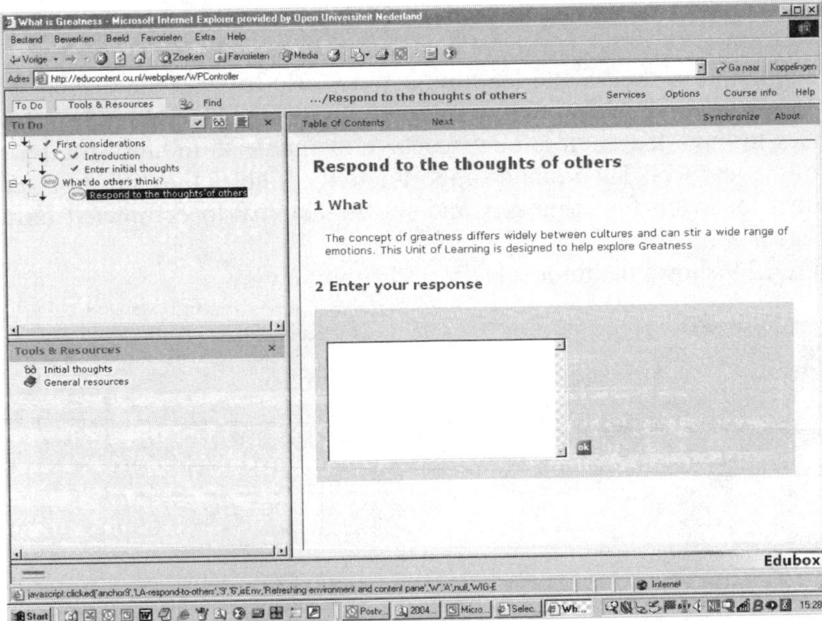

Fig. 22.7. Allowing learners to respond to others

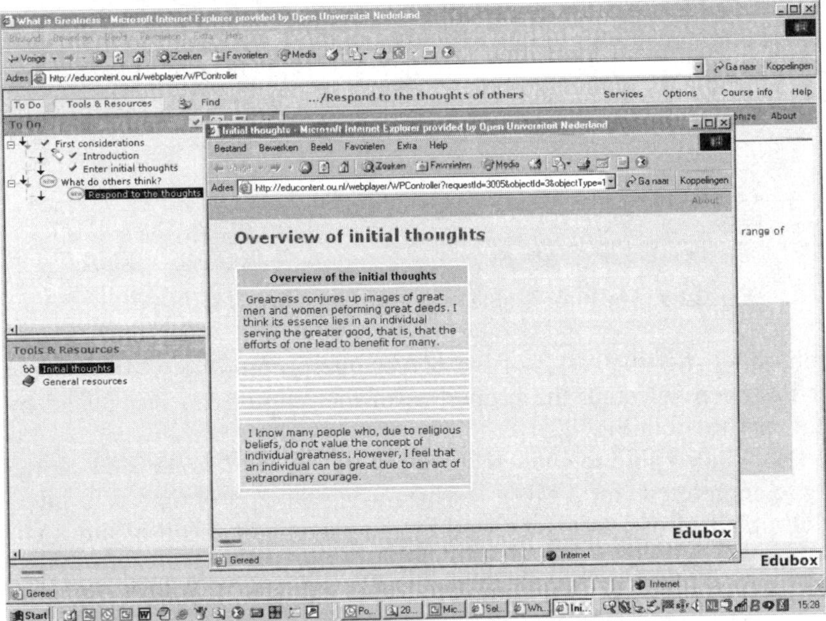

Fig. 22.8. Viewing others' responses

22.3.5 Respond To Initial Thoughts (Tutor)

The completion of the second learning-activity also triggers the display of a new support-activity (*Respond to initial thoughts*) for the tutor. The tutor continues to have the environment resource available to monitor the progress of the learners. The second support-activity enables the tutor to enter individual feedback for each user and set the activity to completed on a per-user basis.

Figure 22.9 shows the tutor selecting a learner to view.

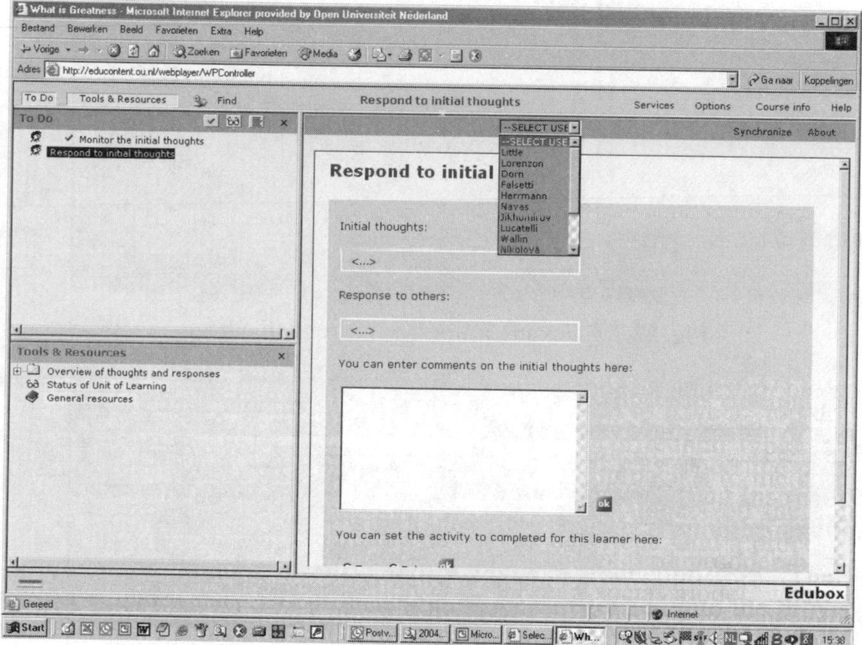

Fig. 22.9. The tutor is able to select from a list of learners

Again, this list is the result of the player interpreting the XML. Once a learner has been selected, the properties of the learner can be viewed by the tutor, as shown in Fig. 22.10.

The tutor is also able to enter some feedback for the learner, and set the activity to completed (for a given learner) using the appropriate user interface control, all of which is generated by the player as a result of the XML code.

Once the support-activity is completed, the UOL is also completed.

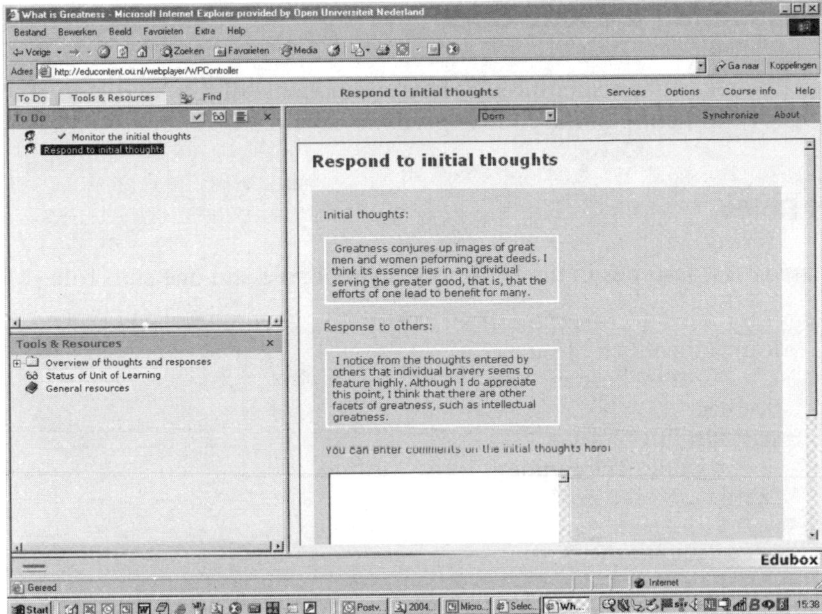

Fig. 22.10. Viewing the answers of a particular learner

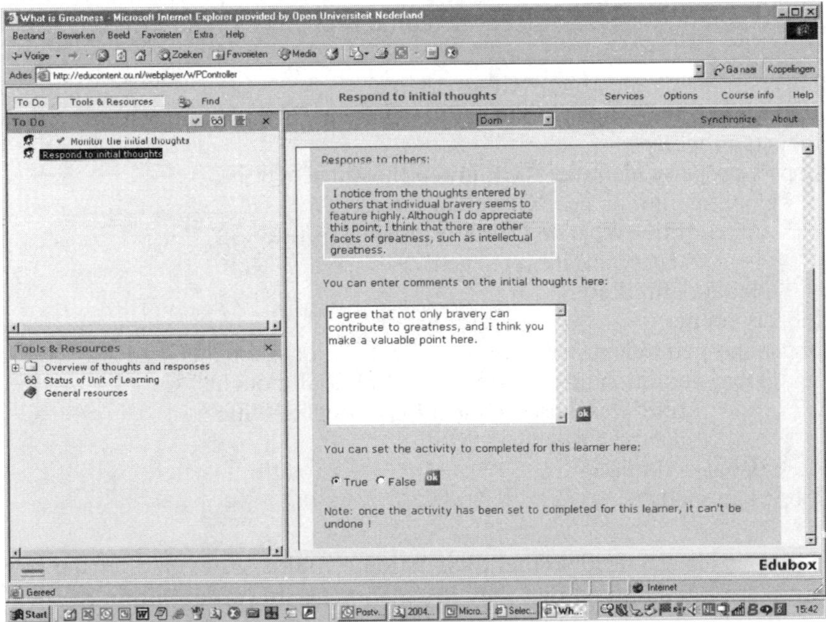

Fig. 22.11. Providing feedback on a learner's responses

22.4 Dissecting the XML Code

This section takes the reader through key components of the XML code for the UOL. A full listing of the code is given in Sect. 22.6.

22.4.1 Roles

There are two role-types in the UOL, one learner role and one staff role:

```
<roles>
        <learner identifier="Learner">
                <title>Learner</title>
        </learner>
        <staff identifier="Tutor">
                <title>Tutor</title>
        </staff>
</roles>
```

22.4.2 Properties

To store the initial thoughts and responses, two global personal properties are defined and one existing global personal property is referenced:

```
<globpers-property identifier="GP-username">
        <existing href="http://eml.ou.nl/dossier/name"/>
</globpers-property>
<globpers-property identifier="GP-initial-thoughts">
        <global-definition uri="GP-initial-thoughts">
                <title>What do I think is greatness</title>
                <datatype datatype="text"/>
        </global-definition>
</globpers-property>
<globpers-property identifier="GP-response-to-initial-thoughts">
        <global-definition uri="GP-response-to-initial-thoughts">
                <title>Responses to the initial thoughts</title>
                <datatype datatype="text"/>
        </global-definition>
</globpers-property>
```

Global properties are used so that their value remains set even after the run has been completed and so that they are also available from within another UOL. As they are personal, the value is set individually for each user. The data type "text" results in a text area being rendered by the player when the <set-property> element is being used. The GP-username property is filled with the username of the current user by the player. To illustrate the difference with these global properties, the feedback given by the tutor is stored in a local personal property:

```
<locpers-propertyidentifier="LP-tutor-comments-initial-thoughts">
        <title>Response by tutor</title>
        <datatype datatype="text"/>
</locpers-property>
```

The result of this choice is that the value is reset for each run of the UOL and is also not available from another UOL.

The UOL uses two additional properties to set the completion of two of the three learning activities of the UOL. One of the properties is a local property, which contains the same value for all users. The other is a local personal property, and is set on a per-user basis. Both properties are Booleans (possible values are true and false) and are initially set to false.

```
<loc-property identifier="LP-activity-2-completed">
        <title>Activity Enter Initial Thoughts completed</title>
        <datatype datatype="boolean"/>
        <initial-value>false</initial-value>
</loc-property>
<locpers-property identifier="LP-activity-3-completed">
        <title>Enter response to initial thoughts completed</title>
        <datatype datatype="boolean"/>
        <initial-value>false</initial-value>
</locpers-property>
```

22.4.3 Learning-Activities

The five activities in the UML Activity Diagram have been translated into three learning-activities and two support-activities:

```
<learning-activity isvisible="true" identifier="LA-introduction">
        <title>Introduction</title>
        <activity-description>
                <item identifier="I-introduction-a" identifierref="R-intro">
                        <title>What</title>
                </item>
        </activity-description>
        <complete-activity>
                <user-choice/>
        </complete-activity>
</learning-activity>
```

The second activity revolves around learners entering their initial thoughts. It arranges for a form where learners can enter their thoughts. The completion of the activity is set by the tutor, in order to ensure that all learners have completed this step, or as many as the tutor feels are necessary, before interaction proceeds to the next activity where learners are asked to respond to each other's thoughts.

```
<learning-activity isvisible="true" identifier="LA-enter-initial-thoughts">
    <title>Enter initial thoughts</title>
    <activity-description>
        <item identifier="I-enter-initial-thoughts"
            identifierref="R-initial-thoughts">
            <title>Consider what you think is greatness</title>
        </item>
    </activity-description>
    <complete-activity>
        <when-property-value-is-set>
            <property-ref ref="LP-activity-2-completed"/>
            <property-value>true</property-value>
        </when-property-value-is-set>
    </complete-activity>
</learning-activity>
```

The third learning-activity (`LA-respond-to-others`) consists of explanation of what to do, together with a form using a <set-property> element to set the global personal property that stores the initial thoughts of the learner. This learning-activity is again set to completed by the tutor. Completion depends on a value change of the property `LP-activity-3-completed` from its initial value of false to true.

```
<learning-activity isvisible="false" identifier="LA-respond-to-others">
    <title>Respond to the thoughts of others</title>
    <activity-description>
        <item identifier="I-respond-to-others"
            identifierref="R-respond">
        </item>
        <item identifier="I-respond-to-others-2"
            identifierref="R-response-to-initial-thoughts-form">
            <title>Enter your response</title>
        </item>
    </activity-description>
    <complete-activity>
        <when-property-value-is-set>
            <property-ref ref="LP-activity-3-completed"/>
            <property-value>true</property-value>
        </when-property-value-is-set>
```

```
    </complete-activity>
</learning-activity>
```

The three learning-activities are grouped into two activity-structures. The first one (`AS-first-step`) consists of the two first learning-activities and makes the environment `E-wig-general-environment` available during both activities. The resource `R-Info-AS-first-step` contains general instructions for the learner, and is displayed when the activity-structure `AS-first-step` (and not the learning-activities within the sequence) is selected. The second activity-structure (`AS-second-step`) contains only one learning-activity (`LA-respond-to-others`) but adds an extra two environments to the already available environment. Here, as with the first sequence, the resource `R-Info-AS-second-step` is displayed when the activity-structure itself is selected.

```
<activity-structure identifier=“AS-first-step” structure-type=“sequence”>
    <title>First considerations</title>
    <information>
        <item identifierref=“R-Info-AS-first-step”/>
    </information>
    <environment-ref ref=“E-wig-general-environment”/>
    <learning-activity-ref ref=“LA-introduction”/>
    <learning-activity-ref ref=“LA-enter-initial-thoughts”/>
</activity-structure>
<activity-structure identifier=“AS-second-step” structure-type=“sequence“>
    <title>What do others think?</title>
    <information>
        <item identifierref=“R-Info-AS-second-step”/>
    </information>
    <environment-ref ref=“E-wig-general-environment”/>
    <environment-ref ref=“E-overview-thoughts”/>
    <environment-ref ref=“E-response-by-tutor”/>
    <learning-activity-ref ref=“LA-respond-to-others”/>
</activity-structure>
```

22.4.4 Support-Activities

There are two support-activities for the tutor. The first one (`SA-first-step`) consists of one activity-description and two environments. The support-activity is set to completed using the same property as used for the completion state of the second learning-activity.

```
<support-activity identifier=“SA-first-step” isvisible=“true”>
    <title>Monitor the initial thoughts</title>
```

```
        <environment-ref ref="E-wig-general-environment"/>
        <environment-ref ref="E-overview-responses"/>
        <activity-description>
                <item identifier="I-sa-first-step"
                        identifierref="R-set-activity2-complete">
                        <title>Set the activity to completed</title>
                </item>
        </activity-description>
        <complete-activity>
                <when-property-value-is-set>
                        <property-ref ref="LP-activity-2-completed"/>
                        <property-value>true</property-value>
                </when-property-value-is-set>
        </complete-activity>
    </support-activity>
```

The second support-activity (`SA-respond`) is notable because of the `<role-ref ref="Learner">` element. By using this construct, the support-activity is repeated for each individual user in the specified role (in this case the Learner role), and is rendered as a list box in the player interface.

```
<support-activity identifier="SA-respond" isvisible="true">
    <title>Respond to initial thoughts</title>
    <role-ref ref="Learner"/>
    <environment-ref ref="E-wig-general-environment"/>
    <environment-ref ref="E-overview-responses"/>
    <activity-description>
        <item identifierref="R-response-to-initial-thoughts-form-tutor" />
    </activity-description>
</support-activity>
```

22.4.5 Plays and Acts

The play is split into two acts:

```
    <play identifier="P-1" isvisible="true">
        <title>What is Greatness - default play</title>
        <act identifier="A-1">
                <title>What is Greatness - Default act</title>
                <role-part identifier="RP-Learner-1">
                        <title>First step</title>
                        <role-ref ref="Learner"/>
                        <activity-structure-ref ref="AS-first-step"/>
                </role-part>
                <role-part identifier="RP-Tutor-1">
```

```
                <title>Support activities for first step</title>
                <role-ref ref="Tutor"/>
                <support-activity-ref ref="SA-first-step"/>
            </role-part>
            <complete-act>
                <when-role-part-completed ref="RP-Tutor-1"/>
            </complete-act>
        </act>
        <act identifier="A-2">
            <role-part identifier="RP-Learner-2">
                <title>Second step</title>
                <role-ref ref="Learner"/>
                <activity-structure-ref ref="AS-second-step"/>
            </role-part>
            <role-part identifier="RP-Tutor-2">
                <title>Support activities for second step</title>
                <role-ref ref="Tutor"/>
                <support-activity-ref ref="SA-respond"/>
            </role-part>
            <complete-act>
                <when-role-part-completed ref="RP-Tutor-2"/>
            </complete-act>
        </act>
        <complete-play>
            <when-last-act-completed/>
        </complete-play>
    </play>
```

22.4.6 Environments

There are four environment elements within this UOL. The first (`E-wig-general-environment`) consists of two static XHTML files combined together in one knowledge-object:

```
<environment identifier="E-wig-general-environment">
    <title>General environment</title>
    <learning-object identifier="lo-E-wig-general-environment">
        <title>General resources</title>
        <item identifier="I-1-wig-general-environment"
                identifierref="R-TextualContent">
                <title>Introduction</title>
        </item>
        <item identifier="I-2-wig-general-environment"
                identifierref="R-TextualContent-2">
                <title>Examples</title>
        </item>
```

```
  </learning-object>
</environment>
```

The environment `E-overview-thoughts` displays the initial thoughts of all the learners in a table. The item file (`R-initial-thoughts-overview`) contains a table with a single row containing a `<view-property>` element. The player renders the table rows needed for the resulting table.

```
  <environment identifier="E-overview-thoughts">
        <title>Overview of initial thoughts</title>
        <service identifier="S-overview-initial-thoughts">
              <monitor>
                    <role-ref ref="Learner"/>
                    <title>Initial thoughts</title>
                    <item identifierref="R-initial-thoughts-overview"/>
              </monitor>
        </service>
  </environment>
```

The environment `E-overview-responses` is available only for the tutor and consists of two services, one of them displaying all the initial thoughts, and the other displaying the responses from the learners. The tutor sees not only the initial thoughts entered by the learners (as displayed in `E-overview-thoughts`) but also the name of the associated learner.

```
<environment identifier="E-overview-responses">
  <title>Overview of thoughts and responses</title>
  <service identifier="S-overview-initial-thoughts-tutor">
        <monitor>
              <role-ref ref="Learner"/>
              <title>Initial Thoughts</title>
              <item identifierref="R-initial-thoughts-overview-tutor"/>
        </monitor>
  </service>
  <service identifier="S-overview-responses">
        <monitor>
              <role-ref ref="Learner"/>
              <title>Responses</title>
              <item identifierref="R-response-to-initial-thoughts-overview"/>
        </monitor>
  </service>
</environment>
```

The final environment (E-response-by-tutor) contains a single learning-object which displays the feedback of the tutor for a single learner. The visibility of this environment is set in the conditions section of the design.

```
<environment identifier="E-response-by-tutor">
        <title>Response by tutor</title>
        <learning-object identifier="lo-E-response-by-tutor">
                <title>Response by tutor</title>
                <item identifierref="R-response-by-tutor"/>
        </learning-object>
</environment>
```

22.4.7 Conditions

Conditions in this UOL are used to show or hide parts of pages using classes, environments, activities-structures and support-activities. They all have a basic structure, consisting of an <if> statement checking a condition, a <then> part which describes what to do when the condition is true and an <else> part which describes what to do when the condition is false.

The following property structure checks to see if a value has been entered into the local personal property that has been defined to contain the response by a tutor (for a single learner). If that property is not empty, the environment that shows the content of both the learner's initial thoughts and the feedback of the tutor is set to visible.

```
<if>
  <not>
        <no-value>
                <property-ref ref="LP-tutor-comments-initial-thoughts"/>
        </no-value>
  </not>
</if>
<then>
  <show>
        <environment-ref ref="E-response-by-tutor"/>
  </show>
</then>
<else>
  <hide>
        <environment-ref ref="E-response-by-tutor"/>
  </hide>
</else>
```

The second condition handles the showing/hiding specific classes based on a check for the completion of a learning-activity (`LA-respond-to-others`). The completion of a learning-activity is controlled on a per-user basis.

```
<if>
        <complete>
                <learning-activity-ref ref="LA-respond-to-others"/>
        </complete>
</if>
<then>
        <show>
                <class class="C-Activity3-complete"/>
        </show>
        <hide>
                <class class="C-Activity3-not-complete"/>
        </hide>
</then>
<else>
        <show>
                <class class="C-Activity3-not-complete"/>
        </show>
        <hide>
                <class class="C-Activity3-complete"/>
        </hide>
</else>
```

22.4.8 Key Resources

The scenario makes use of a number of resources, some of which include so-called global-elements.

`Initial-thoughts-form.xml` is used by the learners to enter their initial thoughts:

```
<?xml version="1.0" encoding="UTF-8"?>
<!DOCTYPE html PUBLIC "-//W3C//DTD XHTML 1.0 Strict//EN"
        "http://www.w3.org/TR/xhtml1/DTD/xhtml1-strict.dtd">
<html xmlns:ld="http://www.imsglobal.org/xsd/imsld_v1p0"
        xmlns="http://www.w3.org/1999/xhtml">
  <head>
        <title>Enter some initial thoughts regarding what is greatness</title>
  </head>
  <body>
        <div class="C-Activity2-not-complete block-in-flow">
                <p>Please enter your initial thoughts on greatness.</p>
```

```
            <ld:set-property ref="GP-initial-thoughts"/>
        </div>
        <div class="C-Activity2-complete block-in-flow">
            <p>You entered these initial thoughts:</p>
            <table border="0" width="50%" cellspacing="1"
                cellpadding="0">
                <tr>
                    <td>
                        <ld:view-property
                        href="GP-initial-thoughts"
                        property-of="self" view="value"/>
                    </td>
                </tr>
            </table>
        </div>
        <div class="C-Activity2-complete in-flow">
            The activity has been completed by the tutor.
        </div>
    </body>
</html>
```

The file contains the classes `C-activity2-complete` and `C-activity2-not-complete`. Visibility of the classes is set in the conditions section of the UOL. If the activity has not been set to complete (that is, the class `C-activity2-not-complete` is visible then), the <set-property> element causes the player to render a form with text area element and an ok-button enabling the learner to enter and, if needed, change his/her initial thoughts. The thoughts are then stored in the global personal property `GP-initial-thoughts`. If the property has a value, that value is shown when the form is being displayed and overwritten when the form is (re-)submitted.

Once the activity has been completed, the visibility of the classes toggles and the form becomes invisible, being replaced by a table showing the contents of the `GP-initial-thoughts property` (read-only). It also sets the text "The activity has been completed by the tutor" to visible.

The file uses the cascading effect of the class property in XHTML to also add the block-in-flow or in-flow style to the <div> element. In XHTML a browser, and thus the player, cascades styles with the later ones taking precedence over previous ones. The block-in-flow style causes the text to be displayed as a text box using a different background, different colouring, etc. while the in-flow style (which is the default style for all text displayed in the player) just applies the default fonts etc. to the text.

This structure of combining <view-property> and <set-property> elements in the same resource file with the visibility controlled by class-visibility is also used in many of the other resources.

The resource `responses-overview.xml` gives an overview of all the initial responses by the learners with their usernames. It is used for the service that gives the overview of the initial thoughts (`S-overview-initial-thoughts`) in the environment `E-overview-thoughts`.

As you can see, the table in the XHTML file only contains a header row and a single table row with the `<view-property>` elements. Rendering of the additional rows needed for all learners is handled by the player.

```
<?xml version="1.0" encoding="UTF-8"?>
<!DOCTYPE html PUBLIC "-//W3C//DTD XHTML 1.0 Strict//EN"
        "http://www.w3.org/TR/xhtml1/DTD/xhtml1-strict.dtd">
<html xmlns:ld="http://www.imsglobal.org/xsd/imsld_v1p0"
        xmlns="http://www.w3.org/1999/xhtml">
   <head>
        <title>The intitial thoughts</title>
   </head>
   <body>
        <table border="0" width="50%" cellspacing="1" cellpadding="0">
              <tr>
                    <th>Learner</th>
                    <th>Overview of the responses to the
                          initial thoughts</th>
              </tr>
              <tr>
                    <td>
                          <ld:view-property ref="GP-username"/>
                    </td>
                    <td>
                          <ld:view-property
                          ref="GP-response-to-initial-thoughts"/>
                    </td>
              </tr>
        </table>
   </body>
</html>
```

22.5 Concluding Remarks

The worked example described above represents only part of the What is Greatness use case but is none the less instructive – it illustrates the use of multiple roles in a collaborative learning situation, a learning service (the monitor), properties and conditions, advanced completion rules, the showing and hiding of content and global elements.

22.6 XML Code

```
<?xml version=“1.0” encoding=“UTF-8“?>
<imscp:manifest xmlns:imscp=“http://www.imsglobal.org/xsd/imscp_v1p1“ xm-
lns=“http://www.imsglobal.org/xsd/imsld_v1p0“ xmlns:xsi=“http://www.w3.org/2001/XMLSchema-instance“
xsi:schemaLocation=“http://www.imsglobal.org/xsd/imscp_v1p1 imscp_v1p1.xsd
http://www.imsglobal.org/xsd/imsld_v1p0  IMS_LD_Level_B.xsd “ identifier=“What-Is-Greatness-Partial“>
    <imscp:organizations>
        <learning-design identifier=“LD-What-Is-Greatness“ uri=“WIGC“ level=“B“>
            <title>What is Greatness</title>
            <components>
                <roles>
                    <learner identifier=“Learner“>
                        <title>Learner</title>
                    </learner>
                    <staff identifier=“Tutor“>
                        <title>Tutor</title>
                    </staff>
                </roles>
                <properties>
                    <globpers-property identifier=“GP-username“>
                        <existing href=“http://eml.ou.nl/dossier/name“/>
                    </globpers-property>
                    <globpers-property identifier=“GP-initial-thoughts“>
                        <global-definition uri=“GP-initial-thoughts“>
                            <title>What do I think is greatness</title>
                            <datatype datatype=“text“/>
                        </global-definition>
                    </globpers-property>
                    <globpers-property identifier=“GP-response-to-initial-thoughts“>
                        <global-definition uri=“GP-response-to-initial-thoughts“>
                            <title>Responses to the initial thoughts</title>
                            <datatype datatype=“text“/>
                        </global-definition>
                    </globpers-property>
                    <locpers-property identifier=“LP-tutor-comments-initial-thoughts“>
                        <title>Response by tutor</title>
                        <datatype datatype=“text“/>
                    </locpers-property>
                    <loc-property Identifier=“LP-activity-2-completed“>
                        <title>Activity Enter Initial Thoughts completed</title>
                        <datatype datatype=“boolean“/>
                        <initial-value>false</initial-value>
                    </loc-property>
                    <locpers-property identifier=“LP-activity-3-completed“>
                        <title>Enter response to initial thoughts completed</title>
                        <datatype datatype=“boolean“/>
                        <initial-value>false</initial-value>
                    </locpers-property>
                </properties>
                <activities>
                    <learning-activity isvisible=“true“ identifier=“LA-introduction“>
                        <title>Introduction</title>
                        <activity-description>
                            <item identifier=“I-introduction-a“ identifierref=“R-intro“>
                                <title>What</title>
                            </item>
                        </activity-description>
                        <complete-activity>
                            <user-choice/>
                        </complete-activity>
                    </learning-activity>
                    <learning-activity isvisible=“true“ identifier=“LA-enter-initial-thoughts“>
                        <title>Enter initial thoughts</title>
                        <activity-description>
                            <item identifier=“I-enter-initial-thoughts“ identifierref=“R-initial-thoughts“>
```

```
                <title>Consider what you think is greatness</title>
            </item>
        </activity-description>
        <complete-activity>
            <when-property-value-is-set>
                <property-ref ref=“LP-activity-2-completed“/>
                <property-value>true</property-value>
            </when-property-value-is-set>
        </complete-activity>
    </learning-activity>
    <learning-activity isvisible=“false“ identifier=“LA-respond-to-others“>
        <title>Respond to the thoughts of others</title>
        <activity-description>
            <item identifier=“I-respond-to-others-1“ identifierref=“R-TextualContent“>
                <title>What</title>
            </item>
            <item identifier=“I-respond-to-others-2“ identifierref=“R-response-to-
initial-thoughts-form“>
                <title>Enter your response</title>
            </item>
        </activity-description>
        <complete-activity>
            <when-property-value-is-set>
                <property-ref ref=“LP-activity-3-completed“/>
                <property-value>true</property-value>
            </when-property-value-is-set>
        </complete-activity>
    </learning-activity>
    <activity-structure identifier=“AS-first-step“ structure-type=“sequence“>
        <title>First considerations</title>
        <information>
            <item identifierref=“R-Info-AS-first-step“/>
        </information>
        <environment-ref ref=“E-wig-general-environment“/>
        <learning-activity-ref ref=“LA-introduction“/>
        <learning-activity-ref ref=“LA-enter-initial-thoughts“/>
    </activity-structure>
    <activity-structure identifier=“AS-second-step“ structure-type=“sequence“>
        <title>What do others think?</title>
        <information>
            <item identifierref=“R-Info-AS-second-step“/>
        </information>
        <environment-ref ref=“E-wig-general-environment“/>
        <environment-ref ref=“E-overview-thoughts“/>
        <environment-ref ref=“E-response-by-tutor“/>
        <learning-activity-ref ref=“LA-respond-to-others“/>
    </activity-structure>
    <support-activity identifier=“SA-first-step“ isvisible=“true“>
        <title>Monitor the initial thoughts</title>
        <environment-ref ref=“E-wig-general-environment“/>
        <environment-ref ref=“E-overview-responses“/>
        <activity-description>
            <item identifier=“I-sa-first-step“ identifierref=“R-set-activity2-complete“>
                <title>Set the activity to completed</title>
            </item>
        </activity-description>
        <complete-activity>
            <when-property-value-is-set>
                <property-ref ref=“LP-activity-2-completed“/>
                <property-value>true</property-value>
            </when-property-value-is-set>
        </complete-activity>
    </support-activity>
    <support-activity identifier=“SA-respond“ isvisible=“true“>
        <title>Respond to initial thoughts</title>
        <role-ref ref=“Learner“/>
        <environment-ref ref=“E-wig-general-environment“/>
        <environment-ref ref=“E-overview-responses“/>
```

```
                <activity-description>
                    <item identifierref=“R-response-to-initial-thoughts-form-tutor“/>
                </activity-description>
            </support-activity>
        </activities>
        <environments>
            <environment identifier=“E-wig-general-environment“>
                <title>General environment</title>
                <learning-object identifier=“lo-E-wig-general-environment“>
                    <title>General resources</title>
                    <item identifier=“I-1-wig-general-environment“ identifierref=“R-
TextualContent“>
                        <title>Introduction</title>
                    </item>
                    <item identifier=“I-2-wig-general-environment“ identifierref=“R-
TextualContent“>
                        <title>Examples</title>
                    </item>
                </learning-object>
            </environment>
            <environment identifier=“E-overview-thoughts“>
                <title>Overview of initial thoughts</title>
                <service identifier=“S-overview-initial-thoughts“>
                    <monitor>
                        <role-ref ref=“Learner“/>
                        <title>Initial thoughts</title>
                        <item identifierref=“R-initial-thoughts-overview“/>
                    </monitor>
                </service>
            </environment>
            <environment identifier=“E-overview-responses“>
                <title>Overview of thoughts and responses</title>
                <service identifier=“S-overview-initial-thoughts-tutor“>
                    <monitor>
                        <role-ref ref=“Learner“/>
                        <title>Initial Thoughts</title>
                        <item identifierref=“R-initial-thoughts-overview-tutor“/>
                    </monitor>
                </service>
                <service identifier=“S-overview-responses“>
                    <monitor>
                        <role-ref ref=“Learner“/>
                        <title>Responses</title>
                        <item identifierref=“R-response-to-initial-thoughts-overview“/>
                    </monitor>
                </service>
            </environment>
            <environment identifier=“E-response-by-tutor“>
                <title>Response by tutor</title>
                <learning-object identifier=“lo-E-response-by-tutor“>
                    <title>Response by tutor</title>
                    <item identifierref=“R-response-by-tutor“/>
                </learning-object>
            </environment>
        </environments>
    </components>
    <method>
        <play identifier=“P-1“ isvisible=“true“>
            <title>What is Greatness - default play</title>
            <act identifier=“A-1“>
                <title>What is Greatness - Default act</title>
                <role-part identifier=“RP-Learner-1“>
                    <title>First step</title>
                    <role-ref ref=“Learner“/>
                    <activity-structure-ref ref=“AS-first-step“/>
                </role-part>
                <role-part identifier=“RP-Tutor-1“>
                    <title>Support activities for first step</title>
```

```
                <role-ref ref=“Tutor“/>
                <support-activity-ref ref=“SA-first-step“/>
            </role-part>
            <complete-act>
                <when-role-part-completed ref=“RP-Tutor-1“/>
            </complete-act>
        </act>
        <act identifier=“A-2“>
            <role-part identifier=“RP-Learner-2“>
                <title>Second step</title>
                <role-ref ref=“Learner“/>
                <activity-structure-ref ref=“AS-second-step“/>
            </role-part>
            <role-part identifier=“RP-Tutor-2“>
                <title>Support activities for second step</title>
                <role-ref ref=“Tutor“/>
                <support-activity-ref ref=“SA-respond“/>
            </role-part>
            <complete-act>
                <when-role-part-completed ref=“RP-Tutor-2“/>
            </complete-act>
        </act>
        <complete-play>
            <when-last-act-completed/>
        </complete-play>
    </play>
    <complete-unit-of-learning>
        <when-play-completed ref=“P-1“/>
    </complete-unit-of-learning>
    <conditions>
        <if>
            <not>
                <no-value>
                    <property-ref ref=“LP-tutor-comments-initial-thoughts“/>
                </no-value>
            </not>
        </if>
        <then>
            <show>
                <environment-ref ref=“E-response-by-tutor“/>
            </show>
        </then>
        <else>
            <hide>
                <environment-ref ref=“E-response-by-tutor“/>
            </hide>
        </else>
        <if>
            <complete>
                <learning-activity-ref ref=“LA-respond-to-others“/>
            </complete>
        </if>
        <then>
            <show>
                <class class=“C-Activity3-complete“/>
            </show>
            <hide>
                <class class=“C-Activity3-not-complete“/>
            </hide>
        </then>
        <else>
            <show>
                <class class=“C-Activity3-not-complete“/>
            </show>
            <hide>
                <class class=“C-Activity3-complete“/>
            </hide>
        </else>
```

```
                    </conditions>
                </method>
            </learning-design>
        </imscp:organizations>
        <imscp:resources>
            <imscp:resource identifier=“R-intro“ type=“webcontent“ href=“dummy.xml“>
                <imscp:file href=“dummy.xml“/>
            </imscp:resource>
            <imscp:resource identifier=“R-TextualContent“ type=“webcontent“ href=“dummy.xml“>
                <imscp:file href=“dummy.xml“/>
            </imscp:resource>
            <imscp:resource identifier=“R-Info-AS-first-step“ type=“webcontent“ href=“activity-seq1-info.xml“>
                <imscp:file href=“activity-seq1-info.xml“/>
                <imscp:file href=“einstein2.gif“/>
            </imscp:resource>
            <imscp:resource identifier=“R-Info-AS-second-step“ type=“webcontent“ href=“activity-seq2-
info.xml“>
                <imscp:file href=“activity-seq2-info.xml“/>
                <imscp:file href=“pencils.jpg“/>
            </imscp:resource>
            <imscp:resource identifier=“R-initial-thoughts“ type=“imsldcontent“ href=“initial-thoughts-
form.xml“>
                <imscp:file href=“initial-thoughts-form.xml“/>
            </imscp:resource>
            <imscp:resource identifier=“R-set-activity2-complete“ type=“imsldcontent“ href=“set-activity2-
complete.xml“>
                <imscp:file href=“set-activity2-complete.xml“/>
            </imscp:resource>
            <imscp:resource identifier=“R-initial-thoughts-overview“ type=“imsldcontent“ href=“initial-
thoughts-overview.xml“>
                <imscp:file href=“initial-thoughts-overview.xml“/>
            </imscp:resource>
            <imscp:resource identifier=“R-initial-thoughts-overview-tutor“ type=“imsldcontent“ href=“initial-
thoughts-overview-tutor.xml“>
                <imscp:file href=“initial-thoughts-overview-tutor.xml“/>
            </imscp:resource>
            <imscp:resource identifier=“R-response-to-initial-thoughts-form“ type=“imsldcontent“
href=“response-to-initial-thoughts-form.xml“>
                <imscp:file href=“response-to-initial-thoughts-form.xml“/>
            </imscp:resource>
            <imscp:resource identifier=“R-response-to-initial-thoughts-overview“ type=“imsldcontent“
href=“responses-overview.xml“>
                <imscp:file href=“responses-overview.xml“/>
            </imscp:resource>
            <imscp:resource identifier=“R-response-by-tutor“ type=“imsldcontent“ href=“initial-thoughts-tutor-
comments.xml“>
                <imscp:file href=“initial-thoughts-tutor-comments.xml“/>
            </imscp:resource>
            <imscp:resource identifier=“R-response-to-initial-thoughts-form-tutor“ type=“imsldcontent“
href=“initial-thoughts-tutor-form.xml“>
                <imscp:file href=“initial-thoughts-tutor-form.xml“/>
            </imscp:resource>
        </imscp:resources>
</imscp:manifest>
```

Appendix

This appendix contains the full XML code for a problem-based learning template. The code is a generalised and extended version of the case discussed in the present chapter. This was done to make the template suitable for other cases than the one discussed above: it is always easier to modify a template than to build one from scratch. The accompanying, generalised scenario consists of the following steps:

1. The coordinator for the course makes a *problem description* available to the group (by uploading a file to a website).
2. Each of the students in the group *reads the problem* (on the website), as does the facilitator. With the help of some synchronous conferencing system which includes the facilitator, the students also decide who is going to be the *chairperson* – the spokesperson for the group, responsible for recording key group decisions. This step corresponds to step 1 in Box 8.1: Discuss what body part or organ the case is about.
3. The chosen representative is *formally appointed* by the facilitator. This allows the facilitator some leeway to override the students' decision if this may be desirable.
4. The students in the group attempt to *clarify the problem*, using each other and the facilitator to discuss and clarify terminology and any open issues, eventually arriving at their own comprehensive statement of the problem at hand. This step corresponds to step 2 in Box 8.1: Discuss what additional information needs to be acquired [...] to obtain a full picture of the problem.
5. The chairperson *states this problem* description in a file uploaded to the website and the group continues by identifying possible solutions or explanations for the problem. This step corresponds to step 3 in Box 8.1: Combine the results of step 1 and 2.
6. These possible *explanations are clustered* and the ensuing clusters will be further explored by the students. This step corresponds to step 4 in Box 8.1: Formulate a causal explanation for the combined results.
7. The *explanations* to be pursued *are listed* in a file uploaded to the web site. This step corresponds to step 5 in Box 8.1: ... make a differential diagnosis.
8. The group then *identifies the learning goals* of the problem, and
9. each individual student *embarks on the required research*. This step and the previous one correspond to step 6 in Box 8.1: Discuss how a more certain diagnosis may be arrived at.

10. Eventually, the students in the group meet up (using a suitable synchronous means of communication) to *discuss their findings*, again assisted by the facilitator. This corresponds to step 7 in Box 8.1: Develop a therapy in the form of a plan.
11. The chairperson *summarises the findings* in a file uploaded to the website.
12. Subsequently, an evaluator and the facilitator discuss the performance of the group
13. and the evaluator provides an evaluation of the group (in a file uploaded to the website).

When working through the code template, one should take note of the following points:

- The template makes use of several acts in the learning flow. Acts are used not only to support parallel activities (e.g. the students and facilitator reading the problem description), but also as synchronisation points when the flow crosses roles (e.g. between the students discussing findings and the chairperson summarising the findings).
- Two environments are defined to support group discussions, both between the students (including the chairperson) and between the facilitator and evaluator.
- The various texts produced during the sessions are 'published' using a mechanism which exploits a property with a file datatype being set in the resource associated with 'publishing' activity. In this way P-Problem-Description is defined as a property (with datatype file) associated with the coordinator role, and is set in the resource (RES-Accompanying-Text-For-Coordinator) associated with the coordinator's support activity of SA-Make-problem-Description-Available.
- The example is at level C due to the use of notifications (e.g. the email notification to the facilitator and students following the coordinator's 'publication' of the problem description, handled with an on-completion element on SA-Make-problem-Description-Available).

Identifiers are chosen such that they help the human reader to keep track of how the design evolves. Thus the learner role is identified as R-student, property identifiers will use a leading 'P', learning activities 'LA', support activities 'SA', etc.

Role	Activity	Environment	Activity completion	Property/ notification	Act	Act completion	Activity-structure	Type
R1-Coordinator	SA1-Make problem description available		User choice	Notify student Notify facilitator (P1-e-mail) P2-problem description	ACT1-Make problem description available	When coordinator is		
R2-Student	LA1-Read problem description		User choice		ACT2-Prepare	When facilitator is done	AS1-Prepare	Sequence
R2-Student	LA2-Choose chairperson	E1-Synchronous group facilities						
R3-Facilitator	LA1-Read problem description		User choice				AS3-Help group	Sequence
R3-Facilitator	SA2-Provide assistance	E1-Synchronous group facilities						
R3-Facilitator	SA3-Appoint chair		User choice	Notify student (P1-e-mail)	ACT3-Appoint chair	When facilitator is done		

Table continued

Role	Activity	Environment	Activity completion	Property/ notification	Act	Act completion	Activity-structure	Type
R2-Student	LA3-Clarify problem	E1-Synchronous group facilities	User Choice		ACT4-Clarify problem	When all students are done		
R3-Facilitator	SA2-Provide assistance	E1-Synchronous group facilities						
R4-Chairperson	LA4-State problem	E1-Synchronous group facilities	User choice	P3-Problem statement	ACT5-State problem	When chair is done		
R3-Facilitator	SA2-Provide assistance	E1-Synchronous group facilities						
R2-Student	LA5-Brainstorm explanations	E1-Synchronous group facilities	User choice		ACT6-Arrive at explanation	When all students are done	AS2-Arrive at explanation	Sequence
R2-Student	LA6-Cluster explanations	E1-Synchronous group facilities	User choice					
R3-Facilitator	SA2-Provide assistance	E1-Synchronous group facilities						

Table continued

Role	Activity	Environment	Activity completion	Property/ notification	Act	Act completion	Activity-structure	Type
R4= Chairperson	LA7-List explanations	E1-Synchronous group facilities	User choice	P4-List of explanations	ACT7-List explanations	When chair is done		
R3-Facilitator	SA2-Provide assistance	E1-Synchronous group facilities						
R2-Student	LA8-Formulate goals	E1-Synchronous group facilities	User choice		ACT8-Formulate goals	When all students are done		
R3-Facilitator	SA2-Provide assistance	E1-Synchronous group facilities						
R2-Student	SA9-Carry out research	E1-Synchronous group facilities	User choice		ACT9-Carry out research	When all students are done		
R2-Student	LA10-Discuss findings	E1-Synchronous group facilities	User choice		ACT10-Discuss findings	When all students are done		
R3-Facilitator	SA2-Provide assistance	E1-Synchronous group facilities	User choice					

Table continued

Role	Activity	Environment	Activity completion	Property/ notification	Act	Act completion	Activity-structure	Type
R4-Chair	LA11-Summarise findings	E1-Synchronous group facilities	User choice	Notify facilitator (P1) Notify evaluator (P1) P5-Summary of findings	ACT11-Summarise findings	When chair is done		
R3-Facilitator	SA2-Provide assistance	E1-Synchronous group facilities						
R5-Evaluator	SA4-Discuss group	E2-Synchronous evaluation facilities	User choice	P6-Group evaluation	ACT12-Discuss group	When evaluator is done		
R3-Facilitator	SA4-Discuss group	E2-Synchronous evaluation facilities						
R5-Evaluator	SA5-Evaluate group		User choice		ACT13-Evaluate group	When evaluator is done		

```
<?xml version="1.0" encoding="UTF-8"?>
<!-- edited by Colin Tattersall, adapted by Peter Sloep (Open University of the Netherlands) -->
<manifest xmlns="http://www.imsglobal.org/xsd/imscp_v1p1" xmlns:imsld="http://www.imsglobal.org/xsd/imsld_v1p0"
xmlns:xsi="http://www.w3.org/2001/XMLSchema-instance"
xsi:schemaLocation="http://www.imsglobal.org/xsd/imscp_v1p1 http://www.imsglobal.org/xsd/imscp_v1p1p3.xsd
http://www.imsglobal.org/xsd/imsld_v1p0 http://www.imsglobal.org/xsd/imsld_level_c_v1p0.xsd" identifier="PBL-
Manifest">
        <metadata>
                <schema>IMS Metadata</schema>
                <schemaversion>1.2</schemaversion>
        </metadata>
        <organizations>
                <imsld:learning-design identifier="Problem-Based-Learning" version="" level="C" sequence-
used="false" uri="">
                        <imsld:components>

                                <imsld:roles>
                                        <imsld:learner identifier="R-student"/>
                                        <imsld:learner identifier="R-chairperson"/>
                                        <imsld:staff identifier="R-facilitator"/>
                                        <imsld:staff identifier="R-coordinator"/>
                                        <imsld:staff identifier="R-evaluator"/>
                                </imsld:roles>

                                <imsld:properties>
                                        <imsld:globpers-property identifier="P-email">
                                                <imsld:existing href=""/>
                                        </imsld:globpers-property>
                                        <imsld:locrole-property identifier="P-Problem-Description">
                                                <imsld:role-ref ref="R-coordinator"/>
                                                <imsld:datatype datatype="file"/>
                                        </imsld:locrole-property>
                                        <imsld:locrole-property identifier="P-Problem-Statement">
                                                <imsld:role-ref ref="R-chairperson"/>
                                                <imsld:datatype datatype="file"/>
                                        </imsld:locrole-property>
                                        <imsld:locrole-property identifier="P-List-Of-Explanations">
                                                <imsld:role-ref ref="R-chairperson"/>
                                                <imsld:datatype datatype="file"/>
                                        </imsld:locrole-property>
                                        <imsld:locrole-property identifier="P-Summary-Of-Findings">
```

```
                    <imsld:role-ref ref="R-chairperson"/>
                    <imsld:datatype datatype="file"/>
               </imsld:locrole-property>
               <imsld:locrole-property identifier="P-Group-Evaluation">
                    <imsld:role-ref ref="R-evaluator"/>
                    <imsld:datatype datatype="file"/>
               </imsld:locrole-property>
          </imsld:properties>

          <imsld:activities>
               <imsld:support-activity identifier="SA-Make-problem-Description-
Available">
                    <imsld:activity-description>
                         <imsld:item identifier="I-Make-problem-Description-
Available" identifierref="RES-Accompanying-Text-For-Coordinator"/>
                    </imsld:activity-description>
                    <imsld:complete-activity>
                         <imsld:user-choice/>
                    </imsld:complete-activity>
                    <imsld:on-completion>
                         <imsld:notification>
                              <imsld:email-data email-property-ref="P-email">
                                   <imsld:role-ref ref="R-student"/>
                              </imsld:email-data>
                              <imsld:subject>Availability of the prob-
lem</imsld:subject>
                         </imsld:notification>
                         <imsld:notification>
                              <imsld:email-data email-property-ref="P-email">
                                   <imsld:role-ref ref="R-facilitator"/>
                              </imsld:email-data>
                              <imsld:subject>Availability of the prob-
lem</imsld:subject>
                         </imsld:notification>
                    </imsld:on-completion>
               </imsld:support-activity>
               <imsld:support-activity identifier="SA-Provide-Assistance">
                    <imsld:environment-ref ref="E-PBL-Group-Facilities-Synchronous"/>
                    <imsld:activity-description>
                         <imsld:item identifier="I-Provide-Assistance" identifier-
ref="RES-Facilitator-Provide-Assistance-Text"/>
```

```
                <\/imsld:activity-description>
            </imsld:support-activity>
            <imsld:support-activity identifier="SA-Appoint-Chairperson">
                <imsld:activity-description>
                    <imsld:item identifier="I-Appoint-Chairperson" identifier-
ref="RES-Appoint-Chairperson"/>
                </imsld:activity-description>
                <imsld:complete-activity>
                    <imsld:user-choice/>
                </imsld:complete-activity>
                <imsld:on-completion>
                    <imsld:notification>
                        <imsld:email-data email-property-ref="P-email">
                            <imsld:role-ref ref="R-student"/>
                        </imsld:email-data>
                        <imsld:subject>Appointment cf chairper-
son</imsld:subject>
                    </imsld:notification>
                </imsld:on-completion>
            </imsld:support-activity>
            <imsld:support-activity identifier="SA-Discuss-Group">
                <imsld:environment-ref ref="E-Evaluation-Facilities-Synchronous"/>
                <imsld:activity-description>
                    <imsld:item identifier="I-Discuss-Group" identifier-
ref="RES-Accompanying-Text-For-Facilitator-Evaluator-Discussion"/>
                </imsld:activity-description>
                <imsld:complete-activity>
                    <imsld:user-choice/>
                </imsld:complete-activity>
            </imsld:support-activity>
            <imsld:support-activity identifier="SA-Evaluate-Group">
                <imsld:activity-description>
                    <imsld:item identifier="I-Evaluate-Group" identifier-
ref="RES-Accompanying-Text-For-Evaluation"/>
                </imsld:activity-description>
                <imsld:complete-activity>
                    <imsld:user-choice/>
                </imsld:complete-activity>
            </imsld:support-activity>

            <imsld:learning-activity identifier="LA-Read-problem-Description">
```

```
                    <imsld:activity-description>
                        <imsld:item identifier="I-Read-problem-Description" identi-
fierref="RES-Accompanying-Text-For-Students-And-Facilitator"/>
                    </imsld:activity-description>
                    <imsld:complete-activity>
                        <imsld:user-choice/>
                    </imsld:complete-activity>
                </imsld:learning-activity>
                <imsld:learning-activity identifier="LA-Choose-Chairperson">
                    <imsld:environment-ref ref="E-PBL-Group-Facilities-Synchronous"/>
                    <imsld:activity-description>
                        <imsld:item identifier="I-Choose-Chairperson" identifier-
ref="RES-Accompanying-Text-For-Chairperson-Choice"/>
                    </imsld:activity-description>
                </imsld:learning-activity>
                <imsld:learning-activity identifier="LA-Clarify-Problem">
                    <imsld:environment-ref ref="E-PBL-Group-Facilities-Synchronous"/>
                    <imsld:activity-description>
                        <imsld:item identifier="I-Clarify-Problem" identifier-
ref="RES-Accompanying-Text-For-Student-Problem-Clarification"/>
                    </imsld:activity-description>
                    <imsld:complete-activity>
                        <imsld:user-choice/>
                    </imsld:complete-activity>
                </imsld:learning-activity>
                <imsld:learning-activity identifier="LA-State-Problem">
                    <imsld:environment-ref ref="E-PBL-Group-Facilities-Synchronous"/>
                    <imsld:activity-description>
                        <imsld:item identifier="I-State-Problem" identifier-
ref="RES-Help-For-Chair-With-Problem-Statement"/>
                    </imsld:activity-description>
                    <imsld:complete-activity>
                        <imsld:user-choice/>
                    </imsld:complete-activity>
                </imsld:learning-activity>
                <imsld:learning-activity identifier="LA-Brainstorm-Explanations">
                    <imsld:environment-ref ref="E-PBL-Group-Facilities-Synchronous"/>
                    <imsld:activity-description>
                        <imsld:item identifier="I-Brainstorm-Explanations" identi-
fierref="RES-Brainstorm-Guidance"/>
                    </imsld:activity-description>
```

```
                    <imsld:complete-activity>
                        <imsld:user-choice/>
                    </imsld:complete-activity>
                </imsld:learning-activity>
                <imsld:learning-activity identifier="LA-Cluster-Explanations">
                    <imsld:environment-ref ref="E-PBL-Group-Facilities-Synchronous"/>
                    <imsld:activity-description>
                        <imsld:item identifier="I-Cluster-Explanations" identifier-
ref="RES-Brainstorm-Guidance"/>
                    </imsld:activity-description>
                    <imsld:complete-activity>
                        <imsld:user-choice/>
                    </imsld:complete-activity>
                </imsld:learning-activity>
                <imsld:learning-activity identifier="LA-List-Explanations">
                    <imsld:environment-ref ref="E-PBL-Group-Facilities-Synchronous"/>
                    <imsld:activity-description>
                        <imsld:item identifier="I-List-Explanations" identifier-
ref="RES-Help-For-Chair-With-Explanations"/>
                    </imsld:activity-description>
                    <imsld:complete-activity>
                        <imsld:user-choice/>
                    </imsld:complete-activity>
                </imsld:learning-activity>
                <imsld:learning-activity identifier="LA-Formulate-Goals">
                    <imsld:environment-ref ref="E-PBL-Group-Facilities-Synchronous"/>
                    <imsld:activity-description>
                        <imsld:item identifier="I-Formulate-Goals" identifier-
ref="RES-Help-With-Goal-Formulation"/>
                    </imsld:activity-description>
                    <imsld:complete-activity>
                        <imsld:user-choice/>
                    </imsld:complete-activity>
                </imsld:learning-activity>
                <imsld:learning-activity identifier="LA-Carry-out-research">
                    <imsld:activity-description>
                        <imsld:item identifier="I-Carry-out-research" identifier-
ref="RES-Carry-out-research"/>
                    </imsld:activity-description>
                    <imsld:complete-activity>
                        <imsld:user-choice/>
```

```
        </imsld:complete-activity>
    </imsld:learning-activity>
    <imsld:learning-activity identifier="LA-Discuss-Findings">
        <imsld:environment-ref ref="E-PBL-Group-Facilities-Synchronous"/>
        <imsld:activity-description>
            <imsld:item identifier="I-Discuss-Findings" identifier-
ref="RES-Discuss-Findings"/>
        </imsld:activity-description>
        <imsld:complete-activity>
            <imsld:user-chcice/>
        </imsld:complete-activity>
    </imsld:learning-activity>
    <imsld:learning-activity identifier="LA-Summarise-Findings">
        <imsld:environment-ref ref="E-PBL-Group-Facilities-Synchronous"/>
        <imsld:activity-description>
            <imsld:item identifier="I-Summarise-Findings" identifier-
ref="RES-Summarise-Findings"/>
        </imsld:activity-description>
        <imsld:complete-activity>
            <imsld:user-choice/>
        </imsld:complete-activity>
        <imsld:on-completion>
            <imsld:notification>
                <imsld:email-data email-property-ref="P-email">
                    <imsld:role-ref ref="R-evaluator"/>
                </imsld:email-data>
                <imsld:subject>Evaluation by group</imsld:subject>
            </imsld:notification>
            <imsld:notification>
                <imsld:email-data email-property-ref="P-email">
                    <imsld:role-ref ref="R-facilitator"/>
                </imsld:email-data>
                <imsld:subject>Evaluation by group</imsld:subject>
            </imsld:notification>
        </imsld:on-completion>
    </imsld:learning-activity>
    <imsld:activity-structure identifier="AS-Prepare" structure-
type="sequence">
        <imsld:title>Prepare</imsld:title>
        <imsld:learning-activity-ref ref="LA-Read-problem-Description"/>
        <imsld:learning-activity-ref ref="LA-Choose-Chairperson"/>
```

```
                        </imsld:activity-structure>
                        <imsld:activity-structure identifier="AS-Arrive-At-Explanations">
                              <imsld:title>Arrive At Explanations</imsld:title>
                              <imsld:learning-activity-ref ref="LA-Brainstorm-Explanations"/>
                              <imsld:learning-activity-ref ref="LA-Cluster-Explanations"/>
                        </imsld:activity-structure>
                        <imsld:activity-structure identifier="AS-Help-Group" structure-
type="sequence">
                              <imsld:title>Help The Group</imsld:title>
                              <imsld:learning-activity-ref ref="LA-Read-problem-Description"/>
                              <imsld:learning-activity-ref ref="SA-Provide-Assistance"/>
                        </imsld:activity-structure>
                  </imsld:activities>

                  <imsld:environments>
                        <imsld:environment identifier="E-PBL-Group-Facilities-Synchronous">
                              <imsld:title>PBL Synchronous Group Facilities</imsld:title>
                              <imsld:service identifier="S-ConferencingSoftware">
                                    <imsld:conference conference-type="synchronous">
                                          <imsld:participant role-ref="R-student"/>
                                          <imsld:participant role-ref="R-facilitator"/>
                                          <imsld:item identifier="I-Conferencing-Text" identi-
fierref="RES-Conferencing-Text"/>
                                    </imsld:conference>
                              </imsld:service>
                        </imsld:environment>
                        <imsld:environment identifier="E-Evaluation-Facilities-Synchronous">
                              <imsld:title>PBL Synchronous Facilities For Evaluator and Facili-
tator</imsld:title>
                              <imsld:service identifier="S-EvaluatorsConferencingSoftware">
                                    <imsld:conference conference-type="synchronous">
                                          <imsld:participant role-ref="R-evaluator"/>
                                          <imsld:participant role-ref="R-facilitator"/>
                                          <imsld:item identifier="I-Evaluator-Conferencing-
Text" identifierref="RES-Conferencing-Text"/>
                                    </imsld:conference>
                              </imsld:service>
                        </imsld:environment>
                  </imsld:environments>
            </imsld:components>
```

```
<imsld:method>
      <imsld:play identifier="PLAY-PBL">
            <imsld:act>
                  <imsld:role-part>
                        <imsld:role-ref ref="R-coordinator"/>
                        <imsld:support-activity-ref ref="SA-Make-problem-
Description-Available"/>
                  </imsld:role-part>
                  <imsld:complete-act>
                        <imsld:when-role-part-completed ref="R-coordinator"/>
                  </imsld:complete-act>
            </imsld:act>
            <imsld:act>
                  <imsld:role-part>
                        <imsld:role-ref ref="R-student"/>
                        <imsld:activity-structure-ref ref="AS-Prepare"/>
                  </imsld:role-part>
                  <imsld:role-part>
                        <imsld:role-ref ref="R-facilitator"/>
                        <imsld:activity-structure-ref ref="AS-Help-Group"/>
                  </imsld:role-part>
                  <imsld:complete-act>
                        <imsld:when-role-part-completed ref="R-facilitator"/>
                  </imsld:complete-act>
            </imsld:act>
            <imsld:act>
                  <imsld:role-part>
                        <imsld:role-ref ref="R-facilitator"/>
                        <imsld:learning-activity-ref ref="SA-Appoint-Chairperson"/>
                  </imsld:role-part>
                  <imsld:complete-act>
                        <imsld:when-role-part-completed ref="R-facilitator"/>
                  </imsld:complete-act>
            </imsld:act>
            <imsld:act>
                  <imsld:role-part>
                        <imsld:role-ref ref="R-student"/>
                        <imsld:learning-activity-ref ref="LA-Clarify-Problem"/>
                  </imsld:role-part>
                  <imsld:role-part>
                        <imsld:role-ref ref="R-facilitator"/>
```

```
                <imsld:learning-activity-ref ref="SA-Provide-Assistance"/>
        </imsld:role-part>
        <imsld:complete-act>
                <imsld:when-role-part-completed ref="R-student"/>
        </imsld:complete-act>
</imsld:act>
<imsld:act>
        <imsld:role-part>
                <imsld:role-ref ref="R-chairperson"/>
                <imsld:learning-activity-ref ref="LA-State-Problem"/>
        </imsld:role-part>
        <imsld:role-part>
                <imsld:role-ref ref="R-facilitator"/>
                <imsld:learning-activity-ref ref="SA-Provide-Assistance"/>
        </imsld:role-part>
        <imsld:complete-act>
                <imsld:when-role-part-completed ref="R-chairperson"/>
        </imsld:complete-act>
</imsld:act>
<imsld:act>
        <imsld:role-part>
                <imsld:role-ref ref="R-student"/>
                <imsld:activity-structure-ref ref="AS-Arrive-At-
Explanations"/>
        </imsld:role-part>
        <imsld:role-part>
                <imsld:role-ref ref="R-facilitator"/>
                <imsld:learning-activity-ref ref="SA-Provide-Assistance"/>
        </imsld:role-part>
        <imsld:complete-act>
                <imsld:when-role-part-completed ref="R-student"/>
        </imsld:complete-act>
</imsld:act>
<imsld:act>
        <imsld:role-part>
                <imsld:role-ref ref="R-chairperson"/>
                <imsld:learning-activity-ref ref="LA-List-Explanations"/>
        </imsld:role-part>
        <imsld:role-part>
                <imsld:role-ref ref="R-facilitator"/>
                <imsld:learning-activity-ref ref="SA-Provide-Assistance"/>
```

```
        </imsld:role-part>
        <imsld:complete-act>
                <imsld:when-role-part-completed ref="R-chairperson"/>
        </imsld:complete-act>
</imsld:act>
<imsld:act>
        <imsld:role-part>
                <imsld:role-ref ref="R-student"/>
                <imsld:activity-structure-ref ref="LA-Formulate-Goals"/>
        </imsld:role-part>
        <imsld:role-part>
                <imsld:role-ref ref="R-facilitator"/>
                <imsld:learning-activity-ref ref="SA-Provide-Assistance"/>
        </imsld:role-part>
        <imsld:complete-act>
                <imsld:when-role-part-completed ref="R-student"/>
        </imsld:complete-act>
</imsld:act>
<imsld:act>
        <imsld:role-part>
                <imsld:role-ref ref="R-student"/>
                <imsld:activity-structure-ref ref="LA-Carry-out-research"/>
        </imsld:role-part>
        <imsld:complete-act>
                <imsld:when-role-part-completed ref="R-student"/>
        </imsld:complete-act>
</imsld:act>
<imsld:act>
        <imsld:role-part>
                <imsld:role-ref ref="R-student"/>
                <imsld:activity-structure-ref ref="LA-Discuss-Findings"/>
        </imsld:role-part>
        <imsld:role-part>
                <imsld:role-ref ref="R-facilitator"/>
                <imsld:learning-activity-ref ref="SA-Provide-Assistance"/>
        </imsld:role-part>
        <imsld:complete-act>
                <imsld:when-role-part-completed ref="R-student"/>
        </imsld:complete-act>
</imsld:act>
<imsld:act>
```

```
				<imsld:role-part>
					<imsld:role-ref ref="R-chairperson"/>
					<imsld:learning-activity-ref ref="LA-Summarise-Findings"/>
				</imsld:role-part>
				<imsld:role-part>
					<imsld:role-ref ref="R-facilitator"/>
					<imsld:learning-activity-ref ref="SA-Provide-Assistance"/>
				</imsld:role-part>
				<imsld:complete-act>
					<imsld:when-role-part-completed ref="R-chairperson"/>
				</imsld:complete-act>
			</imsld:act>
			<imsld:act>
				<imsld:role-part>
					<imsld:role-ref ref="R-evaluator"/>
					<imsld:support-activity-ref ref="SA-Discuss-Group"/>
				</imsld:role-part>
				<imsld:role-part>
					<imsld:role-ref ref="R-facilitator"/>
					<imsld:support-activity-ref ref="SA-Discuss-Group"/>
				</imsld:role-part>
				<imsld:complete-act>
					<imsld:when-role-part-completed ref="R-evaluator"/>
				</imsld:complete-act>
			</imsld:act>
			<imsld:act>
				<imsld:role-part>
					<imsld:role-ref ref="R-evaluator"/>
					<imsld:support-activity-ref ref="SA-Evaluate-Group"/>
				</imsld:role-part>
				<imsld:complete-act>
					<imsld:when-role-part-completed ref="R-evaluator"/>
				</imsld:complete-act>
			</imsld:act>
			<imsld:complete-play>
				<imsld:when-last-act-completed/>
			</imsld:complete-play>
		</imsld:play>
		<imsld:complete-unit-of-learning>
			<imsld:when-play-completed ref="PLAY-PBL"/>
		</imsld:complete-unit-of-learning>
```

```
            </imsld:method>
        </imsld:learning-design>
    </organizations>

    <resources>
        <resource identifier="RES-Accompanying-Text-For-Coordinator" type="imsldcontent">
            <!--Textual content which states that the coordinator should create/find a problem
(named, for example description.txt) and have it stored through <global-elements><set-property identifier-
ref="P-Problem-Description"/></global-elements>-->
        </resource>
        <resource identifier="RES-Accompanying-Text-For-Students-And-Facilitator" type="imsldcontent">
            <!--Textual content welcoming the students and facilitator and including a statement to
allow the problem description to be viewed: <global-elements><view-property identifier-ref="P-Problem-
Description"/></global-elements>-->
        </resource>
        <resource identifier="RES-Accompanying-Text-For-Chairperson-Choice" type="webcontent">
            <!--Textual content: select from your group an individual who will responsible for pub-
lishing the group output and inform the facilitator of your choice. Use the facilities available in the envi-
ronment to communicate with both your fellow students and the facilitator.-->
        </resource>
        <resource identifier="RES-Facilitator-Provide-Assistance-Text" type="webcontent">
            <!--Text: use the communication facilities provided in the environment to help the stu-
dents-->
        </resource>
        <resource identifier="RES-Appoint-Chairperson" type="webcontent">
            <!--Text: guidance on appointing the chairperson-->
        </resource>
        <resource identifier="RES-Accompanying-Text-For-Student-Problem-Clarification"
type="webcontent">
            <!--Text stating that the students should reach as full and unambiguous a decription of
the problem as possible, discussing any uncertainties and issue among themselves and using the facilitator for
assistance;-->
        </resource>
        <resource identifier="RES-Help-For-Chair-With-Problem-Statement" type="imsldcontent">
            <!--Textual content which states that the chairperson should state the problem as the
group understands it in a file (eg problemstatement.txt) and have it stored through <global-elements><set-
property identifier-ref="P-Problem-Statement"/></global-elements> -->
        </resource>
        <resource identifier="RES-Brainstorm-Guidance" type="webcontent">
            <!--Text to indicate to students that they should try to gather explanations/solutions
for the problem and then cluster this information into a smaller set to be more fully researched.-->
```

```
            </resource>
            <resource identifier="RES-Help-For-Chair-With-Explanations" type="imsldcontent">
                  <!--Textual content which states that the chairperson should list the explanations in a
file (eg explanations.txt) and have it stored through <global-elements><set-property identifier-ref="P-List-Of-
Explanations"/></global-elements> -->
            </resource>
            <resource identifier="RES-Help-With-Goal-Formulation" type="webcontent">
                  <!--Text to the tune of: think about the learning goals associated with this problem
prior to carrying out your (desk) research;-->
            </resource>
            <resource identifier="RES-Carry-out-research" type="webcontent">
                  <!--Acccmpanying text to guide the students in carrying cut their research. Could in-
clude links to useful sites, a list of standard reference works etc.-->
            </resource>
            <resource identifier="RES-Discuss-Findings" type="webcontent">
                  <!--Direction for the students following the desk research. Might include core questions
associated with the problem.-->
            </resource>
            <resource identifier="RES-Summarise-Findings" type="imsldcontent">
                  <!--Textual content which states that the chairperson should summarise the findings in a
file (eg findings.txt) and have it stored through <global-elements><set-property identifier-ref="P-Summary-Of-
Findings"/></global-elements> -->
            </resource>
            <resource identifier="RES-Acccmpanying-Text-For-Facilitator-Evaluator-Discussion"
type="webcontent">
                  <!--Textual content along the lines of: Discuss the group and form an evaluation-->
            </resource>
            <resource identifier="RES-Acccmpanying-Text-For-Evaluation" type="imsldcontent">
                  <!--Textual content which states that the evaluator should write up the evaluation in a
file (evaluation.txt) and have it stored through <global-elements><set-property identifier-ref="P-Group-
Evaluation"/></global-elements> -->
            </resource>
            <resource identifier="RES-Conferencing-Text" type="webcontent">
                  <!---->
            </resource>
      </resources>
</manifest>
```

Glossary

Term	Definition
Activity	An action to be undertaken by a role within a specified environment. There are two types of activities: learning activities and support activities.
Activity Structure	A container for activities and/or other activity structures allowing sequencing and selection of its elements, and assigned to a role at a particular point in the learning process. Arbitrarily complex structures of activities can be formed, such as tree hierarchies.
Components	The collection of parts that are reusable within a learning design. The elements role, activity-structure, learning-activity, support-activity and environment are all included in the components section of an IMS Learning Design document instance.
Condition	A rule used to influence the flow of a play in a unit of learning. Used in conjunction with properties, conditions add further refinement and personalization facilities to a learning design. Conditions have the basic format: IF [expression] THEN [show, hide, or change something or notify someone]. The expressions are mostly defined on properties (e.g. IF pre-knowledge-English="4").
Environment	A structured collection of learning objects, services and sub-environments within which activities take place.
Global Elements	A mechanism used in order to be able to set and view properties during the teaching and learning. There are four global elements: set-property, view-property, set-property-group and view-property-group. Global elements are designed to be included in any XML content schema by use of XML namespaces (e.g. for inclusion in XHTML).
Item	When a component, a learning objective or a prerequisite needs a resource, an 'item' element is used in a similar way to the organization part of

Term	Definition
	IMS Content Packaging.
Learning Activity	An activity to be carried out by a learner in order to obtain a learning objective. The notion of a learning activity recognizes that learning can happen with or without learning objects (learning is different from content consumption) and that learning comes from learners being active.
Learning Design	A description of a method enabling learners to attain certain learning objectives by performing certain learning activities in a certain order in the context of a certain environment.
Learning Object	Any reproducible and addressable digital or non-digital resource used to perform learning activities or support activities. Represented in IMS Content Packaging with the element 'Resources'.
Learning Objective	The intended outcome for learners. It is possible to define learning objectives both at the global level of the unit of learning and for every single learning activity in the learning design.
Method	The container element for a play and the conditions governing its execution.
Notification	The triggering of a new activity or the sending of a message in response to an event. Events which trigger notifications include the completion of an activity and the changing of a property value.
Play	Specifies which roles perform what activities in what order. A play is modelled according to a theatrical play with acts and role-parts. In general: a play consists of a sequence of acts. In each act, different activities are set for different roles and are performed in parallel. When an act is completed, the next act starts until the completion requirements for the learning design are met.
Prerequisite	An entry requirement for learners engaging in learning. As with learning objectives, the prerequisites can be provided at the level of the unit of learning and/or for individual learning activities.
Property	A variable used for a variety of purposes including monitoring, personalization and assessment. Learning Design supports five types of properties: local properties, local-personal properties, local-role properties, global-personal properties and global properties.

Term	Definition
Role	A specification of the type of participant in a unit of learning. There are two basic role types – Learner and Staff, which can be sub-typed to allow learners to play different roles in different learning activities (e.g. task-based, role-playing, simulations). Similarly support staff can be sub-typed and given more specialized roles, such as Tutor, Teaching Assistant, Mentor, etc. Roles thus lay the basis for multi-user models of learning.
Service	Facilities used during teaching and learning, for instance a discussion forum or some other communication facility.
Support Activity	An activity carried out in support of a role performing one or more learning activities. For example, a staff role might have the support activity to grade reports made by people in the learner role named 'student'. Each student creates his/her own report and the tutor grades every report (repeating the 'grade report' support activity).
Unit of Learning	An abstract term used to refer to any delimited piece of education or training, such as a course, a module, a lesson, etc. A unit of learning represents more than just a collection of ordered resources to learn—it includes a variety of prescribed activities (e.g. problem-solving activities, search activities, discussion activities, peer assessment activities), assessments, services and support facilities provided by teachers, trainers and other staff members.
XML	The Extensible Markup Language is a simple, flexible text format used in electronic publishing and for the exchange of a wide variety of data on the Web.

References

Abdallah R, El Hajj A, Benzekri A, Moukarzel I (2002) On the Improvement of Course Interoperability in E-Learning Models. In: International Conference on Engineering Education 2002

ADL (2004a) About SCORM. Retrieved January 23, 2004 from http://www.adlnet.org/index.cfm?fuseaction=scormabt

ADL (2004b) Sharable Content Object Reference Model (SCORM) 2004. Retrieved July 2, 2004 from http://www.adlnet.org/index.cfm?fuseaction=DownFile&libid=648&bc=false

AF (2004) IMS Abstract Framework. Retrieved January 22, 2004 from http://www.imsglobal.org/af/index.cfm

Alexander C (1977) A pattern language: Towns, buildings, construction. Oxford University Press, Oxford

Almond R, Steinberg L, Mislevy R (2002) Enhancing the design and delivery of assessment systems: a four process architecture. The Journal of Technology, Learning and Assessment 1 (5). Retrieved September 18, 2003 from http://www.jtla.org and http://www.bc.edu/research/intasc/jtla/journal/pdf/v1n5_jtla.pdf

Altova (2004) XML Spy Integrated Development Environment. Retrieved January 21, 2004 from http://www.xmlspy.com/products_ide.html

Ausubel DP (1968) Educational Psychology: A Cognitive View. Holt, Rinehart and Winston, New York

Barrows H, Tamblyn RM (1980) Problem-Based Learning: An Approach to Medical Education. Springer, New York

Bartz J (2002) Great Idea, but how do I do it? A practical example of learning object creation using SGML/XML. Canadian Journal of Learning and Technology 28 (3), pp 74–75

Bergin J, Eckstein J, Manns M, Sharp H, Voelter M (2000) The Pedagogical Pattern Project. Retrieved June 12, 2003 from http://www.pedagogicalpatterns.org

Berners-Lee T, Hendler J, Lassila O (2000) The Semantic Web. Scientific American, May, Feature article

Biggs JB (1999) Teaching for Quality Learning at University. Society for Research in Higher Education & Open University Press, Buckingham

Bjork S, Lundgren S, Holopainen J (2003) Game design patterns. In: Copier M, Raessens J (eds) Level Up – Proceedings of Digital Games Research Conference, Utrecht, The Netherlands, 4–6 November 2003

Black R, Duncan C, Douglas P, Morrey M, Gondouin D (1999) Accurately tracking the use of distributed Web-based learning courses. British Journal of Educational Technology

Booch G, Rumbaugh J, Jacobson I (1999) The Unified Modeling Language User Guide. Addison-Wesley, Reading, MA

Borland (2004) JBuilder: The Leading Development Solution for Java. Retrieved January 21, 2004 from http://www.borland.com/jbuilder/

Boticario JG, Gaudioso E, Hernandez F (2000) Adaptive Navigation Support and Adaptive Collaboration Support in WebDL. Proceedings of the International Conference on Adaptive Hypermedia and Adaptive Web-based Systems, August 2000 number 1892 in Lecture Notes in Computer Science (LNCS), Springer, Berlin HeidelbergTrento, Italy, pp 51 - 61

Breuker J, Muntjewerff A, Bredewej B (1999) Ontological modelling for designing educational systems. In: Proceedings of the AI-ED 99 Workshop on Ontologies for Educational Systems. IOS Press, Le Mans, Francc

Bruner J (1966) Toward a Theory of Instruction. Belknap Press/Harvard University Press, Cambridge, MA

Brusilovsky P (2001) Adaptive Hypermedia. User Modelling and User-Adapted Interaction 11, pp 87–110

Brusilovsky P, Miller P (2001) Course Delivery Systems for the Virtual University. In: Tschang FT, Della Senta T (eds) Access to Knowledge: New Information Technologies and the Emergence of the Virtual University. Elsevier Science and International Association of Universities, Amsterdam, pp 167–206

Bull J, Dalziel J (2003) Assessing question banks. In: Reusing online resources: A sustainable approach to e-learning. Kogan Page, London, Chap. 14

Butson R (2003) Learning objects: weapons of mass instruction. British Journal of Educational Technology 34 (5), pp 667–669

Canadian Department of National Defence (2003) White paper: SCORM Dynamic Appearance Model. Retrieved January 19, 2004 from http://www.online-learning.com/papers/SCORMModel.pdf

Canvas Learning Ltd (2004) Retrieved January 19, 2004 from http://www.canvaslearning.com/

Carrión MJ, Fuentes C, Rodrigo M, Barrera C, Catalina C, Gaudioso E, Boticario JG, Rodríguez A, Santos O, Martens H, Mofers F, Passier H, Stoyanov S, Vogten H, De Abreu RC (2004) General System Architecture & Design. ALFanet/IST-2001-33288 Deliverable D21. SAGE, Madrid. Retrieved November 10, 2004 from http://hdl.handle.net/1820/258

CEFRL (2001) A Common European Framework of Reference for Languages. Retrieved February 4, 2004 from http://www.culture2.coe.int/portfolio/documents_ intro/common_framework.html

CETIS (2002) Retrieved January 19, 2004 from http://www.cetis.ac.uk

Cockburn A (2001) Writing effective use cases. Addison-Wesley, Boston, MA

Collins A, Stevens AL (1983) A Cognitive Theory of Inquiry Teaching. In: Reigeluth CM Instructional Design Theories and Models: An Overview of their Current Status. Lawrence Erlbaum, Hillsdale, NJ

Constant D, Kiesler S, Sproull L (1994) What is mine is ours, or is it? Information Systems Research 5 (4), pp 400–422

CP (2003) IMS Content Packaging. Information Model, Best Practice and Implementation Guide, XML Binding, Schemas. Version 1.1.3 Final Specification IMS Global Learning Consortium Inc. Retrieved May 26, 2004 from http://www.imsglobal.org/content/packaging/

Cronbach LJ, Snow RE (1977) Aptitudes and Instructional Methods: A Handbook for Research on Interactions. Irvington, New York

Dalziel JR (2003) Implementing Learning Design: The Learning Activity Management System (LAMS). In: Crisp G, Thiele D, Scholten I, Barker S, Baron J (eds) Interact, Integrate, Impact: Proceedings of the 20th Annual Conference of the Australasian Society for Computers in Learning in Tertiary Education. Adelaide, 7–10 December 2003. Retrieved March 1, 2004 from http://www.melcoe.mq.edu.au/documents/ASCILITE2003%20Dalziel%20Final.pdf

Daniel J (1998) Mega-universities and Knowledge Media. RoutledgeFalmer, London

De Croock MBE, Paas F, Schlanbusch H, van Merriënboer JJG (2002a) ADAPT-IT: Tools for Design and Evaluation. Educational Technology Research and Development 50, pp 47–58

De Croock M, Mofers F, van Veen M, van Rosmalen P, Brouns F, Boticario J, Barrera C, Santos O, Ayala A, Gaudioso E, Hernández F, Arana C, Trueba I (2002b) State-of-the-art ALFanet/IST-2001-33288 Deliverable D12. Open Universiteit Nederland, Heerlen. Retrieved November 10, 2004 from http://hdl.handle.net/1820/94

De Krom M, Antheunis L (2002) Blok 3.2 Uitvalsverschijnselen en functieverlies. Onderwijsinstituut Medische Faculteit, Universiteit Maastricht, Maastricht

Dewey J (1900) Psychology and social practice. The Psychological Review 7, pp 105–124

Dougiamas M (2004) Moodle. Retrieved February 27, 2004 from http://moodle.org/

Douglas I (2003) Instructional Design Based On Reusable Learning Objects: Applying Lessons Of Object-Oriented Software Engineering To Learning Systems Design. In: Proceedings of the 31st ASEE/IEEE Frontiers in Education Conference, IEEE

Downes S (2001) Learning Objects: Resources For Distance Education Worldwide. International Review of Research in Open and Distance Learning 2

DR (2003) IMS Digital Repositories Specification. Information Model, Best Practice and Implementation Guide, XML Binding, Schemas. Version 1.0 Final Specification IMS Global Learning Consortium Inc. Retrieved February 29, 2004 from http://www.imsglobal.org/digitalrepositories/

Dufresne A (2001) ExploraGraph: Improving interfaces to improve adaptive support. Paper presented at AIED 2001, San Antonio, TX, USA

Duncan C (2003) Granularisation. In: Littlejohn A (ed) Reusing Online Resources: A Sustainable Approach to E-Learning. Kogan Page, London

Duval E, Robson R (2001) Guest Editorial on Metadata. Interactive Learning Environments, Special issue : Metadata 9.3, pp 201–206

Duval E, Hodgins W (2003) A LOM Research Agenda. The Twelfth International World Wide Web Conference, Budapest, Hungary. Retrieved January 23, 2004 from http://www.2003.org/cdrom/papers/alternate/P659/p659-duval html. html

Eckstein J (2000) Learning to teach and learning to learn. Retrieved January 21, 2004 from http://www.pedagogicalpatterns.org/examples/LearningAndTeaching. pdf

ECLIPSE (2004) eclipse.org. Retrieved January 21, 2004 from http://www.eclipse.org/

Edusource (2004) The Edusource website. Retrieved January 22, 2004 from http://www.edusource.ca

EduSource-Splash (2004) eduSplash. Retrieved January 23, 2004 from http://www.edusplash.net/

E-LEN (2004) A network of e-learning centres (website Socrates/Minerva project). Retrieved January 22, 2004 from http://www.tisip.no/E-LEN/

EML (2000) Educational Modelling Language. Retrieved November 10, 2004 from http://hdl.handle.net/1820/81

Engeström Y (1987) Learning by expanding: an activity-theoretical approach to developmental research. Orienta-Konsultit Oy, Helsinki

ES (2004) IMS Enterprise Services. Public Draft Version 1, Retrieved July 19, 2004 from http://www.imsglobal.org/es/

Ewell PT (2003) An Emerging Scholarship: A Brief History of Assessment. Retrieved January 19, 2004 from http://media.wiley.com/product_data/excerpt/56/07879594/0787959456.pdf

Fischer G, Scharff E (1998) Learning technologies in support of self-directed learning. Journal of Interactive Media in Education 4

Fischer G, Ostwald J (2002) Transcending the Information Given: Designing learning Environments for Informed Participation. Proceedings of the ICCE 2002 International Conference on Computers in Education, Auckland, New Zealand

Fowler M (2000) UML distilled (second edition). Addison-Wesley, Upper Saddle River, NJ

Friesen N (2001) What are Educational Objects? Interactive Learning Environments 9, pp 219–230

Gagné RN (1970) The conditions of learning. Holt, Rinehart & Winston, New York

García-Robles R, Blat J, Sayago S, Griffiths D, Casado F, Martínez J (2004) Supporting usability and reusability based on eLearning standards. ICALT, IEEE, August-2004

Gardner H (1983) Frames of Mind. Basic Books, New York

Gibbons AS (2000) The Practice of Instructional Technology. In: Proceedings of the Annual International Conference of the Association for Educational Communications and Technology 2000 (AECT 2000)

Girard J, Paquette G, Miara A, Lundgren K (1999) Intelligent Assistance for Web-based TeleLearning. Proceedings of AI-Ed'99, Amsterdam, Lajoie S and Vivet M (eds). In: AI and Education, open learning environments. IOS Press, pp 561–569

Gondouin D (1996) EuroMET development for meteorological satellite training, 1996 Meteorological Satellite Data Users' Conference, Eumetsat Publications, EUM P 19

Gorissen P (2003a) Quickscan QTI. De Digitale Universiteit, Utrecht. Retrieved January 19, 2004 from http://www.digiuni.nl/digiuni//download/EA183322-C145-0A52-7B7EF8A4EDFF4655.pdf

Gorissen P (2003b) Quickscan QTI Addendum #1. De Digitale Universiteit, Utrecht. Retrieved January 19, 2004 from http://www.digiuni.nl/digiuni//download/ EA1A1D10-D0D4-9C27-26004CB-F99A92EBC.pdf

Griffiths D, Kearney N, Koper EJR, Layte M, Malmport B, Vyskovsky P (2002) PROMETEUS Paris Conference Proceedings Report, 29–30 September 2002. Retrieved July 13, 2004 from http://www.prometeus.org/PromDocs/nkearney_florida-uni_es_17-03-03_11- 04-46.zip

Hadeli PV, Zamfirescu CB, van Brussel H, Saint Germain B, Holvoet T, Steegmans E (2003) Self-Organising in Multi-agent Coordination and Control Using Stigmergy. Paper presented at the The First Workshop on Self-Organising Engineering Applications (ESOA 2003). Melbourne, Australia

Hermans H, Manderveld J, Vermetten Y, Wagemans L (2000) Assessment. In: Eindrapportage ELO project 1.1 – Nadere uitwerking onderwijsconcept. Onderwijstechnologisch expertisecentrum, Open Universiteit Nederland, Heerlen

Hermans H, Manderveld J,Vogten H (2004) Educational Modelling Language. In: Jochems W, van Merriënboer J, Koper EJR (eds) Open and Flexible Learning. integrated E-LEARNING implications for pedagogy, technology & organization. RoutledgeFalmer, London, Chap. 6, pp 80–99

Hummel HGK, Manderveld JM, Tattersall C, Koper EJR (2004) Educational Modelling Language: new challenges for instructional reusability and personalized learning. International Journal of Learning Technology 1, pp 111–126

Intrallect (2002) Demonstration e-learning materials. Retrieved January 19, 2004 from http://www.intrallect.com/demos/msgcal

Jacobson J (1992) Object-Oriented Software Engineering: A Use Case Driven Approach. Addison-Wesley, Reading,MA

JBoss (2004) JBoss Application Server. Retrieved July 19, 2004 from http://www.jboss.org

Jennings NR, Sycara K, Wooldridge M (1998) A roadmap of agent research and development. Autonomous Agents and Multi-Agent Systems 1, pp 7–38

JISC (2003) Xgrain: cross-searching specialist databases for learning and teaching. Retrieved January 23, 2004 from http://www.jisc.ac.uk/project_xgrain.html

JISC (2004a) Investing in the future: Developing an Online Information Environment. Retrieved January 23, 2004 from http://www.jisc.ac.uk/indexcfm?name=ie_home

JISC (2004b) e-Learning Frameworks and Tools Programme. Retrieved January 23, 2004 from http://www.jisc.ac.uk/index.cfm?name=elearning_framework

Johns G (1996) Organizational behavior: Understanding and managing life at work. Harper Collins, New York

Jonassen DH, Grabowski BL (1993) Handbook of Individual Differences, Learning, and Instruction. Lawrence Erlbaum Associates, Hillsdale, NJ

JORUM+ Project Team (2004) The JISC Learning Materials Repository Service; JORUM Scoping and Technical Appraisal Study, Volume V: Metadata. Retrieved May 26, 2004 from http://www.jorum.ac.uk/vol5_fin.pdf

Key C, Mundell R (2004) LOGIC: Creating online case studies. White Paper. Retrieved June 6, 2004 from http://www.logicproject.ca/text/ LOGIC_Whitepaper.pdf

Kirschner P, Carr C, van Merriënboer JJG, Sloep PB (2003) How Expert Designers Design. Performance Improvement Quarterly 15 (4), pp 86–104

Kolb DA (1984) Experiential Learning: Experience as the Source of Learning and Development. Prentice Hall, Englewood Cliffs, NJ

Koper EJR (2001) Van verandering naar vernieuwing [from change to renewal]. In: Schramade P (ed) Handboek Effectief Opleiden. Elsevier, Den Haag, Vol 26, pp 45--86 (4710-4101–4710-4142)

Koper EJR (2002) Modelling units of study from a pedagogical perspective – The pedagogical metamodel behind EML. Retrieved November 10, 2004 from http://hdl.handle.net/1820/36

Koper EJR (2003a) Learning Technologies in eLearning: An Integrated Domain Model. In: Jochems W, van Merriënboer J, Koper EJR (eds) Integrated E-Learning: Implications for Pedagogy, Technology and Organization. Kogan Page, London

Koper EJR (2003b) Combining reusable learning resources and services to pedagogical purposeful units of learning. In: Reusing online resources: A sustainable approach to e-learning. Kogan Page, London, pp 46–59

Koper EJR, Manderveld JM (2004) Educational modelling language: modelling reusable, interoperable, rich and personalised units of learning. British Journal of Educational Technology 35 (5), pp 537–551

Koper EJR, Sloep PB (2003) Learning Networks: connecting people, organizations, autonomous agents and learning resources to establish the emergence of effective lifelong learning (OTEC RTD Programme Plan 2003-2008). Open University of the Netherlands, Heerlen. Retrieved November 10, 2004 from http://hdl.handle.net/1820/65

Koper EJR, Olivier B (2004) Representing the Learning Design of Units of Learning. Educational Technology & Society 7 (3), pp 97–111

Koper EJR, Giesbers B, van Rosmalen P, Sloep P, van Bruggen J, Tattersall C (in press) A Design Model for Lifelong Learning Networks. Interactive Learning Environments

Koper EJR and Van Es R (in press) How well can we implement existing lesson plans in IMS Learning Design to evaluate its pedagogical flexibility?

Kraan W (2003) IMS and OKI, the wire and the socket. CETIS, July 17, 2003. Retrieved January 23, 2004 from http://www.cetis.ac.uk/content/20030717185453

Lakoff G, Johnson M (1980) Metaphors We Live By. University of Chicago Press, Chicago

Landa LN (1976) Instructional Regulation and Control: Cybernetics, Algorithmization and Heuristics in Education. Educational Technology Publications, Englewood Cliffs, NJ

Laurillard D, McAndrew P (2003) Reusable educational software: a basis for generic e-learning tasks. In: Littlejohn A (ed) Resources for Networked Learning, Kogan Page, London

LD (2003) IMS Learning Design. Information Model, Best Practice and Implementation Guide, XML Binding, Schemas. Version 1.0 Final Specification IMS Global Learning Consortium, Inc. Retrieved May 26, 2004 from http://www.imsglobal.org/content/learningdesign/

Le Moigne J-L (1995) Les épistémologies constructivistes (ed). PUF Que sais-je? Paris

Leshin C, Pollock J, Reigeluth Ch (1992) Instructional Design Strategies and Tactics. Educational Technology Publications, Englewood Cliffs, NJ

LIP (2001) IMS Learner Information Package. Information Model, Best Practice and Implementation Guide, XML Binding, Schemas. Version 1.00 Final Specification IMS Global Learning Consortium Inc. Retrieved January 22, 2004 from http://www.imsglobal.org/profiles/

Littlejohn A (ed) (2003) Reusing Online Resources: A Sustainable Approach to eLearning. Kogan Page, London

LOM (2002) Standard for Learning Object Metadata. Learning Technologies Standards Committee of the IEEE 148.41.21

Lundgren-Cayrol K, Paquette G, Miara A, Bergeron F, Rivard J, Rosca I (2001) Explor@ Advisory Agent: Tracing the Student's Trail. Paper presented at WebNet'01 Conference, Orlando, FL, USA, 2001

Lynch C (2003) Institutional Repositories: Essential Infrastructure for Scholarship in the Digital Age. ARL Bimonthly Report 226, February 2003. Retrieved July 13, 2004 from http://www.arl.org/newsltr/226/ir.html

Mack RL, Nielsen J (1994) Usability Inspection Methods. Executive Summary. In: Baecker RM, Grudin J, Buxton WAS, Greenberg S (eds) Readings in Human-Computer Interaction: Toward the year 2000. Morgan Kauffman, San Francisco

Martinez M (2001) Using Learning Orientations to Design Instruction with Learning Objects. In: Wiley D (ed) Instructional Use of Learning Objects. Association for Educational Communications & Technology. Retrieved January 19, 2004 from http://reusability.org/read/

Martinez M, Bunderson CV (2000) Building Interactive Web Learning Environments to Match and Support Individual Learning Differences. Journal of Interactive Learning Research, 11 (2). Retrieved January 19, 2004 from http://www.aace.org/dl/files/JILR/jilr-11-02-163.pdf

Masciarelli A (2004) Beginning of the Year or Semester Review for Returning Spanish students (lesson plan). Retrieved January 20, 2004 from http://www.lessonplanspage.com/LABeginningOfYearSpanishAssessmentOrReviewActivity68.htm

Maturana H, Varela FJ (1992) The Tree of Knowledge: The Biological Roots of Human Understanding (revised edition). Shambhala/New Science Press, Boston, MA

Mayer RH (1999) Designing instruction for constructivist learning. In C. Reigeluth (ed) Instructional-design theories and models (volume II). Lawrence Erlbaum Associates, London, pp 141–160

McGreal R (ed) (2004) Online Education Using Learning Objects. Routledge/ Falmer, London

MD (2001) IMS Meta-Data. Information Model, Best Practice and Implementation Guide, XML Binding, Schemas. Version 1.2.1 Final Specification IMS Global Learning Consortium Inc. Retrieved January 22, 2004 from http://www.imsglobal.org/meta-data/

Merlot (2004) Online database with courses and learning objects. Retrieved January 22, 2004 from http://www.merlot.org

Merrill MD (1994) Principles of Instructional Design. Educational Technology Publications, Englewood Cliffs, NJ

Merrill MD (2003) First Principles of Instruction. Retrieved October 2, 2003 from http://www.1.moe.edu.sg/itopia/download/abstracts/Applying%20First Principles of Instruction to Technology-Based Education.pdf

Merrill MD, Reigeluth C, Faust G (1979) The instructional quality profile: Curriculum evaluation and design tool. In: O'Neil H (ed) Procedures for Instructional Systems Development. Academic Press, New York

Mislevy RJ (2000) A sample assessment using the four process framework. US Department of Education

Molyneux S (2000) Where Technology Enables Open Learning Today. The Journal of the British Association for Open Learning, July

Montessori M (1912) The Montessori Method Scientific Pedagogy as Applied to Child Education. In: George AE (ed) The Children's Houses. Frederick A. Stokes, New York

Morgan G (2003) Faculty Use of Course Management Systems: Key Findings. EDUCAUSE Center for Applied Research

Morrison GR, Ross SM, Kemp SE (2004) Designing Effective Instruction. Wiley, Jossey Bass, Hoboken, NJ

Mwanza D, Engeström Y (2003) Pedagogical Adeptness in the Design of E-learning Environments: Experiences from the Lab@Future Project. Proceedings of E-Learn 2003 - International conference on E-Learning in Corporate, Government, Healthcare, & Higher Education. Phoenix, AZ, USA. Retrieved January 21, 2004 from http://www.aace.org/dl/index.cfm?fuseaction= toc& start_row=301&id=13897

Nielsen J (1992) Finding usability problems through heuristic evaluation. Proceedings of CHI'92. ACM Press, New York, pp 373–380

Nielsen J (1994) Usability Inspection Methods. CHI Tutorials 1994. ACM Press, New York, pp 413–414

Nokelainen P, Tirri H, Kurhila J, Miettinen M, Silander T (2002) Optimizing and profiling users online with Bayesian probabilistic modeling. In: Proceedings of The NL 2002 Conference. Berlin, Germany, May 2002

Nulden U (2001) Education: research and practice. Journal of Computer Assisted Learning 17, pp 363–375

OAI (2004) Open Archives Initiative Protocol for Harvesting Metadata. Retrieved January 23, 2004 from http://www.openarchives.org/OAI/ openarchivesprotocol.html

OASIS (2002) DocBook Version 4.2. Retrieved July 2, 2004 from http://www.oasis-open.org/docbook/xml/4.2/indexs.html

OKI (2004) Open Knowledge Initiative Open Service Interface Definitions. Retrieved July 2, 2004 from http://web.mit.edu/oki/specs/OSID_table.pdf

OMG-UML (2003) UML Specification Version 1.4. Retrieved October 14, 2003 from http://www.omg.org/technology/documents/formal/uml.htm

Paiva A (1996) Communicating with Learner Modeling Agents. Position Paper for ITS'96 Workshop on Architectures and Methods for Designing Cost-Effective and Reusable ITSs, Montreal, Canada

Paquette G (1995) Modeling the Virtual Campus, Innovative Adult Learning with Innovative Technologies A-61

Paquette G (1996) La modélisation par objets typés: une méthode de représentation pour les systèmes d'apprentissage et d'aide a la tâche. Sciences et techniques éducatives, France, avril

Paquette G (1999) Meta-knowledge Representation for Learning Scenarios Engineering. Proceedings of AI-Ed'99. Lajoie S and Vivet M (eds). In: AI and Education, open learning environments. IOS Press, Amsterdam

Paquette G (2001a) TeleLearning Systems Engineering – Towards a new ISD model. Journal of Structural Learning 14, pp 1–35

Paquette G (2001b) Designing Virtual Learning Centers. In: Adelsberger H, Collis B, Pawlowski J (eds) Handbook on Information Technologies for Education & Training. International Handbook on Information Systems. Springer, Berlin Heidelberg, pp 249–272

Paquette G (2002a) L'ingénierie pédagogique, pour construire l'apprentissage en réseau. Presses de l'Université du Québec, Québec

Paquette G (2002b) La modélisation des connaissances et des com-pétences, pour concevoir et apprendre. Presses de l'Université du Québec, Québec

Paquette G (2003) Instructional Engineering for Network-Based Learning. Pfeiffer/Wiley

Paquette G, Rosca I (2002) Organic Aggregation of Knowledge Objects in Educational Systems. Canadian Journal of Learning Technologies, 28 (3), pp 11–26

Paquette G, Tchounikine P (2002) Contribution à l'ingénierie des système conseillers: Une approche méthodologique fon-dée sur l'analyse du modèle de la tâche. Science et Techniques Educatives, 9/3-4/2002, pp 409–435

Paquette G, Pachet F, Giroux S, Girard J (1996) EpiTalk: Generating Advisor Agents for Existing Information Systems. Artificial Intelligence in Education. USA

Paquette G, Rosca I, De la Teja I, Léonard M, Lundgren-Cayrol K (2001) Web-based Support for the Instructional Engineering of E-learning Systems. Paper presented at WebNet'01 Conference, Orlando, FL, USA

Paquette G, Lundgren-Cayrol K, Miara A, Guérette L (in press) The Explor@-2 Learning Object Manager. Chapter in Rory McGreal (ed) Online education using learning objects. Routledge/Falmer, London

Permanand M, Brooks C (2003) Engineering a Future for Web-Based Learning Objects. In: Lecture Notes in Computer Science Number 2722. Springer, Heidelberg, pp 120–123

PHP-Nuke (2004) PHP-Nuke. Retrieved February 27, 2004 from http://www.phpnuke.org/

Porter D (2001) Object Lessons From the Web. In: Farrell G (ed) The Changing Faces of Virtual Education. The Commonwealth of Learning, Vancouver, pp 47–69

Preece J (2000) Online Communities: designing usability, supporting sociability. Wiley, Chichester

QTI (2003) IMS Question and Test Interoperability Information Model, Best Practice and Implementation Guide, XML Binding, Schemas. Version 1.2.1 Final Specification IMS Global Learning Consortium Inc. Retrieved January 19, 2004 from http://www.imsglobal.org/qti/

QTI (2004) IMS Question and Test Interoperability. Public Draft Version 2. Retrieved July 19, 2004 from http://www.imsglobal.org/question/

QTI-Lite (2001) IMS Question & Test Interoperability QTI Lite Specification. Final Specification Version 1.1. Retrieved June 28, 2004 from http://www.imsglobal.org/question/index.cfm

Rawlings A, van Rosmalen P, Koper R, Rodriguez-Artacho M, Lefrere P (2002) Survey of Educational Modelling Languages (EMLs) Version 1. September 19, 2002, CEN/ISSS

Raymond ES (2000) The Cathedral and the Bazaar, Revision 1.57. Retrieved May 31, 2004 from http://www.catb.org/~esr/writings/cathedral-bazaar/

RDCEO (2002) IMS Reusable Definitions of Competencies and Educational Objectives. Information Model, Best Practice and Implementation Guide, XML Binding, Schemas. Version 1.0 Final Specification IMS Global Learning Consortium Inc. Retrieved July 19, 2004 from http://www.imsglobal.org/competencies/

Reigeluth CM (ed) (1983) Instructional Theories in Action: Lessons Illustrating Selected Theories and Models. Lawrence Earlbaum, Hillsdale, NJ

Reigeluth CM (1999) Instructional Design Theories and Models Volume II: A New Paradigm of Instructional Theory. Erlbaum, Hillsdale, NJ

Reigeluth CM, Rodgers CA (1980) The Elaboration Theory of Instruction: Prescription for Task Analysis and Design. NSPI Journal 19, pp 16–26

Rein D (2000) What is Effective Integration of Technology, and Does it Make a Difference? Apple Computer Inc, Cupertino. Retrieved May 30, 2004 from http://www.l2l.org/iclt/2000/papers/181a.pdf

RELOAD (2004) RELOAD Project. Retrieved January 23, 2004 from http://www.reload. ac.uk

Respondus Inc (2004) Retrieved January 19, 2004 from http://www.respondus. com/

RLI (2004) IMS Resource List Interoperability Specification – Public Draft Version 1.0. Retrieved July 19, 2004 from http://www.imsglobal.org/rli/

Rumbaugh J, Blaha M, Premerlani W, Eddy F, Lorensen W (1991) Object-Oriented Modeling and Design. Prentice Hall, Englewood Cliffs, NJ

Rumbaugh J, Jacobson I, Booch G (1999) The Unified Modelling Language Reference Manual. Addison-Wesley Object Technology Series, Upper Saddle River, NJ

Salen K, Zimmerman E (2004) Rules of play: Game design fundamentals. MIT Press, Cambridge, MA

Sampson D, Karagiannidis C (2002) Incorporating Learning Styles Research for Personalised Access to Educational e-Content. 14th World Conference on Educational Multimedia, Hypermedia and Telecommunications (ED-MEDIA 2002). Denver, Colorado, USA

Sampson D, Karagiannidis C, Kinshuk (2002) Personalised Learning: Educational, Technological and Standardisation Perspectives, Interactive Educational Multimedia. Special Issue on Adaptive Educational Multimedia, 4 (invited paper)

Sayago S, Martinez J, García R, Blat J, Casado F, Griffiths D (2004) Evaluación de una aplicación sencilla de e-learning, presented at INTERACCIÓN 2004. V Congreso Internacional Interacción-Persona Ordenador, May 3–7, 2004, Lleida, Spain. Retrieved May 30, 2004 from http://www.tecn.upf.es/scope/

Scandura JM (1973) Structural Learning I: Theory and Research. Gordon & Breach, London

SCOPE Project (2003) Training Course Prototype report. Retrieved May 31, 2004 from http://www.tecn.upf.es/scope/showcase/documentation/SCOPE_D4.pdf

Segers M, Dochy F, Cascallar E (2003) Optimising New Modes of Assessment. In: Search of Qualities and Standards. Kluwer Academic Publishers, Dordrecht

Shute VJ (1993) A Comparison of Learning Environments: All that Glitters... In: Lajoie SP, Derry SJ (eds) Computers as Cognitive Tools. Lawrence Erlbaum, Hillsdale, NJ, pp 47–74

Shute VJ, Towle B (2003) Adaptive e-Learning. Educational Psychologist 38 (2) , pp 105–114

Simon HA (1973) The Organization of Complex Systems. In: Pattee HH (ed) Hierarchy Theory, The Challenge of Complex Systems. George Braziller, New York, pp 1–27

Sipser M (1997) Introduction to the Theory of Computation. PWS Publishing , Boston, MA

Skinner BF (1974) About behaviorism. Knopf, New York

Sloep PB (2003) The Language of Flexible Reuse: Reuse, Portability and Interoperability of Learning Content or Why an Educational Modelling Language. In: McGreal R (ed) Online Education Using learning Objects. Kogan Page, London

South JB, Monson DW (2002) A university-wide system for creating, capturing and delivering learning objects. In: Wiley DA (ed) The instructional use of learning objects. Agency for Instructional Technology and Association for Educational Communications and Technology, Bloomington, IN

Spector JM, Polson MC, Muraida DJ (eds) (1993) Educational Technology Publications. Englewood Cliffs, NJ

SS (2003) IMS Simple Sequencing Specification. Information Model, Best Practice and Implementation Guide, XML Binding, Schemas. Version 1.0 Final Specification IMS Global Learning Consortium Inc. Retrieved February 29, 2004 from http://www.imsglobal.org/simplesequencing/

SSP (2004) IMS Shareable State Persistence Specification – Public Draft Version 1.0. Retrieved July 19, 2004 from http://www.imsglobal.org/ssp/

SToMP (2004) Retrieved January 19, 2004 from http://www.ph.surrey.ac.uk/stomp/downldem.htm

Tattersall C (2004a) Presentation at joint SURF SiX/CETIS Assessment SIG meeting, January 12, 2004 in Amsterdam. Retrieved January 20, 2004 from http://e-learning.surf.nl/docs/six/colin_tattersall.ppt

Tattersall C (2004b) Input for IMS Question & Test Interoperability: Item, Version: 2.0, Public Draft Document, Integration Guide, 21 April 2004. Retrieved May 20, 2004 from IMS members website at http://www.imsglobal.org/

Tattersall C, Manderveld J, van den Berg B, van Es R, Janssen J, Waterink W, Bolman C (2003) Road Mapping (ROMA) (OTEC/LTD Project Plan).Open University of the Netherlands, Heerlen. Retrieved November 10, 2004 from http://hdl.handle.net/1820/86

The Assessment Reform Group (2002) Assessment for Learning: 10 Principles. Retrieved December 17, 2003 from http://www.assessment-reform-group.org.uk/CIE3.pdf

Thibaut J, Kelly H (1959) The Social Psychology of Groups. Wiley, New York

Thorne S, Shubert C, Merriman J (2004), Architectural Overview. Retrieved January 22, 2004 from http://web.mit.edu/oki/learn/whtpapers/ArchitecturalOverview.pdf

TIBCO (2004) TIBCO TurboXML. Retrieved January 21, 2004 from http://www.tibco.com/solutions/products/extensibility/turbo_xml.jsp

TOIA project (2003). Retrieved January 19, 2004 from http://www.toia.ac.uk/

UNFOLD Project (2003) Understanding New Frameworks of Learning Design/IST-2002-1_507835. Retrieved July 19, 2004 from http://www.unfold-project.net

Van der Klink M, Boon J, Rusman E, Rodrigo M, Fuentes C, Arana C, Barrera C, Hoke I, Franco M (2002) Initial Market Study. ALFanet/IST-2001-33288 Deliverable D72. Open Universiteit Nederland, Heerlen. Retrieved November 10, 2004 from http://hdl.handle.net/1820/93

Van Es R (2004) Overview of online databases with lesson plans and other learning design methods. Retrieved January 22, 2004 from http://hdl.handle.net/1820/102

Van Es R, van der Baaren J, van Rosmalen P, Manderveld J, Koper R, Boticario J, Barrera C, Rodriguez A, Santos O (2003) Existing Standards Analysis. ALFanet/IST-2001-33288 Deliverable D31. Open Universiteit Nederland, Heerlen. Retrieved November 10, 2004 from http://hdl.handle.net/1820/95

Van Merriënboer JJG (1997) Training Complex Cognitive Skills: A Four-Component Instructional Design Model for Technical Training. Educational Technology Publications, Englewood Cliffs, NJ

Varela FJ, Thompson E, Rosch E (1991) The Embodied Mind: Cognitive Science and Human Experience. MIT Press, Cambridge, MA

VDEX (2004) IMS Vocabulary Definition Exchange Specification. Information Model, Best Practice and Implementation Guide, XML Binding, Schemas. Version 1.0 Final Specification IMS Global Learning Consortium Inc. Retrieved July 19, 2004 from http://www.imsglobal.org/vdex/

Virvou M, Tsiriga V (2001) An object-oriented software life-cycle of an intelligent tutoring system. Journal of Computer Assisted Learning 17, pp 200–205

Visscher-Voerman JIA (1999) Review of Design in Theory and Practice. Universiteit Twente

Vogten H, Martens H (2004) CopperCore. Retrieved February 27, 2004 from http://www.coppercore.org

W3C (1999) XML Transformations (XSLT) Version 1.0. Retrieved January 21, 2004 from http://www.w3c.org/TR/xslt

W3C (2001) Web Services Description Language (WSDL) Version 1.1. Retrieved January 22, 2004 from http://www.w3c.org/TR/wsdl

W3C (2002) XHTML 1.0 The Extensible HyperText Markup Language (Second Edition) W3C Recommendation. Retrieved July 2, 2004 from http://www.w3.org/TR/xhtml1/

W3C (2003) SOAP, Version 1.2 Part 1: Messaging Framework. Retrieved January 22, 2004 from http://www.w3c.org/TR/SOAP

W3C (2004a) XML Inclusions (XInclude) Version 1.0. Retrieved November 8, 2004 from http://www.w3.org/TR/xinclude/

W3C (2004b) XML Schema Part 1: Structures Second Edition. Retrieved November 8, 2004 from http://www.w3.org/TR/xmlschema-1/

Warmer J (2004) Introduction to OCL. Retrieved January 21, 2004 from http://www.klasse.nl/ocl/index.html

Waters R, McCracken M (1996) Problem-Based Learning in Computer Science, 5th Annual Conference on Problem-Based Learning. Retrieved July 28, 2004 from http://fie.engrng.pitt.edu/fie97/papers/1454.pdf

Webber C, Bergia L, Pesty S, Balacheff N (2001) The Baghera project: a multi-agent architecture for human learning. Workshop - Multi-Agent Architectures for Distributed Learning Environments. Proceedings International Conference on AI and Education. San Antonio, TX, USA

Weller MJ, Pegler CA, Mason RD (2003) Putting the pieces together: What working with learning objects means for the educator. Proceedings of Elearn International Edinburgh, February 2003. Retrieved January 21, 2004 from http://www.elearninternational.co.uk/2003/docs/presentations/ref_papers/wel.zip

Wenger E (1987) Artificial Intelligence and Tutoring Systems. Morgan Kaufman San Francisco

Wiley DA (2002) Connecting learning objects to Instructional design theory: a definition, a metaphor, and a taxonomy. In: Wiley DA (ed) The Instructional Use of Learning Objects. Agency for Instructional Technology and Association for Educational Communications of Technology, Bloomington, IN

Wooldridge M, Jennings N (1995) Intelligent Agents: Theory and Practice. Knowledge Engineering Review 10 (2), pp 115–152

Xerces (2004) XML Parsers in Java and C++. Retrieved July 19, 2004 from http://xml.apache.org/#xerces

Index